A PROTEST HISTORY
OF THE
UNITED STATES

A PROTEST HISTORY OF THE UNITED STATES

**GLORIA J.
BROWNE-MARSHALL**

BEACON PRESS, BOSTON

BEACON PRESS
Boston, Massachusetts
www.beacon.org

Beacon Press books
are published under the auspices of
the Unitarian Universalist Association of Congregations.

28 27 26 25   8 7 6 5 4 3 2 1

This book is printed on acid-free paper that meets the uncoated paper
ANSI/NISO specifications for permanence as revised in 1992.

Text design and composition by Kim Arney

Library of Congress Cataloging-in-Publication Data
is available for this title.
ISBN: 978-0-8070-1081-5; e-book: 978-0-8070-1082-2;
audiobook: 978-0-8070-1811-8

To my mother "Lady Bradshaw"

and

Great-Great-Grandmother
Eliza Broadnax Bradshaw

CONTENTS

AUTHOR'S NOTE

Protest matters. Protests have led to changes in political will and winds. One person chooses to courageously defy, question, or demand change from the powerful in relative anonymity where masses of people, with song and soulful sharing, are moved to stand shoulder to shoulder, chanting in unison, collectively presenting their grievances against injustice by law or by tradition. Despite possible consequences, they all want to make a difference. Protest, to me, is spiritual.

My first protest outside of my family was in third grade. I marched through the streets with classmates, carrying signs demanding that the adults vote to pass a tax levy to finance public school renovations. We laughed, sang a protest song I had written, and watched the sun set feeling ourselves champions of a cause we believed all adults would be foolish to ignore. The measure failed miserably. Some White parents had started their abandonment of the city's public schools in the wake of racial desegregation. Learning in integrated classrooms, living in mixed neighborhoods, perhaps having a person of color in leadership who made decisions affecting their lives was anathema. They crept away into the suburbs to create secluded White havens, taking their children and a flawed notion of democracy with them. Now their children and grandchildren have come to the cities as "urban settlers" estranged from or unaware of the history of colonial settlers, redlining, busing, or environmental racism. I am writing this book because activists are soldiers for social justice, deserving of recognition for their service and sacrifice, perhaps even via a special day or designated cemetery. Far too many community organizers become elderly without a pension, pass away without enough money for a casket, with lives shortened by constant self-deprivation, giving their time to the cause of others instead of to themselves or their families. Fannie Lou Hamer was a Mississippi sharecropper, forced out of her home, clothes thrown out on a dirt road because she had registered to vote. As a voting activist, she was arrested then beaten after leading other African Americans in Mississippi to the polls. Employers refused to hire her, and death threats were constant, as were money worries and stress. I am writing this book for her and others.

A Protest History of the United States is an interdisciplinary telling of the obstacles, protests, and protesters that braids together law, memoir, events, and interviews into an account of centuries of history. This book is for you, the reader, who may remember particular protesters or participated in activism yourself, in one form or another. As you read this book, I urge you to think about generations of your family and the kinds of protest and resistance they engaged in without realizing it. Our achievements speak to their tenacity. This book is important to me because I, like each generation of my family, have been Davids facing the Goliaths of oppression, racism, sexism, and classism. We have done so with tenacity, intelligence, faith, and a well-aimed rock.

Protest is an investment. My African American high school music teacher, Mrs. Baskins, tried to explain the debt we all owe to the next generation. I apologize on behalf of a raucous concert choir class that failed to embrace the songs of freedom, struggle, and resistance. Only later did I realize those songs contained history, life skills, and protest. She, like me, had been integrated into the White school across town. Only as a working adult did I understand the racial and gender challenges she must have faced and how she used "Black Excellence" as protest. My teachers gave me the gift of self-expression.

I am a playwright and writer, a social justice attorney and teacher. Music, theater, song, dance, film, sculpture, and drawing can all be protest. Art has long been a part of activism. Protests can be on canvases or billboards; sung in deep-throated jazz or opera; danced in ballet, tap, or modern; ignited in theaters and in the streets. Do something! In art or academia, take a knee or walk the picket line, whether lawyer or librarian, be the first or refuse to be last but recognize a responsibility to keep progress moving. An investment of sweat and blood allowed me the time to write and you the time to read this book. It is humbling to realize so many made sacrifices without ever knowing our names.

Progress comes from public pressure creating equality under law, because for most of this nation's history the Rule of Law was a grand idea whereby every person was equal under law. However, historically, the "role of law" is too often to control the labor class, people of color, women, the poor, immigrants, the marginalized, queer people, disabled people, and their allies until a critical mass of people rise up and convince stakeholders, influencers, attorneys, and politicians to join their fray. For many, there is little connection between the freedoms they enjoy and the protests needed to make these rights a reality. For example, the eight-hour work week was not readily handed to workers; lives were lost to achieve it. The US Constitution may provide the right on paper, but I was able to enter the once segregated main library in Kansas City, Missouri, because of protests against discrimination. A source of pleasure for me during hot Midwestern summers was taking the bus downtown and nurturing my curiosity and love of books at the library or walking to the local museums that would have turned me away a generation before.

Protest is primal. This book expands protest and resistance to include the precisely planned labor protests by the mill girls in the nineteenth century, the 1963 March on Washington for Jobs and Freedom, the 1975 Chinatown protests in New York City, and the Women's March of 2017. Protest includes the spontaneity of slave uprisings, West Virginia coal mine gunfights, anti-war marches, and urban rebellions. Protest can be the act of doing one small thing: refusing to move, standing up or staying seated, speaking up or remaining silent with one's fist in the air, signing a petition, waging a sit-in or a boycott. Protest can mean resistance or surviving horrendous wrongs. This book is an extension of my research, writing, and speaking on protest, law, and violence in colonial America and the United States from 1607 to the present.[1]

Indigenous peoples studied the colonial statutes and treaty laws, as did some fugitives from slavery, newly arrived immigrant workers, women seeking the vote, and those not formally educated, who learned to bend the power of law to their needs. The rule of law remains an American ideal, a concept that protest brought into the realm of reality.

Unfair laws are usually at the heart of protests, triggering demonstrations, civil disobedience, strikes, rallies, and sometimes armed combat. Wealthy people have learned how to command the necessary laws and politicians to protect their positions and business interests. But the unified power of the people is a force strong enough to battle tycoons, slaveholders, industrialists, magnates, billionaires, and the One Percenters, and this book shows the laws and social conditions confronting the common person before they gather with others and channel rage, frustration, and desperation into strategy and action.

"Your silence will not protect you." Audre Lorde's words sing with a burning truth. Silent good people allow bad things to happen as they try to wait out the controversy—until it comes for them. Women in human resources offices across the nation know that female employees earn less for the same job, but they remain silent. Police officers know that fellow cops spew racism and assault civilians, but they say nothing. Bank employees watch qualified borrowers be denied loans or become burdened with higher interest rates and poor terms, and they only complain privately. Realtors quietly watch prospective tenants and homebuyers get steered to marginalized communities. Courage is being afraid but acting anyway. Protests need not be mass meetings, bull horns, and big painted signs. That is fine and necessary. However, sometimes activism means one just needs to act.

I have stood in the cold, marched in the heat, and been drenched in the rain for issues concerning African American voting rights, women's pro-choice rights, police-involved civilian deaths, book banning, housing rights, and gun violence. I have marched sometimes and written letters to the editor other times, filed complaints, boycotted stores, spoken up, remained vigilant, donated funds, stopped donating funds, joined a group, quit a group, signed petitions, or simply avoided businesses that offer second-class service, and you can do so as well. "Do not spend money in places where respect is not served" remains my motto. This can be a personal everyday act of protest. Use your power within your sphere of influence to start a ripple effect that brings social change.

The Ancestors gave their livelihoods, and some their very lives, without ever knowing our names. Protesters, as warriors, are marching to a different drummer and are drawn to a light just beyond the horizon, some pushing forward despite personal fears and possible professional suicide. Courage is a superpower. Rest in power, ancestral protest leaders, rabble-rousers, conscience raisers, advocates of change, martyrs for equal rights, and conscientious objectors who built the freedoms about which this conflicted country boasts and blindly enjoys. For those who fought the good fight, finished the race, and kept the faith, thank you for your service.[2]

OUR CONFLICTED PROTEST HISTORY

When Emma Lazarus's poem "The New Colossus" beckoned immigrants to enter our nation's "golden door" and breathe free, we were in a time of post–civil war racial terrorism, western expansion confiscating Indigenous land, Chinese exclusion under law, female oppression, and the brutal suppression of workers' rights. This poem of freedom, placed deep within the Statue of Liberty, inextricably connected this nation to that "mighty woman with a torch, whose flame is the imprisoned lightning, and her name Mother of Exiles," but it sheds no light on all that would be needed, and by whom, for this conflicted country to keep such bold promises. This book speaks to the protests and protesters who made this nation the country it is today.

The United States of America was conceived by gunfire and born in rebellion. It was a breech birth, fraught with near-death labor pains and lasting scars. Brought to the New World was a fatherless child fed on conflicted dreams of commerce and liberty whose mass grew faster than its mind. This United States of America has maintained a dual personality, writing of freedom in a Declaration of Independence with one hand, lashing the backs of enslaved people with the other, and all while on stolen Indigenous land. These deep and abiding contradictions have marked the country's laws and traditions, which offer the hope of inclusion and opportunity if one only works hard enough. At the same time, the country kills dreams with obstacles of discrimination, classism, and violence that are intentionally placed along the path, making protest a natural response.

This nation abhorred the abuse of law by England, so a Bill of Rights was created, only to repress the rights of others. The United States of America is a country at war with itself. There is America, the split personality's mythicized benevolent side, that has, from the earliest days, called to the world's poor to seek shelter and opportunity on her shores. At the same time, the brutish United States, showing an early bloodlust and quick temper, crushes any opposition with a thick fist and ruthlessly uses their backs for empire building.

America says that one has free speech and the right to petition the government for a redress of grievance. Then, the nation's arrogant other half, the United States, calls on law enforcement to quash challenges by citizen and immigrant alike, fixed on raw avarice and delusions of superiority. Between these battling Goliaths stand the nation's huddled masses and, among them, the activists who believe enough in the uplift of regular human beings to resist, push, and protest for progress. Throughout this book, the use of "America" reflects the full name of the country—the United States of America—and draws on this dualism between the nation's ideal of liberty for all and its history of narcissistic capitalism. One side of this country's personality extends a right to protest and the other gives the reason.

This nation's conception was from an unnatural union. To the dueling drama of conflicting nation-state personalities, add the experiment of a country artificially made and maintained. If this book were a novel, the unnatural conception of our country would be the inciting incident. Europeans chose to brutally wrest a rich land away from its natural inhabitants, then kidnap and subjugate people from a faraway continent, forcing them to labor for the Europeans for free for centuries, on penalty of death. It was intended to be a Euro-American-dominated land mass, controlled through class-based dogma and with an artificially made White majority, using biased laws and medieval violence.

For people of color, workers, women, and the poor, American idealism was a myth called "liberty" that founders used as a blanket to cover their bloodshed. Protests rose from disillusionment over America's inability to control her power-hungry twin, the United States. Protesters challenged the United States and the dreams that were promised in this Great Experiment. Protests rose to counter settlers' greed and slaveholding debauchery, to demand a place for regular people at the table, to live free. Today, as in centuries past, protesting authority, the elite, and their minions can lead to economic distress, arrest, physical assault, and even death. Human beings, regular people, met the challenge in the face of these obstacles. Our rights and privileges today were produced by their sacrifice.

There is a great deal of good in the United States, and most of it came by way of protest. Notably, the word "protest" is not in the US Constitution; instead, our practice of it comes from a combination of guaranteed rights regarding free speech, freedom of assembly, and the petitioning of the government for a redress of grievances. Protesters prodded this nation toward enlightened humanity by placing their bodies on the line. Often the response to shining a light on injustice has been termination from one's job, divide-and-conquer tactics, and unrestrained brutality. This book will provide examples of abuse resulting from challenges to power, in a nation that boasts about her liberty to the rest of the world.

Protest will be explored expansively and beyond traditional definitions. Therefore, an interdisciplinary approach is used in telling this protest story, going beyond macro-historical methods to include biography, memoir, and interviews. Protest history includes nonviolent and violent rebellions, sit-ins and uprisings, marches and slave revolts, big and small acts of defiance. Protests, in this book, are nonviolent prayer vigils as well as acts of self-defense.

This protest history involves the curious cycle of repression in which those who were once oppressed protest, work their way up, and then attack another vulnerable group or racial minority. The oppressed climb the ladder only to oppress others. Some believe that a second-class membership in White American circles is earned by subjugating people of color. White women exclude women of color. Some Indigenous tribes look down on other tribes and exclude mixed-race Blacks from tribal membership, while colorism besets Latino, Asian, African American, and South Asian communities. The city folk in office buildings look down on the farmers and factory workers, ignoring their plight, until a protest stops the supply chain of food and products needed for the city to run.

It is impossible to include the thousands of uprisings and rebellions that have taken place in US history. This book cannot note all the countless individuals who have protested and all that has been gained from their sacrifices. The individuals who decided on the day of that protest to risk their lives and livelihoods as members of the crowd, standing up for change, risking arrest, assault, or even death, have played a part in the making of a democracy. They must not be forgotten. Too often, when the protester risks life and livelihood, the bystander watches and waits to benefit from the fruits of activism. Protests usually involve a minority within a marginalized group. The number is relatively small. But the impact can make history.

Although the United States prides herself on being a society that embraces freedom, this country has treated protesters with disdain. Yet Rev. Dr. Martin Luther King Jr., speaking on behalf of African American sanitation workers in Memphis, Tennessee, stated that America is a nation that gives a right to protest for our rights.[1] The self-appointed leaders of White patriarchy refused to recognize the constitutional rights of African Americans to protest for full citizenship. They met these protesters with race-based violence and murder. This malevolent fate is a tradition in the United States. Protesters for equal justice under the law, and those fighting institutional power, understood the stakes.

When the poor protest for economic fairness, some wealthy respond by citing Matthew 26:11—"the poor will always be with us"—however, that does not mean the poor deserve low wages or that their suffering should be ignored. As the income gap widens between the upper classes and the struggling class, tensions increase too. Parents will not allow their children to go hungry. Throughout time, they have taken to the streets demanding better jobs, higher pay, and safer working conditions. Attempts to form labor unions have often been met with full-scale layoffs, low-wage replacement workers, bloodshed, eviction, and employer-led violence backed by federal troops, police, and passage of anti-union laws.

From a silent march in New York City, in 1917, against lynching and mob attacks against underpaid workers to college sit-ins for civil rights and boycotts to picketing and traffic blockades, those protesting injustice have had to rely on diverse strategies and tactics. Also, racial prejudice has not been limited to African Americans. Attacks on Asians in America began over one hundred fifty years ago. In San Francisco, California, and Tacoma, Washington, Whites brutally attacked Chinese workers intent on purging them from the state. Resistance and refusal to comply with American hypocrisy has led to murder as punishment for breaking the unstated rules of White supremacy.

When Indigenous peoples of North America protested the original European settlers and their descendants about the taking, renaming, and distributing of their native land, it spurred a government-led propagandist campaign. Native people fought negotiation, treaties, combat, and the courts using all forms of resistance. Newspapers, radio, television, and movies depicted the Indigenous, who were in their right to defend themselves, as the attackers. The White settlers and militia were portrayed as innocent defenders of their homesteads. The US Cavalry massacres of Native peoples were characterized as heroic acts of bravery in a one-sided narrative.

Protest can be finely orchestrated civil unrest, as well as the very simple feat of staying alive while facing genocidal forces. Militia groups and military regiments, working as tools of the presidency, the Congress, the US Supreme Court, and wanton constituents, descended upon Native peoples, seeking their annihilation and the conquest of their lands, but the Indigenous held onto life and resisted these forces of destruction. For groups under constant assault, like Native Americans, African Americans, the working class, and women, to continue to love, to resist, to maintain a cultural heritage, and carve out a life, are all acts of protest. To live under siege and still thrive and find joy, despite the oppressive and unnatural conditions of this country, is an immeasurable victory.

Africans in America resisted servitude through escape, uprisings, petitions to governments, and self-defense; and they fought against colonial powers and then the full regime of state, local, and federal governments infused with religious bigotry and social hierarchies, all intent on creating a perpetual underclass based on skin color. Once citizenship was assured for the African American, the protests for legal protections began. Every aspect of American life became a point of protest. White people in the United States reserved their most violent acts for protesters of color, especially if the protest challenged racial discrimination.

Activists embraced being arrested as a protest strategy and the use of civil disobedience to call attention to their cause through the media, filling jails to capacity and clogging the criminal justice system until their grievances were recognized. Jail did not automatically lead to change; however, it did provide leverage for the protest leaders who sought a place at the negotiation table. Key changes to US laws and major protest cases were later decided by the US Supreme Court, and such outcomes were often part and parcel of the activists' strategy. Throughout history, the highest court has been conservative more often than liberal in its rulings on social justice issues. Unfortunately, the Court has been restored to its conservative moorings. Protesters have taken to the streets to demonstrate against Supreme Court decisions that have undermined the autonomy of women and the voting rights of young Americans and people of color.

The United States of America is made better when her people demand better. Using the ideals of the US Constitution as a lantern, small groups and national organizations have often cobbled together a vision of freedom beyond the status quo, and then set out into the streets to make it a reality. The protesters who make up a movement's vanguard bear the greatest weight and may fail miserably. But they are driven and are especially blessed for the sacrifices that will make it less difficult for future generations. One needs to learn about the protests that secured the liberties enjoyed daily, even as the nation fails to recognize the awful price paid to gain them.

The global power that is the United States was raised from childhood to be a bully, with an arrogant belief that God blessed this nation, alone, with great abundance, and it matters not how people were oppressed to achieve greatness. Ignoring its brutality, the United States boasts a benevolence and brilliance rarely balanced with regret for the sins of Manifest Destiny, enslavement, worker abuses, gender inequality, the ravaging of the natural world, and war upon unnecessary war. Although a working democracy was not the plan of the Founders or Framers, the people protested their way into the Constitution, and the people took the United States from a democracy only on paper to one that actually protected its people.

When the rule of law is used merely to play a role in legal subjugation, then prepare for the rebellion, for it will surely come. It is protest that awakens the apathetic owners of corporations, stirs the college campus, shakes the sleeping justices, inspires leaders, and induces politicians to action. The resistance of thousands in the streets changes the value of Wall Street stocks and draws the international news stations. A trifecta of litigation, legislation, and protest can create social change using the power of the people. And if ordinary people do not have access to litigation or legislative bodies, they can use their voices to make the earth tremble until the laws are changed or lawsuits are brought.

The First Amendment makes clear that people in this country are granted free speech, freedom of assembly, and the right to petition the government for a redress of grievances. Ratified in 1791, the Bill of Rights was assumed, until the twentieth century, to apply to upper-class White Protestant men. Slaveholders did not grow so tired of the riches they gained from slavery that they simply gave up their human property and profits. Men did not realize the error of their ways and magnanimously hand rights to women. Christians were not visited by three ghosts and become convinced that wars should end. Indigenous land was not returned or treaties respected based on the goodwill of the federal government. Litigation and demonstrations forced the recognition of rights under law.

Uprisings are protests that chart a jagged course over generations. For many groups in this country, their protests were riots, their history was consistently taught inaccurately, their achievements were disregarded, and their attributions went missing. When books are banned, now that the truth is finally being told, then reading to understand the complex myths and often violent past of this country is a strong act of protest. Reading is resistance against an educational system that often whitewashes the past and denies young people the truth. Freedom is not free, and each generation must sacrifice to make it theirs. I have written about these topics in *Race, Law, and American Society*, *The Voting Rights War*, and *She Took Justice*, as well as in essays, articles, and even stage plays, but *A Protest History of the United States* is uniquely positioned to be an interdisciplinary exploration of events, people, and places, in historical context, over five hundred years.

Protest helps connect current social justice issues with past battles for freedom, equality, fair wages, the end to wars, and desegregation. This historical context is crucial for readers, for activists, and for those questioning the forces aligned against progress, forces that fear inevitable change. Their use of violence, by even the seemingly staid members of the status quo, is evidence of a simmering rage against the inclusion of others. It is the lives and livelihoods lost in this war of attrition that propels the writing of this book.

In a country brought forth in rebellion, there have been tens of thousands of protests from colony to independence to the present day. There has rarely been a time, from the colonial era to the twenty-first-century empire, without an uprising, revolt, boycott, strike, or movement for social change. So it was impossible to include in this book but a small fraction of the historic protests and protesters. The definition of a protest movement utilized here involves direct action, political activism taking the form of a strike, uprising, riot, economic demand, legal challenges, boycott, civil disobedience, or demonstration, and it is still not broad enough. That is why I have included individual and group resistance, thriving, and survival as protest.

Some readers are aware that by the year 2045, people of color will outnumber the White population in the United States (however "White" is defined by then). History has shown that the law, brutality, and divide-and-conquer tactics will probably play a role in maintaining White supremacy, despite the changing demographics. I wrote this book to give the present generation of protesters a historical tool kit from which to build a movement. To them, I say, take what is needed to be empowered, to create strategies, and to envision a future worthy of the sacrifices their challenges will require.

Our Ancestors gave the shoulders upon which we stand; out of their blood, sweat, and tears, a place was created for us, without ever knowing our names or destinies. We must do the same.

The world will be made better by those who refuse to be silent. *A Protest History of the United States* connects past battles and leaders with twentieth-first-century conflicts and activists. History reveals that the opposition's response, whether cruel or dismissive, will in time yield to protest and progress. We stand in the flickering light of ancestral work. Protest!

CHAPTER ONE

INDIGENOUS DEFENSE OF LAND, LIFE, AND CULTURE

GREETINGS TO THE NATURAL WORLD:
THE EARTH MOTHER

We are all thankful to our Mother, the Earth, for she gives
us all that we need for life. She supports our feet as we
walk about upon her. It gives us joy that she continues
to care for us as she has from the beginning of time.
To our mother, we send greetings and thanks.[1]

K ansas is the land of the Kansa, Pawnee, Osage, Wichita, Comanche, Arapaho, Cheyenne, and other Indigenous peoples. My mother's ancestors arrived in Kansas in 1879 as Exodusters. They were the first wave of African Americans who migrated north as post–Civil War terrorism spread across the South. Their surname is Bradshaw, and they were farmers of the southwest Kansas plains. Before trekking north to Kansas, Eliza and Lewis Bradshaw had been enslaved in Kentucky and, after the Civil War, tried to live there peacefully, seeking to raise a family, build schools, farm the land, and embrace the United States as a republic bound by its stated constitutional promises. But when Reconstruction ended, in 1877, and federal troops were pulled from the South, Confederate terrorism was unleashed. Our US protest history entails countless stories of triumph, failure, resilience, and survival. My family's journey is one intertwining thread.

As post-Reconstruction violence stretched across the South, the US Army was carrying out its final phases of attacks on the Indigenous. Eliza, Lewis, and their family chose to leave Kentucky to start anew in Kansas. The Cheyenne were fighting for their lives, culture, and land in Kansas. Cheyenne chief Dull Knife was a strategic military master and fierce warrior who outsmarted the US military in multiple battles. He had piercing eyes and pronounced cheekbones, but his wavy hair gave him a handsome softness. One particular battle, fought on a rocky expanse named Punished Woman's Fork, left US Army lieutenant colonel William H. Lewis with wounds he would later die from. After the fighting, Chief Dull Knife, whose men had also suffered, decided to take his people, hundreds of women, children, and elders, into the Dakotas. The Battle of Punished Woman's Fork was the last of the Indigenous wars in Kansas.

The Indigenous met the incursions by colonial Europeans and, later, White Americans with resistance, in the form of diplomacy as well as warfare, court cases, and counterattacks, treaties, and the continuation of cultural traditions, including maintaining identities, religions, and practices despite forced assimilation. The history of Indigenous resistance includes petitions, lobbying, demonstration marches, lawsuits, boycotts, and the "illegal" occupation of federal land, with the political power of the Indigenous always ebbing and flowing. For five centuries, Indigenous peoples fought an enemy—first Europeans, then Americans—intent on creating an unnatural empire on stolen land. This chapter presents only a small piece of the immense history of Indigenous resistance to colonization.

"Greed is an amazing driving force in the history of America," writes activist Winona LaDuke. Through exemplary works such as *All Our Relations: Native Struggles for Land and Life*, LaDuke recounts the history of how this vice led to colonization and its unending consequences for Indigenous peoples.[2] "Gaining access to Indian lands in order to secure railway development had guided Indian policy before the Civil War, and the goal was quickly achieved during it," she explains.[3] Railroad tracks were laid across Kansas, connecting New York to California. Stolen land was granted to European immigrants, enticing them to populate Indigenous land as homesteaders. Europeans were drawn to the United States with posters boasting "Free Soil, Free Labor, Free Men," even though, as scholars have pointed out, it was only the wealthy elite males who were free.[4] They came to be part of a Great Experiment, making a new country on top of other people's homeland.

Like millions of people of African descent worldwide, my ancestors had been forced by violence to labor for free, on this land, until the Emancipation Proclamation ended their bondage. They, as homesteaders, were given title to land purchased from the government through a broker, not knowing the duplicitous history.

It is impossible to overstate the tenacity of spirit required for a people to maintain culture, religion, and identity—or reclaim them when they've been stolen—while being subject to the crushing systems of law, political propaganda, capitalistic corruption, and societal hypocrisy, first in the American colonies and later in the American republic, for over five hundred years. Therefore, I cannot detail the myriad forms of Indigenous resistance in full here, though this book offers some key examples.

While war can be protest, protest is not always the rationale for war. To reiterate, throughout this book, I expand the concept of protest to contain a multitude of forms, large and small, that speak to resistance to subjugation. Indigenous battles were a means to protest European invasion, the taking of Indigenous land, and the undermining of Indigenous sovereignty.[5] Diplomacy, as well as armed resistance, could also be a form of protesting assimilation, invasion, the destruction of culture, and murderous aggression. The act of war as a measure of self-defense is considered a form of protest in particular situations where violence has been inflicted on a people and options are limited. Indigenous nations are sovereign and have the right to wage war. Historically, the oppressed who use violence as self-defense are judged more harshly than the oppressors who enter brutally and maintain pride of place by utilizing any despicable means possible.

The word "Indigenous" does not always provide a proper context for the many cultures and languages of the different tribes of the United States and the rest of North America.[6] There is too much to properly cover in a single chapter. Ned Blackhawk's *The Rediscovery of America: Native Peoples and the Unmaking of U.S. History* and several other excellent resources provide a more in-depth telling of how Indigenous history and US history intertwine.[7] Native peoples persevered through violence from the military and civilian militias, federal divide-and-conquer tactics, diseases, and forced assimilation policies. They resisted, revolted, rose up, and rebelled, and continue to do so today.

RESISTANCE NOW. RESISTANCE FOREVER.

Neither colonial settlers nor their descendants living in the early republic contemplated the extent of Indigenous resistance they would encounter, the protests that would become a mainstay, or the counterattacks by those they sought to oppress. The Indigenous stood their ground as their land was commandeered by explorers, then colonists and settlers from Europe drawn to North America under royal charters and private incentives of free land and, later, free labor—the African enslaved laborer.[8] Resistance was protest. For over six hundred years, Indigenous peoples of North America have fought to protect their land and way of life from invaders intent on procuring their land. Those protests have taken many forms through the centuries, led by men and women with vision.[9] Forces behind settler colonialism labeled Indigenous people as undeserving of their land—land with which they had been in special relationship from time immemorial.

In the words of historian Roxanne Dunbar-Ortiz, author of *An Indigenous History of the United States*, "The history of the United States is a history of settler colonialism—the founding of a state based on the ideology of White supremacy, and the widespread practice of African slavery, and a policy of genocide and land theft."[10] There is also a history of Indigenous being sold into slavery and sometimes subjugating other Native people into slavery.[11]

All manner of legal machinations, public contempt, violence, propaganda, political tactics, economic subjugation, criminal injustice, theories of White superiority, and civilian militia and military attacks were used against Indigenous resistance.[12] They fought back in myriad ways, and survived.

RESISTING JAMESTOWN

The origin story of the United States of America begins in Virginia. Indigenous resistance to the building of Jamestown, the first permanent English settlement in North America, began soon after the English landed. Before the arrival of Europeans, the Indigenous population in that region was estimated at twenty thousand.[13] This was before explorers claimed swaths of North America in the name of their monarchs, and before settlers created colonies and lured millions to purchase land from sellers who asserted their claim to the land was legitimate—when, in fact, unilateral charters had been given to corporations in cities across the Atlantic. Given that there were thousands of Indigenous tribes in North America and hundreds of European explorers from various nation-states arriving in the fifteenth century, this book could commence in any region. But it begins with the Jamestown settlement of Virginia and the Powhatan people, indigenous to the land called Tsenacomoco, and their resistance to settler expansion. By 1669 only 1,800 Powhatans were left in the Virginia Colony.

On April 10, 1606, King James granted a charter to English investors to establish a profit-generating company in North America. Born in Scotland to the ill-fated Mary Queen of Scots, King James had an erratic reign. The royal decision to grant a charter took place in a reign that spanned between 1603 and 1625, ending with his death. A Protestant, James I was nearly assassinated by a group of Catholics, led by Guy Fawkes, incensed over the king's unyielding stance on Catholicism. James was embattled, constantly at odds with Parliament, and belittled as the "wisest fool in Christendom" by Henry IV of France.[14]

However, James holds an irrefutable place in history for ordering the translation of the Bible from Latin into English and for founding the first successful English settlement in North America, thereby laying the foundation for the United States of America. In deciding to conquer Native land in the name of King James, a hardy band of English colonists triggered a vortex of events that led to the nadir of human depravity and the creation of myths to cover it up. Africans from Angola arrived in Virginia in 1619, a year before the *Mayflower* landed. Multiple sins—of both commission and omission—abounded.

Europeans had been aware of the existence of Indigenous peoples in North America as early as 1492, when a misguided Christopher Columbus encountered the Arawak, Taíno, and Lucayan in the Bahamas, a Caribbean island, on a mission to India financed by Spain. Columbus left the Old World for a new one, finding inhabitants who welcomed him and a land rich with resources. In a letter to King Ferdinand and Queen Isabella, sent first to the Vatican and published in 1493, Columbus described with covetous candor the rich natural resources he saw in the New World.

To say that Columbus's intent was murderous is not hyperbole, as evidenced by the fact that after he unceremoniously unfurled the Spanish flag, declaring the land to be a Spanish possession, he put the plot for subjugation in writing. Although he had met with no resistance, it was evil that guided his thoughts toward those who had demonstrated kindness. He wrote:

> I came into the Indian Sea, where I discovered many islands inhabited by numerous people. I took possession of all of them for our most fortunate King by making public proclamation and unfurling his standard, no one making any resistance. . . . The inhabitants . . . are all, as I said before, unprovided with any sort of iron, and they are destitute of arms, which are entirely unknown to them, and for which they are not adapted. . . . They would make fine servants. . . . With fifty men we could subjugate them all and do whatever we want.[15]

Taking their land in the name of Spain was his foremost objective. Columbus, by his own words, plainly characterizes the murderous mindset and tactical scheming that would confront Indigenous people for five hundred years. The first settlement by the Spanish in North America was a fort community called St. Augustine, established in 1565, though Spanish explorers had sailed along the coasts of Texas as early as 1528.

The Jamestown colonists arrived aboard three English ships aptly named *Discovery*, *Susan Constant*, and the *Godspeed*, which had set sail from London on December 6, 1606, their voyage lasting 144 days. They were the pride of the United Kingdom and burdened with the expectations of eager investors in the Virginia Company of London.[16] On May 13, 1607, when the three ships carrying one hundred and four men and boys arrived, they had been warned about antagonizing the native people. After sailing along the coastal region, and fifty miles up a waterway later named the James River, these English colonists landed at the Powhatan hunting grounds, a grassy peninsula with seemingly no signs of people but with abundant wildlife and water deep enough to allow large ships to dock. Since the peninsula was surrounded by water on three sides, it was thought to be a strategic location for defending against a possible attack by the Spanish. This humble settlement was named Jamestown in honor of King James I.

The English settlers arrived at a point of entry that was flat and grassy but led to a swampy marsh of mosquitos and a creek. The Powhatan wondered why the European men would choose their hunting ground, a place where they themselves would not live, as a site to rest and assumed it would be a temporary stay for supplies and food. However, as we know, the colonists were more than explorers of the land, as they had been given an edict to survive, thrive, and colonize. In 1606, the newly crowned King James I had given a royal charter to the Virginia Company of London to expand the United Kingdom into North America by taking land, growing a profitable crop, and creating a thriving English colony.

It was a commercial venture from the start, with settlers seeking a source of revenue to sustain and grow a population that had no planned return to England once they ensconced themselves on foreign soil. A failed Roanoke Colony in 1590 gave this second royal investment in the New World an unspoken directive to succeed or die trying. However, the Powhatans, under the impression that the colonial travelers were merely passing through to other lands and needed temporary assistance, found themselves giving aid and comfort to Europeans who were secretly intending on appropriation and conquest.

Additionally, the monarchs of Portugal, The Netherlands, Spain, and France had planted their flags in Indigenous lands at least a century earlier. Powerful forces in Italy, allegedly guided by holy Catholic monarchs, had given instructions to invade the lands and subsume all territory belonging to non-Christian people. It began with Pope Nicholas V, born Tommaso Parentucelli, who decreed in the papal bull of 1455 that the Portuguese king Afonso V had the right "to invade, search out, capture, vanquish, and subdue all Saracens and pagans whatsoever" and reduce them to perpetual slavery, taking all their wealth for the good of Christians and vanquishers.[17] Later, Pope Alexander VI on May 4, 1493, supported Christopher Columbus and Spain's colonization as it was deemed a religious "duty, to lead the peoples dwelling in those islands and countries to embrace the Christian religion; . . . appoint to the aforesaid mainlands and islands worthy, God-fearing, learned, skilled, and experienced men, in order to instruct the aforesaid inhabitants and residents in the Catholic faith and train them in good morals." The Vatican's papal bull fed the pervasive ideology of settler colonialism in the New World of North and South America as well as Africa, in the name of monarchs using European commoners, governed by a wealthy class loyal to the crown, to populate foreign lands. The impoverished colonial settler was made a weapon—at once indispensable and disposable—against Indigenous peoples and a near-perfect tool for colonialism.

CHIEF POWHATAN AND THE ANGLO-POWHATAN WAR

Although he was the leader of an empire, his name has changed with time and whoever is narrating events. To the Indigenous people of the Powhatan villages, he was Wahunsenacock; to the English, he was Chief Powhatan.[16] A tall, muscular man with gray hair and a thin beard, he carried himself with a royal bearing. When he interacted with the English, he did so with the lives of over 150 villages and dozens of lower chiefs on his shoulders, but Chief Powhatan was a diplomat and seasoned warrior.[17] He had ambitiously created a network of some thirty different tribes, with a population estimated to be over twenty-five thousand and villages that may have spanned as far as Maryland.

The Europeans had come to North America to begin new lives but refused to accept the self-determination of Indigenous and other peoples. Violent resistance to English incursions would come only after diplomacy failed, and, in 1607, the Powhatans were abruptly confronted by English colonists intent on depleting precious resources without explanation, apology, or plan for departure. The battle was over England's efforts to control the region's land and resources. Although the Powhatan tribes had a nomadic lifestyle, following the fertility of the land according to the seasons, Indigenous peoples had occupied the region for thousands of years.

The Powhatan people had governmental structures and systems advanced enough to include female leaders—as did the Iroquois—as well as a thriving economy, educational system, and religious beliefs. The Europeans did not bring "civilization" to the Indigenous. Before the Europeans arrived, the Powhatan grew vegetables, fished along the river, and hunted deer on the grounds later occupied by the settlers, who cut trees, built forts, trapped animals, and killed deer, the latter not only being an Indigenous source of food but also used for clothing, tools, and ceremonial tributes.[18]

Chief Powhatan oversaw a network of various tribes that had been formed two years before the arrival of the English into the hunting grounds on the peninsula, which the settlers branded. There were Eastern Woodland Indians, called the Algonquian by some of the English settlers. Chief Powhatan was relatively new to his role, but a seasoned man estimated to be in his fifties, he soon faced one of the greatest challenges in his life when the tribes came together for mutual protection and to share food. Chief Powhatan was kept apprised of English ships and their movements. He must have initially viewed this intrusion with curiosity, not knowing the English had selected the area because it was open and unoccupied.[19]

Chief Powhatan met with his leadership to discuss the English. It was not their first encounter with Europeans, as Spanish explorers had come the century before the English. Their ships traveled down the coast, settling on the farthest southeast shores, named for Spain's Easter celebration, the "Pascua Florida." There, and in other regions, battles between the Indigenous ensued. The British Museum holds watercolor drawings of a Powhatan village named Secoton, by John White, dated as early as 1587.[20] The orderly life then must be appreciated or else an assumption that Europeans brought civilization to the Indigenous would persist. One image depicts orderly schemata of corn fields, gardens, roads, and clearings where meetings are taking place, children are playing, and carved thatched-roof structures are built; other drawings show a round compound of thatched structures.

As with Columbus and his interactions with the Indigenous of the Bahamas, the English had taken Chief Powhatan's generosity as a sign of weakness. War did not break out immediately. However, the European men remained. Over two years, more foreign men and then foreign women arrived, and a larger compound was built. They overhunted the area's animals, which threatened to deplete the primary food source for them and the Indigenous. Chief Powhatan's efforts at diplomacy had failed, and, having seen the Europeans' avarice, he realized the invaders meant only harm to him and his people. He told them: "Your coming is not for trade, but to invade my people and possess my country. . . . I know the difference of peace and war."[21] He was correct. The European invasion precipitated the Anglo-Powhatan War, which began in 1609 and did not end until 1614. Here, as in other moments in history, war served as a form of Indigenous protest.

Yet despite the facts about what caused the war, historically, the Indigenous are portrayed as the aggressors and are also blamed for the near disappearance of the Jamestown colony in the winter of 1609, commonly referred to as "the Starving Time." Weakened by malaria, the region experienced a drought, followed by what was then one of the longest winters in Virginia's history. After a poor harvest, food was scarce. Tensions rose, and skirmishes between the Powhatan and the colonists became battles. Frigid temperatures and the Powhatans' attacks kept the settlers trapped within the Jamestown fort. Drinking water was contaminated and food supplies ran out. Desperation brought the English to madness, murder, and even cannibalism.[22] Starving settlers dug up "dead corpses out of graves" to eat and "licked upp the Bloode," while a young girl's skeletal remains lay in state at the Historic Jamestowne museum bearing the marks of a cleaver or axe.[23]

Food supplies dwindled quickly as nearly five hundred hunkered down in a shabbily built fort that was meant to house about half that number. The English ate the horses and even vermin. One of the settlers, George Percy, wrote of that time: "Having fed upon horses and other beasts, as long as they lasted, we were glad to makeshift with vermin, as dogs, cats, rats, and mice."[24] Unbearable thirst drove some to drink contaminated water. Of life inside the fort, John Smith wrote, "There remained not just sixtie men, women, and children, most miserable and poore creatures; and those were preserved for the most part, by roots, herbs, acorns, walnuts, berries, now and then a little fish . . . yea even the very skins of our horses."[25] Meanwhile, Chief Powhatan's men lay in wait, knowing hunger would draw the English out of the fort. Percy wrote: "Some were enforced to search the woods, and to feed upon serpents and snakes, and to dig the earth for wild and unknown roots, where many of our men were cut off and slain."[26]

Only sixty colonists survived the Starving Time; however, the Powhatan, too, had a harsh summer and poor crops and experienced a long, frigid winter. In occupying the Powhatans' natural hunting ground, the English had chased away the deer, and they hunted without concern for preserving the food supply. The Powhatans were left unable to store adequate amounts of meat and vegetables. Indigenous children went hungry, while elders fell to diseases brought from Europe and for which there was no ready cure. It was a tragic irony that the Indigenous peoples, after giving hospitality and making sacrifices by sharing their food with the Europeans, also had to struggle to survive.

The Anglo-Powhatan War ended in 1614 with the marriage of Chief Powhatan's favorite daughter to the widower John Rolfe in Jamestown. Amonute was her given name, yet she was better known by her nickname, Pocahontas (or "Playful One"), as well as Matoaka; she was born about 1596. In 1607, John Smith was captured and brought before Chief Powhatan. The details are murky, but, according to most accounts, Smith was freed when Pocahontas, who was considered kind-hearted, begged for his life. The colonists, led by need and greed, made further demands on Chief Powhatan for land and food. When relations between Chief Powhatan and the colonists deteriorated, the colonists laid a trap.

The events leading to the union of Pocahontas and Rolfe were initiated by Captain Samuel Argall, who, through a scheme using the local chief of the Patawomeck tribe, took Pocahontas hostage and held her for ransom. During months of captivity, under the influence of Rolfe, Pocahontas converted to Christianity and agreed to marry him. This union brought the "Peace of Pocahontas" that secured the end of the Anglo-Powhatan War. Rolfe took Pocahontas to England as a showpiece for the Virginia Company of London, the financier of the expedition to Virginia. The only known portrait of her shows the "Playful One," as Chief Powhatan fondly called her, now a severe, worn-looking woman at only twenty years old, bound in tight English fabric, throat covered in a lace brocade collar as high as her chin, with fingers awkwardly holding a feather as a symbol of her people and former self. This was the face of assimilation.

European invaders plotted for the acquisition of Indigenous lands as well as their souls, intent on making them adherents to Christianity and European culture. Assimilation had diminished Pocahontas, now baptized with the Christian name Rebecca. On March 21, 1617, during a return trip to Virginia, she died—likely from an infection, probably tuberculosis or pneumonia.[27] Although life in the seventeenth century was precarious, and early deaths were common, some have suspected there were more nefarious factors in her death because she planned to reveal to her father all she had seen and heard abroad. Chief Powhatan followed her in death just a year later.

Many years after the fact, the story of this Indigenous girl's life was molded by John Smith, perhaps borrowing from a Scottish tale and then retold as myth. But as Camilla Townsend stresses in her *Pocahontas and the Powhatan Dilemma*, Pocahontas's life serves as a case study of Native American agency and strategies of defiance in the face of overwhelming odds.[28] In the propogandist retelling of the Europeans' invasion, the focus on Pocahontas and Chief Powhatan's role is limited, overlooking the fact that, as leader of thousands, he was an effective diplomat and military strategist who thwarted early European conquest.

Unlike Chief Powhatan, Chief Opechancanough was not a peacemaker with long patience but a charismatic and dynamic leader whose diplomacy skills included the threat of war. Chief Opechancanough represented the more militant contingent of lower chiefs, who had tired of the settlers' betrayals and lies as they took Indigenous land.[29] He angrily watched as a growing European population harmed his people and the land. Tobacco plantations were spreading across the colony, depleting the soil, requiring more workers for the labor-intensive tobacco crops. Responding to the call, the Virginia London Company sent more ships filled with laborers. Settlements were growing, spreading Europeans across Indigenous land while the Powhatan confederation of tribes was shrinking from disease. Disarray among the once-orderly tribes revealed fault lines where European divide-and-conquer tactics caused in-fighting among the lower chiefs. The emboldened English plantation owners turned to military measures to secure their profitable business enterprises.

Into rising antagonisms between the Indigenous and Europeans, a heavily damaged English privateer ship arrives with "20 and odd Negroes" from Angola (formerly Ndongo), in the heat of August of 1619.[30] The Angolans carried on the ships were to serve as laborers for the landholders and middle-class tradesmen, supplementing the indentured Europeans who had been living as "White slaves," working unpaid and abused until their contracts or indentures terminated. If these laborers managed to escape this brutality, some attempted to live among the Indigenous while others were killed by them, further exacerbating tensions.

Chief Opechancanough could see that only by waging war could they end the continuing invasion of his land. There was no Pocahontas to broker peace. Besides, her untimely death while living among the English served as a harsh lesson about what lay ahead when someone's most precious gift is entrusted to English hands. In 1622, after the murder of a member of Opechancanough's inner circle by an English settler, Chief Opechancanough declared war. On March 22, the chief led what was planned to be a surprise attack on thirty English settlements and plantations. However, an Indigenous youth who lived with the English is credited with warning the colonists. In a letter to the Virginia Company of London, he is described as "one . . . who had lived much amongst the English, and by revealing yt pl[ot] . . . appon the day of Massacre, saved theire lives."[31] (Despite growing tensions, there were Indigenous people, like this youth, so endeared to the English and willing to betray his people.) Jamestown readied for attack, but despite being forewarned, nearly four hundred Whites were killed, twenty White women were taken hostage, and dozens of structures burned. Chief Opechancanough believed that in winning this battle, a defeated English would sail away within two months' time. Not only did the English not leave, but more arrived. The Euro-White population grew larger, causing more bloody battles over land and deeper Indigenous resistance against White oppression.

Of course, some Europeans interacted peaceably with numerous Indigenous people, like the Monacan Indians, located in the town of Monasukapanough, in what is believed to be present-day Albemarle County, Virginia. This focus on the conflicts between Chief Powhatan and the English is not meant to diminish other tribes or European incursions. Nor were these Virginia battles the first or the bloodiest. But given the early foundational importance of the Powhatan and English in the Virginia Colony, this moment in history remains symbolic of colonial oppression and continued Indigenous resistance during that early time.

DEFENSE IS PROTEST: 1700S

Historical accounts reveal dozens of skirmishes, battles, and outright wars between the Indigenous and the European invaders—and the word "invaders" accurately captures the role the Europeans played, in South America and Africa as well as North America. In fact, since declaring its independence in 1776, the United States government has authorized at least 1,500 wars, attacks, and raids on American Indian tribes.[32] Law, religious belief, and violence were the tools of European conquest. Propaganda was promulgated then and continues to be today: White-led battles against the Indigenous have been called "wars," while Indigenous victories against Euro-White invaders have often been referred to as "massacres" of innocent Whites.

The names for the wars between the Indigenous and the European settlers depended on who told the story. Metacom's Rebellion in New England, for example, was also known as King Philip's War and the First Indian War, which is an inaccurate name. Metacom was chief of the Wampanoag and had taken the name Philip during the early amicable times with the colonists. The rebellion ended with the signing of the Treaty of Casco Bay in 1678 in New Casco, Maine. It was an agreement that required the settlers to pay for use of the land, and restricted trade and river rights. Of course, the settlers later betrayed the treaty and the Wampanoag, which led to more battles and a second treaty, which the French then undermined using divide-and-conquer tactics to incite hostilities both among Indigenous tribes and between New England settlers and the Native signers of the treaty.

THE FRENCH AND INDIAN WAR

Sometimes resistance involved war between Indigenous groups. One such conflict was the French and Indian War, part of a bloody, all-encompassing Seven Years' War (1756–63). Indigenous nations fought on different sides of the war, for the French and for the British. It began with Great Britain declaring war on France in 1756. As with any rebellion, there were military tactics, political measures, violent acts, and many sides to the story. The Indigenous of the Ohio Valley sought an alliance with the French, hoping it would result in greater protection of their shrinking homeland and fur trade.

There were simmering conflicts, betrayals, and longtime alliances within the Indigenous communities. Europeans pitted tribal nations against one another in conflicts whose principal combatants were Great Britain and France and, later, France's ally Spain. One cannot forget that but for settler colonialism, these tribes would not have attacked Euro-White settlers. France and Britain fought over control of Indigenous land, leaving Indigenous leaders to decide which side would best protect their interests.

Algonquin, Lenape, Wyandot, Ojibwe, Ottawa, Shawnee, and Mi'kmaq allied with France. The Iroquois sided with England, but some French had respected Indigenous practices and taken time to learn their languages and religions, and even intermarried with them.

Pontiac said: "The French familiarized themselves with us, Studied our Tongue, and Manners, wore our dress, Married our Daughters, and our Sons their Maids, Dealt honestly, and well supplied our wants."[33]

But France found it difficult to finance the war and thus had to ally itself with Austria, Sweden, Russia, and, later, Spain. Less than two centuries later, Winston Churchill referred to the Seven Years' War as the first world war, during which nearly a million people died. It laid a bloody trail through western Pennsylvania and exploded into Canada, with battles waged as far afield as India. The Seven Years' War was not resolved until 1763 with the Treaty of Paris. In the agreement, France ceded to England, as victor, all lands except for what today is Quebec.

Missing from the negotiation table were the Indigenous nations. Despite being on the land for a millennium, and fighting and dying in this protracted war, they were not parties in making the treaty. Their land was divided and distributed as spoils of war. The concept of ceding Indigenous land to French and English ownership and control was nonsensical to Indigenous leaders. By the signing of the Treaty of Paris, England had controlled North America and westward expansion began quickly thereafter. Roxanne Dunbar-Ortiz makes a critical distinction about European colonization that must be emphasized:

> Had North America been a wilderness, undeveloped, without roads, and uncultivated, it might still be so, for the European colonists could not have survived. They appropriated what had already been created by Indigenous civilizations. They stole already cultivated farmland and the corn, vegetables, tobacco, and other crops domesticated over centuries, took control of the deer parks that had been cleared and maintained by Indigenous communities, used existing roads and water routes in order to move armies to conquer, and relied on captured Indigenous people to identify the locations of water, oyster beds, and medicinal herbs.[34]

PONTIAC'S REBELLION

Britain's control of the land included the treatment of all Indigenous peoples as subjects of the British Empire. Although King George III's Royal Proclamation of 1763 recognized Indigenous lands not controlled by Britain to be sovereign, the settlers did not recognize Indigenous rights. By May 1763, another war had broken out over the encroachment of Whites, and again, the Indigenous peoples were forced to resist the European rulers and fight back.

Pontiac, also known as Obwaandi'eyaag, was chief of the Ottawa and the namesake of a conflict that lasted from 1763 to 1766. Known by some historians as Pontiac's War or Pontiac's Rebellion, and by others as Pontiac's Conspiracy, it was a conflict waged against Euro-White settlers who were drawn to the Ohio Valley to establish an English colony.[35] Up until the Revolutionary War, it was the largest and longest revolt against British rule. Chief Pontiac had believed that after the Seven Years' War, life would be stable with established boundaries for Indigenous land, allowing his people to resume their independence, way of life, and spiritual practices. He was quickly disillusioned.

When Pontiac was born, about 1714, he was surrounded by battles with settlers over his people's lands. He was a demanding leader and persuasive speaker, and many were drawn to hear him speak against British rule and the proud heritage of his people before the Europeans. He said:

> It is important for us, my brothers, that we exterminate from our lands this nation which seeks only to destroy us. . . . Therefore, my brothers, we must all swear their destruction and wait no longer. Nothing prevents us; they are few in numbers, and we can accomplish it. . . . The French are subdued, But who are in their Stead become our Lords? A proud, imperious, churlish, haughty Band.[36]

In May 1763, he led a surprise attack on Fort Detroit. Despite numbering nearly a thousand men, his forces could not take the fort. But this attempt on British soldiers, known as the Battle of Bloody Run, was enough to send a message to the British that led to their Proclamation of 1763, but its restriction on settlements west of the Appalachian Mountains could not be enforced. There were few real consequences for ignoring treaties, except for the lack of protection available to settlers if Indigenous people, furious with the expansion of Whites into their designated lands, decided to attack. Indigenous peoples of the Ohio Valley wanted to trade with Europeans without giving up their way of life and land. But to gain the gunpowder and metal objects that made hunting easier, they had to interact with settlers who desired their animal skins. It was a Faustian bargain with deadly consequences.

Pontiac was said to have been a leader who possessed courage and vision but lacked self-control and humility, for which he paid a deadly price. He boasted of personal relationships with British diplomats and was invited to private meetings with Sir William Johnson, British superintendent of Indian Affairs. This was in 1766, three years after the Siege of Detroit. Although the attacks on settlements continued, Chief Pontiac ended his siege against the British. To some, he was perceived as arrogant and too friendly with the enemy, which led to rising hostility. It is unclear whether his assassination in 1769 occurred in response to his bombastic personality, out of jealousy over the power he had acquired within the British circles, or because he ignored Indian tradition and took the title of chief, which had not been rightfully given to him.[37]

Pontiac was killed by a nephew of Makatchinga, a rival and Peoria chief of the Illinois Confederation. For some, Pontiac was a self-proclaimed chief riding high on past battle victories that were overblown by the Europeans who catered to him. But history says his courage and diplomacy were pivotal factors in the unification of tribes across the Ohio Valley.[38] Unbeknownst to King George III, the restrictions under his Proclamation of 1763 laid the groundwork for disgruntled American colonists to begin a pursuit of independence and fulfill a quest for land with little thought of Indigenous people.

A PROTEST DECLARATION FOR INDEPENDENCE

Colonists rebelled against British taxes and burdensome laws, such as the unpopular Stamp Act of 1765, which required the colonies to source paper products used for newspapers, cards, and legal documents from London and pay for them using British currency.[39] The purpose of the Stamp Act was to raise funds to pay off British debt left over from the French and Indian War. Grumbling over taxation without representation led to secret discussions about independence and boycotts of British goods. It was December of 1773 when a group of colonists in Boston, Massachusetts, masquerading as Indigenous people, boarded a British ship and dumped 342 crates of highly taxed tea imported by the British East India Company into the harbor.

The irony is that they shamelessly disguised themselves as Indigenous with whooping cries and blackened faces to protest a tax from Britain. They protested taxation without representation while Africans were enslaved, Indigenous lands were being taken, and both groups were murdered with impunity for challenging these crimes. Thomas Jefferson's Declaration of Independence used the king's Proclamation of 1763 as a royal instigation for war. The proclamation held back new settlements and respected the territory that was designated Indigenous land. To the signatories of the Declaration, by not allowing settlers on the land, the king was refusing "to encourage their migrations hither, and raising the conditions of new Appropriations of Lands."[40]

The land referred to in the Declaration was Indigenous land and protected by treaty, yet the Declaration calls the Indigenous, acting in self-defense, barbarians whose actions were instigated only by the Royal Proclamation of 1763. The Declaration of Independence charges King George with inciting the Indigenous to commit violence against American colonists by claiming:

> He has excited domestic insurrections amongst us, and has endeavoured to bring on the inhabitants of our frontiers, the merciless Indian Savages, whose known rule of warfare, is an undistinguished destruction of all ages, sexes and conditions.[41]

One person's freedom fighter is another person's terrorist, depending on who is recording the history. The Declaration of Independence is a celebrated protest document lifted up as a symbol of freedom, yet it is rarely read, and rarer still is it criticized for the hypocrisy inherent in colonists demanding freedom from English tyranny while terrorizing Indigenous peoples and Africans.

REBELLIONS, WEAPONS, AND THE CONSTITUTION

The US Constitution was drafted in 1787 and ratified in 1789, providing three branches in the federal government and control over Indigenous lands. The Bill of Rights, guaranteeing individual freedoms, was ratified in 1791. Framers of the Constitution, especially Benjamin Franklin, were influenced by the 1744 treaty conference with Chief Canassatego of the six-nation Iroquois Confederacy.[42] They met in Lancaster, Pennsylvania, to discuss settler encroachment on Indigenous land and to possibly work together against the French. Chief Canassatego's philosophy on leadership helped inspire the federalist system, the balance of power between states and a central government, embodied in the Constitution.

Article 1 of the Constitution did not include Indigenous in counting a state's population to determine Congressional representation. "Excluding Indians not taxed" recognized Indigenous sovereignty, in word only. They were not considered part of the union. The Preamble to the Constitution ensured jittery Americans and European immigrants seeking a stable new home that a central government would "insure domestic Tranquility, provide for the common defense, promote the general Welfare" by quelling Indigenous resistance to the usurpation of their land and controlling African slave revolts. The Constitution also stated, in Article 6—referred to as the Supremacy Clause—that the "Constitution, and the Laws of the United States . . . and all Treaties made, or which shall be made, under the Authority of the United States, shall be the supreme Law of the Land." Treaties with Europe were recognized as legally binding documents, while treaties with sovereign tribes were ignored when it came to protecting Indigenous lands from settlers. Financial requirements and restrictions in treaties were overlooked for Whites and duly enforced against the Indigenous who rebelled against this double-standard.[43]

States and the federal government enacted laws to limit Indigenous movement, trapping people who believed in a living relationship with nature. They were corralled onto reserved lands, only to be pushed onto smaller and smaller tracts of land. Not only were they physically removed from their tribal land, hunting territory, and burial grounds, but they were also separated from their farming traditions and cultural practices.

These reckless actions by Euro-White Americans sparked rebellions, but successful revolts require supplies and weapons, which the Indigenous generally lacked. By 1800, the Indigenous population had been decimated by smallpox, murder, and starvation. Census estimates showed that the population, once numbering in the millions in pre-colonial times, was decreasing quickly. By contrast, the White population had increased by 35 percent from 1790 to 1800. Cities such as New York, Philadelphia, Baltimore, and Boston had grown larger. The kidnapped enslaved population was nearly a fifth of the country's total population. European laborers had escaped a feudal caste system just to reinvent it in a new country while boasting of liberty and ignoring their cruel hypocrisy, which denied others who craved freedom.

As early as 1610, unfair laws were passed prohibiting the sale of weapons to Indigenous people. But they gained rifles and defended themselves. Wagon trains of armed settlers were allowed to expand westward over the Appalachian Mountains into the Ohio Valley and beyond the Missouri River and were protected by federally funded squadrons, hired hands, and civilian militias allowed to kill Native Americans under criminal codes created for White self-defense. During an era of expansion that extended to California, settlers constructed homesteads that became towns and built roads through reserved Indigenous lands.

FROM COLONIAL SETTLERS TO HOMESTEADERS

Westward expansion onto Indigenous land was resisted using many tactics—including the law, even if it was often manipulated against the Indigenous. They challenged the government, and the president, in court, all the way to the US Supreme Court, to defend their treaty rights as land was taken with abandon and laws were passed to prevent them from reclaiming it.

The US Constitution has several direct and indirect references to Indigenous peoples, one of which is coincidently placed within the same provisions determining that an African in America would be counted as three-fifths of a person. Article 1, Section 2, states in part:

> Representatives and direct Taxes shall be apportioned among the several States which may be included within this Union, according to their respective Numbers, which shall be determined by adding to the whole Number of free Persons, including those bound to Service for a Term of Years, and excluding Indians not taxed, three fifths of all other Persons.

In concept, Indigenous people living on their designated lands were not taxed because their land was considered a separate nation, a tribal nation, or sovereign territory within the United States.

Agreements between the US and Indigenous nations are binding treaties and under Article 6, the Constitution, federal law, and all treaties with nations inside and outside its borders "shall be the supreme Law of the Land." Also, under the Commerce Clause of Article 1, Section 8, Congress has the power to "regulate Commerce with foreign Nations, and among the several States, and with the Indian Tribes." Yet the federal government entered into hundreds of treaties with various Indigenous nations and consistently failed to honor their legally binding obligations.

The first treaty between the newly formed American government and Indigenous peoples was under the Articles of Confederation. It was signed on September 17, 1778, in hopes of maintaining an extended peace between the Delaware Tribe and the government, but it fell apart within weeks due to ongoing violence and a lack of communication.[44] The treaty was negotiated in good faith by attorneys Andrew and Thomas Lewis representing the United States of North America and John Kill Buck representing the Delaware Nation.[45] The highly ambitious document laid out how "a perpetual peace and friendship shall henceforth take place, and subsist between the contracting parties. . . . The Delaware Nation would give free passage through their country to the [United States] troops."[46]

However, the forces of settler colonialism, the lack of local enforcement, and the breadth of territory undermined even the few sincere federal efforts to respect Indigenous land rights. Then, Shays's Rebellion, a White, farmer-led uprising in Massachusetts, exposed further weaknesses in the Articles of Confederation, resulting in the historic 1787 Convention, in Philadelphia, to produce a constitution that established a strong central government; it was ratified in 1789. The first treaty with the Indigenous under the second government, the United States of America, was the Indian Trade and Intercourse Act of July 22, 1790, passed by Congress, to give the federal government control over commercial interactions, called intercourse, between non-Natives and the Indigenous people.[47] Unfortunately, the Intercourse laws, and there would be many—1793, 1796, 1799, 1802, and 1834—soon became known as the Indian Non-Intercourse Act. This collection of laws laid the foundation for unequal federal policies governing US-Indigenous affairs, trade, criminal justice, displacement, acquiring lands, and even "civilizing" Native peoples through assimilation to White Protestant culture.

The Seneca Chief, Cornplanter, brilliantly set out the history of concerns over land, violence, and broken promises on December 1,

1790, when the murder of two Seneca men received no justice from the federal government and settlers continued to build homes on Seneca land. Chief Cornplanter said:

> We must know from you, whether you mean to leave us, and our children, any land to till. Speak plainly to us concerning this great business. All the Lands we have been speaking of belonged to the Six Nations: no part of it ever belonged to the King of England, and he could not give it to you. The Land we live on our Fathers received from God, and they transmitted it to us, for our Children and we cannot part with it. . . . Was it intended that your people should kill the Seneccas, and not only remain unpunished by you: but be protected by you against the next of kin?[48]

One year after the constitutional creation of the new national government, and weeks after the Seneca letter, President George Washington gave a speech responding to the Seneca Nation on December 29, 1790, in Philadelphia. He sought their trust in a new federal system and the Intercourse Act to solve disputes, punish nonnative offenders before conflicts became bloody wars, and designate "Indian Country" as a safe haven.[49] Travel across Native land required a system of passports controlled by the federal government. But frustrated tribal leaders watched as land-grab settlements continued legally and illegally on designated Indigenous lands with few consequences for White interlopers. As the eighteenth century ended, what was clear from all of these laws and treaties was the tightening grip and endless greed—despite the flowery words in the Constitution—of a government hellbent on executing a multigenerational plan to take Indigenous land and remove Native peoples so that the US could realize the fullness of its supposed Manifest Destiny. In response to this war on the Indigenous was a century of resistance in defense of land and culture against settler colonialism that was upheld by federal laws, murder, rape, military violence, and a complicit federal court system.

TRAIL OF BETRAYALS

An estimated 1.5 billion acres of land was confiscated from the Indigenous through unfair treaties and executive orders between 1776 and 1887, when the Dawes Act was passed.[50] The infamous Trail of

Tears was decades in the making. Removal of Native people had taken place in fits and starts. Always, there was Indigenous resistance to divide-and-conquer tactics fomenting intra-tribal violence, a devastating strategy utilized on people of color and oppressed groups that must be countered successfully by unity. With the creation of a strong central government, the practice of government-planned removal began. Indigenous leadership did not anticipate that a government founded on a constitution, touted as a document of liberty, would be used as a tool for their removal and near annihilation.

In President Thomas Jefferson's First Annual Message, delivered in 1801, he spoke of selling public land to raise needed revenue: "The success which has attended the late sales of the public lands, shows that with attention they may be made an important source of receipt." Those Indigenous peoples who would be affected were to be assimilated into American culture, their land confiscated by treaty and redistributed to White American settlers expanding the country westward. Peace may have been well intentioned, but it was not long-lasting.

By 1802, the Indian Trade and Intercourse Act was regulating the interactions between Indigenous people and settlers. The ostensible plan was to preserve peace on the frontier, but it only further restricted Indigenous people's freedom to buy from, sell to, or trade with Whites living near them, including prohibiting the sale of liquor to Native people on or off their own tribal land.[51] Segregation and starvation must have been the motives behind such legislation, because as the settler population expanded, abusing natural resources, the Indigenous found hunting more difficult, which forced them to rely on "illegal" trade. Federal non-Intercourse laws criminalized trade between the Indigenous and White settlers, leading to starvation and crime. Chief Cornplanter's concerns were realized, leading to wars and litigation as promises made by George Washington fell away.

The US Bureau of Indian Affairs was created in 1823 to "oversee Treaty negotiations, manage Indians schools, and Indian trade." In *Johnson and Graham's Lessee v. William McIntosh*, an 1823 case, the US Supreme Court was presented with a private dispute involving Indian land.[52] The land was inherited from British relatives who bought it in 1775 from the Piankeshaw Indians. The opposing party, William McIntosh, contended he had bought the land directly from the US government. The court ruled in favor of McIntosh, explaining that the Piankeshaw, and all Indigenous for that matter, never had a legal right to their land. It was a dubious logic at best, and self-serving for the US settler government at worst.

Chief Justice John Marshall wrote the opinion on behalf of the Court, which ruled that because the Piankeshaw never "owned" the land in the traditional European-based commercial sense, they could not sell it. Indigenous peoples did not own the land they had occupied for at least a millennium; there was no deed of sale given to them by a higher authority, no proof of sale. Therefore, it was not their land, which meant the Indigenous were prohibited from selling their land to private parties. They could only sell land to the federal government. The prevailing attitude toward Indigenous property rights would question if one owned land merely by having lived on it for hundreds of years. The court determined, "Probably, however, their title by occupancy is to be respected, as much as that of an individual, obtained by the same right, in a civilized state."[53] The court is referring to the Indigenous as uncivilized and reducing land rights to mere occupancy rights, as if they were squatters. Since the Court had ruled the Indigenous did not "own" their land, the federal government and President Andrew Jackson were in position to move them from ancestral land to reserved land or reservations.

The court would only allow the Indigenous a restricted interest in their own land—and to be thus restricted by the federal government meant a loss of sovereign right to the land of their birth the moment the Europeans invaded and "discovered" that land. The court stated:

> Discovery is the foundation of title, in European nations, and this overlooks all proprietary rights in the natives. . . . Even if it should be admitted that the Indians were originally an independent people, they have ceased to be so. A nation that has passed under the dominion of another, is no longer a sovereign state.[54]

The law was being used to incrementally dispossess the Indigenous using murder by a thousand cuts. In 1830, Georgia enacted laws that ignored Native land rights and gave parcels out to create and expand White settlements.

Thinking the US courts would abide by their own laws, Native Americans protested by suing to protect their land rights and refusing to leave it, disputing the endorsed deeds.[55] The US Supreme Court decided *Cherokee Nation v. Georgia*, a case in 1831, and the next year, *Worcester v. Georgia*.[56] In both these decisions, the Court fell back, capitulating to political pressure by President Jackson and assuming a position that would be used in future slavery cases. In the Cherokee case, the Court said it lacked jurisdiction to determine claims concerning an Indian nation within the United States.[57] The Indigenous witnessed betrayal by the rule of law and oppression as the role of law.

The *Worcester* case involved a dispute over the Georgia legislature's decision to outlaw the presence of any non-Indians on Indigenous land without a license. When White missionaries refused to leave Indigenous land, they were arrested, convicted, and sentenced to four years of hard labor by Native courts. The Supreme Court ruled that Indigenous people had no right over their own land or the people on it. Neither Georgia nor the Indigenous people had the authority to control who could reside on their land; only the federal government had that authority. After this ruling, now that Indigenous people had no right over their land, President Jackson pushed for federal legislation to allow their removal. Jackson signed nearly seventy treaties removing fifty thousand Indigenous people from their land.[58]

FIGHTING A TRAIL OF TEARS

An arrogant hardliner, Andrew Jackson remains a hero to those who believe the Indian Wars and violent removal of Indigenous from their land was a necessary betrayal to build a White empire on foreign soil.[59] Jackson was a lawyer and rough-hewn plantation owner, a military man who rose up through the ranks, known for his vicious battle strategies in the Indian Wars.[60] As the seventh president of the United States, he inherited a fledgling nation still finding its footing as the Great Experiment. Jackson held more than one hundred and fifty enslaved human beings on his Tennessee plantation, though some records place the number near three hundred.

Jackson had survived the first attempted assassination of a president of the United States. It's been rumored that he raised three Indigenous children from the Creek Tribe and was said to have referred to them as his "pets." In the evolution of this nation, "Jackson was the Dark Knight in the formation of the United States as a colonialist, imperialist democracy."[61] He gained Indigenous land through politics, military action, and law, as well as through bribes, violence, and other tactics. The majority of Cherokee refused to sign the removal treaties.

On May 28, 1830, Jackson signed the Indian Removal Act into law, authorizing him to grant lands west of the Mississippi in exchange for Indian lands within existing state borders. A few tribes volunteered to give up land, but most resisted.[62] During the fall and winter of 1838 and 1839, the Cherokees were forcibly moved west by the US government. Approximately four thousand Cherokees died on this forced and brutal march, which became known as the Trail of Tears. Some have argued that the act did not specifically give the federal government the right to take the land or remove Indigenous people. However, the act did allow the Jackson administration "to freely 'persuade, bribe, and threaten' tribal leaders to sign removal treaties."[63]

When Congress passed the Indian Removal Act, it gave President Jackson power to extricate the Indigenous people and populate their land with settlers, just as Powhatan had predicted would happen. Over two centuries, there were too many betrayed treaties, lost battles in court and on the battlefield, and internal skirmishes, while the population of lawless interlopers grew across the Great Plains. European immigrants arrived eager for their free land and share in the mythologized American Dream. The Removal Act states:

> That it shall and may be lawful for the President of the United States to cause so much of any territory belonging to the United States, west of the river Mississippi, not included in any state or organized territory, and to which the Indian title has been extinguished, as he may judge necessary, to be divided into a suitable number of districts, for the reception of such Tribes or nations of Indians as may choose to exchange the lands where they now reside, and remove there.[64]

This allusion to an "exchange" of lands was a malevolent lie that falsely suggested the Indigenous had a choice in the matter. By May 1838, the removal of Indigenous people had begun, as reservations in Georgia, Arkansas, and the Carolinas were emptied of Indigenous residents. It was Jackson's final solution. The Cherokee, Choctaw, Chickasaw, Seminole, and Creek tribes were forced to walk thousands of miles while White soldiers on horses rode beside the milelong line of four thousand children, women, and men.[65] They were held at gunpoint for the entire journey to Oklahoma territory, without adequate food, warm clothes, or shelter. They walked north for six months, dying by the hundreds along the way. By winter, President Martin Van Buren said he was pleased to inform Congress that the Cherokee were in "their new homes west of the Mississippi" and that the Removal Act had "had the happiest effects."[66]

Still, the Indigenous were resolute in their spiritual resistance and acts of self-determination. Strategies of engagement varied with the personality of the tribal leaders, the terrain, traditions, resources, and relationship with the oppressor. Indigenous peoples differed in terms of customs, government structure, language, religion, and tribal history, but a common bond remained. The Indigenous who were once pivotal to European survival had become an impediment to White progress. Laws were enacted to protect the lives and land holdings of the settlers over the Indigenous.

The Indigenous fought to maintain their hereditary homeland, culture, religion, hunting grounds, and basic freedom. As battles over land increased, Native Americans were demonized through colonial laws that labeled them "savages" and smeared them as being without a true god or any redeeming value. As Europeans expanded westward, settlers of Indigenous lands were ready to fight the Indigenous over the land they took through government sanction. Because European settlers held deeds to land belonging to Indigenous people, who had no rights or representation in a court of law, the simple defiant act of fighting to hold on to Indigenous land was an act of war. Similarly, the United States deemed the deaths of military officers or civilians in such conflicts as the tragic outcome of self-defense. To assimilate Native Americans, Congress passed numerous laws to oppress, such as the Dawes Severalty Act in 1887. Also known as the General Allotment Act, this act prohibited Indigenous governance of tribal land. Depredation Acts reimbursed settlers for land and property destroyed or taken back by Indigenous people.

THE MASSACRE AT WOUNDED KNEE—1890

On the banks of Wounded Knee Creek in South Dakota was the site of the last traditional military battle between the federal government and Indigenous peoples, fought on December 29, 1890.[67] The Indigenous possessed a small fraction of the land before first contact with

Europeans. Culture and customs were taken underground out of fear of attack by White supremacists in and outside the government. Forced assimilation was threatened on all sides. The "Trail of Tears" had taken many on a grueling journey from as far as Georgia to reservations in Oklahoma. Two centuries of battles, wars, and military conflicts with soldiers and settlers had decimated Native American tribes.

In South Dakota, the Sioux were awaiting some redeeming end to the tragic fall of their proud people. The US Army arrived to disarm the surviving warriors. In search of weapons, they groped women and children. Young warriors, perhaps hotheaded or disgusted, refused to accept this indignity. Shots were fired by the trigger-happy soldiers, and the young warriors fired back in self-defense. Eventually, Chief Sitting Bull was killed. The military had opened fire on every Native American man, woman, and child in sight, the majority of whom were not armed. A total of one hundred sixty-six Native Americans were killed. Nearly half were women and children. Many others were wounded. Of the five hundred Army soldiers, thirty died, probably by friendly fire.[68]

Although the military claimed to have peacefully sought to resolve the standoff at Wounded Knee, the resulting deaths of Native Americans can be viewed as a massacre. The commanding officer was acquitted at court-martial. In a cruelly ironic move, the army chose to honor the soldiers of Wounded Knee with medals for valor.

FORCED ASSIMILATION AND INDIAN BOARDING SCHOOLS

Some languages have become extinct, but as of this writing, there are two hundred forty-five distinct Indigenous languages in the United States, of which sixty-five have gone extinct and seventy-five are nearing extinction.[69] Indian boarding schools were created to assimilate Indigenous children into a White American mindset.[70] After centuries of attempted genocide against the Indigenous, President Andrew Jackson created a new policy of assimilation in order to pry Native Americans from their land and their culture. The boarding schools had been around for several decades, but the federal government began significantly expanding the program in the 1870s, when the US was still at war with the Indigenous people. An army officer, Richard Pratt, founder of the Carlisle Indian Industrial School, based his curriculum on the programs developed in an Indian prison. Pratt said, "A great general has said that the only good Indian is a dead one. In a sense, I agree with the sentiment, but only in this: that all the Indian there is in the race should be dead. Kill the Indian in him, and save the man."[71]

Native American children were forcibly taken from their parents and placed in White-controlled boarding schools, established by private citizens such as Pratt, Christian missionaries, or the federal government. The children were not allowed to speak, read, or write in their native language and were forbidden to dress in any clothing other than Western attire. At one time, nearly a hundred Indian schools were in operation, from Wisconsin to California. The majority were built in Oklahoma to educate the children in reservations there, following the Trail of Tears.

The federal government oversaw most aspects of life on reservations, including the education of children. Attendance at government schools was mandated, even at gunpoint if necessary. Dr. Lewis Meriam, a government researcher, wrote of the harsh conditions and privations in Indian boarding schools including the scarcity of nutritious food, inadequate clothing, and child labor supporting the facility. The emphasis was on punishment and discipline. The Meriam Report, a survey of conditions on Indian reservations in twenty-fix states, was published in 1928. Officially titled *The Problem of Indian Administration*, which in its very name placed blame for the schools on the Indigenous, recommended that Indigenous children attend schools closer to their families and that the education be infused with elements of Indian culture.

The food and clothing for the children improved somewhat, but the educational program did not. Protest had led to some progress, such as the Indian Reorganization Act of 1934, which reversed certain provisions of the Dawes Act, which itself had limited self-governance, yet Indian boarding schools remained well into the twentieth century. *Plessy v. Ferguson* prevented Native American children from attending White public schools. For many tribes, the boarding schools were the only means of educating their children. The choice between boarding schools and no school at all was a painful one, especially since the families knew that the federal government's interest in Indigenous children was primarily in their assimilation and labor, not in a quality education to prepare them for an accomplished future. Change occurred because parents complained.

In urban areas, segregationist laws applied to Indigenous people, as with all people of color, subjecting them to lack of access to employment, housing, and education. Even in urban areas, children of color were segregated from White children. In California, "Indian children" had been segregated by law until 1947, the year a lawsuit challenging the policy led to the integration of the state's public schools. The original California law stated:

§ 8003. Schools for Indian children, and children of Chinese, Japanese, or Mongolian parentage: Establishment. The governing board of any school district may establish separate schools for Indian children, excepting children of Indians who are wards of the United States Government and children of all other Indians who are descendants of the original American Indians of the United States, and for children of Chinese, Japanese, or Mongolian parentage.

§ 8004. Same: Admission of children into other schools. When separate schools are established for Indian children or children of Chinese, Japanese, or Mongolian parentage, the Indian children or children of Chinese, Japanese, or Mongolian parentage shall not be admitted into any other school.[72]

The famous 1954 *Brown v. Board of Education* desegregation decision ended legal racial segregation for public school children of all races, not just African American children. However, the de facto practices and traditions of segregation remained.

In 1968, the Navajo Nation founded Navajo Community College, later renamed Diné College, becoming America's first tribally controlled college. In 1975, the Indian Self-Determination Act gave tribes the authority to prioritize federal funds for Indigenous education. Despite the allegations against them of sexual abuse, maltreatment, and racism, Indian boarding schools remain, albeit in far fewer numbers.

Ten years later, the practice of White families taking Indigenous children from their homes for adoption was ended by the 1976 ruling in the case *In the matter of the Adoption of John Doe v. Heim*.[73] The adoption of Native children through state agencies was a vestige of the earlier boarding school policy. Removing the child from all Indigenous cultural influences meant placing these children only in White homes.

Through advocacy that won the passage of the Indian Child Welfare Act of 1978, activists succeeded in having tribal adoption and foster care agencies oversee the placement of Indigenous children.

Protests in the streets, litigation in courts, and the lobbying of Congress led to a continued rise in Indigenous political power. In 1996, Elouise Cobell filed suit over the federal government's failure to abide by its treaties and agreements, in this case regarding the use of trust funds for five hundred thousand Indigenous people. In 2009, after years of litigation, the celebrated case of *Cobell v. Salazar* was finally resolved. The settlement with Indigenous tribes included the creation of a scholarship fund to give more Native Americans access to higher education. This was an excellent challenge to racial policies dating back centuries. Indigenous protests were an important part of the waves of demonstrations taking place during the Vietnam War, era when there were not only demonstrations against the war but also for women's, immigrant, and civil rights, as well as the urban uprisings that followed the assassination of Dr. Martin Luther King Jr. The arts gave expression to the pain and rage.

OCCUPYING ALCATRAZ

The former prison of Alcatraz in the San Francisco Bay became the focus of a struggle over Indigenous sovereignty and self-determination between 1969 and 1971. Richard Oakes, an Akwesasne Mohawk activist and the director of Indian Studies at San Francisco State, and a group of Indigenous students took a boat to the island and for nineteen months occupied the notorious former prison, demanding its return to Indigenous people.[74] Alcatraz Island, commonly known as "The Rock" but also by its Spanish name La Isla de Los Alcatraces (Island of the Pelicans), is located about a mile and a half from the shore of San Francisco.[75] It was symbolically important to the nearly one hundred Indigenous women and men who began their occupation of the site on November 20, 1969.[76] Demanding the return of the island by "right of discovery," the occupiers created a news frenzy and struck against the image of Indigenous victimization, reigniting an international struggle over appropriated lands, the recognition of treaties, and Indigenous peoples' right to self-determination.[77]

Oakes and his fellow occupiers, including members of the activist group the American Indian Movement (AIM), founded in 1968, called themselves "Indians of All Tribes." They demanded the return of Alcatraz Island for the creation of a Native American university and cultural outpost.[78] "We Are Indians of All Tribes! WE HOLD THE ROCK!" they declared in their proclamation.[79] At the protest's height, more than fifty tribes and nearly six hundred activists were engaged. The occupation drew international attention to the poverty on reservations and their substandard healthcare and poor sanitation and water quality. They pointed to "the Rock," an abandoned, fetid federal prison, as a useful point of comparison for the conditions that millions faced on reservations.[80]

In January 1970, Oakes's stepdaughter tragically fell to her death from a stairway in the prison. Oakes left Alcatraz, and his departure, along with internal struggles in the group, signaled that what had been a successful movement of "Indians of All Tribes" had turned into a cause collapsing under the weight of personality clashes, drug use, competing agendas, and, possibly, spies planted by President Richard Nixon's administration to foment turmoil, which would be in keeping with the government's age-old divide-and-conquer strategy.[81] Nixon had feigned patience, fearful of losing votes when the movement was well supported, but when the occupation lost popularity, the government disconnected the island's electricity and telephone lines, cut off its water supply, and sent in officers to arrest the remaining occupiers.[82]

Nonetheless, the Alcatraz protest spurred other demonstrations and occupy movements to reclaim Indigenous lands in Northern California, Alaska, New Mexico, and at Wounded Knee in South Dakota, as well as at the Bureau of Indian Affairs in the Department of the Interior headquarters in Washington, DC. This resulted in the hiring of Indigenous people by the BIA, which oversees the administration of tribal lands, law enforcement, economic development, governance, and natural resources.[83] Later, the National Park Service would admit that although "the Trail of Broken Treaties did not accomplish all that its organizers had hoped, it would be a mistake to call the demonstration a failure. Though Nixon's task force initially rejected the demands set forth by protesters in the Twenty Points, many of these objectives were later incorporated into American Indian policy in the coming years, setting a new course for self-determination and tribal recognition, a reversal of the disastrous policies of the past."[84]

A REBELLION AT WOUNDED KNEE

Nearly a century after the massacre at Wounded Knee, ten of the twenty poorest counties in the United States were reservations in the Lakota and Dakota territories.[85] In 1973, hundreds of members of the Sioux Nation led an uprising to protest the squalid conditions on the reservation at Wounded Knee, on the Pine Ridge Indian Reservation in southwestern South Dakota.[86] As highlighted earlier, Wounded Knee was the notorious site of the 1890 battle between the Sioux Nation and the US military that left 30 soldiers and 166 Indigenous men, women, and children dead. It was the final formal battle between the Indigenous and federal troops.

Two vocal AIM members, Dennis Banks and Leonard Peltier, charged the Pine Ridge administration with corruption and led a protest against the conditions on the reservation and the non-Indian police's treatment of residents. They chose Wounded Knee as the site of their protest because of its historic and symbolic significance. On February 27, 1973, gunfire was exchanged between AIM and federal officers. Seventy-three days later, the protest ended. Officially, two Native Americans were killed, and a federal marshal was permanently paralyzed by a bullet wound. Hundreds of arrests were made. The leaders of AIM surrendered and were acquitted at trial. AIM's protest had drawn national and mainstream attention to the horrific conditions on Pine Ridge and other reservations.

In 1975, there was another outbreak of violence between AIM and the administrators of Pine Ridge's reservation, resulting in assaults and murders, with more than one hundred dead. After an exchange of gunfire, two FBI agents lay dead. Leonard Peltier was convicted and sentenced to two consecutive life sentences. To date, Peltier has been imprisoned for nearly fifty years, his appeals denied, and he is considered by many a political prisoner.

CASINO OWNERSHIP AS DEFIANCE

There is progress despite the poverty on most reservations. In 2021, American Indians and Alaska Natives had the highest poverty rate of any US ethnic group, with poverty at around 22 percent, while the national poverty rate was 13 percent.[87] However, the reservation has political, cultural, emotional, historical power (and economic power

for some), countries within a country and an autonomous governmental structure based on the will of the leadership of the tribe or
clan and its members. Tribal laws dictate how the land is used. In
recent decades, casinos and other legalized gambling ventures have
been chosen as a means to create Indigenous jobs and wealth. As with
any casino, establishing a tribal casino often includes purchasing a
liquor license—a symbolic act of defiance given the history of racist
stereotypes by the paternalistic federal government, state governments,
and the US Supreme Court, which once barred the Indigenous from
having access to alcohol on Native land. The first Indigenous-owned
casino opened in 1979 on Seminole land in Florida. Today, according
to the Partnership with Native Americans, more than 150 tribes have
high-stakes bingo or casino businesses.

CHALLENGING RACIST MYTHS

Oppressing people is less difficult once the hard work of convincing
society that certain groups deserve to be oppressed has taken place.
Throughout this book, propaganda and negative stereotypes about
people of color, immigrants, women, and working-class laborers remain that unspoken underlying element supporting the laws and traditions of subjugation due to the lingering pervasive power of early
American propaganda. Depictions of the Indigenous as godless and less
than human was driven by fear and mythologized stories in colonial
years, biased books, articles, lectures during the land wars, and then
comic books, radio, movies, and television in the twentieth century.

Like chasing a ghost, protesting a pervasive myth or stereotype
is an ever-evolving task but necessary because lawmakers can create
legislation and mobs commit murder based on myths. Prohibitions on
Indigenous people drinking alcohol or purchasing liquor was official
law based on a stereotype that was upheld by the US Supreme Court.
In the case of *United States v. Sandoval,* the Court allowed Congress to
prohibit "any intoxicating liquors" on Pueblo Indian territory in New
Mexico.[88] The ruling affected a large population, as Pueblo Indians
numbered over eight thousand and lived on over seventeen thousand
acres of land. The paternalistically racist language of the 1913 decision
provides an insight into how Native Americans were viewed.[89] The
Pueblo people are described as

sedentary, rather than nomadic, in their inclinations, and disposed to peace and industry. . . . [They] are nevertheless Indians in race, customs, and domestic government. Always living in separate and isolated communities, adhering to primitive modes of life, largely influenced by superstition and fetishism, and chiefly governed according to the crude customs inherited from their ancestors, they are essentially a simple, uninformed, and inferior people.[90]

Even as good, law-abiding people, they are, nevertheless, "Indians," the Court writes, and therefore cannot drink alcohol.

In ruling that no alcohol could be bought or sold on Indigenous lands, the Court supported the myth of substance abuse as singularly an Indigenous problem. That argument does not square with the fact that Alcoholics Anonymous, today an international organization, was founded in 1935 by two White men—a New York City stockbroker and an Akron, Ohio, surgeon.[91] Although this negative stereotype about the Indigenous lingers, it is being challenged, as are negative depictions in media and the lack of attribution in US history. During the Civil Rights Movement of the 1960s, Indigenous artists, singers, musicians, and writers claimed their space to tell their own stories, giving birth to the Institute of American Indian Art (IAIA) in Santa Fe, New Mexico, which opened in 1962, and Native media across the nation.[92]

TENACITY TO VICTORY

Persistence is protest. There was gold in the hills of Montana, and thousands invaded Indigenous land, ignoring treaties to get their share of it with a complicit federal government. Acknowledgment and compensation would take over one hundred and fifty years. The land was taken via the 1868 Fort Laramie Treaty, signed to end the bloody Powder River War (1866–67) between the US military and a victorious alliance of Sioux, Cheyenne, and Arapaho led by Red Cloud, the tenacious and visionary war chief of the Sioux nation, who used the battlefield as well as the courtroom to fight gold-obsessed interlopers prospecting the Black Hills.

By taking the best land, including the Black Hills, the government had allowed the Sioux to starve.[93] In 1876, 10 percent of the Sioux entered into an "agreement" in which they relinquished their rights to the Black Hills in exchange for food rations, ending the Fort Laramie Treaty, which had promised education for Indigenous on the reservation, as well as the provision of seeds and farm tools.[94] But the Sioux would not relinquish their land in the face of a US Congress that controlled the appeals process, part of a strategy in which tribal sovereignty was only respected when it was convenient for the government. In 1920, half a century later, a new law was passed allowing the Sioux to successfully challenge the taking of the Black Hills.

In 1947, the Indian Claims Commission awarded $17.5 million—without interest.[95] Nothing was forthcoming to cover the damages that, under the 1946 Indian Claims Commission Act, should have been awarded for the gold taken by the trespassing prospectors. In 1980, the Supreme Court ruled in *United States v. Sioux* that in taking the Black Hills of South Dakota from the Sioux Nation, the federal government had violated the Fifth Amendment's "Takings" Clause, which requires compensation for the taking of private land by the government, even if it is for public good. Food rations did not qualify as "just compensation" for the stolen land of the Black Hills of South Dakota and the stolen gold. The Sioux were entitled to the $17.5 million from the 1947 judgment, but this time *with* interest.[96] This was but one example of many in which several decades would pass before federal and state governments would recognize their obligations to treaties they had signed. But the spiritual force, generation after generation, to survive, hope, and gain the victory was ceaseless.

In the twenty-first century, Indigenous land rights and treaties are under constant litigation as the government is made to pay old debts and precious metals are discovered on reservations or corporations deem it expedient to lay a pipeline through Indigenous lands. Then the old tactics of unfair laws, divide-and-conquer, and violence are employed in ways reminiscent of the railroad barons stealing thousands of miles of Indigenous land to lay railroad track for settlers expanding west.

STANDING TALL AT STANDING ROCK

The Dakota Access Pipeline was the modern battleground where an alliance of Indigenous activists and allies stood their ground in a year-long protest. The plan for the pipeline's route spanned four states and some 1,200 miles, crossing under the Missouri River reservoir and near the Standing Rock Sioux Reservation in North Dakota. Under the Trump administration, permission to construct and maintain a portion of the Dakota Access Pipeline one hundred feet under the bed of Lake Oahe was upheld. Lake Oahe is a large reservoir lying behind a dam on the Missouri River between North and South Dakota.

Fearing severe environmental consequences, an alliance of tribes on nearby reservations fought to invalidate federal easements allowing the Dakota Access Pipeline to carry oil under the lake. Activists and residents believed the pipeline would jeopardize the water supply for the reservation and for millions of people in North Dakota and neighboring states, and that, since its path was across ancestral grounds, the pipeline would destroy sacred Indigenous religious sites in violation of treaty rights.

For years, arguments were made that the US Army Corps of Engineers had failed to conduct proper environmental impact statements. President Barack Obama's administration had halted construction, but when Donald Trump became president, his administration's engineers found there was nothing "injurious to the public interest."[97] The Standing Rock Sioux brought a lawsuit against the US Army Corps of Engineers to protect their cultural sites and the water.[98] Protesters faced off against bulldozers, dogs, and private security forces. The National Guard, activated by North Dakota governor Jack Dalrymple, a Republican, stood with law enforcement. Members of Standing Rock were joined by hundreds of protesters from other tribes, and the encampment swelled to a population of over ten thousand.

"Standing Rock was part of the culmination of Indigenous resistance combined with a movement for human rights around the country," observed Judith LeBlanc, member of the Caddo Nation and executive director of Native Organizers Alliance, which played a significant role in the protest. In an interview for this book, LeBlanc analyzed the significance of the protest at Standing Rock and its greater meaning to the Indigenous people. LeBlanc has spent her life as an activist working for voting rights, educational equity, and women's rights, and as a leader in Indigenous movements.[99]

LeBlanc sees her mission of empowerment and protest in multiple causes—the Black Lives Matter movement against police killings; the immigrant struggle, including those with family members in cages at the border; the Dreamers who, though undocumented, take a stand despite the risk of drawing the attention of law enforcement; and the fast-food workers' struggle for the right to a living wage. "All of these movements, all these issues, created the landscape for Standing Rock. It's amazing when you understand how no movement, no community, stands alone. We are all having an impact on one another." When she looks back on George Floyd, the African American suffocated to death on a Minneapolis street by White police officer Derek Chauvin on May 25, 2020, it is with an eye toward the spirit of protest that filled the street in response to his murder. That spirit propelled a demand for change that spread widely. "I am so proud of what happened in Indian country to take our stand to continue to build this movement of resistance to the crisis of capitalism."

In the modern era, the Standing Rock rebellion over the Dakota Access Pipeline turned the tide for Indigenous protests in America. LeBlanc recalled, "Museum directors are supporting the right of Standing Rock to protect its sacred sites. Actors Leonardo DiCaprio and Jane Fonda, elected officials, leaders of diverse backgrounds came to show support. We were there to ensure our ancestral responsibility, our inherent role as caretakers of Mother Earth." After so much had been lost, taken, and stolen, the Standing Rock protests were an attempt to re-establish justice and traditional ways of governance. LeBlanc explained:

> Water is life. The world began to see us as who we really are in the twenty-first century, exerting our power and our right to defend water and land and to use our power for the good of all people. We are the only peoples in the United States that have collectively been self-governing since the beginning of time. We are the ones that can represent the Missouri River and the concerns of farmers and others in federal court because we have treaties, a constitutionally guaranteed right. Standing Rock was a real mass public education, but not only who we are externally, but also who we were.

The protesters remained at Standing Rock as long as they could, but the occupation ended because of the severe winter weather, not a faltering of their spirit. North Dakota, known for its weather, was experiencing sustained winds and blizzard conditions. Unfortunately, a federal judge ruled that the pipeline could not be enjoined because there was no proof of future injury to the plaintiffs or the water.

Although the corporate interests were ultimately protected, the protests inspired and empowered Indigenous communities nationwide. LeBlanc believes that the protest at Standing Rock raised the consciousness of Indigenous people and allowed them to realize their power—power they held through their spirituality as well as through their dual citizenship as citizens of the US and an Indigenous nation, which always engenders a sense of ancestral responsibility. Protest rarely provides an immediate, direct line to victory, but it is effective nonetheless, especially when obstacles are historical and multilayered.

To LeBlanc, Indigenous protest at Standing Rock sharpened much-needed activist skills such as advocacy and lobbying, which she believes played a role in Deb Haaland's appointment in 2021 as the first Indigenous secretary of the interior, a federal cabinet post responsible for public lands, environmental justice, and nation-to-nation diplomatic relations with Indigenous tribes. In 2019, Haaland, a Democrat, along with Representative Sharice Davids of Kansas, became the first two Indigenous women elected to Congress. In the hotly debated 2020 presidential election, Indigenous votes made a difference in Arizona and turned the tide in that state's Senate election. They also made a difference in elections in New Mexico and Kansas.

Indigenous people did not become recognized citizens of the United States until 1924, and even then, for decades afterward, their voting rights were suppressed. The Voting Rights Act of 1965 protected their right to vote along with African Americans. Judith LeBlanc said the Indigenous "never had our Barbara Lee, our Maxine Waters [Black female politicians] for our children to see." But they do now. The current Indigenous movement is reminiscent of the energy at the Wounded Knee standoff. Resistance and protest ebbs and flows, but they're never going to be able to eradicate Indigenous cultures. "Our peoples, our awareness, our consciousness, our will to have cultural continuity cannot be destroyed," LeBlanc said. "And we still are thriving." The pipeline was built, but Indigenous self-confidence and structure were also built at Standing Rock and will be paying dividends for generations to come. In the words of LeBlanc—and history supports this statement—"we will always continue." Thriving, against odds, is protest.

CONCLUSION

Five hundred years of struggle have been a crucible and an unwelcome badge of honor. Indigenous people have been and remain spiritually joined to the land as caretakers of Mother Earth. They stand tall in a culture grounded in the land, the waters, wildlife, in a spiritual connectedness that fed a powerful strength to resist and fight back against settler colonialism in all of its diabolical forms of invasion. The forces of law, violence, and populations from abroad artificially created a United States of America on stolen Indigenous lands, forcibly removing the people to make way for European occupation and then proclaiming themselves lovers of liberty. Facing this truth is protesting historical lies. Indigenous resistance became this nation's original protest. Theirs is the longest struggle against oppression, using revolts, violence, direct action, and uprisings to challenge authoritarianism, maintain their culture, and continue their caretaking of this land.

Today, the United States recognizes five hundred sixty-six Indigenous tribes. However, there are over four hundred tribes the United States does not recognize for various reasons of history, geography, and politics. Federal and state investigations into abuses at Indian boarding schools have been sporadic as best. Treaty negotiations continue in court and Congress, as the tides have turned by the force of those Indigenous who resisted all forms of settler colonialism, or White superiority, upon which land theft and forced assimilation were based. As Leroy Little Bear of the Blackfeet Nation has asserted, "Individually, each tribe may have limited resources and influence. . . . However, our combined voice and expressed political unity will help us achieve broader support for ecological restoration and the enrichment of tribal cultures."[100]

There is nothing White colonists or state and the federal governments have not done in the effort to create and maintain an empire called the United States of America. When unearthing the past, surreal discoveries reveal how much harm was sustained and overcome, but they also expose the depth of the country's wickedness. In 2022, Harvard University's Peabody Museum of Archaeology & Ethnology issued a written apology for its collection of hair samples cut from the heads of seven hundred Indigenous children who had been forced into boarding schools. Their hair had been given to the Peabody Museum in 1935 by anthropologist George Edward Woodbury.[101] In the official statement, director of the museum Jane Pickering apologized for

Harvard's "complicity in the objectification of Native peoples and for [their] more than 80-year possession" of this macabre collection.[102]

Teaching the history of this nation is protest, because young people should not become blind carriers of America's myth of immaculate conception. It seems that in these hair clippings, White elites had sought to possess the very spirit of the Indigenous. Not satisfied with occupying their land, they sought to collect their essence too. It evokes memories of when the actual skins of the Indigenous were collected, which is the origin of the term "redskin."[103] After years of protests and litigation, activist Suzan Harjo has led successful efforts to end the use of disparaging and racist terms such as "redskin" and "squaw" by many sports teams, street names, towns, and high schools. Protests against racist images and names are ongoing.

Longtime activist Winona LaDuke has led battles and strategies to defend religious sites. "Native American religions, sacred sites, languages, and ways remain under assault," says LaDuke.[104] Indigenous populations are increasing despite government, commercial, and socio-cultural attempts to halt their growth, and they are thriving as resistance remains a shield and buckler for sustaining self-determination. Continued existence can be protest, after five hundred years of government-led violence. From first contact with Europeans to Standing Rock, the Indigenous tribes of America have been fending off attacks. Indigenous resistance is eternal—past, present, and future.[105]

The phrase "Free Soil, Free Labor, Free Men" still haunts me. My ancestors witnessed the diminishing Indigenous populations of Kansas. Declined but not gone. As a child, my mother attended public schools, together with Indigenous children, other African Americans, native-born White Americans, and European immigrants. She said they were taught reading, writing, and arithmetic along with the origin story of a United States that, relying on White male ingenuity, grit, hard work, and through God's grace, became an empire. Outside of propagandist programs on the radio and later television, such as *The Lone Ranger*, the westerns where cowboys and the cavalry always won, there was no mention of those for whom the land belonged.

Protests against racist images and names, and continued litigation to regain Indigenous land, are ongoing. Stolen land and kidnapped people made the United States, and those abolitionists, freedom fighters, and believers in justice who opposed the laws, violence, and oppression that flew in the face of America's idyllic claims faced the wrath of an empire-building nation. Yet, they spoke up alone or in conventions, rose to defend values beyond the law and lawlessness, and laid the foundation for a modern democracy.

Protest can provide for the passing down of cultural traditions while resisting assimilationist deceptions, teaching all young people the true history of their country, and keeping self-love aflame despite generational trauma and the ever-changing winds of oppression.

Indigenous American history overlaps with African American history, each having distinct battles, defeats, and triumphs. Both groups suffered colonial and national oppression in unimaginably barbaric forms. But it was their opposition to subjugation that laid the foundation for a modern democracy. Stolen land and kidnapped people made the United States of America. In the century after its founding, the price for tyrannical nation building would trigger countless revolts by those for whom freedom and equality were human rights that existed without legislation. It would take freedom fighters who opposed slavery as a man-made evil based in greed that flew squarely in the face of America's idyllic claims, as well as a civil war, to extricate this sacrilege from the land.

CHAPTER TWO

"WHAT TO THE SLAVE
IS THE FOURTH OF JULY?"

There was nothing unusual about seven-year-old Eliza, an enslaved girl born in Mercer County, Kentucky, about 1827. In need of a quick influx of money to pay off a $1,000 debt, Eliza's owner, J. A. Lewis, sold her to Thomas and Harriet Christian, a couple looking for a house slave. Eliza was my great-great-grandmother on my mother's side. Mattie Leatha Bradshaw, her granddaughter, wrote an account of Eliza in a 1907 student essay when Eliza was still alive and Mattie, a graduate of Topeka High School, was studying to be a teacher at Kansas Normal School.

Mattie's essay, titled "My Grandmother's Story," was published in the October 18, 1907, edition of the school paper of the Kansas State Normal School, now Emporia State University. Dr. Sam Dicks, a history professor at Emporia State University, found Mattie's article about Eliza and researched her story as a descendent of the Exoduster movement in "Eliza Bradshaw: An Exoduster Grandmother."[1] Mattie's essay of 1907 was written as a protest of this country's heinous past, but she shared Eliza's humanity and act of defiance as protest, as well.

Lewis, the man who sold Eliza to pay a debt, was also her father, and since her African mother's name was unknown, she must have been sold away when the child was a toddler. At seventeen years old, the Christians allowed Eliza to marry an enslaved man named Lewis, probably as an investment in farmwork, breeding, and eventual selling, as was the custom in the chattel slavery system at this time.[2] Marriage and children were seen as a stabilizing anchor to reduce escapes and increase the probability of children as more enslaved laborers. The marriage of Lewis and Eliza was not recognized by law, because enslaved people were without legally recognized free will to enter marriage contracts.[3] Caring for each other as human beings, however, was a form of protest against an unconscionable fallacy that non-Whites were devoid of human feelings.

Eliza, in addition to being a mother herself, was forced to be Harriet's seamstress, cook, laundress, housekeeper, gardener, dishwasher, and a wetnurse to Harriet and Thomas's children, laboring from sunrise to sunset at any task that the mercurial Harriet gave her. One day, Eliza, exhausted by endless demands, sat down to rest for a moment, only to find Harriet immediately pick up a thick wooden broomstick handle and strike Eliza, beating her until blood oozed down her face, after which this sadistic woman poured salt into those wounds, demanding that Thomas Christian beat Eliza with a rawhide whip after dinner.[4] A rawhide whip is made of cow skin but was not used on animals—only inmates and the enslaved—and it cuts through skin and muscle. Many enslavers kept a rawhide whip above the kitchen door as an ever-present warning.

After dinner, Thomas Christian raised his whip, with Harriet Christian looking on greedily. Eliza responded by throwing a pot of scalding hot water that, along with her rage, had been boiling over a large fire. The Christians screamed, cursed, and called Eliza crazy, but the incident convinced them to leave her alone. From that point until she gained her freedom, at fifty-nine years old, she was never beaten again. She and her husband, Lewis, chose the last name Bradshaw. After such a life of bondage, dreaming of a future can be considered protest. However, when African Americans sought to peaceably begin anew as citizens with constitutional freedoms, White terrorism by night and segregation by day was intent on keeping them enslaved. Night riders torching the community's newly built school for African American children, and threatening murder, led Eliza and Lewis to join others emigrating north, by train and then horse-drawn wagon, leaving Kentucky forever for the plains of Kansas. The Bradshaws became Exodusters, the first large-scale migration of African Americans and named in homage to the biblical book of Exodus.[5]

One Exoduster poster proclaimed:

Come!
To the Colored People of the United States:

We, the undersigned, having examined the above county and found it best adapted to our people, have applied to the proper authority, and have obtained a Charter, in the name and style of "The David City Town Company," in the County of Hodgeman. State of Kansas. Thomas P. Moore, part salesman, part and explorer, led the migration of families, including the Bradshaw tribe, from Kentucky to Kansas.[6]

John F. Thomas, minister of the First Baptist Church (Colored) of Lexington, chose Hodgeman County and was a local leader of the Kentucky migration.[7]

I take pride in the independence and tenacity shown by the African Americans who created a life from the earth, living in dugouts in the ground, and warmed by campfires until their homes could be constructed. My ancestors made a living farming the land of Larned, Kansas, a half day's walk from the legendary Wild West town of Dodge City. The railroad brought workers from the East Coast, Europe, and Asia. Desolate Fort Larned was a military compound built to appease railroad magnates fearful that attacks by angered Indigenous might slow construction. There were no such attacks.

As Africans in bondage, Lewis and Eliza had no legal protection against abuse and were expected to witness and withstand diabolical violence without uttering a word of protest or act in self-defense. But the enslaved were, indeed, human and resisted, fought back, used diplomacy and deception, escaped from bondage, and tried to maintain traditions and identities despite the systemic prohibition—enacted first by the abominable English and then the Americans—against African names, religions, and traditions. Mattie graduated from Topeka High School in 1905 and received a Life Teaching Certificate from the Kansas State Normal School in 1908. She went about her work stoically, like many Midwesterners, educating African American children as best she could, in a segregated school, in a nation of legalized racial oppression.

Without slavery and the Indigenous land grab, the United States would not be the nation it is today. This world-class economy relied on immoral, greed-based systems based on propagandist notions of supremacy, created to provide Euro-American elites the means to build intergenerational wealth from the unpaid work of cradle-to-grave African laborers. Although subjugated under threat of murder, rape, and torture, those Africans resisted, revolted, and rose to claim their citizenship. There must be an examination of their protests of enslavement and subjugation on every front, through escape, education, petitions, litigation, uprisings, and basic survival. In addition, when post–Civil War promises were quickly broken, African Americans continued to protest and disrupt capitalist thought and strongholds that attempted to relegate them, again, to a laboring class, through legal strategies, organization building, and direct action to lift themselves to citizenship—albeit one lacking in the full guarantee of proper rights.

SIN, SALVATION, AND SLAVERY

Sin began early in what would become the United States, back when the "Old World" monarchs embarked on an exploration and then invasion of North America, or the New World. Religion arrived in Virginia with its founding in 1607. But sin followed a year of drought and a blistering summer, a stormy fall, a frigid winter, and attacks by Powhatan forces. The colony began to fail, confined within a small fort without fresh water, supplies, or food. As detailed in the previous chapter, most of the Virginia Colony starved to death between 1608 and 1609, known as the Starving Time, with deprivation leading to desperation and even cannibalism.

When the colony's deputy governor, Thomas Dale, arrived in the wake of the Starving Time's debauchery, he was appalled by what he considered shameless immorality as well as misplaced anger of the colonists. Although they felt themselves abandoned by England, it was around 1611, that Dale chose to address these concerns by issuing the "Lawes Divine, Morall and Martiall," a legal doctrine to re-establish order under a moral code and severely punish critics. Any criticism of government and religious leaders or the corporate interests financing the Virginia Colony of London was met with violence.

The European elite wielded immense social, legal, and economic power over the poor masses and indentured servants who lived in fear of the lash, stockade, banishment, and even death for criticizing colonial authorities. Article 12 of "Lawes Divine, Morall and Martiall" states:

> No manner of person whatsoever, shall dare to detract, slaunder, calumniate, or utter unseemely, and unfitting speeches, either against his Majesties Honourable Councell . . . or against the Committees, Assistants unto the said Councell, or against the zealous indeavors, and intentions of the whole body of Adventurers for this pious and Christian Plantation.[8]

The first offense carried the penalty of a public flogging with a horse-whip. The second got three years in jail, and the third, death. There were no jury trials or appeals. These cruel orders added extensively to the existing Divine Laws. Governor Dale considered criticism of the powerful an offense equal to robbery and thus deserved the same punishment. In July of 1619, the leaders of Virginia Colony, tired of awaiting word from Parliament in London, went ahead and created the House of Burgesses, their own legislative body. The landholders created laws favoring themselves, subjugating both Europeans and Indigenous people.

Into this colonial madness, some "20 and odd Negroes" arrived from Angola in August of 1619 and were forced to somehow make a life. They had been kidnapped in Angola, which at that time was being invaded by the Portuguese, torn from their homes, and forced onto slave ships, which were attacked on the high seas by an English priva-teer ship named the *White Lion*, who succeeded in stealing the enslaved from the Portuguese. The English ship, needing repairs and provisions, then sought out the Virginia Colony, at that time the only English settlement in North America. The legal status of the first Africans in North America was either quasi-enslaved or indentured, depending on the whim of their owner. Enslavement meant perpetual labor without rights while being quasi-enslaved was closer to indenturement, which carried the possibility of freedom as indentured Europeans worked for free until the termination of their labor contract.

Landholding English lawmakers in Virginia understood that legal oppression would provide them with free labor and prevent Africans who had arrived with superior farming skills from becoming com-petitors. Since the viability of the colony was far from guaranteed, success required legal manipulation despite settler proclamations of their morality. The same incremental laws that based the status of a child on that of the mother, and severed inheritance rights if the child was born of a European, prohibited the land rights of African farmers who had legally gained property after their servitude.[9]

Since Jamestown was founded as a charter, an English business venture, the selling of human beings quickly undermined their sanctimonious divine laws when Africans arrived. The need for the Africans' expertise in agriculture was crucial to the growing of crops for consumption and for riches. However, there were no laws permitting slavery at the time these Africans arrived in 1619, a year before the *Mayflower* arrived in Plymouth, Massachusetts. This is significant because the treatment of the Africans in the colony deteriorated as tobacco plantation owners grew wealthy, ignoring their early religious doctrine.

The hypocrisy was stunning: Africans were being kidnapped, raped, and murdered under law, by invaders who loudly professed to being virtuous people. Nonetheless, there were some European indentured servants who were allies to the Africans and protested the abuse against them. Some even escaped together with them, as evidenced by a 1660 statute that extended the length of any indentured servant's sentence if they were caught doing so:

> BEE itt enacted That in case any English servant shall run away in company with any negroes who are incapable of makeing satisfaction by addition of time, Bee itt enacted that the English so running away in company with them shall serve for the time of the said negroes absence as they are to do for their owne by a former act.[10]

Other statues directly affected Africans, including those permitting enslaved people to be severely beaten, even to death. A statute passed in 1669 established that there were no legal consequences for any White person if they assaulted or killed an African:

> If any slave resist his master, or owner, or other person, by his or her order, correcting such slave, and shall happen to be killed in such correction, it shall not be accounted felony; but the master, owner, and every such other person so giving correction, shall be free and acquit of all punishment and accusation for the same, as if such accident never happened.[11]

These colonial laws served as the foundation of oppression in America and were thus the root cause for protests challenging racial violence for at least three hundred years.

AFRICANS AND EUROPEANS IN BACON'S REBELLION

Sir William Berkeley, governor of Virginia and a former friend of King James, was a wealthy scholar. Nathaniel Bacon, a distant relation to Berkeley, was an ill-tempered recent immigrant to the Virginia Colony who felt an affinity with the common man. He resented the English caste system and the fact that indentured White servants were ridiculed as scum and only gained their freedom after years of laboring without wages.

Some who were eventually released from servitude could purchase land and try to grow rich from tobacco crops, using their experience from having worked on the plantations of the wealthy. However, many struggled under heavy taxes and with the area's rocky land on the colony's edges, which were vulnerable to attacks from the Powhatan's warriors. Indentured servants and Africans were forced to defend the colony from these attacks, while the wealthy elite remained safely ensconced on their plantations.

Governor Berkeley and Nathaniel Bacon's conflict arose over several issues, including the need to respond to Indigenous attacks. In 1675, Bacon, embittered about the Native Americans' retaliations against the settlers, began a campaign of verbal insults against Berkeley, which then escalated into class warfare, the burning of Jamestown, and many casualties. Bacon demanded that Berkeley remove all Indigenous people from the colony, but Berkeley instead sought a diplomatic resolution, which some believed catered to non-Europeans in order to maintain favorable trade deals. In Nathaniel Bacon's Declaration of the People of Virginia, he claimed that Berkeley was selling the "country and the liberties of his loyal subjects to the barbarous heathen."[12] It was in this manner that Bacon rallied the masses against the elite.

Bacon's rebellion of the masses against Governor Berkeley and the wealthy class was unique in that it joined White farmers—both those formerly and currently indentured—to fight alongside African enslaved people and other servants. On September 19, 1676, Bacon's men burned the colonial capital and several other buildings to the ground. Berkeley called for British reinforcements. The uprising ended abruptly with Bacon's sudden death, from dysentery, and the surrender of his followers. When English troops finally arrived, they ultimately arrested Berkeley, who was taken back to England, where he died less than a year later.

Powerful lessons for protesters of African descent, and all oppressed people, can be found from this odd rebellion that took place one hundred years before the Declaration of Independence and Revolutionary War. Unity is crucial, and identifying common issues of concern will bring together seemingly disparate groups so they can outnumber oppressive forces. The application of this lesson is core to protest, but is often forgotten or dismissed, leaving unrealized the potential for unified power.

Importantly, in defeating the rebellion, the elite gained a counterstrategy, which was to use divide-and-conquer schemes to split the masses, preventing alliances and dissipating the people's strength. Colonial laws were enacted based on a racial hierarchy that gave pride of place to poor European servants, thus severing their common economic interests with Africans. Also, Africans were not granted the right of self-defense, and by 1705, chattel slavery laws had made them human property in the colonies.

By 1789, when the Constitution of the United States was ratified, America had made itself a hostage to an economy based on human bondage. The divide-and-conquer tactics devised after Bacon's Rebellion were infused in laws and traditions giving the poorest European immigrants a particular form of American identity, one that equated whiteness with freedom and required complicity in the subjugation of Africans and the Indigenous. Although divide and conquer has been an essential tool to undermine progressive movements, the myriad forms of protesting enslavement ensured the immorality and illegality of this institution gained momentum. Abolitionists were fighting commercial interests as well as provisions of the US Constitution. Under the Constitution's Article Four, Section 2, a slaveholder could send bounty hunters to claim fugitives who had escaped into another state and extradite them back into slavery. These bounty hunters, the poor White American and European immigrants, had power over African fugitives under the Fugitive Slave Act of 1793. These legal measures not only subjugated African enslaved people but also ensured that the bounty hunters had a modicum of relative privilege in the racial hierarchy.

Protesters and resistance groups, in the era of enslavement, were abolitionists, formerly enslaved Africans, the religious, and others who defied the Fugitive Slave Law by helping escaped people become free. Each ingenious tactic struck a blow against this despicable system. Through acts of defiance and revolt both large and small—making individual escapes; waging armed uprisings; publishing poetry, slave narratives, and other books; filing lawsuits; writing petitions; starting an abolitionist newspaper; founding learning societies, libraries, and schools; attending conferences—Africans in the United States rebuked the propaganda that they were an inferior people.

STANDING AGAINST A SLAVE EMPIRE

African battles against European invaders while in Africa continued at sea and challenged their forced servitude in the courts by law and violence once in North America.[13] Frederick Douglass, one of the most famous protesters of the antebellum era, stated:

> Power concedes nothing without a demand. It never did and it never will. Find out just what any people will quietly submit to and you have found out the exact measure of injustice and wrong which will be imposed upon them, and these will continue till they are resisted with either words or blows, or with both. The limits of tyrants are prescribed by the endurance of those whom they oppress.[14]

Douglass was a public speaker, newspaperman, and lobbyist for the abolitionist movement who rose to be an adviser to President Abraham Lincoln. Douglass was an intellectual born about 1817 as the property of Aaron Anthony—his birth year is not certain because birth certificates for enslaved people were not kept, and inventory records and census allowed for approximate birth dates.

Naming oneself can be a form of protest, and Douglass chose Valentine's Day as a birthdate because he recalled being called "Little Valentine" by his enslaved mother, Harriet Bailey, who died when he was about seven years old.[15] He only saw her a few times during his life, as she worked and lived on a different plantation, several miles away. Her love for young Douglass gave Harriet Bailey the strength to walk miles after working, from before sunrise to after sunset, to visit him. This bond for her child was a testament to and a form of protest against the forces that would stand between a mother and her child. Douglass didn't know his father but believed him to be a White man.[16]

Frederick Douglass was sent to work on the Hugh and Sophia Auld plantation.[17] At this time, laws prohibited an enslaved person from being taught to read, and to deter them, brutal punishments were doled out to those caught reading. Sophia began to teach him to read—though she could have been fined for doing so—and eventually, the Aulds realized that reading would lead Douglass or any enslaved person to yearn for freedom. Although the lessons ended abruptly, Douglass was determined to read and found snatches of letters that would supplement the basic alphabet Sophia Auld had taught him.[18] Reading, for Douglass, was protest. Douglass knew there was a power in reading that White people feared would break the bond of slavery.[19] Learning in the face of a probable beating with a rawhide lash was protest.

Slaveholding Europeans in America, led by greed and avarice, through their control of laws created a separate category for an entire race called quasi-humans. Enslaved Africans in North America were deemed movable property or chattel, and property did not need an education. The institution of slavery boasted an ideology of White supremacy provided by God and nature, and it held that Africans were unable to learn anything beyond what was required for performing menial tasks.[20] The myth that God had made all non-Christians lesser humans who were only meant for servitude owed greatly to Pope Nicholas V and his edicts, known as papal bulls, which gave his blessing to enslavement for profit. Pope Nicholas's papal bulls of 1452 and 1455 endorsed the invasion and enslavement of all non-Christians for the profit of Christian Europeans, and his charging of King Afonso of Portugal with the duty to enslave non-Christians is the first recorded case of an edict giving a Christian nation the right to promote and profit from the slave trade.

RAISING THEIR VOICES

Many Africans refused to dwell in quiet suffering and smiling submissiveness. It should be noted that not all White people believed in slavery, but even White abolitionists believed they spoke on behalf of the fugitive and free African. The famous friendship between William Lloyd Garrison, a White abolitionist and newspaperman, and Frederick Douglass ended as Douglass rose in prominence and refused to be controlled by Garrison as a symbol of slavery paraded at abolitionist conventions to evoke White pity. Douglass, like other fugitives from bondage, placed his torment on the page through first-person narratives, detailing the assaults and suffering he faced at the hands of callous Whites as acts of protest.

Poems and theatrical works dramatized the heartbreak of mothers having children torn away and sold, of men beaten and women raped or bred for salacious profit. Douglass wrote his autobiography—*Narrative of the Life of Frederick Douglass, an American Slave*—to dispel rumors that he had never been enslaved and to protest lies about African ignorance, such as the notion that an articulate Black man was an impossibility. The suspicion that Douglass was lying motivated him to provide precise details of the brutal life he had spent in forced labor, and he gave specific names and dates as accurately as he could. The book was wildly successful, leading to threats of Douglass's recapture, which forced him to flee the country for Europe in 1845 and not return to his wife, Anna, and children, until 1847.

SPEAKING AS PROTEST

Frederick Douglass nervously eyed the hundreds of abolitionists who had travelled to Rochester, New York, and waited in the summer's heat to enter Corinthian Hall where the nation's foremost orator would chastise America for its celebration of independence while millions of Africans suffered in slavery. It would become one of Douglass's most famous speeches. Delivered on July 5, 1852, it is titled "The Meaning of July Fourth for the Negro" and in modern times known under the title "What to the Slave Is the Fourth of July?" in which Douglass indicts the US, stating "This Fourth of July is yours, not mine, You may rejoice, I must mourn."[21] it renounced the hypocrisy of America's parades amid "the mournful wail of millions! whose chains, heavy and grievous yesterday, are, to-day, rendered more intolerable by the jubilee shouts that reach them. If I do forget, if I do not faithfully remember those bleeding children of sorrow this day, may my right hand forget her cunning, and may my tongue cleave to the roof of my mouth!"

Given his renown and how much he had already contributed as an intellectual, a newspaperman, an adviser, and an abolitionist leader, Douglass could have chosen to retire and live comfortably. Instead, he insisted on using his position and power to demand justice and try to change hearts and minds. He proclaimed: "I will, in the name of humanity, which is outraged, in the name of liberty, which is fettered, in the name of the constitution and the Bible which are disregarded and trampled upon, dare to call in question and to denounce, with all the emphasis I can command, everything that serves to perpetuate slavery, the great sin and shame of America! 'I will not equivocate; I will not excuse'; I will use the severest language I can command."[22] Douglass spoke to the issue of protest and belonging, addressing the enslavers as well as the formerly enslaved. Douglass hoped his message would reach those who remained in bondage as the children of the kidnapped, taken from Africa and made to build an ungrateful America. It would become a message read on the Fourth of July, in African American communities, more than a century later.

BURY ME IN A FREE LAND

Born free in Baltimore, Frances Ellen Watkins Harper was a suffragist, a public speaker, an educator, and one of the first African American poets published in America, and was among many African women who protested slavery. In her poem "Bury Me in a Free Land," Harper states her opposition to slavery and the country that condones it: "You may make my grave wherever you will, in a lowly vale or a lofty hill; / You may make it among earth's humblest graves, but not in a land where men are slaves."[23] Another Black woman, Phillis Wheatley, was the first published poet of African descent in America, but she was challenged by those Whites whose skepticism prevented them from ascribing such talent to an African person.

Most Whites, by law and practice, had limited access to people of color and believing their own theories of superiority would not accept Wheatley's educability, intellect, and creativity. Beautiful works of art, complex literature, and in-depth political analysis were produced by many Africans during this dark time. William Cooper Nell cofounded the Histrionic Club, through which he wrote, produced, and directed stage plays. The production of concerts, operas, lectures, and other works served to defy prevalent notions of African American ignorance and explore the talents of Africans whose lives were deemed fit only for physical labor.[24] Antebellum African society indicated a certain level of financial independence as well as racial pride, all despite and in defiance of the prejudices of White America.

REVOLTS ON PLANTATIONS

Slave revolts are acts of protest. Enslaved Africans, free African Americans, and White advocates protested the brutality of slavery and the many laws enacted to enforce it in various ways. The enslaved fought back often and creatively. When, for instance, meals for enslavers were intentionally burned or poisoned, tools of labor broken, clothes poorly sewn, or the food of the enslaved hidden away, these were acts of rebellion.[25]

Running away from forced labor meant torture or death if the enslaved were caught, as bounty hunters were paid to bring back a fugitive slave dead or alive. Their dogs would hunt the woods, howling and barking, trained to seek out human prey. Escapes were best carried out by moonless night, though total darkness in thick woods and swamps meant poisonous snakes, with the enslaved moving slowly through treacherously thick foliage, thorns tearing at their flesh, no fresh water or food, and possibly walking in circles, hopelessly lost.[26] It is unknown how many escapes were successful, though one's proximity to the North or to a train station or port increased their chances and opportunity to gain freedom. Frederick Douglass was able to escape enslavement because his freeborn wife, Anna Douglass, sold all her possessions and hatched a plan to have Douglass board a ship in Maryland disguised in uniform so as to look like a free African sailor. He boarded a ship docked in Baltimore and sailed away to freedom. After writing his autobiography, however, he had to flee the country to avoid bounty hunters who were intent on putting him back in bondage.

The numbers of escapes ending in failure were viciously celebrated by overseers ready to give torturous beatings to send a warning through torn flesh by horsewhip; amputated fingers, ears, or toes; branded faces; or maliciously devised murder.[27] Castration was meted out to the prized male worker who would not be tamed by torture.[28] No punishments, no matter how cruel and evilly executed, prevented some enslaved Africans in America from fighting against their bondage and rebel against a depiction as nonhuman.

POOR WHITES AND ANGRY AFRICANS

Insurrections continued even when laws limited the actions of free African Americans and punishments for the enslaved escalated with growing White upper-class fear. Slave rebellions were suspected at every turn as fear or guilt made any unexplained death, fire, or strange illness within the slaveholder's family was an act of rebellion in the minds of shameless White slaveholders. For instance, the New York City fire of 1741, in which wood warehouses and churches blazed in the April night for four days, was blamed on Caesar John Hughson, accused of leading fellow enslaved African men and conspiring with poor hungry Whites. New York's upper classes feared that Africans and "the vulgar," as poor Whites were called, would join together.[29] A crippling fear rekindled memories of Bacon's Rebellion in 1676 and the aligned power of Africans and poor Whites.

"The negroes were rising" was one explanation for the thirteen fires that set New York City aflame in 1741 in a conspiracy with Spanish sailors taken by force to the colony from a captured mercantile ship and sold into slavery.[30] Or were fires on the waterfront an insurrectionist plot by poor Irish who were starving in this British stronghold and wealthy city of eleven thousand where an underground economy in fencing stolen goods led prosecutors to believe looting stores was a motive. Known as the New York Conspiracy of 1741, scholars have studied it from many angles and believe that this uprising was multiracial effort involving Irish soldiers, enslaved Africans, and mixed-race Cuban sailors who came very close to capturing New York City.[31] The value of immigrant labor had been undercut by the fact that enslaved people were paid nothing, and the White elite had ignored the suffering of workers of every race. Some theories place poor Whites at the center of the New York City fires, venturing that they set them in the hope that, once Africans were blamed, the poor Whites would have an even better image relative to Africans and would subsequently receive higher wages. It is still unknown if the Africans participated willingly or were set up by poor White laborers.

Given that White colonists would in other situations throw off suspicion for their acts by masquerading as non-White people—for instance, disguising themselves decades later as Native Americans in the 1773 Boston Tea Party—it is possible that White arsonists acted alone in setting New York City ablaze. Enslaved people were arrested daily and taken to the dungeon. New York City was under English rule. Some believed a Catholic conspiracy was afoot. *A Journal of the Proceedings in the Detection of the Conspiracy Formed by Some White People, in Conjunction with Negro and Other Slaves*, written in 1744 by Judge Daniel Horsmanden, who oversaw the New York Conspiracy trials, shows there was little evidence and only one real witness.[32]

In the end, Horsmanden imposed brutal sentences that supported the belief that White enslavers and slavery sympathizers were aligned as oppressors of the enslaved. In what would become a pattern for centuries in America, the accused went through fake proceedings known as "slave trials." Slave trials did not follow legal due process or rules of evidence. The accused were rarely given any opportunity to testify under oath. Horsmanden wrote, "We have not been able entirely to unravel the Mystery of this Iniquity; for 'twas a dark Design, and the Veil is in some Measure still upon it!"[33]

Africans were accused of arson and crimes against slavery, and the punishments varied only in degree of barbarity. Thirteen were burned alive, eighteen were hanged, and seventy enslaved Africans were banished to Caribbean island plantations.[34] Slave rebellions increased due to the inspiration of slave uprisings in Haiti led by Toussaint L'Ouverture (1791–1804).[35] In that conflict, Haitian slaves rose up to defeat General Napoleon Bonaparte's army and gain their independence.

Slave laws, laws of indenture for poor Whites, and legislated attacks on the Indigenous formed the basis for the rule of law in the United States. Haiti's shadow followed White lawmakers into Congress and state houses. Slave revolts were a nightmare haunting a slave master's nights and resulted in more repressive slave laws.[36]

STONO REBELLION AND DENMARK VESEY'S PLOT

Owing to the sheer number of revolts and rebellions that occurred during slavery, it is difficult to decide which to share here. There were revolts on the high seas, such as the one aboard the ship *Amistad*. Although that revolt ended in the murder of the ship's captain, it made its African leader, Cinqué, a hero and resulted in a national media campaign for abolitionists and a decree of freedom for Cinqué and the others in an 1841 US Supreme Court case argued by former president John Quincy Adams. There was also the slave rebellion of 1811, which took place in the Territory of Orleans (present-day Louisiana), home at that time to sixteen hundred plantations. The rebellion ended in the massacre of dozens of Africans by White mobs and soldiers. The surviving African freedom fighters were executed, with dozens beheaded and their heads placed on poles in a display of White moral depravity and warning to any future African rebels. There were also female-led African uprisings, though they were largely forgotten by history.[37]

Compared with slavery in other places, slavery in South Carolina is often overshadowed, despite the state's outsize role in the slave trade, reputation for repressive laws, and historic slave rebellions waged there. The Stono Rebellion (1737) and Denmark Vesey's plot (1822), two South Carolina revolts nearly a century apart, indicate the entrenched battle waged by the enslaved to break the chains of bondage. Most of South Carolina's population was composed of enslaved Africans, working in the fields or homes of Whites. The port of Charleston buzzed with enslaved Africans who had survived the trauma of their kidnapping and the diseased ships of the Middle Passage only to be sold in auction houses down the street from exports such as rice, cotton, and tobacco, planted and harvested by their enslaved brethren. The bullwhip served to break in new slaves and punish the disobedient, making cruelty the standard.

By 1739, the institution of chattel slavery was building personal empires in which death was an everyday consequence because the importation numbers of the enslaved were so high. The Stono Rebellion, named for the Stono River that flows southwest of Charleston, started on September 9, 1739, and ended in the deaths of twenty-five Europeans and dozens of Africans. The leader, known as Jemmy or Cato, and his compatriots had been headed to freedom in the Spanish colony of Florida when they launched the rebellion. Jemmy, a fierce and charismatic leader who was probably from the Congo or Angola, led an intrepid group of sixty to one hundred individuals. They were outmatched by an armed mob who tracked the group of escaped bondsmen, killing dozens; those not killed in battle were executed, after a slave tribunal, which, presided over by slave owners, was an unjust trial, like all slave trials.

Restrictive laws for enslaved and free Africans in South Carolina, such as the Negro Act of 1740, prohibited group meetings, writing, reading, and travel and permitted the murder of Africans with impunity.[38] These laws remained in place until the end of the Civil War. They maintained that all persons deemed slaves would forever remain so, including "all Negroes, Indians, mulattoes, and mestizos."[39] One individual who fell under this legal definition and who dedicated himself to the cause of freedom was Denmark Vesey, born in Saint-Domingue (now Haiti) in 1767. Before settling on the name of Denmark, he was Telemaque, then Telmak, and his "beauty, alertness and intelligence" was noted early in life as a cabin boy under a slave trader named Captain Joseph Vesey.[40] Enslaved in South Carolina, Vesey eventually won a lottery in 1799 or 1800 and used the money to purchase his freedom.[41] He was influenced by the uprising in Haiti as well as the French Revolution, which toppled the country's monarchy, and he read about the Missouri Compromise of 1820, which allowed free and slave states into the Union.[42]

FREE, AND RISKING ALL FOR THE ENSLAVED

Vesey could have lived free but chose to lead a rebellion against slavery. Although Vesey was free, he was rejected by other Black freemen in Charleston who looked down on him for his prior status. Instead of begging to be a part of what he considered an apathetic free Black society, or going north to start a new life, Vesey chose to risk his freedom to liberate other Africans who were in bondage, declaring, "We Shant be Slaves to these damn rascals any longer!"[43] The lack of political will in the North and the obstinance of Southern slaveholders made him aware that African freedom would not come through the courts. Vesey was a formidable orator and intellect, and if law and racial discrimination had not denied him the opportunity, he would have been an excellent lawyer.[44] He also was a prosperous carpenter and could have continued on that path, but he believed that God had told him to lead an attack against slavery.[45]

Vesey and his compatriots developed an elaborate plan of revolt, deciding they would poison Charleston's wells, thereby sickening the entire White population. Once the people were weakened by poison, his army of five hundred to one thousand Africans would subdue and kill them.[46] The rebels created a map that divided the city into particular sections that would become rebel strongholds, and their first plan of attack was to overwhelm guards at the armory in order to secure weapons. Vesey made clear they must kill any White person they encountered, then obliterate the city and its residents with "fire and sword [so that] not a single white soul would survive."[47] The plan entailed looting the banks and then sailing to Santo Domingo, on the island of Hispaniola. In the event that South Carolina's militia grew too strong, Vesey's backup plan was to fight "man to man" and escape into the hills.

The rebels swore not to reveal the plot on pain of torture and death, but fear broke their resolve, and the plot was discovered. One by one, details emerged, and Vesey, along with hundreds of others, was arrested. White Charleston was shocked by the intricacy of Vesey's plan. The trial began on June 19, 1822, and as it extended into August, Vesey was betrayed by a slave, and those freed men with mixed loyalties, and anyone who mistakenly believed betrayal would save them from the gallows.[48] They were wrong to do so, as the innocent and conspirator alike would be charged with "attempting to raise an Insurrection amongst the Blacks against the Whites."[49] The seven White men—lawyers, planters, and slave owners—who presided over this case involving the era's most shocking slave revolt would decide the fate of men who detested bondage.

In the trial, the court reporter refused to write down Vesey's statements against slavery. The trial transcript recorded only a summary from Black witness testimony. Vesey and seventy-two others were tried and convicted of attempting to overthrow slavery.[50] Upon Vesey's sentencing, the court had the audacity to chastise him as the leader of a plot "to trample on all laws, human and divine." Rather than being outraged about slavery, he should have stayed satisfied with the comforts compatible with his situation.[51] The judge added: "To that Almighty Being alone, whose Holy Ordinances you have trampled in the dust, can you now look for mercy, and although 'your sins be as scarlet,' the tears of sincere penitence may obtain forgiveness at the 'Throne of Grace.'"[52]

Vesey never divulged the names of any co-conspirators.[53] The court did not record the elegance of his mighty last words in order to limit his reach, remove his voice from history, and erase the threat that his plot posed. He was hanged, along with thirty-five others both innocent and guilty, according to slave laws.[54] Thirty-seven other co-conspirators were deported to plantations on Caribbean islands.[55] Learning about Vesey's plot and other slave revolts is an act of protest, especially for students in an educational system that hides the ever-deepening story of American slavery behind myths, and that often limits examples of bravery to those who upheld unjust laws, which meant supporting enslavement, murder, and assault for money.

Slave revolts terrified slaveholders because they demonstrated people of color had a working intelligence, leadership ability, and, given that self-defense in all forms was outlawed on pain of death, tremendous courage. Slave masters and lawmakers enacted more restrictive laws for free and enslaved Africans based on both paranoia and the real threat of revolts. They failed to recognize the spiritual nature of protest, that it was a natural response by oppressed human beings that could not be legislated away. It was a reality they wished to ignore for the sake of profits. Slave masters and politicians also realized that executing the leaders of slave revolts would not end rebellions for those who believed death in the battle for freedom was well worth the risk.

MURDER IN JERUSALEM

Nathaniel "Nat" Turner led the bloodiest recorded slave revolt in US history. Turner must have known of Vesey's plot, as well as other rebellions, and watched stricter laws get tightened around enslaved people, with harsher punishments to quell the threat of revolt. Turner, a devoutly religious Christian preacher, considered himself safely absorbed in the White slave master's version of the Bible, never spoke of rebellion until, he said, God guided him to rise against slavery.

Turner was born enslaved in 1800, in Jerusalem, Virginia, and worked first on the farm of Benjamin Turner.[56] Turner's mother, who had been kidnapped from Africa, despised enslavement and instilled in her son a sense of self beyond the White man's bondage. Nat Turner would not allow himself to believe his condition was natural or ordained by God, believing instead that God meant him for better, and it was his Christian belief that inspired the revolt of 1831.[57] A sign from God instructed Turner when to attack White slaveholders—men who had kidnapped, raped, and beaten enslaved Africans.

In 1831, Turner was sold to Joseph Travis, a farmer in the area. Later that year, the sign from God that Turner had awaited came: an eclipse of the sun.[58] On August 21 of that year, he initiated the rebellion with the murder of the Travis family, the first of over fifty murders committed by his followers.[59] Turner did little of the actual killing, serving instead as the murderous uprising's leader, carrying a large, dull sword of justice, attacking only slaveholding White families and then fleeing into the darkness, across miles of farmland, through woods and fields. With amazing speed and agility, the rebels went from farm to farm until over fifty bodies were bludgeoned and stabbed. By the time they finished, the pitch-black night had faded into morning.[60]

In the morning, bodies were found, and an alarm was sent across Virginia and surrounding states that their worst nightmare, a slave uprising, was taking place. White masters and over three thousand deputized soldiers amassed to search the woods and capture anyone who had dared resist bondage and its atrocities. Turner was found on October 30, 1831, and brought back to Jerusalem alive. Unfortunately, innocent enslaved people were the victims of retaliation by enraged Whites who needed to send a message to all enslaved Africans to stave off any further rebellions.[61] There was a slave tribunal pretending to be a lawful execution of justice, but, as in all slave trials, Turner and the others were not afforded due process and a fair trial.

Turner was prohibited from testifying on his own behalf at his tribunal, as no person of color was afforded that right. Instead, Thomas Gray, a White lawyer, was sent to Turner's cell to take his "confession," which has been the basis for most accounts about the uprising, except there are books, such as William Styron's 1968 novel *The Confessions of Nat Turner*, and films that falsely purport Turner's raid was based on his lust for a White woman, which allowed a cover for White guilt. Turner was not allowed to speak directly to the three men who presided over the tribunal. The slave court found Turner guilty and sentenced him to hang. Gray, meanwhile, would become a celebrity, speaking about the murders, the tribunal proceedings, and, of course, Turner's confession to the insurrection.[62]

According to the 1831 pamphlet *The Confessions of Nat Turner, the Leader of the Late Insurrection in Southampton, Va.*, published by Gray, Turner believed himself a prophet:

> I was thirty-one years of age the 2d of October last, and born the property of Benj. Turner, of this county. In my childhood a circumstance occurred which made an indelible impression on my mind, and laid the ground work of that enthusiasm, which has terminated so fatally to many, both white and black, and for which I am about to atone at the gallows. It is here necessary to relate this circumstance—trifling as it may seem, it was the commencement of that belief which has grown with time, and even now, sir, in this dungeon, helpless and forsaken as I am, I cannot divest myself of. Being at play with other children, when three or four years old, I was telling them something, which my mother overhearing, said it

had happened before I was born—I stuck to my story, however, and related somethings which went, in her opinion, to confirm it—others being called on were greatly astonished, knowing that these things had happened, and caused them to say in my hearing, I surely would be a prophet.[63]

Like Vesey, Turner refused to give the names of co-conspirators, and on November 11, 1831, he was hanged along with thirteen others, including a woman who that fateful night believed that she was going to be freed by Turner. Her only crime was wearing her slave mistress's dress the night of the uprising.[64] Later, pieces of Turner's dead body were taken as souvenirs and family heirlooms. They cut off his head and placed it on a pike as a public display of warning to other enslaved people. These upholders of law and morality pulled the skin off Nat Turner's body and dissected it. Next, they took Turner's head and boiled it to use the skull as a souvenir.

There were so many Whites who believed Turner's head had mystical powers that, according to a *New York Times* op-ed, it remained out of the possession of his family members for nearly 185 years. It was finally returned in 2016: "Richard Hatcher, a former mayor of Gary, Ind., delivered what researchers suspect is the skull of Nat Turner, the rebel slave, to Turner's descendants. The skull had been kept as a relic, sold and probably handed down through generations."[65]

Turner's skin remained with the Mallory family. William Mallory was in the mob in Jerusalem, Virginia. He openly bragged about skinning the body of Nat Turner, a fact that was even noted in Mallory's obituary in 1860:

Mr. William Mallory, an old citizen of Southampton County, died a few days ago, immediately after returning from a visit to this city. Mr. Mallory was 80 years of age, and figured in the suppression of the Southampton massacre. He was the identical "Buck Mallory" who skinned Nat Turner, the leader of the rebellion, and the hide having been tanned, portions of it are now extant in the "curiosity shops" of many residents in and about Southampton. While in the store of Mr. John R. Davis, in this city, a week or two since, he remarked that "he had skinned Nat Turner, and he would have skinned old John Brown if he could only have had the opportunity."[66]

For Mallory and other pro-slavery Americans, Turner's execution was not punishment enough. The town's decision to change its name from Jerusalem to Courtland, Virginia, did not erase the stain. White rage, panic, and paranoia about insurrections led to ever more restrictive laws.[67] Conspiracies about uprisings would be formulated if free African Americans were seen simply talking in small groups on a street or attending certain social functions. Maryland prohibited free African Americans from entering the state.[68] Even the church was under scrutiny. In Virginia, a law enacted in 1832 stated:

> No slave, free negro, or mulatto, whether he shall have been ordained or licensed, or otherwise, shall hereafter undertake to preach, exhort, or conduct, or hold any assembly or meeting, for religious or other purposes either in the day time, or at night.[69]

In Maryland, the gathering of Africans could result in thirty lashes.[70] Africans could not possess weapons. In Virginia, the law prohibited free and enslaved people from bearing arms despite the Second Amendment.

> CHAP. XXII. Para. 4. No free negro or mulatto shall be suffered to keep or carry any firelock of any kind, any military weapon, or any powder or lead; and any free negro or mulatto who shall so offend, shall, on conviction before a justice of the peace, forfeit all such arms and ammunition to the use of the informer; and shall moreover be punished with stripes, at the discretion of the justice, not exceeding thirty-nine lashes.[71]

A punishment of thirty-nine lashes on the bare back was probably a death sentence. Yet, the enslaved escaped and planned revolts as protest even when they understood the consequences could be a rawhide whip, torture, and hanging.

In spite of the clear penalties of resistance, the enslaved persisted. In Missouri, for instance, an enslaved woman named Celia decided she no longer would be sexually assaulted by her master, Robert Newsom. He had first raped her at fourteen, newly purchased, on the wagon ride to his home, and then had a special cabin built to have full access to her. Celia murdered Newsom on his Fulton plantation. When she confessed to the murder, no due process rights were afforded to her. Under the law, she was not a woman whose virtue needed to be protected. Convicted of first-degree murder, Celia was hanged on December 21, 1855.[72]

The United States had a bloodlust for money rooted in the institution of slavery, even as this young nation rising to global prominence touted the American ideals of individualism, Christian virtue, hard work, and inventiveness. Hiding in plain sight was its engine of productivity: slavery. One pious man, recognizing how the lust for power and money enthralled this nation, believed that grip could only be loosened through death and destruction.

NOT WITHOUT BLOOD

John Brown sacrificed all he had in a failed attempt to end slavery. He remains an abolitionist in US history not merely because he was White and lost his life, as well as the lives of two sons, fighting against slavery but because his rebellion speaks to the advent of religious zeal among abolitionists. Like Vesey and Turner before him, Brown led his rebellion, an 1859 attack on a Virginia armory, hoping to trigger a national uprising that would finally end slavery.

Born in 1800 in Torrington, Connecticut, to a deeply religious abolitionist family, John Brown believed violence was necessary to end the grip of slavery in America. He showed his deadly side first in the "Bleeding Kansas" conflict of the 1850s. The 1820 Missouri Compromise, which sought to balance Northern and Southern interests, had given hope to Africans and abolitionists that the Kansas territory would enter statehood as a place of freedom. However, the government reneged on the compromise. In 1854, Congress passed the Kansas-Nebraska Act, which allowed voters to decide whether Kansas would be a free state or a slave state. "Bleeding Kansas" was the name for the murderous confrontation between pro-slavery and abolitionist forces that began in 1855. Lawrence, Kansas, was sacked by pro-slavery forces in May of 1856, and in retaliation, John Brown, a White anti-slavery minister, and his four sons allegedly kidnapped and butchered to death a group of pro-slavery men, in what was known as the Pottawatomie massacre.

John Brown's raid on the US arsenal at Harpers Ferry, Virginia, was a meticulously planned rebellion. On October 16, 1859, Brown, his sons, sixteen other Whites, and five African Americans, broke into the arsenal.[73] According to Brown's plan, once inside, they would steal the arms and distribute them to African Americans, enslaved and free, then mobilize them to lead a national slave revolt. Although the group had successfully entered the armory and held sixty men as hostages, they also had inadvertently alerted the town, and soon thousands of militiamen surrounded the armory. Brown, in a standoff and badly outnumbered, was cornered, shot, and captured, and his sons were killed. Later, when he was tried, he had to lay on a stretcher for much of his trial, weakened by his wounds and extensive blood loss.

After forty-five minutes of deliberation, Brown was sentenced to death for leading the enslaved in the treasonous raid. Upon hearing his sentence, Brown stated: "Now, if it is deemed necessary that I should forfeit my life for the furtherance of the ends of justice, and mingle my blood further with the blood of my children and with the blood of millions in this slave country whose rights are disregarded by wicked, cruel, and unjust enactments, I submit; so let it be done!"[74]

Spectators held coveted spots for Brown's execution, on December 2, 1859, in Charles Town, Virginia. Mysterious fires and letters promising Brown's rescue had prompted Virginia's governor, Henry Wise, to call up 1,500 soldiers in case they were needed.[75] On execution day, they stood in formation, some standing and others on horseback. Soldiers surrounded wooden gallows, whose plank stood ten feet above the ground, with a lone trap door in the center.[76] The noose swayed in the cold breeze as thousands of eyes looked on.

For those sentenced to execution, the custom at that time was to force them to ride to the gallows sitting on their own coffin. John Brown sat stoically atop his black walnut casket in the back of a wagon. On the gallows, he was hooded and politely waited through delays before the trap door was released. He did not even cry out when the noose, which should have instantly broken his neck in the fall, strangled him to death instead. It took over four minutes. Perhaps those moments of hanging, kicking the air were Brown's final protest. In the end, the soldiers were not needed because no one tried to thwart the execution.

Perhaps the enslavers thought Brown's legacy would end there on that clear, chilly afternoon in Charles Town. While Brown's raid had failed miserably, it inflamed the question of slavery in America.

Although he had been wounded in the raid and had to lay on a stretcher during his trial, he gained strength to stand to speak on his own behalf.

His body arrived in upstate New York to curious men and silent women who entered the red brick courthouse in Elizabethtown, New York, on December 6, where he lay in state, guarded through the night by loyal residents with rifles.[77] Long-bearded and white-haired, John Brown still looked like the fiery preacher he was and the revolutionary he had become. As a White ally, he had sacrificed all. He had purchased land for Africans in New York to build a livelihood and have access to the right to vote. Brown had Africans at his dinner table as equals and had fought to the death to free the enslaved, sacrificing himself and his sons at Harpers Ferry, Virginia, to end the burning evil of human bondage.

Outside of his statement in court, Brown made no statement of remorse or guilt about the lives taken in the raid, saying, "I have stated from the first [day] what was my intention and what was not." His only disappointment, he said, was underestimating the amount of bloodshed needed to break this country's addiction to the powerful profit system of free labor, wicked legal protections, and a euphoric sense of racial superiority. Later, it was revealed that a final note handed to Brown's jailer, Franklin Sanborn, who became a follower after Brown's death, revealed Brown's prescience. The noted stated: "I, John Brown am now quite certain that the crimes of this guilty land will never be purged away, but with Blood. I had . . . vainly flattered myself that without very much bloodshed, it might be done."[78] He knew it would take the blood of hundreds of thousands, and that is what happened in the Civil War, which began in 1861, just two years after his death.

To undermine Brown's effort at Harpers Ferry, Whites called him a madman. They would rather believe he was insane than recognize the insanity of a system that forced human beings to labor a lifetime, under threat of death, for free, to profit a so-called superior people. After Brown was arrested, and news of the failed raid spread, abolitionists who had once admired Brown rebuked and condemned him, including William Lloyd Garrison, who in the abolitionist newspaper the *Liberator* dismissed the raid as "misguided, wild, and apparently insane."[79] Horace Greeley, a noted abolitionist in New York, berated the attack, calling it a "deplorable affair" and "the work of a madman."[80] Greeley blamed Brown's upbringing in Kansas as having been one of "madness, rapine, cruelty and murder to produce such a man, to the Pottawatomie incident, in which Brown had killed White enslavers, while the abolitionist Gerrit Smith condemned all slave insurrections as a terrible remedy for a terrible wrong.

Frederick Douglass heard that investigators were coming to interview him about the slave revolt at Harpers Ferry, and, to avoid being implicated as a co-conspirator and possibly arrested, he fled to England. Along with Brown's detractors, there were a handful of supporters, including Henry David Thoreau. In his essay "A Plea for Captain John Brown," Thoreau interrogated those who had turned their backs on Brown: "Is it not possible that an individual may be right and a government wrong? Are laws to be enforced simply because they are made?"[81]

Even though John Brown correctly predicted it would take bloodshed and a civil war to end slavery, his rebellion was condemned and often is still dismissed as one White man's act of insanity. However, Brown is not a madman in the eyes of those who recognized the hypocrisy inherent in Whites killing people of color with lavish impunity and then being shocked that anyone would strike back. His gravesite in upstate New York is visited by those who know his legacy as a White person who sacrificed his life and that of his family to end slavery in America. Activist groups like John Brown Lives! and the John Brown Farm Museum in the Adirondacks keep Brown's name alive by educating the world about the man and his rebellion and raising social awareness about racial justice.[82]

On that cold December morning in 1859, John Brown's funeral procession left the church. The solemn quiet was broken by clomping horse hooves on the town's cobblestone main street. Had he been there, it's likely that old sinner Mallory would have tried to take the skin of John Brown with a sick pleasure. Two horses pulled that walnut coffin containing the body of John Brown, heavy with American history and betrayal, along twenty-five miles of steep, muddy, mountainous hillside to North Elba, New York. Mary Brown, his weary wife, rose before sunrise to take her husband's body back to the farm. Their home was acres of difficult farmland, with a simple two-story wood home and livestock. John Brown, and his two martyred sons, would be buried near a remarkably tall protruding black stone on a landscape of snow-covered soft slopes of a peaceful place. In a later interview,

Salmon Brown, one of the surviving sons, explained why violence was needed and that his father had intended for the raid on Harpers Ferry to trigger a civil war. "Father's idea in his Harper's Ferry movement, was to agitate the slavery question," he said. "He wanted to bring the war. I have heard him talk of it many times."[83]

WHITE ALLIES

Slavery was rooted in US identity, seeping beyond economy, religion; it was American culture to oppress by law and violence. Abolitionists of all backgrounds, including wealthy Whites and the formerly enslaved, gave fervent speeches condemning enslavers, participated at their peril in the Underground Railroad, and voted against slavery laws. It was a business enterprise that had propelled the United States to prosperity, using violence and the law to maintain order. It was not a new point of view to assert that slavery fed commerce and wealth. Frances Ellen Watkins Harper, an orator, a poet, and an abolitionist, among other titles, understood that breaking the hold of slavery meant toppling slaveholders from their commercial thrones by recognizing that the business of slavery was deeply ingrained in every aspect of the country.[84]

In Congress, Thaddeus Stevens, a quick-witted Radical Republican born in 1792 in rural Vermont, was a vocal abolitionist, as was Senator Charles Sumner, who was attacked and beaten unconscious by pro-slavery congressman Preston Brooks on the Senate floor in May of 1856. It was abolitionist William Lloyd Garrison who embraced a brilliant young fugitive from slavery named Frederick Douglass after hearing him speak about the horrors of life in bondage at a gathering shortly after his escape. Born on December 10, 1805, Garrison grew up poor in Newburyport, Massachusetts, where he worked as a printer and learned the difficulties of life as an underpaid laborer.[85] At twenty-five years old, he founded the abolitionist newspaper *The Liberator*. One year later, in 1831, he created the New England Anti-Slavery Society and then the American Anti-Slavery Society, in 1833.

William Lloyd Garrison fended off death threats by pro-slavery factions of both the upper and lower classes. Steeped in religious and revolutionary spirit, Garrison pushed for immediate freedom for the enslaved, turning away from an early belief in gradual emancipation.[86] While thousands of White abolitionists protested slavery, some were unsure about equal rights once slaves were emancipated, and they were similarly unsure about Black suffrage. In short, the majority of White abolitionists felt a moral burden to protest slavery but otherwise silently accepted the privileges that the system afforded them. As to the question regarding the inherent worth of Black people, they generally believed they were a lesser human class but also part of God's creation, and thus should be pitied but not harmed.

Congress capitulated to slaveholders when it passed the Fugitive Slave Act in 1850. This federal law assigned high fines and prison time to anyone who hid a slave fugitive or failed to report the fugitive to the authorities, which forced Whites who had been ambivalent to take sides on the issue of slavery, creating some allies for abolition. Some will not protest unless their personal stake is clear and in high immediate danger. Douglass warned, "Those who profess to favor freedom, and yet depreciate agitation, are men who want crops without plowing up the ground. They want rain without thunder and lightning. They want the ocean without the awful roar of its many waters."[87]

THE SLAVE MASTERS' RELIGION

Although religion was a tool of subjugation, slave rebellions meant the enslaved refused to fully accept the doctrine of submission as the will of God. The enslaved were forbidden from practicing their religions from Africa or practicing any religion other than Christianity, since non-Christian religious practices were denigrated as pagan. At first, both Christian doctrine and the law allowed an enslaved person to gain their freedom, on earth and in heaven, by converting to Christianity. However, this practice ended when people realized the value of free labor. Enslaved men and women were encouraged to follow the Christian tenet of obedience while remaining in bondage. Religion, faith, and prayer were mechanisms of solace for the enslaved and the free during these horrific times.

Only Bible passages that could be interpreted to support African American debasement and inferiority were allowed in a book called the "Slave Bible." This was an annotated Bible, with any passages about equality, love, and fighting back removed. Slaveholders gave this Bible to Christians in bondage with the lie that God required that Africans remain submissive and accept enslavement as an atonement for inherited sins. The Slave Bible was published in 1807, in London, and is the first instance of an abridged Holy Bible with selected passages omitted specifically for the enslaved for fear certain Bible stories would incite a rebellion. There are 1,189 chapters in a standard Protestant Bible. This Bible contains only 232. Nonetheless, African Americans took the opportunity provided by this invitation into the Christian faith to find spiritual sustenance, exchange information, and even plan revolts.

Africans in the colonies endured, rebelled, and built the foundation for what would become America. Their number rose into the millions and their labor was indispensable. Their pain was incomprehensible, their future uncertain. Yet, they survived. A Virginia law stated that to prevent insurrections "no master or overseer shall allow a Negro slave of another to remain on his plantation above four hours without leave of the slave's own master."[88] The enslaved could only meet for specific purposes, granted by the owner in a letter of permission providing the time of return and with whom the enslaved could associate. Any enslaved people who were caught in clandestine meetings faced severe punishment, so such meetings had to be highly covert.

EIGHTEENTH-CENTURY ACTIVISM

Prince Hall has a long and intriguing story as an activist in the eighteenth century because the idea of activism seems a twentieth-century concept. Hall was born between 1735 and 1738. Accounts of his birthplace vary: some say Bridgetown, Barbados, while others say western Africa. Records indicate that Hall was enslaved when brought to the island but booked passage to Boston of his own volition, as opposed to being brought to Massachusetts by slaveholder William Hall.[89] In 1765, Prince Hall resided in Medford, Massachusetts, working as a tradesman. Sara, his first wife, died young. At the age of twenty-five, he had earned enough money as a leatherworker to buy land, which allowed him to vote. When the Revolutionary War began, Prince Hall, like many Black free men in the Northern colonies, fought against England, engaging the British enemy in the Battle of Bunker Hill.[90]

The first known African member of the prestigious and secretive Freemasons, Hall boasts a legacy of intelligence, cultural pride, and faith in freedom.[91] Historically, Freemasons, whose members include President George Washington and other US presidents, have had a reputation for being well-respected, elite members of society. Prince Hall wanted to be a Freemason because of its creed of brotherhood without regard to one's status or race, heritage, or level of wealth.

Hall was determined to prove the humanity and intellect of Africans to White men through the interactions that would come from membership in the Freemasons. Racism in the American colonies forced Hall to join a British contingent of Freemasons. In 1775, he joined the Grand Lodge of Ireland, which was a military lodge under the British forces stationed at Boston's Castle William (now Fort Independence).[92] He was fully made a Freemason with all rights and privileges. However, the White American lodges refused to recognize him as their brother. Once again, it was Britain that allowed Hall to found and be granted a charter in 1784 for African Lodge #459, now known as the Prince Hall Lodge.[93]

Hall presented several anti-slavery petitions to the Massachusetts legislature invoking law and religion and asserting the humanity of those deemed less than human. His early writings cite the masonic creeds of equality among all men. Hall declared in "Petition Against Slavery Addressed by Prince Hall to the Counsel and House of Representatives of Massachusetts Bay, January 13, 1777":

> The Petition of A Great Number of Blacks, who are detained in a state of Slavery in the Bowles of a free & Christian Country Humbly showing: That your Petitioners apprehend that they have, in Common with all other Men, a Natural and Unalienable Right to that freedom which the great Parent of the Universe hath bestowed equally on all mankind and which they have never forfeited by any compact or agreement whatever. But they were unjustly dragged by the hand of cruel Power from their dearest friends and some of them even torn from the embraces of their tender parents—From a populous and plentiful Country—and in violation of the Laws of nature and of nations and in defiance of all the tender feelings of humanity, brought together to be sold like beasts of burden & like them condemned to Slavery for Life, among a People professing the mild Religion of Jesus.[94]

FIRST RECORDED REPARATIONS CASE

Prince Hall's protest on behalf of Belinda Sutton, a Ghanaian-born woman also known as Belinda Royall, may be the first reparations petition. Sutton had been enslaved by the Royall family in Medford, Massachusetts, as stated in her campaign for slave reparations, presented on February 14, 1783, to the Massachusetts General Court.[95] Her enslaver, Isaac Royall, died in war, and Hall wrote eloquently about the fifty years of grueling work she did for him, as well as Belinda's suffering as an elderly woman without any means of financial support. The petition reads:

> Fifty years her faithful hands have been compelled to ignoble servitude for the benefit of an Isaac Royall, untill, as if Nations must be agitated, and the world convulsed for the preservation of that freedom which the Almighty Father intended for all the human Race, the present war was Commenced. The terror of men armed in the Cause of freedom, compelled her master to fly—and to breathe away his Life in a Land, where, Lawless domination sits enthroned—pouring bloody outrage and cruelty on all who dare to be free.
>
> The face of your Petitioner, is now marked with the furrows of time, and her frame feebly bending under the oppression of years, while she, by the Laws of the Land, is denied the enjoyment of one morsel of that immense wealth, apart whereof hath been accumulated by her own industry, and the whole augmented by her servitude.
>
> WHEREFORE, casting herself at the feet of your honours . . . she prays, that such allowance may be made her out of the estate of Colonel Royall, as will prevent her and her more infirm daughter from misery in the greatest extreme, and scatter comfort over the short and downward path of their Lives—and she will ever Pray.[96]

Demanding reparations was protest then, and it remains so today.

Hall has also been connected to the first recorded campaign by free African parents to gain access to public schools. In 1787, Hall presented a petition to the Massachusetts legislature requesting that the City of Boston provide an education for the children of African American taxpayers. African American parents of free children argued that since their taxes helped finance Boston public schools, their children should have the benefit of those schools. Hall's petition stated:

> As by woeful experience we now feel the want of a common education. We, therefore, must fear for our rising offspring to see them in ignorance in a land of gospel light . . . and for not other reason can be given this they are black. We therefore pray your Honors

that you would in your wisdom some provision would be made for the free education of our dear children.[97]

The petition was denied, but African parents in Boston continued to push for the education for their children.

In the North and South, free African Americans petitioned state legislatures, protesting slaveholding and their ill-treatment. In February 1788, Hall presented a petition to the Massachusetts legislature protesting the slave trade and the kidnapping of free people into slavery. Hall's petition asked, "What then are our lives and Lebeties [liberties] worth if they may be taken away in [such] a cruel & unjust manner as these." That year, African Americans and Whites protested the kidnapping of several African American men from Massachusetts who were taken to the island of Martinique, a French colony, and sold into slavery. John Hancock, governor of Massachusetts, protested to the governor of the island, and the men were returned. Hall's petition led to the passage of Massachusetts's anti-slavery legislation in March 1788.[98] The fight in Massachusetts for equal rights for African Americans continued over the decades. In 1844, a group petitioned the state government to desegregate public schools while intellectual societies fought "Jim Crow" images used by black-faced White actors.

Similar state-based protest movements unfolded elsewhere. In 1791, African Americans in South Carolina submitted a petition to the state legislature to protest their treatment. "[Free African Americans] have been and are considered as free citizens of this state, they hope to be treated as such," the petition stated.

Meanwhile, individuals released petitions and appeals that acted as compelling arguments against slavery. Robert Alexander Young's attack on slaveholding, *The Ethiopian Manifesto, Issued in Defence of the African Americanman's Rights, in the Scale of Universal Freedom*, was published in 1829. "Hearken, therefore, oh! Slaveholder, thou task inflicter against the rights of men, the day is at hand, nay the hour draweth nigh, when poverty shall appear to thee a blessing, if it but restore to thy fellow-man his rights," Young wrote.

That same year, abolitionist and writer David Walker disseminated a petition seeking African American unity against oppression. In *Walker's Appeal*, he asked: "Can our condition be any worse?—Can it be more mean and abject? If there are any changes, will they not be for the better, though they may appear for the worst at first?" On August 6, 1830, David Walker was found dead near the doorstep of his shop.[99] No one was charged with the crime.

In 1842, the US Supreme Court upheld an expansion of fugitive-slave laws. The decision in *Prigg v. Pennsylvania* allowed bounty hunters to apprehend an escaped person and return her and her children, including children born in freedom, to slavery in their state of origin. The court ruled that the rights of slave owners to regain "property" superseded any Northern state's attempt to abolish slavery. In 1850, Congress passed harsher fugitive slave laws that gave even greater authority to slave owners and bounty hunters in retrieving fugitives escaping slavery. In response, abolitionists held the Fugitive Slave Convention in Cazenovia, New York, to propose strategies for the enslaved to defend themselves against those seeking their return to bondage.

At the convention, free and fugitive African Americans drafted militant resolutions rebuking the enactment of racially repressive laws. A similar resolution was adopted at a meeting of the Colored Citizens of Springfield, Massachusetts, in 1850. Two points in the resolution stated:

2. *Resolved*, That we will repudiate all and every law that has for its object the oppression of any human being, or seeks to assign *us* degrading positions. And, *whereas*, we hold to the declaration of the poet, "that he who would be free, himself must strike the blow," and that resistance to tyrants is obedience to God, therefore,

3. *Resolved*, That we do welcome to our doors every one who feels and claims for himself the position of a man, and has broken from the Southern house of bondage, and that we feel ourselves justified in using every means which the God of love has placed in our power to sustain our liberty.[100]

These were daring words of reprisal and resistance, published for Whites to take note of the vulnerability of free Africans and to assert the need for action "using every means" to end slavery, including violence. These petitions and declarations of rights, as well as all the mobilization of people behind them, were testaments to African Americans' agency and courage to protest.

OBSTACLES TO VOTING RIGHTS

Voting and political participation was worth the battle in court and on the streets. Protest against voting rights discrimination began in this nation's colonial infancy. Virginia had restricted voting rights to landholders in colonial days, and by 1705, African Americans in Virginia were prohibited from holding political office even if they owned land.[101] Even though free African Americans paid taxes, most were prohibited from voting. For example, in 1723 Virginia enacted a statute prohibiting free African landholders from voting in any election. Of course, enslaved African Americans, as nonpersons, were precluded from voting; however, the Delaware legislature even passed a statute that prohibited African Americans from being in the vicinity of voting in progress.[102]

Even free people of African descent had no due process rights and could not sit on a jury or testify in court against a White person. Indigenous peoples suffered the same fate. In Maryland, the General Assembly passed an act in 1717 stating

> That from and after the end of this present session of assembly, no Negro or mulatto slave, free Negro, or mulatto born of a white woman, during his time of servitude by law, or any Indian slave, or free Indian natives, of this or the neighbouring provinces, be admitted and received as good and valid evidence in law, in any matter or thing whatsoever depending before any court of record, or before any magistrate within this province, wherein any Christian white person is concerned.[103]

The South arrived at a compromise in which states would count African Americans as three-fifths of a person, which enabled the South to gain additional seats in the House of Representatives owing to the large numbers of African Americans enslaved in their region. Native Americans received a different status regarding their suffrage. In 1831, the US Supreme Court ruled that they were part of a "domestic dependent nation," and thus each state could decide their level of suffrage or exclude them from voting. In the 1857 decision *Dred Scott v. Sandford*, the Supreme Court decided that African Americans were never meant to be a part of the political community.[104] The issue of African American suffrage remained hotly contested in Congress and within state legislatures during the Civil War and even afterward. Each state could decide the voting rights of African Americans and women.

The Civil War, while at its core a political and economic conflict between White men in the North and the South, also demonstrated the power of African Americans armed to defend themselves, their rights, and the country. Free of the fetters of bondage, they could create their own economic path and reach for the American Dream that millions had immigrated to the country to find. The North, embracing the Industrial Revolution and its factories, could leave behind the system of bonded farm labor. But to gain a primary political as well as economic position over the South, it needed the African American vote. They had been counted in the population as three-fifths of a person to determine the number of representatives to Congress, which served to benefit Southern politicians. Now, their voting strength was large enough to change the outcome of state, local, and national elections, and this political power frightened White supremacists.

President Lincoln had evolved as a politician and person by 1863 and, when he signed the Emancipation Proclamation and the words of the Gettysburg Address flowed from him a few months later, he was led by more than just the pragmatic need for more African American soldiers. These executive actions finally freed the enslaved in the Confederate states and denounced human bondage.[105] African Americans in Confederate states fled to Union forces when soldiers overtook Confederate plantations. Benjamin Butler, a balding but long-haired, mustached lawyer from Massachusetts, created the legal theory of contraband of war to provide enslaved fugitives safety among the Union soldiers. Since enslaved people were chattel, or human property, and in war an opponent's property can be seized, thousands of the enslaved who sought solace with the Union troops from Confederate states became contraband of war, despite federal extradition laws. The formerly enslaved persons provided a crucial infusion of troops and resources to a beleaguered Union military, fighting for their own liberation.

General Gordon Granger delivered the Juneteenth Order, General Order No. 3, which gave absolute equality to all of the formerly enslaved, stating:

> The people of Texas are informed that, in accordance with a proclamation from the Executive of the United States, all slaves are free.

> This involves an *absolute equality* of personal rights and rights of property between former masters and slaves, and the connection heretofore existing between them becomes that between employer and hired labor. The freedmen are advised to remain quietly at their present homes and work for wages. They are informed that they will not be allowed to collect at military posts and that they will not be supported in idleness either there or elsewhere.[106]

President Lincoln stated that without the military help of the black freedmen, the war against the South could not have been won.

After President Lincoln's death on April 15, 1865, and despite efforts by a pro-slavery administration, courageous members of Congress rallied to enact the Civil Rights Act of 1866, granting citizenship to African Americans. This was done over the veto of President Andrew Johnson, a Democrat turned Independent and with roots in North Carolina and Tennessee who was impeached in 1868 but missed conviction by one vote.[107] Before his death, Lincoln had overseen passage of the Thirteenth Amendment to the US Constitution. It was with a lawyer's understanding that he decided to make a constitutional amendment his imperative and his legacy. Through this strategy, he bypassed a US Supreme Court that was loyal to the Confederacy, knowing it would overturn any federal law enacted to grant freedom to enslaved persons. The court did, indeed, manage to undermine the Civil Rights Act of 1875 passed by Congress, but it could not deny citizens the freedoms granted under the Thirteenth, Fourteenth, and Fifteenth Amendments. President Johnson had no intention of protecting African American rights and sought to appease a recalcitrant South for political gain.

However, Congress pushed forward and ratified the Fourteenth Amendment to secure African American citizenship at birth, as well as granting privileges and immunity, equal protection, and due process for all citizens, formally overturning the *Dred Scott* ruling.[108] The next issue Congress addressed was suffrage, or the right to vote, for African Americans, a highly contested issue in the North as well as the South and among suffragist White women who believed they deserved to receive the vote before Black men. After a series of spirited congressional debates, the Fifteenth Amendment was passed, securing African American men the right to vote.[109] The amendment states: "The right of citizens of the United States to vote shall not be denied or abridged by the United States or by any state on account of race, color, or previous condition of servitude."[110]

Congress enacted the Ku Klux Klan Act of 1871 in response to the White terrorism of African Americans and because prosecutors refused to enforce basic criminal laws. The Supreme Court, however, responded by using its power to weaken this crucial legislation.[111] Despite being the object of White hate, and being outnumbered and abandoned by the high court and targeted by state laws, African Americans demonstrated a courage and unity that led to court cases defending their rights, as well as economic and educational achievements when they were refused political access. They understood it was the progress they had made, after centuries of enslavement and in the face of extreme adversity, that motivated the country's murderous terrorism and segregation laws.

RESISTANCE TO EARLY SEGREGATION

Many Whites could not accept African Americans as equals, even after slavery was abolished in 1865, and Congress ratified the Fourteenth Amendment, in 1868, re-establishing citizenship for African Americans. Acting individually as well as collectively as mobs or members of organized terrorist groups like the Ku Klux Klan, White racists used violence in attempts to return to the socio-racial hierarchy of slavery and halt the social, economic, and political progress of African Americans.

Southern power rose with the dissipation of Northern resolve and a Supreme Court of White supremacists intent on undermining African American progress. In 1883, the Court ruled in a group of major cases known as the Civil Rights Cases that the protections granted by Congress under the Civil Rights Acts would not apply to privately owned businesses such as theaters, hotels, or restaurants.[112] It was a blow to racial justice felt by African Americans in all stations of life. In 1894, two years before the *Plessy v. Ferguson* decision, Ida B. Wells refused to move from a ladies-only White car to the overcrowded smoking car reserved for African Americans and other people of color. The enraged conductor and then other men tried pulling Wells from her seat. She held on to the seat and bit the conductor's hand when he grabbed her, but the men forcibly pulled her from the seat, dragged her down the aisle, and threw her off the train. The fact that Wells had purchased a first-class ticket meant nothing.[113]

Wells brought a successful action against the railroad and was awarded damages, but the railroad appealed the decision.[114] Tennessee's high court overturned Wells's victory in the earlier verdict and then ordered her to pay the court costs for bringing the lawsuit in the first place.[115] In a newspaper article, Wells pointedly summarized the meager justice afforded African Americans, stating, "[Left to] the State courts for redress of grievances . . . I was given the brand of justice Charles Sumner knew Negroes would get when he fathered the Civil Rights Bill during the Reconstruction period."[116]

In 1890, the Louisiana state government passed the Separate Car Act, officially legalizing segregated train cars. It marked yet another piece of a growing web of state and national laws, such as the Chinese Exclusion Act, stitched together with racist violence such as the Colfax Massacre and military-led campaigns against the Indigenous. The web served to brand the United States a White country even as it maintained an illusion of American liberty. However, just as anti-slavery activists before him had placed themselves in harm's way, Homer Plessy chose to take an anti-segregationist stand against the ever-encroaching racial divide in his beloved New Orleans.

PLESSY WAS AN ACTIVIST

Homer Adolph Plessy was an activist who had not intended to be forever known for bringing the case that created legal segregation across the United States. Plessy was a shoemaker and activist in New Orleans creole society, an octoroon who was proud of his mixed-race heritage; it was said he could pass for White. As the shadow of segregation crept across America, Plessy chose to face it head-on.

Louisiana had been a colony of the Spanish and the French, and New Orleans was a port city of mystery and magic where Creoles, or *gens de couleur*, were living in relative freedom with some political rights owing to the strong presence of a free educated class of African Americans in Louisiana.[117] But the former slaveholders who largely made up the Louisiana legislature wanted a return to slavery, and they were ready to use voter suppression and violence to get their way. The law relegated all Negroes into a designated train car; exceptions were made only for servants caring for White passengers. The "colored car" was a ramshackle, unclean, smoke-filled, crowded container with splintered wooden seats that paired well with the train's wood-burning engine.

On June 7, 1892, tired of the indignities of segregation, and in defiance of the Separate Car Act of 1890, Homer Plessy purchased a first-class ticket and sat on the leather seats among the White passengers. Under the law, the train's conductors, who were all White males, would be fined if they did not remove a passenger who violated this act.

When Plessy was discovered in the White car, he was dragged from the train, arrested, and fined. The case could have been dropped; however, Plessy chose to appeal his fine and challenge this segregationist law. He claimed it violated his Thirteenth and Fourteenth Amendment rights. When these amendments, along with the Fifteenth Amendment, which gave African American men voting rights, were ratified after the Civil War, they granted full citizenship rights to African Americans, both the newly freed enslaved and free persons. But a wave of racist laws and terrorism followed the assassination of President Abraham Lincoln in 1865. Plessy's challenge to the Separate Car Act was watched by conservatives afraid of the rise in African American socioeconomic and political power, especially the power of the African American vote.

Plessy argued that racial segregation placed a badge of inferiority on him as an African American person, but he was told he could not win the case since the law was stacked against him. A. W. Tourgee, a White civil rights attorney, argued the case before the Supreme Court on behalf of Plessy.[118] Tourgee was an ally to African Americans who had fought for the Union, and he had been wounded in the Civil War. While he fought on legal grounds, the Supreme Court chose racial ones, ruling that the states could decide to segregate the races to avoid violence. The reasoning was that it was within the government's police power to maintain peace, and Whites would not riot if people of color existed separately in all social settings.

The federal government, by law, could not segregate the races, but this power was given readily to the former Confederates and racists. The well-earned, fought for, long awaited rights of African American citizens were dismantled by the high court in 1896, setting the stage for the next century of protest, resistance, and litigation by all people of color, especially people of African descent.

CONCLUSION

Beginning in Africa, "20 and odd" Africans were brought from Angola (then Ndongo) to Virginia, enslaved. Their descendants met law and violence with courage and creativity, using petitions, lawsuits, revolts, the arts, lectures, and escape to rebuke bondage and let it be known they were human beings, with free will, demanding freedom. The bloodshed and death of the Civil War brought freedom and legal protections, but the sins of the founding fathers were embraced by too many of their sons.

Plessy v. Ferguson ushered in a regime of segregation that spread to schools and cemeteries, restaurants and hospitals. With racial segregation came terrorism and the lynching, with impunity, of African Americans and other people of color. Subsequent generations of African American people and their allies used the courts, legal petitions, legislation, and street protests in a feverish fight to overturn the *Plessy* decision of "separate but equal."

Supreme Court justices, like anyone else, can protest injustice, and the sole dissent of Justice John Marshall Harlan in *Plessy v. Ferguson* was a prescient outcry against a United States that remained rooted in an ideology in which the power of whiteness reigned over all other racial identities, and any fear of African American progress could be met with violence and legal discrimination. Justice Harlan's famous dissent, his protest, stated:

> But in view of the Constitution, in the eye of the law, there is in this country no superior, dominant, ruling class of citizens. There is no caste here. Our Constitution is color-blind, and neither knows nor tolerates classes among citizens. In respect of civil rights, all citizens are equal before the law. The humblest is the peer of the most powerful. The law regards man as man, and takes no account of his surroundings or of his color when his civil rights as guaranteed by the supreme law of the land are involved. It is therefore to be regretted that this high tribunal, the final expositor of the fundamental law of the land, has reached the conclusion that it is competent for a State to regulate the enjoyment by citizens of their civil rights solely upon the basis of race.

> I am of the opinion that the statute of Louisiana is inconsistent with the personal liberty of citizens, white and black, in that State, and

hostile to both the spirit and letter of the Constitution of the United States . . . by sinister legislation, to interfere with the full enjoyment of the blessings of freedom to regulate civil rights, common to all citizens, upon the basis of race, and to place in a condition of legal inferiority a large body of American citizens now constituting a part of the political community called the People of the United States.[119]

Over the course of the twentieth century, Harlan's dissent was taken as a rallying cry to overturn the *Plessy* decision and its horrific damage to the nation before it was too late. Racial segregation sparked protest movements across the nation.

———————

When Eliza threw scalding water on her slave masters, it was a small private victory with a miraculous ending that would have disappeared, as did most acts of courage by the enslaved, were it not for a curious granddaughter and our family records. Keeping family history alive is protest. The stories of those enslaved who rebelled, fought back, and lived were hidden, buried by slaveholders for fear these heroics would ignite courage in others. It is remarkable that Eliza survived enslavement, especially given the violence and barbaric laws, costing millions of innocent lives and forever tainting the soul of this nation.

When Frederick Douglass was in bondage, long before he was a revered leader of the battle against slavery, he set his mind on the fight of life against Edward Covey, a notorious slave-breaker and overseer who was known for his brutality. Covey attempted to break Douglass's willful mind and control his spirit. They squared off with Covey determined to show his reputation was well-earned. It ended hours later with two exhausted, bloody, sweat-drenched men as Douglass stood before Covey, unbroken.

Eliza Broadnax Bradshaw died in Jetmore, Kansas, on July 26, 1913, and in homage to her legacy, my young cousin, who is both African American and Indigenous, traveled to Kentucky. She took with her to Kentucky the only known photograph of Eliza, in which she appears as an elderly woman in royal pose, seated serenely with hair neatly parted down the middle and hands folded. My cousin had herself photographed holding the photo of Eliza and standing between the rounded gray headstones of Eliza's enslavers, Thomas and Harriet

Christian. Eliza's indomitable spirit was revealed, burning bright in the steady gaze of my young cousin, who took a survivor's defiant stance between those Christian tomb markers, displaying gratifying and righteous rage. It is a rage I share on behalf of my family and all people of the African diaspora who toiled to build nations that refuse to acknowledge their debt and shame.

When confronted with the fact of their racism and sexism, my opponents do not understand that our bloodline traces back to resisters like Eliza who fought back, throwing scalding water at their enslavers. It is an act of patience and protest to channel anger into positive action. I think of Eliza, Lewis, and the countless post–Civil War African American families the federal government abandoned to be massacred by Confederates, and my life as a descendant of those Exodusters who protested terrorism in Kentucky by migrating to Kansas.[120]

There was no mention on the advertisements to homesteaders that the land was stolen by the federal government, bloodied by military battles, and left fallow after the forced migrations of Indigenous peoples to Oklahoma reservations. Eliza and Lewis Bradshaw arrived penniless in Kansas in 1879, a disease-filled year of drought that was its own "Starving Time." Lewis died of consumption, babies died of hunger, and crops failed.[121] Through hard work, tenacity, and resilience they made it through with none resorting to the cannibalism that overtook the Jamestown settlement during their difficult "Starving Time."[122] As a widow myself, I think of Eliza losing her husband within a year of arriving in Kansas and how the lingering pain of his loss must have made the hardships of starting a new life even more difficult.

Eliza Bradshaw represents one miracle among millions of African Americans who outlived slavery. Mattie Bradshaw gave her grandmother Eliza roses for her ashes, as the biblical saying goes, providing love and care, until the matriarch's last days. My mother, Ardythe Bradshaw, told me stories of Eliza and other enslaved relatives, some whom she met or heard about when a child growing up on one of the family farms in Kansas. Those stories continue to enrage and strengthen me; they calm me and fuel my journey. With tenacity and faith, overcoming natural and unnatural obstacles, the Bradshaw families began their ascent in America, making a life in a land of opportunity, racism, and war, where "lifting as we climb"—to quote the motto of the National Association of Colored Women's Clubs—is protest.

CHAPTER THREE

LABOR RIGHTS AND UNION STRIKES

My father was a union member, a machinist, and my mother was an administrative clerk with the Social Security Administration. In grade school, when negotiations broke down between the machinists' union and Allis-Chalmers Manufacturing Company, my father and his union brethren went on strike. He was out of work for over a year. At the time, I thought Allis-Chalmers was a woman and did not know it was a company formed in the nineteenth century by Edward P. Allis, with a history of building steam engines, farm equipment, and munitions for war, along with having a notorious reputation for breaking unions, which it earned beginning in 1946.[1] My father worked at an Allis-Chalmers plant in a rural outskirt of Kansas City, Missouri, where racism was as deep as the Mississippi and people pretended *Brown v. Board of Education* never happened. I remember sitting in the backseat of a neighbor's car on a blisteringly cold, overcast day, headed to deliver a message and dinner to my father out on the picket line.

As we left the city, I watched houses give way to isolated farms and then miles of bright snow on the open, flat plains of rural life. Missouri's seasons brought ice storms in the winter, flooding in spring and fall, and scorching summers above 100 degrees Fahrenheit. There had been heavy snowfall recently, and the car swayed as tires crunched on unshoveled snow into the lot where my father stood with a dozen men wearing "On Strike" signs tied across their coats, warming bare hands over barrels of burning wood. The image of those men on strike for higher wages and job security, standing in the cold, sat next to me on the long car drive home, during which I felt a sense of pride, anchored in foreboding.

The strike had already lasted longer than predicted, and as it dragged along, large parts of my already troubled Black middle-class life fell away until foreclosure took our home. Although my father would find another job and work his way up the ladder, my sense of the world had been shaped by a feast-or-famine mindset. There was an ever-present feeling of forces beyond my control waiting to crush whatever was built, no matter how hard one worked. I believed in a higher power, having been raised in the Church of God in Christ, with my father's father at the pulpit, a big dark-skinned man who would lose his legs to racism and diabetes. He anointed my forehead with oil, while Gran, my father's mother, led the deaconesses with a smile and iron hand. Somewhere between God and disaster, there was the labor union. No matter what I achieved, my early values spurred me to side with the working people who, like me, were trying to navigate a blessedly beautiful yet humanly hostile class-based world of racism and sexism.

Years later, when I was in law school, the classes initially had little to do with my view of the world, given that the parties in employment cases were still known as "master and servant," and it was assumed we all wanted to be masters. Constitutional law intrigued me with its history and power. But my hallelujah moment came while taking a labor class, at which point I saw how the law was also a tool for change. Subsequent courses in gender rights, environmental law, and civil rights confirmed that my career would focus on liberation, using the law, the arts, and, of course, activism, to make a difference in the world. I believed in the philosophy and practicality of unions, and whenever possible, in my role as a lawyer, writer, and professor, I joined the union or a guild.

Unions are far from perfect, but when organized workers sit at a bargaining table with the business elite, they are using the power of the masses. Given that land barons and the owner classes have ruled for thousands of years, unions are a relatively young phenomenon, still finding their way. Despite the racism and sexism in unions, past and present, I stand with organized labor. The prejudice I have seen and experienced in employment, housing, education, and every aspect of my American life tells me that unity is the strongest weapon with which to fight labor oppression, making unions a great vehicle for worker progress.

We begin this chapter with the Gilded Age, when wealthy factory owners treated workers as serfs forced to labor twelve hours a day in unsafe conditions, unsure of the wages they would receive and vulnerable to termination for merely filing a complaint. Workers formed unions to protest the master-and-servant system, and, by organizing labor despite violent opposition, political undermining, and legal obstacles, they shifted the power dynamic. This examination provides insight into some of the many battles, defeats, and victories of the labor movement.

GILDED AGE GREED

It was an era of ravenous industrial expansion lasting from post–Civil War Reconstruction into the early twentieth century. During this period, former slaveholders became masters of a free-market economy and all workers were nearly chattel. Industrialists were kings, bolstered by their corrupt monopolies, which enjoyed full legal protection, controlled the basic elements of daily life, and capitalized on their workers' starvation wages.

John D. Rockefeller, founder of the Standard Oil Company, was the richest man in the world and reviled for the blatant ways he monopolized the market.[2] Whether it was Rockefeller's oil holdings or Andrew Carnegie's control of the steel industry or Cornelius Vanderbilt's monopoly of the railroads, the New World barons amassed fortunes and control over industries essential to everyday American life. Immense wealth brought tremendous political influence and protection.[3]

While workers toiled and suffered in the factories, mines, and rail yards, six days a week, twelve to fourteen hours a day, the wealthy minority lived as American royalty.[4] Walter Licht's *Industrializing America: The Nineteenth Century* explores the abuse of workers and rise of the industrial tycoons.[5] It was called the Gilded Age, a name coined by Mark Twain, because the post-slavery era in the United States boasted massive wealth and glittering trappings that covered over corruption, poverty, and oppression.[6] The "Robber Barons and Rebels" chapter of Howard Zinn's *A People's History of the United States* speaks to those who challenged the powerful abusers of labor, while Sean Cashman's *America in the Gilded Age: From the Death of Lincoln to the Rise of Theodore Roosevelt* provides a long-range view of the era.[7]

The unions and guilds that emerged during this period of industrialization came as imports to the United States, brought by European immigrants seeking the American Dream of wealth, independence, and freedom. Guilds operated as associations of weavers, bakers, painters, and shoemakers. They were craftsmen as well as merchants. The guild system had begun in the early eleventh century and flourished in Europe until the Industrial Age of factories. Guilds allowed individuals to have a stronger voice, set prices, and control the quality of merchandise or services. The early generations of guilds were organized for an economy based on agriculture, but the nineteenth century witnessed a dramatic shift. This once fully agrarian nation, with its slave-based profit machine, had entered the age of factories, while Europe was well on its way.

NORTH AMERICAN SERFS

Early US laborers, like indentured servants from the colonial past, served at the pleasure of enterprise owners and managers. Contracts of indenture set the number of years. One such contract read: "In 1799, in England, John Smith, orphaned son of John Smith, as an apprentice to John Latham, as a mariner or seaman, signed on third of August 1799 by the above parties, and Robert Brough, Chamberlain of Norfolk."[8] Unfortunately, Europe's classism and indifference followed the immigrant worker to the North American colonies. But so had the immigrant worker's bitter opposition to oppression and poverty. Even then, there were malcontents who questioned their leaders' orders. Religious doctrine has served as an agent of social control determining acceptable behavior and punishment for those who run afoul of those dictates. The Divine Laws meted out death to the men and women who questioned the authority, dictates, and hierarchy handed down by their economic betters.

During the enslavement of Africans, their free labor undermined any effort by newly arrived European immigrants to make demands. The labor of the enslaved produced tobacco, rice, and sugar. Tobacco was the first golden crop in North America's colony to become a global enterprise. This labor-intensive crop begat the need for the experienced labor that plantation owners needed but did not want to pay. Indentured European servants began their own competing tobacco farms once their labor contracts ended. But African enslavement meant that plantation owners, who were also lawmakers, could retain experienced labor for their tobacco crops, without payment, in perpetuity, under penalty of death. Later, cotton, considered the "white gold" of the United States, would account for half of US exports and, as a product sold on the New York Stock Exchange in Manhattan, made White Northern financiers even wealthier.

Cotton was grown through the labor of enslaved men, women, and children, making wealth for textile factory owners and their corporate investors from New Jersey to Maine. Immigrant textile workers spun tons of plantation cotton into fabric in the New England mills, where they were treated like serfs. Before the cotton gin, the enslaved were forced to pull the white cotton threads laboriously and painfully from the thorny plant in order to pick out its dry seeds. It took thousands of bruised hands and painstaking days to do it. Morally bankrupt plantation owners bred African women and girls to create the free labor needed to produce cotton. With the advent of the cotton gin in 1793, a machine believed to have been invented by Eli Whitney that could pull and separate seeds from cotton, cotton production increased exponentially.

The steamboat's arrival in 1807 allowed the delivery of cotton up the Mississippi River to Northern buyers and investors, saving weeks of travel. Before coal became the dominant fuel of the industrializing US, enslaved workers also had to feed wood into the steam engines of ships and trains, which devoured woodlands where Indigenous lived, forcing them to either starve or move. This socio-racial hierarchy featured a layer of White laborers who did all manner of jobs in every industry, which combined to create enormous wealth for a relative few.

At the same time, the westward expansion of the country needed the labor of immigrants. As factories proliferated on the landscape, their insatiably greedy owners demanded the government assist in providing more laborers in the textile factories. Immigrant workers were called from Europe to "the land of milk and honey." Each entrepreneurial change, patented invention, and nation-building policy brought a new call for foreign laborers and a greater dependence on them. To meet this great demand for labor in the factories and fields, immigrants—then and today—have been enticed here by the American Dream, only to be crushed with discriminatory laws, racialized policing, and nativism when the US economy slows.

But their lives were considered inconsequential despite the value of their labor. Textile factory workers were people of all ages, including children and elders. They were locked in hastily built hovels that were drafty and cold in the winter and smoldering and hot in the summer. They worked in enclosed spaces that were always noisy, the air thick with lint.[9] There were no limits on working hours, no protections from unsafe conditions, and no guarantee of being able to negotiate acceptable wages. The factory boss, like the overseer on the slave plantation, dispensed penalties and reported any infraction to the owners. He kept his cold eye on female workers, ever watchful for troublemakers, slow workers, and sexual prey. Rabble-rousers were fired without recourse.

STRIKING LOWELL MILL GIRLS

The mill girls formed a union in 1834. The textile mills of New England were rumored to be heaven on earth for country girls seeking an independent living beyond farm life.[10] Francis Cabot Lowell led the formation of the Boston Manufacturing Company based on the textile factories in England and is credited with hiring young women as textile workers. The mills of Lowell, Massachusetts, thirty miles from Boston, were portrayed as having a safe environment and enviable working conditions for the women. Although they worked at least twelve hours a day, six days a week, the mill girls were expected to also improve their minds by attending talks by local writers and intellectuals, including Ralph Waldo Emerson.[11] The Lowell factories were meant to be better than the vile workhouses of London made famous by Charles Dickens in *Oliver Twist*, published a few years later.

However, a downturn in the world market for cotton led to the factory owners cutting the wages of the mill girls by 12 percent. It was winter, and the once sought-after cloth produced in the Lowell factories was no longer in demand. The warehouses were full of inventory.[12] Mill owners decided to reduce the wages of female mill workers across the entire city, without providing a warning or taking the time to discuss with the women how they were going to afford their living expenses on less income. Owners expected the mill girls to quietly accept their unilateral decision, but the women fought back, meeting in the evenings to plan a response. Led by mill worker Julia Wilson, they sent out petitions titled "Union Is Power" to women at various mills, seeking unity in concerted action against the owners. Wilson was summarily fired by the owners, but she continued to lead the women in a walkout. Eight hundred women from the mills around Lowell protested their wage cuts and demanded that Wilson be rehired.

Nearly one-sixth of the workers protested by walking out of their mills early and stopping at other mills in the city to recruit women to the cause.[13] The mill owners, appalled by the tenacity of the mill girls, called them "unseemly" and "unwomanly." William Austin, a chief agent of Lawrence Mills, referred to them as violent "amazons."[14] Determined to set an example, the owners dismissed many of the protesters and did not rehire Julia Wilson, improve working conditions, or reinstate the workers' wages. Although the strike was unsuccessful, the women gained confidence from taking a stand. They based their arguments on those of America's Founding Fathers, who had fought the oppression of King George and "preferred privation to bondage."[15]

Two years later, in October of 1836, the mill girls initiated a second strike. The economy was vibrant, and textile factory owners were making a profit. But the workers received no share of this financial boom. Instead, additional money was taken from the women's earnings to increase the wages of the boardinghouse housekeepers—the women in charge of cleaning, cooking, and caring for the workers living on factory grounds. Since a third of wages were deducted by the owners for boarding house expenses, this meant a pay cut. Between fifteen hundred and two thousand workers protested. Unlike the prior action, this strike lasted for several months. A fund was developed to supplement lost wages through an organization called the Factory Girls' Association. The workers scored a small victory when some of the factory owners agreed to reduce the boardinghouse expense.

DEMANDING CHANGE

Replacement workers have long been used to undermine a labor action, and by January of 1845, factory owners had tired of the mill girls' demands. Instead, they took advantage of immigrants, many of whom, because of their dire need to earn money, worked for less and tolerated harsh treatment. However, work stoppages and walkouts were taking place from Paterson, New Jersey, to upstate New York and Lowell, with women demanding a ten-hour per day work week. The Lowell Female Labor Reform Association (LFLRA) was founded, ratifying a constitution containing firm demands for better working conditions and an end to labor oppression in the textile factories.

The preamble of the LFLRA constitution stated:

> Whereas we, the Operatives of Lowell, believing that in the present
> age of improvement, nothing can escape the searching glances of
> reform; and when men begin to inquire why the Laborer does not
> hold that place in the social, moral and intellectual world, which
> a bountiful Creator designed him to occupy, the reason is obvious.
> He is a slave to a false and debasing state of society.[16]

The LFLRA raised money and set out principles for protecting
female workers. This was an age when girls and women had little
access to education. According to societal expectations, they had no
roles beyond being a wife, mother, and daughter. Yet, the mill girls
demanded time to rest and pursue their own personal interests.

Their *Voice of Industry* newspaper had as its masthead logo "Organ
of the New Labor Reform League."[17] The logo image depicted three
women in various stages of work and a globe pronouncing "Freedom
for All."[18] The women of the LFLRA, which featured elected officers,
business meetings, dues, and a constitutional structure, were the fore-
runners of grassroots organizers, direct action campaigns strategists,
and government lobbyists. They protested in the streets and hounded
politicians. And all of this took place in an era when women did not
have the right to vote.

The LFLRA also created and funded a mutual aid society. The Lowell Female Industrial Reform and Mutual Aid Society had a mission to

> unite together and protect each other. In health and prosperity we
> can enjoy each other's society from week to week—in sickness and
> despondency share in and kindly relieve each other's distresses. The
> young and defenceless female, far away from home and loving hearts,
> can here find true sympathy and aid. We do hope and confidently
> believe that many of our toiling sisters will come in next Tuesday,
> sign the Constitution, and engage heart and hand in this benevolent
> cause.[19]

In 1847, the women of Lowell met to address necessary reforms
in the textile industry. Reducing the workday was an immediate goal.
One LFLRA petition that was sent to the Massachusetts State House,

featuring over four thousand signatures, demanded legislation for a ten-hour workday. It would take nearly a decade for widespread change. But the ten-hour workday law was finally passed in New Hampshire—though it was rarely enforced.

The Lowell mill girls strike paved the way for future labor movements.[20] It is much more than a coincidence that these movements for equal rights under the law were most prevalent in New England and New York. The mill girls strikes in Lowell and surrounding cities and towns laid the foundation for the first Women's Convention in Seneca Falls, New York, in 1848, the Temperance Movement, the child labor laws movement, the government reformist movement, and the national suffragists' fight for voting rights. The hiring of female textile and factory workers would spread into New York and Pennsylvania, across the Midwest into Wisconsin, and down south to North Carolina, Georgia, and Alabama, where girls as young as three worked in mills.

THE MACHINES

An industrial revolution in the North was underway when the Civil War ended slave-based labor with a corporate structure and heavy reliance on machines instead of agrarian labor. Those machines, however, would still need human beings to operate them. Enticed from their farms and villages by adventure and steady wages, these workers were ready to transition from farming to factory work. They had abandoned the uncertainty of farming's soil only to toil for twelve to sixteen hours a day, doing repetitive, mind-numbing drudge work in dust-filled factories with nights sleeping in overpriced dormitories, two to a bed, with every move ruled by male overseers, factory managers, and dormitory matrons.

The barons of steel, textiles, railroad, and coal colluded to make their riches off the bent backs of working people who had been watching their greed with growing resentment. Building a railroad to connect the westward expansion of the United States required labor, government backing, and collaboration with other major industries. Feudalism, as a flawed system that benefited the landholder, at least entailed the understanding that the master would provide sustenance to his serfs to fend off hunger. As the replacement to feudalism, capitalism promised greater personal freedom, though there was no longer the guarantee of a master's protection from deprivation, as immigrants to the US would find out during this era. Thus, when calamity struck Europe or Asia, laborers tried to walk through America's Gold Door of opportunity but too often found only a gilded cage of unsafe conditions, meager wages, and violence.

RAILROADS AND COAL MINES

Labor strikes made the eight-hour workday a reality. President Ulysses S. Grant, who had led the Union Army to victory during the Civil War, established the eight-hour workday for all federal employees in 1869.[21] The proclamation he issued stated,

> Whereas the act of Congress approved June 25, 1868, constituted, on and after that date, eight hours a day's work for all laborers, workmen, and mechanics employed by or on behalf of the Government of the United States, and repealed all acts and parts of acts inconsistent therewith. Now, therefore, I, Ulysses S. Grant, President of the United States, do hereby direct that from and after this date no reduction shall be made in the wages paid by the Government by the day to such laborers, workmen, and mechanics on account of such reduction of the hours of labor.[22]

Slavery had ended free labor, which had been depressing wages for White workers. African American men gained the right to vote in 1870, with the Fifteenth Amendment, and were creating organizations to protect the vote. The nation was at a crossroads, and tensions between workers and the rich set aflame the friction between democratic ideals and unbridled capitalism. That year, Cornelius Vanderbilt, the railroad and shipping baron, was the richest person in the United States, and John D. Rockefeller had just incorporated the company that would make him even wealthier than Vanderbilt.

Upon his death in 1877, Vanderbilt's wealth was valued at $100 million. The construction of railroads, built through Indigenous lands, was a military operation using former soldiers from the Civil War. They created towns and vigilante justice in those lands. "There was no law in the country, no courts," with companies owning and controlling entire towns, writes Manu Karuka in *Empire's Tracks: Indigenous Nations, Chinese Workers, and the Transcontinental Railroad*.[23] The book speaks to the confluence of traumatic conditions from the perspective of Chinese railroad workers and the Cheyenne, Lakota, and Pawnee Native American tribes displaced by the railroads.

The Panic of 1873, from which the nation struggled to emerge over four years, caused the railroad barons to cut wages. By 1877, pressing workers to continue to lay tracks as fast as possible and run the trains, feed families, pay rent, and stay healthy enough to work twelve-to-fourteen-hour days for half their wages. That year, Rutherford B. Hayes became president, gaining the office through backhand compromises with Southern politicians to gain the votes of the former Confederacy. The Hayes administration removed the federal troops protecting African Americans in the former Confederate states, leading to the end of Reconstruction and the beginning of the slaughter of African Americans, with impunity.

CHINESE IMMIGRANTS BATTLE EXCLUSION

Workers were enticed by placards describing a land of freedom and opportunity, milk and honey. With the abolition of slavery ending free labor, the United States now needed replacement workers. Moguls sent agency men beyond Europe to the Orient, as it was then called, to take advantage of the civil wars, drought, and ethnic strife there with offers of work in America, where streets were paved with gold. US industrialists used Asian laborers, who were paid less than White workers, to undercut union demands.

True to history's racial precedents, White workers attacked the Chinese, not the wealthy industrialists. Even though in 1880 Chinese immigrants made up only about 0.21 percent of the fifty million US residents, they were still blamed for White unemployment.[24] Segregated Chinatowns were neglected by the government, provided minimal city services, and then ridiculed for their unsanitary conditions. The Chinese in America faced discrimination and violence at every turn. Yet, the United States looked greedily at trade with China, allowing Chinese diplomats to enter the US in the hopes of taking advantage of the country's market.[25]

The Chinese needed to endure in the harsh land that existed on the other side of that golden door of opportunity. They, too, had a culture, language, and heritage to maintain, which thus made survival in the United States, for an immigrant, a form of protest against those who refused to accept them. The Chinese laborer took menial jobs, for less pay, and started laundry businesses, doing the tasks that Whites believed were beneath them. For their sacrifices, they were only paid with racist violence. When White mobs attacked, they were often rewarded with jobs and anti-Asian laws. Congress interceded on behalf of Whites who were angered by Asian competition at any level.

The first Chinese Exclusion Act was enacted on May 6, 1882, and was an absolute ten-year ban on Chinese laborers immigrating to the United States.[26] President Chester A. Arthur capitulated to racist demands by White laborers to enact the ban.[27] Then, in 1884, Congress passed a law preventing Chinese laborers from entering the United States for another ten years.

> CHAP. 220—An act to amend an act entitled "An act to execute certain treaty stipulations relating to Chinese approved May sixth eighteen hundred and eighty-two." . . . Be it enacted by the Senate and House of Representatives of the United States of America in Congress assembled, That from and after the passage of this act, and until the expiration of ten years next after the passage of this act, the coming of Chinese laborers to the United States be, and the same is hereby, suspended, and during such suspension it shall not be lawful for any Chinese laborer to come from any foreign port or place, or having so come to remain within the United States."[28]

Hundreds of state, local, and federal laws would follow with their own exclusionary legislation. The Chinese were thus forced to enter the country surreptitiously, from Canada and Mexico. However, after Canada enacted its own Chinese exclusion laws, Mexico was left as the only possible entry point.[29]

Lawsuits are protest, especially in a litigious nation such as the United States, where wronged parties learn quickly to avail themselves of the courts, even if success is against all odds. In response to the exclusion and discrimination, the Chinese began to bring lawsuits. They challenged a discriminatory California law passed in 1880 that sought to close Chinese laundries, a lucrative business, wherever they competed with White laundries. San Francisco was home to many Asian communities who were running laundries because the Chinese Exclusion laws closed other opportunities to them. Then, it became a crime to have a laundry in any building made from a material other than brick or stone, a requirement that exclusively favored the White-owned establishments because Chinese laundries were made of wood timber. Violation meant a $1,000 fine, six months in jail, or both. Once the law was passed, the police proceeded to raid the laundries, jailing Chinese laundry owners, workers, and family members.

But the Chinese community fought back. They pooled their money, hired an attorney, and appealed their convictions to the US Supreme Court. An 1886 unanimous decision in *Yick Wo v. Hopkins* found that the law was written with discrimination in its intent even if it was without discrimination on its face. For a law to have the appearance of impartiality is not enough; if it is "applied and administered . . . with an evil eye and an unequal hand," it is unconstitutional, the Court ruled.[30] Many White laborers had embraced a sense of superiority despite a lack of any economic proof to support it. The strategy of Bacon's Rebellion, to divide and conquer based on race, was once again a viable one for factory owners, railroad tycoons, and industrialists when labor fails to resist the trap.

BEATING BACK THE BENEVOLENT DICTATOR

They would rise to prominence as a union of railroad porters and cooks wielding national power for half a century. The sleeping-car porters were African American men who resented being called "George," a nickname stemming from the benevolent dictator George M. Pullman, the railroad magnate some called the "Messiah of a New Age." Pullman's elevated version of the sleeping train car made the uncomfortable long rail ride a luxurious experience, and it made him rich. However, this grand service was made possible due to the African American men who cooked delicious meals in overheated kitchens, carried heavy bags, and serviced passengers' needs by fulfilling their every whim and to do so with a smile.

George Pullman was born in 1831, in a village called Salem Cross Roads (present-day Brocton), New York, near Lake Erie. The country he was born into was wrestling with slavery as well as facing westward expansion into Indigenous lands, a budding bourgeois class, and entrepreneurial opportunities. Pullman was an energetic man who saw America on the move. He made his first small fortune with an engineering business that used technology to move whole buildings.[31] Pullman was drawn to Chicago for his operation, as the city had many hastily built buildings, prone to flooding, that needed to be moved.[32]

Passengers scrambled for luxury, and when Pullman began, riding the train was the best means of transportation, and being served by Black waitstaff was expected. After finding success with his Chicago construction business, Pullman founded Pullman's Palace Car Company, which manufactured railcars that provided private and luxurious upgrades. Only Black men from the South were hired to serve White passengers, who called these working men "George's boys" or "George," as if they were Pullman's personal property, hearkening back to the slavery era.[33] Pullman became the largest employer of African Americans, many of whom were formerly enslaved, in the United States. Paid poorly, these waiters and porters lived off cash tips earned through long shifts, lifting heavy suitcases, shining shoes, feeding passengers, and feeding racist White egos, in a setting that recreated the plantation.[34]

Outside Chicago, Pullman had built a segregated company town named after him. White workers who built his luxury train cars got to live in the town of Pullman, while a handful of African American workers could only hope to be waiters in the town's hotels.[35] The wealthy adored him, and Pullman adored himself. "Future generations will bless his memory," the *Chicago Times* wrote of the near-saint.[36] Pullman walked in those rare social circles of Chicago; he even was able to hire President Abraham Lincoln's son Robert as his personal lawyer.

Towns were named after him, and all was divine until Pullman's greed and a bad economy led to his downfall. Working conditions and fluctuating wages led White railroad workers to form the American Railway Union, which prohibited Black membership. When the depression of 1893 halted extravagant spending on luxury Pullman train tickets, working-class spending fell altogether and could only cover necessities. Times were hard for all the Pullman workers. Pullman lowered worker wages and had the rent that workers paid for their company-town homes taken directly from their now meager wages.

The next year, on May 12, 1894, Eugene V. Debs, leader of the American Railway Union, called a strike for higher wages and lower rents. Adoration for Pullman as a benevolent baron had turned to scorn. It became one of the greatest labor strikes of the nineteenth century. Railway workers across the country honored the Pullman strikers. Commerce was brought to a halt, yet Pullman refused to negotiate with the strikers. President Grover Cleveland was convinced by industrialists fearing the loss of business to send federal troops, with bayonets, to hotspots of union rebellion. In the Midwest, the uniformed men lined up in foot-high snow against workers. Bloody battles ensued, feeding rumors of an anarchist takeover.

In the end, Debs spent six months in jail for defying injunctions to end the strike. But he was hailed as a hero for taking his stand. George Pullman died in 1897, at age sixty-six, of a massive heart attack, despised as a paternalistic tycoon. To prevent people from robbing his grave, his casket was lined with lead, covered with quick-drying asphalt and concrete, then nailed into place with rail spikes.[37] Robert Lincoln led the company after Pullman's death, but the battle was not over, as African American workers at the Pullman Company now sought admission into the all-White trade union. Facing a wall of racism, Black sleeping-car Pullman porters protested union segregationists and Pullman Company's poor working conditions by forming a formidable union of their own.

DON'T CALL ME GEORGE

The Black men bore the insult of being called "George" by the White passengers, smiling as they labored twelve to sixteen hours a day because cash tips from those passengers sustained the men and their families. African American Pullman porters needed union protection from the vagaries of feudal train service. But de jure and de facto segregation extended to the trade unions that should have provided that protection, as *Plessy v. Ferguson*'s racist, ugly reach extended to the country's laborers. The same White laborers beaten down by the money elite were keeping people of color out of the union by their vote and with violence. Union contracts included provisions excluding Black members. Eugene Debs had tried to integrate the Pullman workers' union, unsuccessfully. Racial division was rampant in Chicago among native White citizens and European immigrants alike. However, Asa Philip Randolph was determined to launch a union of Black porters.[38]

Randolph's dream for what would become known as the Brotherhood of Sleeping Car Porters had long struggled under crippling betrayals and underfinanced attempts.[39] Unions throughout the labor sector excluded African Americans, and other people of color, from membership. The American Federation of Labor had rebuffed Black membership.[40] The Brotherhood of Railway Carmen turned its back on Black workers as well. In 1930, only fifty-six thousand out of over one million African American workers were members of a union. Meanwhile, owners continued to use divide-and-conquer tactics. The Pullman Company, for instance, hired Chinese and Filipino workers in order to undercut African American workers' demands for better wages. There was power in numbers, however, and Randolph seized that economic and political power on behalf of Black workers who had been paid less and burdened by racism in all aspects of their working lives.

Combining forces with the men and women who had been left at the fringes of organized labor, the Brotherhood called a mass meeting on October 3, 1926. Ahead of the meeting, Randolph had worked with African American women, led by the formidable Ida B. Wells-Barnett, educator, journalist, suffragist, and founder of the Alpha Suffrage Club.[41] Wells-Barnett had investigated Southern lynching before arriving in Chicago, fleeing a murderous mob herself.[42] Another of the Brotherhood's allies was Mary McDowell, the first president of the Women's Trade Union's Chicago branch and advocate for foreign-born workers.[43]

Paternalism pervaded the Pullman Company, even after George Pullman's death. The company was seen as a "friend of the Negro" because it provided African Americans with relative security and employed them in large numbers. Even if the wages were poor and conditions oppressive, some African American workers agreed with Pullman's philosophy that railway work offered opportunities other businesses did not. It took time, but in 1937, A. Philip Randolph's valiant efforts were rewarded when the Pullman Company recognized the Brotherhood. Despite great odds, Randolph and others had created the largest union of African American workers in the world. The Brotherhood then used its economic and political power to branch out. Unity in the face of "divide and conquer" provided safety in numbers and power at the negotiation table.

African American men working for the Pullman Company in Illinois shared more in common with White coal miners in West Virginia than what appeared on the surface. As with Bacon's Rebellion, both groups comprised workers oppressed by the elite and in danger of being fired or met with violence if they attempted to bring labor grievances to the table. Their meager wages kept them quiet, exhausted, and begging until a leader organized them into a cohesive union willing and able to protest higher wages and assert their dignity. In the Midwest, A. Philip Randolph was that galvanizing force for the porters. In Appalachia, it was Mother Jones leading the beleaguered coal miners of West Virginia.

MAKING MOTHER JONES

She was short, some say, five foot, or less, with a kind, soft face, penetrating eyes, and white tufts of hair pinned up or hidden in a bonnet. Workers rejoiced when they heard Mary Harris "Mother" Jones had come to battle injustices in their town. She wore a frumpy black frock, matronly shoes, and carried a cane, making herself look every bit like an old Irish grandmother. But when she spoke, she shook the souls of those privileged to hear.

Once, while speaking in a church to mourners of coal miners killed by mining-company gangs while trying to form a union, Mother Jones urged them to "pray for the dead and fight like hell for the living."[44] She had faced down gun-toting thugs, traveled alone to isolated coal towns erupting in violence, been arrested many times, and chastised government officials for failing the working class. Once she spoke, it became clear why Mother Jones came to be known as the most dangerous woman in America. She embraced the posture of a hell-fighter.[45]

But many still wonder who this woman warrior for unions and working men, with a voice that cut through crowds and the courage to challenge armed men, was. The story of Mother Jones is a mix of real-life heroism and fable, embellished by Jones herself. Mary Harris was born in the city of Cork, Ireland, to impoverished parents; in her autobiography, she claims to have been born in 1830.[46] She was among the many Irish immigrants who fled a homeland plagued by failed crops, insurrections, and brutal British domination for a life of promised freedom in North America. Harris told little of her young life as a teacher and seamstress and how it led her to Memphis, Tennessee. That is where, in 1861, she married George Jones, a staunch member of the Iron Moulders Union.[47]

They had four children. As members of the working class, they struggled. The Jones family was sustained by somewhat steady work, church, and friends. Port cities like Memphis were prone to diseases brought by passengers and sailors. In 1867, yellow fever swept through the city, with its residents suffering from fever, bleeding from the eyes and mouth, excruciating headaches, and their skin turning a yellow tint, which gave the disease its name. There was no treatment for yellow fever, only quarantine, and contracting it typically meant death within three to five days. One by one, Mary's four children faded into death, and then yellow fever came for her husband. The bodies of her children and husband were taken away and burned while Mary remained, by law, in quarantine, grieving. She would never be a grandmother.

She had survived the yellow fever epidemic. Mary Harris Jones found her way to Chicago. Jones held fast to the side of laborers, who faced starvation and were pitted against police, militia, courts, and soldiers. Whether forged from the traumatic clashes between workers and police in Chicago or culled from personal tragedies, Mother Jones emerged a crusader for coal miners ready to wage war against exploitative companies that deprived families of food and adequate housing.

Clarence Darrow was an activist lawyer and was nationally revered as one of the best legal minds of the early twentieth century. Lawyers can use their talents for progressive causes, for good. Darrow's father was an ardent abolitionist, and his mother was a suffragist.

Darrow rose to prominence as the attorney for coal miners and represented the acclaimed union boss Eugene Debs, who led the Pullman Strike of 1894. A gruff man who played on his country upbringing in rural Ohio, Darrow argued history-making criminal cases, defending Ossian Sweet, an African American homeowner in Detroit who stood his ground against a White lynch mob. In the Scopes "Monkey" Trial, Darrow defended the teaching of evolution in court. He and Mother Jones crossed paths in Chicago and made a fearless team of advocates for the working person, but she kept her own counsel even among peers.

Mother Jones was a mystery of her own making, with questions remaining unanswered concerning her true age and early adult life. However, her transformation from a grieving widow and seamstress into a hellfire activist for labor rose from the Haymarket riot of 1886.[48]

Her cause was the enforcement of the eight-hour workday. Chicago at that time was a melting pot of immigrants from Europe, African American migrants from a South tormented by terrorism, Asians escaping civil war and famine in China, and nativists suspicious of labor competition. They had poverty in common, as well as the watchful eye of police, intent on controlling this rambling of humanity on behalf of the industrialists.

Chicago's Haymarket was a crowded, crude epicenter of clamoring voices shouting out their wares for sale—pots and pans, vegetables, fish from Lake Michigan, slaughtered beef, chickens in cages, and hogs fresh from the stockyards—mixed with the clatter of horses pulling vendor carts over cobblestones. Workers felt a collective sense of anxiety, disappointment, and resentment as a hard-fought law that would finally reduce the workday from ten or more hours to eight was largely ignored by factory owners. The eight-hour workday was supposed to begin and when it did not, workers were pushed by leaders to act. On May 1, 1886, what would later be known as May Day, the Federation of Organized Trades and Unions called for a national strike demanding an eight-hour workday.[49]

Chicago's factory owners, who represented the country's new wealthy class, along with slaughterhouse owners, railroad titans, land speculators, and stock market investors, built massive homes on Lake Michigan and drove among the poor wearing silk top hats, mimicking the English aristocracy surveying their landholdings. Meanwhile, the workers lived in squalid, serf-like misery, laboring in dangerous, low-paying jobs butchering animals in meat-packing plants, smelting iron and steel, making furniture, and running printing presses and all other types of machinery in this growing city.

A BOMB IN HAYMARKET

The strike that overtook the city's factories had been planned for weeks.[50] Some estimate that between thirty thousand and eighty thousand workers sat out on May 1, 1886, to protest the factory owners' failure to recognize the eight-hour workday and show solidarity as the laborers confronted the owners and Chicago's elite. The strike continued, and two days later, as peaceful protesters gathered for another rally, the elite sent police to break it up, resulting in one death, others wounded, and mass arrests. The next day, May 4, speakers assembled again, standing on a wagon bearing speakers in Haymarket Square to protest police brutality, with flyers that read "Workingmen Arm Yourselves and Appear in Full Force."[51] Between fifteen hundred and three thousand were on hand, but the speeches were long and repetitive, leading the crowd to dwindle to some six hundred gathered around the wagon. At about 10:20 p.m., on that clear, starry night, police on horseback attacked the crowd with clubs.

Minutes later, a handmade bomb was thrown from a tenement window at the police and exploded. Police officers then started shooting into a crowd of women, men, and children, who screamed and ran away. Bodies fell from gunshot wounds or shrapnel from the bomb, and some were trampled by the mob. The dead, dying, and wounded, which included moaning animals, all lay strewn on Haymarket Square. In the end, seven officers were dead and sixty wounded (perhaps by friendly fire). Civilian losses were higher, though the tally was less accurate as there was little interest in civilian casualties. The bombing shook the country, and newspapers stoked fear with sensational stories of an anarchist conspiracy to overthrow the government.[52]

Mary Harris Jones was in Chicago at the time, drawn by the feverish vilification of union organizers and random arrests of workers. Socialists and anarchists were blamed by politicians and the wealthy for the bombing, and she witnessed the growing paranoia become manipulated by factory owners eager to turn back labor's victories, especially the eight-hour workday. Unions lost support and were shunned as havens for murderous anarchists and immigrant troublemakers. Mother Jones shared with other labor organizers a helpless fury over the fact that they were now indiscriminately labeled as criminals unworthy of basic rights. "The workers' cry for justice was drowned in the shriek for revenge," she said.[53] Newspaper headlines demanded a speedy execution for the alleged bombers, then trials. The bombing set back the labor movement, as detailed in James Green's *Death in the Haymarket: A Story of Chicago, the First Labor Movement and the Bombing That Divided Gilded Age America.*[54]

Jones saw hundreds arrested and beaten, especially foreign-born protesters.[55] There was no evidence against the eight men tried, convicted in August of 1886, and sentenced to death for the Haymarket bombing and murder of Mathias Degan, a policeman, nor was there evidence against the three who were given life sentences. However, they each had held leadership roles in the eight-hour workday movement, and, for the city's factory owners and silk top hat–wearing investors, that was the men's motive for killing. Fear of anarchists and hatred for immigrants drove politicians to see plots on every corner. The defendants would not be intimidated into abdicating their beliefs. Instead, their stance hardened against the government as it pressed on with a prosecution without evidence.

At trial, defendant Michael Schwab shouted at the prosecutors and businessmen who looked on from the front seats that "the ground is on fire upon which you stand."[56] Judge Joseph Gary pronounced his sentence: they were to be hanged by the neck until dead. Another defendant, Louis Lingg, turned to Judge Gary and said bluntly, "I despise you and I despise your laws. Hang me for it!" Defendant Albert Parsons argued that the trial was instigated by "the capitalist press" and that his death sentence was "judicial murder." Parsons's demand for a new trial was denied. There had been public outcry about the lack of evidence and flawed prosecution, in a trial that took place only months after the bombing. The men appealed to higher courts.

After several months, word finally arrived from the US Supreme Court, but it too turned a blind eye to justice. Citing a lack of jurisdiction, the Supreme Court's chief justice, Morrison R. Waite, read a unanimous decision refusing to take the case on appeal. Despite a lack of evidence connecting the defendants to any crime, the high court found the state court judges had not deprived these men of a trial by a fair and impartial jury.[57] Defendant Louis Lingg, a twenty-three-year-old, mustached German-born activist, committed suicide while in jail by biting on a blasting cap.[58] Four of the men were hanged on November 11, 1887. On the day of execution, police guarded the jail from street to rooftop, standing shoulder to shoulder, until the perimeter of the building was black with police.[59]

THEY DIED FOR NOTHING

Protesters have long been martyred in their quest for justice, and Haymarket's executions remain a nadir in labor organizing. Despite the collection of one hundred thousand petition signatures demanding mercy for these labor activists, they were still executed. Illinois executed German-born Adolph Fischer, German-born George Engel, American newspaperman August Spies, and American Albert Parsons, a Confederate soldier turned advocate for the formerly enslaved and husband to Lucy Parsons, a woman of African descent. On June 26, 1893, Governor John Peter Altgeld, at great cost to his political reputation, pardoned the remaining men unfairly serving life sentences for the Haymarket bombing: Samuel Fielden, Michael Schwab, and Oscar Neebe.[60]

Perhaps because of the cruelty she witnessed, the Haymarket incident was when Mary Harris Jones became Mother Jones. She had lost everything in Chicago's devastating Great Fire of 1871, and, like the skyscrapers that the city built from the charred earth, so too did Mother Jones build her new persona. Without children or a romantic partner, Jones could travel freely to the places that called to her heart and needed her unique voice. Those lives and deaths in Haymarket Square and on the gallows burnished in her a resolve to invoke the courage inside the working people.

As the persona Mother Jones, she traveled to mining towns in Pennsylvania, Colorado, and, most notably, deep into the deadly coal country of West Virginia. In that state's isolated mountainous camps, coal miners and their family members were indiscriminately arrested and beaten by law enforcement, fired from their jobs, and evicted from company housing if they made any complaint. The coal company owned their homes, churches, stores, and schools. Losing a job meant losing everything, as mining families had no savings or actual money because owners would pay them against their wages in scrip, or pieces of paper redeemable only at the company store. Into this world, Mother Jones brought her unique brand of hellfire and redemption. She never held a steady job and rarely had a stable residence; however, wherever there was a fight for workers' rights against the powerful corporate interests, Mother Jones was there too. Her work as a champion for unions and as a labor organizer was legendary.

"I have been in West Virginia more or less for the past twenty-three years," Jones wrote in her autobiography, "taking part in the interminable conflicts that arose between the industrial slaves and their masters. . . . There is never peace in West Virginia because there is never justice. Injunctions and guns, like morphia, produce a temporary quiet, and then the pain, agonizing and more severe, comes again."[61] Jones, like many who rise to national prominence, left behind a conflicted legacy. She reserved her protests and lobbying for working

White men, ignoring the fight for women's rights and remaining silent instead of raising her ample voice against racial segregation, at a time when African American coal miners struggled with the double bind of poverty and racism, fending off both hunger and White vigilantes.

Mother Jones knew that, as Black miners worked alongside White ones, the two groups could also fight together, but rectifying discrimination within unions did not figure highly in her work or her writing. African American miners continued to live in segregated, dilapidated housing and were the first to be laid off and left unprotected by their unions when injured. But there was less racial strife than in other parts of the country as photos abound of Black miners working shoulder to shoulder, as illustrated in William H. Turner's *The Harlan Renaissance: Stories of Black Life in Appalachian Coal Towns*, which tells the "Affrilachian" story.[62] Dr. Carter G. Woodson, the founder of Black History and a graduate of Harvard University with a PhD in history, was born in Huntington, West Virginia, to a mining family and spoke of the hardships suffered by Black miners whose contributions were ignored.

Mother Jones, a complicated woman devoted to uplifting laborers, died in Silver Spring, Maryland, on November 30, 1930, and was buried in the Union Miners Cemetery in Mount Olive, Illinois. Driven by rage and personal loss, she reached deep within the labor movement and made a profound difference in the lives of miners and workers across America. Jones spent her adult life advocating for unionized labor, safety in the coal mines, and the eight-hour workday, which she would live to see. In 1905, the fight over labor rights and owner power went before the nation's highest court in the case of *Lochner v. New York*.

This ruling illustrated the push and pull of a society wrestling over the welfare of the worker and the power of the elite. Finally, after decades of protests, lobbying, and court filings, workers received reduced work hours as a result of the *Lochner v. New York* decision.[63] The Supreme Court ruled it as an unconstitutional violation of the freedom of contract for states to decide how long a company can work an employee. Corporations, of course, opposed the decision and would fight back in the coming decades.

Writers, protesting on behalf of overburdened workers, told the story of workers in such persuasive prose so as to move readers and lawmakers. Upton Sinclair's Pulitzer Prize–winning fiction touched the public in ways speeches and demonstrations could not. Early in his career, Sinclair wrote of the savagery in the coal mining industry in *King Coal* (1917), and the haunting images of Chicago's unsanitary meatpacking industry in *The Jungle* (1906) were said to have led to the passage of the 1906 Pure Food and Drug Act and Meat Inspection Act. His books spoke of the early immigrants' experience navigating the harsh realities of factory work, discrimination, and sexual coercion that was found beyond the golden door of opportunity.

URBAN INDENTURE

Too often a predicted tragedy is the catalyst to create the change protesters had demanded but were denied. When the Thirteenth Amendment abolished slavery in 1865, it also abolished indentured servitude. Indentured servants were essentially White slaves from Europe, working under contract for free under a tradesperson or master. Industrialists sought compliant, low-wage workers, and White women and children, especially immigrants, fit that criterion. They became the foundation of factory labor. Young women, seeking independence and perhaps adventure in cities, left behind the drudgery of country farm life, promising their families they would send money home, stay safe, and protect their virtue, all of which proved nearly impossible.

The horrific Triangle Shirtwaist Factory fire in New York City's Triangle Building was a preventable disaster waiting to happen. A *New York Times* newspaper headline read "141 Men and Girls Die in Waist Factory Fire; Trapped High Up in Washington Place Building; Street Strewn with Bodies; Piles of Dead Inside."[64] In all, one hundred forty-six died in the March 25, 1911, blaze that trapped textile workers in a ten-story, supposedly fireproof building. The building only had one fire escape, which the New York City fire chief had warned was a hazard. The doors to the sweatshop had been locked and some chained.[65] Managers wanted to prevent the women, most of whom were sixteen to twenty-three years old, from getting fresh air or taking a rest from being hunched over sewing machines, for twelve-hour shifts, with poor lighting, choking on fabric dust.[66]

Fire spread so quickly that, according to the *New York Times*, the victims "suffocated or burned to death within the building, but some who fought their way to the windows and leaped met death as surely, but perhaps more quickly, on the pavements below." In the short span of thirty minutes, the fire burned itself out. Owners Isaac Harris and Max Blanck, their children, and the governess escaped by fleeing to the roof of the building. "The victims, mostly Italians, Russians, Hungarians, and Germans, were girls and men" who had been hired after a strike in which the former workers were fired for forming a union to demand better working conditions. The Triangle Building had already experienced four prior fires and had been reported by the fire department to be unsafe.[67]

However, Harris and Blanck were found not guilty of any of their manslaughter charges.[68] The fire ignited fervent activism, however, as David Von Drehle details in *Triangle: The Fire That Changed America*.[69] Too often, it takes tragedy and the protests that ensue from it to bring changes. The Triangle Shirtwaist Fire investigations, commissions, and women-led protests for workers' rights led to stronger labor laws, building standards, and factory safety regulations.[70] These protests occurred amid a general wave of women-led protests. However, as women protested for voting rights and safe working conditions, their organizations remained segregated by race under *Plessy* and personal choice. African Americans responded by forming their own organizations and were forced to protest in every aspect of American life as they faced the headwinds against their enjoyment of their citizenship rights.

BLACK LABOR LEADER AND PRESIDENTIAL CANDIDATE

Protest leaders are trailblazers with a vision of society beyond the reach of most of the people they wish to lead. Born in Arkansas to an enslaved father and free mother, George Edwin Taylor rose from the labor movement in the Midwest to run for president of the United States.

Destiny beckoned Taylor when he was living in Iowa, and the National Negro Liberty Party chose him to be its nominee on the 1904 NNLP presidential ticket.

Taylor had been an activist in the voting rights struggle out of his frustration over the fact that Black voters were often ignored, assaulted, or disenfranchised. Taylor and his wife traveled across the Midwest, from Iowa and Missouri to Wisconsin, where he was educated, but he maintained an affinity with the Black working class. Taylor was a journalist who published the *Wisconsin Labor Advocate*, a labor newspaper. In 1886, the writing skill and oratory talents that Taylor had demonstrated in the battle over the eight-hour workday won him the role of secretary in the La Crosse chapter of the Knights of Labor, a predominately White union.

A few decades later, he was presenting the Negro National Liberty platform at the party's national convention in St. Louis, which demanded criminal penalties for lynching, equal accommodations, universal suffrage, and reparations in the form of pensions for ex-slaves.[71] After his bid for the White House, Taylor retired from politics, embittered by workers who had refused to support his candidacy, but he remained a labor activist and newspaperman.

Appalachian workers used their union membership in the United Mine Workers of America, one of the nation's most powerful unions, to challenge corporate masters of the railroad and coal mines. By 1900, union membership had increased tenfold. However, digging inside the bowels of the earth to extract coal was dangerous, with few safety protections, as became tragically evident on December 6, 1907. Shortly after 10 a.m., a fiery blast tore across the mountain of Monongah, West Virginia, blowing away part of the mountainside and entombing hundreds of coal miners inside, forever. Davitt McAteer's *Monongah: The Tragic Story of the 1907 Monongah Mine Disaster* places blame for the fatal explosion, which was caused by the combustion of mining dust, at the feet of the Consolidation Coal Company.[72]

Monongah was the worst coal mining disaster in US history. McAteer estimates that four to five hundred men and boys were killed instantly or later died of injuries, with those hundreds trapped inside the mine dying of their wounds and poisonous gases. Many of the workers were immigrants with families in other countries. After the disaster, bodies were taken directly from the mine to gravesites, without a funeral ceremony.[73] The Red Cross offered relief but, under "yellow dog" employment contracts, widows and their children were evicted from company-owned tenement housing because their husbands were dead, thus no longer employees under contract with the mine. This is but one example of the challenges that faced workers in this era of abundance—but only abundance for the privileged few. Following the Monongah disaster were protests, investigations, and legislation, though it amounted to little enforcement of proper safety regulations in the dance of two steps forward and one back, with the miners facing the worst possible outcome.

MINING BLOOD MONEY

West Virginia was blessed with an abundance of coal. With the outbreak of World War I, the US suddenly required a stable supply of metal. Congress began to take a role in labor relations to ensure wartime productivity. In 1917, with postwar prosperity in mind, President Woodrow Wilson, the segregationist intellectual, appeared to be a supporter of organized labor. However, by 1919, Wilson's support shifted to the corporations. With the government's support, corporations increased their pressure on workers to do more for less. The workers responded with over three thousand strikes and work stoppages in 1919 alone. West Virginia became a flashpoint for the struggle between workers' unions and corporations. But in a small state, with a population of only 1.4 million in 1919, union organizers found West Virginia a difficult place to gain a foothold because mining towns were isolated in mountain regions, which gave coal mining corporations extensive political and economic power.

The federal government believed that the companies needed this power to maintain a stable supply of coal for the nation. The United States' dependency on coal gave politicians in coal-rich states and coal mine owners an outsize role. The workers suffered as low wages kept them in company housing, where the costs for heat and lighting, rent, doctor bills, and groceries, all of which were deducted directly from their wages, left them in deeper debt each month.[74] Miners labored in pitch-black mines with foul air, and the threat of explosion or asphyxiation was constant.

In company towns, indebted workers owed their jobs, homes, schools, churches, and food, which were purchased with the company's currency, to their employers. West Virginia was filled with company-owned towns where the simple act of meeting with a union representative could lead to immediate dismissal and eviction, at the gunpoint of the local sheriff, from company tenements. The contract was a core issue of workers seeking union protection.

Employment contracts, called yellow dog, demanded that workers "while employed . . . [would] not become a member of, or connected or affiliated with, or aid, assist or encourage in any way, the United Mine Workers of America . . . or any other labor union, . . . or attempt to unionize."[75] And if employment was terminated, with or without cause, the miner must "immediately surrender possession of any such tenement house" because it was owned by the company.

A miner's song lamented the sixteen tons of coal that were dug, and still the miners owed their soul to the company store, a store that only accepted the company's scrip paper as currency, regularly resulting in overwhelming debt for the miners. The company owned the saloon on Saturday night, the church on Sunday, and the schoolhouse on weekdays. When the workers fought thugs hired by the company to enforce this feudal system, the company paid law enforcement to arrest the workers, which led, of course, to termination from their jobs and eviction from their homes.[76]

Yet, the coal miners could find inspiration from the success of other striking workers, including the women of the 1912 Lawrence textile strike, also known as the Bread and Roses Strike. News of other triumphs, as well as successful strategies, traveled to the miners via railroad workers. Union organizers "Big Bill" Haywood and Elizabeth G. Flynn, in Massachusetts, sent the workers' hungry children to New York to protest on behalf of their parents. It worked, as Bread and Roses represented one of the first times children were intentionally part of a social justice movement. Through the Industrial Workers of the World (IWW) union, the women—both immigrants and US citizens—had stuck together, standing their ground against thugs and police paid by the mill owners to foment fear. As a result, the women won higher pay and better working conditions.

In West Virginia, after the United Mine Workers shootout in 1912, miners had learned that violence was possible in any encounter with the mining company. But since the women in Massachusetts had stood strong with the IWW, then the United Mine Workers could stand firm, as well.

Mining companies began to rely on outside protection, or strike-breakers. The Baldwin-Felts Detective Agency was a private security firm founded by William Baldwin and Thomas Felts. They climbed to prominence from starting positions as mine guards and informants to become deputized thugs willing to do whatever was needed by the mining company, which paid them well. Whether as railroad detectives or deputy sheriffs, members of Baldwin-Felts could strike fear in union miners. The agency was known for serving eviction notices for terminated mine workers living in company housing.

Baldwin-Felts met its match in Sid Hatfield, the police chief who had become friendly to the union.[77] He was a lean man nicknamed "Smiling Sid" because of his mouthful of gold teeth. Hatfield carried himself with the assurance of a man who had killed before and would do it again. By early May of 1923, hundreds of courageous miners had joined unions despite having yellow-dog contracts.[78] Baldwin-Felts sent its men to evict those miners from company tenements. The two brothers of Thomas Felts, Albert and Lee, arrived with notices of eviction. But Sid Hatfield and Mayor Cabell Testerman were there, and they instead tried to execute arrest warrants on Baldwin-Felts. According to eyewitness accounts, Albert Felts presented an arrest warrant for Sid Hatfield, and all the men were armed.

THE MATEWAN MASSACRE

History is unclear as to who shot first. May 19, 1920, began as an average day for Baldwin-Felts. Thirteen Baldwin-Felts agents, led by Albert and Lee Felts, had gone to the Stone Mountain coal camp and, after evicting striking miners from their homes, went to the Matewan train depot. It was around 3:30 p.m., and the notorious Baldwin-Felts men were waiting for the 5 p.m. train.[79] Albert and Lee Felts decided to wander over to the restaurant and then to the hardware store nearby.

It was at this time that Sid Hatfield appeared with union members, who had been gathering rifles and pistols to stop the Baldwin-Felts men from evicting more miners.[80] Mayor Testerman and Police Chief Sid Hatfield turned the corner, an arrest warrant in Sid's hand for the Felts brothers.[81] One of the Feltses pulled out a warrant for Sid Hatfield's arrest. Both sides disputed the legitimacy of the other's warrant. Shots were fired. Mayor Testerman fell first. Albert Felts fell next, dead. Bullets rang out, hitting the red brick buildings, the station, and five Baldwin-Felts agents, killing them. One miner, as well as an innocent bystander, lay dead. Lee Felts ran to the post office on the far side of the tracks, by the bank near the squat one-story jail, and tried to hide. But Sid stalked him, gunning Lee down.[82] Bodies were sprawled alongside the railroad tracks when that 5 p.m. train arrived. Sid Hatfield placed his warrant on the dead body of Al Felts, saying, "Now, you son of a bitch, I'll serve it on you."[83] For Matewan's beleaguered miners, the massacre was a symbolic victory and Sid Hatfield became their new hero.[84]

In the end, Mayor Testerman died of his wounds. Membership in the United Mine Workers doubled, but union members were outraged about the miners who had been fired and evicted from their homes simply for joining the union. In 1921, coal miners went on strike for higher wages and better working conditions. Families were evicted by the thousands, creating tent towns without sanitation and, ironically, only small wood fires, as there was no coal for heat. Despite the evictions and dire conditions, the strikers refused to return to work. Scabs, a derogatory term for nonunion workers willing to "cross the line" during a strike, took their places.[85]

REBEL REDNECKS

Bullets from the Matewan shootout struck a brick wall near the train station and remain as a testament to the danger facing coal miners. The Tug River, which flows slowly from Kentucky into West Virginia, snaking in curves with dense trees and bushes, was the site of the battles between the strikers and strikebreakers in 1921. Baldwin-Felts' men swarmed into the union strongholds to arrest strikers. Meanwhile, Sid Hatfield was on trial, charged with having a role in the death of Mayor Testerman, killing by accident or intentionally to have a relationship with the mayor's wife.

Hatfield was walking up the stairs of the courthouse, unarmed, with his wife when he was struck by a barrage of bullets from Thomas Felts, avenging his brothers' deaths. Felts's cold-blooded murder of Hatfield spurred a rally of more than five thousand miners seeking vengeance. The men retrieved weapons they had used in World War I and stole others, including a machine gun called a Gatling gun, as Blair Mountain became a battleground between union and anti-union forces. To distinguish themselves from the enemy forces, the union miners wore red bandanna scarves around their necks, from which the word "redneck" stems.[86]

Union miners feared that the anti-union soldiers were equipped with planes and homemade bombs. West Virginia governor Ephraim Morgan begged President Warren G. Harding to provide federal troops. Harding instead sent a negotiator to convince union leadership to persuade the strikers to turn back by appealing to their patriotism. Many miners tried to turn back, but the trains to take them home were late. Then, enraged, they turned back after learning their wives and children were being served with eviction notices, forcing entire families with infants out of their flimsy tents and onto the roads because the company owned the ground under the tent city.

Gunfire was exchanged throughout the night. Private planes flew overhead, dropping heavy metal objects and nails on the miners. At the point when there were nearly one hundred casualties, Governor Morgan was forced again to ask President Harding to intervene. Harding issued a proclamation on August 30, 1921, authorizing military force to put down the insurrection.[87] Then, on September 1, President Harding ordered the US Air Force to fly over the battle on Blair Mountain in a show of governmental force. But the airplanes did not arrive due to bad weather.

WEST VIRGINA FEARS TULSA-LIKE ATTACK

Fear of bombardment by air was realistic because, only months earlier, in Tulsa, Oklahoma, the African American community had been attacked by air and by mob violence on the ground. For two days, White mobs in Tulsa ravaged Black residents and business owners, destroying their vibrant and wealthy community. On the morning of May 30, rumors circulated that Dick Rowland, a young Black man, had touched a White woman in a crowded elevator. What was merely a moment of incidental contact between Rowland and the woman in the elevator became an assault. When the incident was told by Whites, and then retold, it became attempted rape. Rowland was arrested. The *Tulsa Tribune* distorted the story to sell papers, further inflaming a growing White mob. By May 31, a bloodthirsty crowd was gathering. Shots were fired. Whites in Tulsa had long envied the prosperous African American community of Greenwood, with its beautiful two-story homes and wide boulevard of banks, real estate offices, attorneys' offices, grocery, and movie theater. It was affluent enough to be known as "Black Wall Street." Tennessee governor James B. A. Robertson declared martial law.

Thousands of enraged Whites descended on the segregated wealthy side of Tulsa. When Black men defended themselves, the mob was deputized. By June 1, the night sky was lit with the burning homes and businesses of African Americans. African American historian John Hope Franklin's father, an attorney newly arrived in Tulsa, witnessed the attack. He later recounted tar being dropped from low-flying airplanes onto the roofs of Black people's homes and then set afire by White mobs carrying torches. The death toll is unknown, as the sites of mass graves were hidden, but the murders were certainly as many as three hundred.

Over thirty-five square blocks were burned to the ground. Eight hundred Black people were injured, thousands were left homeless. Prosperous Greenwood was gone. Insurance companies refused to honor their policies. Demands for reparations or financial assistance were ignored. The 1921 Tulsa Massacre was the first aerial assault on civilians in US history. Litigation, legislation, and protests over the attack on Greenwood have continued to the time of this writing. In June 2024, a lawsuit was filed by the remaining survivors of the 1921 Tulsa Race Massacre, who saw the Oklahoma Supreme Court deny their claims for reparations. Lessie Benningfield Randle and Viola Fletcher had witnessed the destruction of their vibrant community and the dismissal of their lawsuit. Yet they plan to appeal and maintain a flame of outrage, faith, and unfathomable endurance after years of crushing setbacks to protest this nation's injustice.[88]

Therefore, given what had transpired in Tulsa, miners in West Virginia had reason to fear an aerial assault. Federal troops arrived as the miners retreated. A ceasefire was called. The army held the groups apart. Later, Governor Morgan blamed socialism as the motivation behind the strikers' battle on Blair Mountain. But a government investigation revealed that the men wanted only to provide for their families so they could live in dignity. Union membership in West Virginia decreased during the wave of corporate greed of the Roaring Twenties, leading to the Great Depression of 1929. The Great Depression was a worldwide economic crash of stock prices that began a decade of unemployment and business failures that coincided with a drought. The drought and poor crop rotation led to the collapse of the agriculture market and tornado-sized storms of topsoil called dust bowls. Under President Franklin Roosevelt's New Deal, the government took an active role in protecting labor unions and workers' rights through federal legislation, for which Roosevelt was labeled by the wealthy as a traitor to his class.

The Great Depression's devastating effect on tens of millions of workers who were evicted from their homes, driven off their farms, foreclosed upon, unemployed, hungry, and desperate was captured in John Steinbeck's *Grapes of Wrath*. Steinbeck's book speaks of a poor White tenant farm family who, facing drought and eviction from a callous agriculture industry that treated the ordinary laborer with disdain, trekked from Oklahoma to California. Steinbeck's mission with *Grapes of Wrath* was to speak up for the working-class person while shoveling shame on the plutocrats who triggered such a calamitous financial crash. For his politically engaged fiction, John Steinbeck received the National Book Award and the Nobel Prize for Literature.

PROGRESS AT A PRICE

Imprisoned laborers of all races were ignored by the many biographies and histories of steel magnates and coal barons, which failed to expose their dependence on convict lease workers. This diabolical prison peonage supplied US industrialists with free imprisoned laborers who suffered and even died in their coal mines, forests, quarries, and steel plants. One would think the magnates' wealth flowed from the heavens, when in fact much of it stemmed from exploited labor, including a system of forced penal labor. "Slavery by another name" is a phrase used by Douglas Blackmon and other historians as a label for this system.[89] Blackmon's 2008 book, taking that phrase as its title, describes the suffering of incarcerated labor that municipalities, corporations, and businessmen would lease out from prisons in order to rebuild the South and fuel the Industrial Revolution.

Booker T. Washington, president of Tuskegee Institute, was tall, handsome, dark, and brilliant. As arguably the most respected Black person in the nation during this era, he loomed large in the African American community and beyond. Washington chastised working Black people, only one generation from slavery, for wanting a life that entailed more than physical labor and racial isolation.[90] Washington, enslaved as a child, was known as "the Wizard of Tuskegee" for his savvy ability to navigate virulent White racial hatred and a rising free Black population. The Wizard was considered the leader of Black people, adviser to presidents, and a sounding board to sympathetic wealthy Whites who sought ways to assist the country's downtrodden Black people while still coming short of securing racial equality.

In his infamous speech at the Cotton States and International Exposition in Atlanta, Georgia, on September 18, 1895, Washington promised Whites that poor African American laborers would "cast their buckets where they are" and that the Black middle classes would also remain satisfied with segregation. He received thunderous applause. Washington refused to acknowledge the country's oppressive system of racial incarceration and the men, women, and children barely fed and crushed into the South's lumber mills, steel plants, coal mines, and plantations.[91]

The coal mines of the Tennessee Coal, Iron and Railroad Company were some of the largest employers of convict laborers. Coal mines were dangerous for all workers. Collapsing mines, suffocation, gas poisoning, explosions, and heavy-machinery accidents were daily risks. Before electricity, men often worked standing in water, swinging their sharp pickaxes and shoveling coal in the flickering light of their gas headlamps. Once electricity was introduced into the mines, they had to avoid touching the live wires. For those who survived those hazards, long-term exposure to poor air caused chronic diseases such as black lung.

Working conditions for those in general manual labor were bad during this time. For convict laborers, they were even worse and included poor food rations, cramped sleeping quarters, and inadequate health care, which led to waves of epidemics. Violent convicts bullied and abused weaker ones. For those who were insubordinate or did not meet mining quotas, physical punishment included whippings, being tied up and tossed into solitary confinement, and water torture. The "water cure" was infamous in the penitentiary at Moundsville, West Virginia, and at the branch penitentiary of Eddyville, Kentucky. Men were stripped, blindfolded, and placed twenty to twenty-five feet in front of a hose with water pressure turned to two hundred eighty pounds. Then, under this terrific force, the temperature would be steadily lowered until the water was ice cold. The agony it caused would make the men do any task the warden or prison contractor required.[92]

Shackles, chains, and other methods were used to prevent escape. The convict lease system was called the "crime of crimes" by Clarissa Keeler in 1907 in her book of the same name.[93] This small volume details how the convicted were forced to work in mines in Tennessee,

Georgia, Alabama, Texas, District of Columbia, Missouri, Mississippi, Florida, Virginia, Kentucky, Delaware, and Arkansas. They were all leased from county jails to put money in the jailers' pockets and industrialists' coffers. Those in the system included many who had been acquitted or who had served their time but were reincarcerated for failure to pay court fines.

Keeler's report pleaded for prison reform and protested a merciless system, one in which other laborers turned a blind eye to the convicted men working at their side in the mines, even though their free labor drove down wages for free workers. Rev. Dr. Francis Wayland, a theologian, a medical doctor, an abolitionist, and an early prison reformer, spoke to the hypocrisy of a system that incarcerated the poor and allowed criminal industrialists to flaunt justice: "We punish a man who steals a loaf, if he steals an entire railroad, we say a financier; let us ask him to dinner."[94] Although Keeler's investigation did little to effect permanent change in conditions in convict leasing, it served as a record of a system thick with avarice that would later sully family reputations and institutions. The convict lease system was in its death throes during World War II. The advocacy of the NAACP and other organizations, which included letters to the president and petitions by family members of the convicted, had brought the necessary pressure to end a system that had affected tens of thousands of people, mainly African Americans, including women and girls.[95] This diabolical system that began in slavery ended, unofficially, but the strategies of exploitation endured. Instead of working for free as leased labor, the incarcerated were now paid pennies. The prison system had managed to sidestep the label of slavery, but in the process, it also birthed the prison-industrial complex.

The end of convict leasing was a small step forward. In the era of World War II, there were other gains for the working class, but people of color had to remain vigilant. What was given to working-class Whites was often denied to similarly situated African Americans. Unions were desegregating, slowly. The federal government had acted, finally providing aggrieved workers with the legislative power to form unions. Hoping to stem the violence of strikes and stabilize corporate labor agreements, Congress passed the Wagner Act, signed by Franklin Roosevelt. The act created the National Labor Relations Board, making it a vital player in union negotiations.

When great literature speaks of law and American wealth, there must be more than a mention of the heinous convict lease system, which was enslavement by another name.

PROTEST GAINS LABOR RELATIONS ACT

Working was killing and maiming workers due to hazardous job conditions that were without remedy or financial recourse. It is impossible to give a full recounting of the sacrifices—the lives lost, abuses, bloody battles, worker actions, and workplace disasters—that led to the federal legislation that allowed for open union organizing and provided worker protections on the job.

The NLRB was tasked with deliberating on the complaints and rights of private-sector workers to unionize and engage in collective bargaining. In 1938, Roosevelt signed another piece of labor legislation, the Fair Labor Standards Act, which established a federal law that set a minimum wage, maximum work hours, and overtime pay for most US workers, and banned most forms of child labor. However, these laws had carve-outs that left workers without protection, including many people of color who were sharecroppers, domestic service workers, or had other service jobs.

This was the year of the Pecan Shellers Strike. On January 31, about twelve thousand workers, most of them Mexican American women, organized a strike to protest the low pay and working conditions at a San Antonio, Texas, pecan-shelling plant.[96] The plant's Latina employees were working ten-hour days, seven days a week, some for only two dollars a week, while breathing the dust from the shelled pecans. Tuberculosis was prevalent. Then the corporation lowered their meager pay. Organizer Emma Tenayuca responded by forming the Texas Workers Alliance and leading a strike against the plant.

The peaceful line of strikers was met with company-supported police officers, who arrested hundreds and kept them detained in crowded cells where corporate leaders, who refused to recognize their union, hoped their jailed condition would frighten them back to work. But the strike lasted only thirty-seven days. A federal court found in favor of the laborers, recognized their union, and ordered higher pay. The Southern Pecan Shelling Company responded by laying off all the women and replacing them with pecan-shelling machines. This company's show of force and the firing of the women was, of course, not the intended outcome of their peaceful protest and reasonable request for a livable wage. Yet, the result is consistent with that of most labor struggles, and the heroic effort of these women should be applauded and remembered, because their strike emboldened others and provided valuable lessons to labor activists.

SILENCE WILL NOT PROTECT YOU

Filipinos stood up for the immigrant nurses falsely accused of killing patients in Michigan in 1975. A steady flow of Filipino immigrants into the US served the purpose of easing a nursing labor shortage. The women were selected particularly for their "soft-spoken and friendly" personality as well as their medical skills, as their training in the Philippines was prioritized specifically so that many women could work as nurses abroad, usually in Europe or the United States. However, the nation's initial gratitude for the nurses turned malevolent. The racism simmering beneath the surface boiled over when over thirty-five patients in Veterans Administration Hospital, in Ann Arbor, Michigan, suffered cardiopulmonary arrests, several of them dying. It was suspected that the patients were subjected to the injection of a muscle relaxant. There were ten counts of poisoning, five counts of murder, and one count of conspiracy to commit murder. Two Filipina women were indicted. The case was tried in federal court in 1977 in *United States of America v. Filipina Narciso and Leonora Perez*.[97] It was a bizarre case without any stated motive, yet Ms. Narciso and Ms. Perez were questioned without counsel and demonized in the media. Both were ultimately convicted in a highly publicized trial and incarcerated in a West Virginia prison.

However, on appeal, the verdict was set aside, despite the testimony of one hundred witnesses, because there was only very weak circumstantial evidence supporting the convictions of Narciso in the poisoning of Mark Hogan, John McCrery, and Russell Fletcher, and Perez's conviction in the poisoning of Charles Gasmire and Benny Blaine; both were charged with poisoning William Loesch. Unusual turns continued in this controversial case when a twenty-page memorandum was submitted by US attorney James K. Robinson, the prosecutor, who realized it was not a matter of justice to retry the women and requested a dismissal of the charges.[98] Asian American organizations, including the Japanese American Citizens League, advocates in the Philippines, and others who protested, petitioned, and publicly questioned the case against Narciso and Perez, all helped make a difference in Robinson's decision.[99]

MEXICAN AND FILIPINO WORKERS: STRONGER TOGETHER

On September 7, 1965, Filipino farmworkers in Delano, a small farming community in central California, voted to go on strike. Then, those Filipino farmworkers were joined by Mexican workers seeking to protest conditions. Roger Gadiano, who was a young activist at the time, refers to the Delano strike as "our Selma." He recalled how Cesar Chavez, the hero of the farmworkers' labor movement, and the charismatic Larry Itliong, who became known as the "father of the Delano Grape Strike," made history together.

Filipinos in the United States have had a long and complex history with the US military and the American labor system. In the latter part of the nineteenth century, while racial segregation swept the nation domestically, White supremacy fostered an arrogance about people of color internationally. In the Pacific, the "New Manifest Destiny" sparked a quest for empire building that fomented wars intended to expand US territories. The United States invaded the Philippines during the Spanish-American War of 1898 and occupied it for several decades after the war. Immediately, the nation was forced into near slave conditions. President William McKinley promised kinship with the Filipinos but in reality practiced forced assimilation.

On December 21, 1898, McKinley signed an executive order to the secretary of war regarding the control of the Philippines. It was titled the "Proclamation of Benevolent Assimilation"—as if the forced assimilation of a people could ever be benevolent.[100] It read:

> SIR: The destruction of the Spanish fleet in the harbor of Manila by the United States naval squadron commanded by Rear-Admiral Dewey, followed by the reduction of the city and the surrender of the Spanish forces, practically effected the conquest of the Philippine Islands and the suspension of Spanish sovereignty therein. . . .
>
> Finally, it should be the earnest and paramount aim of the military administration to win the confidence, respect, and affection of the inhabitants of the Philippines by assuring to them in every possible way that full measure of individual rights and liberties

which is the heritage of free peoples, and by proving to them that the mission of the United States is one of benevolent assimilation, substituting the mild sway of justice and right for arbitrary rule.[101]

But the Filipino people were not seeking a new identity. Filipino Americans were once the second-largest immigrant group, from the 1990s to early 2000s, but they are now outnumbered by Indian and Chinese Americans.[102] Asian Americans were considered a "model minority" by many White Americans, who would also often condemn them in the next breath as untrustworthy.[103]

As immigrants in the US, many Filipinos maintained their cultural identity while laboring invisibly in grimy conditions planting and harvesting massive fields. For many middle-class Americans, fruits and vegetables appeared in sparkling grocery stores simply as a course of nature. They had little interest in who produced the cornucopia. Filipino and Mexican workers picked the precious grape crops that were the backbone of the wine and fruit industries.[104] Yet, the working conditions and hours were deplorable. It was backbreaking work, in rain and sun, picking tons of grapes without access to toilets or schools for their children, under the watchful eye of guards, breathing pesticides, and with no pay for time lost to illness or injury.

Filipinos were organized by Itliong, who convinced Chavez to organize Mexican laborers and form what would become the United Farm Workers. Together, they walked off the fields, and thus began the Delano Grape Strike. For five years, farmworkers withheld their labor from the corporations, protesting the exploitative working conditions until their demands were met. The strike was a powerful moment in the agricultural labor rights movement given the incendiary labor history of the West Coast. In San Francisco and Tacoma, Washington, Whites brutally attacked Chinese workers intent on purging them from the state. Latinos had been targeted for centuries. In the West, Mexicans who had been promised citizenship under the Treaty of Hidalgo found themselves landless and without rights in America because the Mexican border was moved after America's war with Mexico.

Under Cesar Chavez's leadership, the Delano Grape Strike of 1965–70 drew attention to farmworkers' poverty, particularly that of Mexican immigrants. After the strike, tensions remained between White workers and immigrants, who continued to have trouble gaining entry into higher-skilled union jobs. Their protests for recognition of land rights, reparations, and citizenship seemed endless. Over five hundred thousand acres became part of the United States, used, once again, for the betterment of White American settlers.

Among the many civil rights leaders who supported Cesar Chavez in protesting the working conditions of fieldworkers was Rev. Dr. Martin Luther King Jr. Dr. King's Poor People's Campaign is often overlooked in US history. For instance, it is well known that King was assassinated in Memphis, Tennessee. However, it was his work with sanitation workers protesting horrific labor conditions that took him to Memphis and led to the series of fateful events ending in his murder.[105]

STRIKING SANITATION WORKERS AND MLK

The workers called on the King, and he gave his life for the sanitation workers of Memphis, who called him. On February 1, 1968, two Black men, Echol Cole and Robert Walker, were crushed to death when their sanitation truck malfunctioned. Sanitation workers in Memphis had no health insurance, survived on handouts and what they found in the trash barrels they picked up, and were paid so far below what other government workers received that they had to work second jobs or receive welfare to support their families. The deaths of Cole and Walker infuriated the sanitation workers, who had often complained about working conditions and faulty truck mechanisms to no avail. Their frustration led them to reach out to the American Federation of State, County and Municipal Employees (AFSCME).

Memphis mayor Henry Loeb was a paternalistic Southerner suspicious of change and enraged by Northern interference in Memphis's two-tier racial system. As an initiative focusing on economic uplift as well as civil rights, Dr. King's Poor People's Campaign was created to fight the type of economic oppression that was keeping workers down in Memphis. Dr. King's Poor People's Campaign was created to focus on economic uplift as well as civil rights. To King, being able to sit at the lunch counter meant little if one was unable to make a purchase.

The sanitation strike, which began less than two weeks after Cole's and Walker's deaths, was led by the hefty and charismatic T. O. Jones, a sanitation worker and natural labor organizer who persuaded Jerry Wurf, the fast-talking New Yorker and president of the national union AFSCME, to come to Memphis. Thirteen hundred sanitation workers walked out, but their strike was ignored by Loeb, who refused to replace the dilapidated trucks or raise wages.

The protesters wore white signs with black letters that stated boldly "I AM A MAN" to remind some of the White population of Memphis of the strikers' humanity. In the meantime, local ministers, including Rev. James Lawson, realized the strike needed national attention, and they persuaded King to lend his voice to the Memphis sanitation strike. These events occurred during a low point in Dr. King's Poor People's Campaign and the Civil Rights Movement generally. The Poor People's Campaign was fighting a worthy cause, as neighborhoods had been deemed blighted by White city planners. Across the country, urban planners appeared to have little interest in the families of color who lived and loved there and who could not access governmental services that should have come with their tax dollars. African Americans had been forced into highly concentrated urban areas, which became firestorms for violent riots in the 1960s, when young, frustrated African Americans in places like Newark, New Jersey, grew tired of fighting despair from under-employment. They also felt that Dr. King's philosophy of nonviolence was doing little to end the regular dose of racist violence administered daily by police.[106]

By 1968, a small but growing Black middle class was looking toward individual opportunities that desegregation had brought, and they were turning away from fighting on behalf of poorer members of the Black community. King's stance against the Vietnam War had made him unpopular among veterans of all backgrounds and most of the leadership of his Southern Christian Leadership Conference. Dr. King saw Memphis as a place to reconnect to the call for justice that still eluded many working-class people. The sanitation workers marched through downtown Memphis, led by a worn thirty-nine-year-old Dr. King, to demand higher wages, better working conditions, and recognition of their union.

Though no fault of Dr. King's, the march turned violent, as factions of young Black protesters battled with White disruptors. When people began breaking store windows, police moved in, and Dr. King was ushered away as mayhem erupted. He was at that time vilified in the media as a troublemaker and—after all King had withstood—called a coward who had placed the striking workers in a worse position than they were already in. Despite warnings not to return to Memphis,

Dr. King did so anyway, and it was there that he delivered his thunderous final speech, known as "I've Been to the Mountaintop."

The next day, April 4, 1968, at Memphis's Lorraine Motel, Dr. King was standing on the balcony when he was struck by an assassin's bullet. Black communities erupted in pain and rage. The king of peace, the world's premier protester, was dead. A second march in Memphis took place, in honor of Dr. King, without incident, in reverent silence. In the end, sanitation workers received their raises and union recognition. Sanitation workers across the United States should annually commemorate the sacrifices made by these men and Dr. King.

Countless acts of courage and protest, revolts and rebellion, followed the death of Dr. King, despite the stunning shock and sadness that engulfed the nation after his murder. In 1970, after fierce lobbying by several unions, an education campaign, documented injuries on hazardous worksites, and street protests, Congress passed the Occupational Safety and Health Act (OSHA). OSHA was intended to ensure safe working conditions for employees. The law sets standards and mandates that inspections are conducted, and training is provided to improve workplace safety. However, such laws require faithful execution and application, which in turn rely on the political will of a president and their administration. That political will isn't always guaranteed, especially when presidents show little concern for workers' welfare.

AIR TRAFFIC CONTROL VS. THE PRESIDENT

Air travel had replaced the train, but protests by the air traffic controllers' union were met with a response similar to those of the overworked and underpaid workers in the nineteenth century. In 1978, President Jimmy Carter, a Democrat from Georgia, signed the Airline Deregulation Act, removing the airline industry from federal government oversight to allow fares and flight routes to be based on the market and competition.[107] The US economy was struggling with a recession, an energy crisis, tense foreign relations, and 8 percent unemployment that had triggered labor protests.

Shortly after his inauguration, in 1981, President Ronald Reagan, a Republican from California, watched as contract negotiations between the thirteen-thousand-member Professional Air Traffic Controllers Organization (PATCO) and the Federal Aviation Administration stalled. Reagan became a symbol for conservatives and a key figure in ending the Cold War. However, he was not considered a friend of the working class. His administration's policies ended many financial aid policies for the poor and working class that would result in forcing them to stay in menial jobs. The Reagan administration relied on a "trickle down" economic theory. The wealth at the top was expected to trickle down to the working classes, though when that trickling down fails to materialize, it is disastrous for the poor.

Weary, overworked air traffic controllers, who were responsible for the safe travel of thousands of planes daily, believed the lives of passengers, crew, and anyone on the ground were in jeopardy due to the long schedules they were forced to work. After heated debate, PATCO members went on strike August 3, 1981, demanding higher pay and better working conditions. After they walked off the job, their absence caused disruptions in air travel that infuriated Reagan, who ordered an end to a strike that he considered a violation of federal law and a danger to national safety.[108] When the majority of workers refused to return until the FAA met to discuss their demands, Reagan used his power to break the air controllers' union as federal employees, despite the deregulation act.

He fired the striking controllers and decertified their union, sending a troubling message to organized labor and signaling an era of governmental support for corporations.[109] On appeal, the courts sided with the federal government, and most of the workers were not re-hired. After the PATCO strike, and the scandals within unions, union membership began to decline. PATCO's historic defeat represented a protest that faced unforeseen circumstances and a culmination of economic and political forces requiring time and renewed strategies.

THE EBB AND FLOW OF CHANGE

The tide turned against unionization following the Reagan era and into the twenty-first century as corporations moved their factories overseas or to nonunion states, membership fell, and strikes failed. It would take a Great Recession for labor to gain power once again. With any social justice movement, it is two steps forward and one step back. There should always be a strategy anticipating the inevitable backlash against progressive movements, which comes from those who have been challenged and wish to maintain the status quo of owner supremacy and underpaid workers.

The labor movement faced challenges, as have all efforts to create progressive change, but renewed energy and strategies come by seeking ideas from traditional and nontraditional sources, activists of all generations, and from history. As Noam Chomsky explains it, some of the most fanatical attacks are against organized labor because "they are a democratizing force."[110] Chomsky is a brilliant activist intellectual whose prodigious work provides an extraordinary example of how writing, lectures, and examining social justice issues as an academic are forms of protest. Chomsky's *Requiem for the American Dream* and other works share his expertise on the intricacies of economic tyranny.[111]

Barbara Ehrenreich's 2001 book, *Nickel and Dimed: On (Not) Getting By in America*, sheds light on working-class struggles, especially the women juggling part-time jobs and families, reminiscent of the mill girls.[112] The groundbreaking works of Chomsky, Ehrenreich, Howard Zinn, and John Hope Franklin, to name a few, analyze the pitfalls of capitalism, the media, the mythologizing of American history, gender bias, racism, and the politics of powerbrokers. In sharing their intellectual gifts, they help fuel the fight of the masses.[113] All told, these four authors have written over one hundred books on the oppression of the working class from the perspectives of race, gender, immigration, and ethnicity.

TWENTY-FIRST-CENTURY GILDED AGE

A new century with old ways of manic money-making and unabashed greed. Telecommunications expanded, and technology replaced many traditional jobs. Champagne pedicures and apartments bought sight unseen illustrated the aspiration and foolishness of the time. But economic uncertainty lurked on the edges. Then, the crash came, as corruption in the financial services and real estate sectors, combined with an ever-growing wealth gap between the very rich and everyone else, changed the landscape in nearly every economic sector, undermining the retirement of seniors and futures of young people.

When news broke in 2008 of Bernie Madoff's $65 billion Ponzi scheme perpetrated by his Wall Street firm, it epitomized the corruption of this Second Gilded Age. Madoff was sentenced to 150 years in federal prison for money laundering, fraud, and other crimes. The Great Recession, a worldwide economic downturn, caused unemployment to double and waves of home foreclosures, as discussed in Bethany

McLean and Joe Nocera's book, *All the Devils Are Here: The Hidden History of the Financial Crisis.* The book's title, paraphrasing a line from William Shakespeare's play *The Tempest*—"hell is empty and all the devils are here"—rightly describes the greedy wickedness behind the financial crisis that devastated so many families.[114] Thousands of individuals, charitable organizations, retirement funds, and investors suffered huge losses.

Michael Lewis's *The Big Short: Inside the Doomsday Machine* and Andrew Ross Sorkin's *Too Big to Fail* explain how the exploitative subprime mortgages that were issued by banks were at the cold heart of the crisis.[115] The Great Recession fueled the frustration of young people who saw their prospects diminish as a result of corporate greed and exorbitant college tuition rates that had left them burdened with tens of thousands of dollars in student loan debt but which Congress specifically deemed ineligible for bankruptcy relief. Because there were few jobs available for young workers, financial insecurity forced them to move back home with their parents, who in turn were forced to retire later in life.

In 2011, young people's frustration drew them into the belly of the beast, Wall Street, to protest corporate greed. Crowds took over a privately owned but publicly accessible space named Zuccotti Park, in Manhattan's Financial District. Spanning about half a block, featuring very few trees, and surrounded by towering business and apartment buildings, the park (previously named Liberty Plaza Park) was named after John Eugene Zuccotti, who rose from a working-class family to become a major influence in government and real estate. It became the platform for a generational standoff known as Occupy Wall Street.

At its height, Occupy Wall Street was a committee-run movement without a hierarchy that sparked national conversations about income inequality and the soaring wealth of the top 1 percent of the population, as explored by Arindrajit Dube and Ethan Kaplan's 2012 article "Occupy Wall Street and the Political Economy of Inequality."[116] Occupy Wall Street protests spread internationally among college-educated young people with similar frustrations around the lack of opportunities in their countries.

On November 15, 2011, citing unsanitary conditions, police raided Occupy Wall Street, under the orders of billionaire mayor Michael Bloomberg and the owner of Zuccotti Park, Brookfield Properties.

Several such confrontations had occurred before this raid, with the protesters always returning afterward, but this time, after nearly two months, the "1 percent" billionaire class had finally razed the tent city created by Occupy Wall Street.

However, also in New York City, empowered fast-food workers organized to demand an increase in the minimum wage, which had been stagnant for years even as inflation and the cost of living rose. As of this writing, the federal minimum wage is $7.25 per hour and has not increased since 2009, though New York State has increased its minimum wage, as have other states. The federal minimum wage only serves as a universal minimum; each state can require employers to pay its employees more, based on calculations by its Department of Labor.

In the wake of the movement, union membership has increased as laborers organized to improve working conditions and increase the minimum wage, echoing the protests against income inequality during the first Gilded Age. This has included workers at Amazon, one of the largest corporations in the world, who have strived to unionize. They started slowly but over fifty stores have discussed starting a union.

PANDEMIC CHANGES

Unions rose from the ashes of a global disaster. Service workers died in the tens of thousands. In January 2020, the Centers for Disease Control confirmed that a travel-related infection of the SARS-CoV-2 or coronavirus had entered the country from Wuhan, China. Although a US travel alert was put in place, this highly contagious virus spread across the country with frightening speed, and there was no vaccine. By March 2020, the coronavirus death toll was in the thousands, with the virus taking lives globally, causing the World Health Organization to declare it a pandemic. Those who interacted with the public or with large groups were more susceptible to contracting this deadly airborne virus. The lives of teachers, nurses, doctors, store clerks, factory workers, receptionists, delivery persons, waitstaff, entertainers, bus drivers, civil servants, and emergency responders were at higher risk. To save lives, emergency medical service unions called for community-based governmental action.[117]

In New York City, the epicenter of the pandemic in the US, mortuaries were overrun, bodies were stacked in refrigerator trucks, Broadway went dark, and the streets were quiet except for the sirens. "Stay-at-home orders" did not pertain to essential workers who faced a disease with no cure or known vaccine and had only hand washing, a mask, and social distancing as the official defensive tactic. Those workers without the luxury of sick pay or an option to work from home risked death. Many of the one hundred thousand service workers laid off during Covid were forced to take gig jobs to supplement their unemployment payments or replace income if they did not qualify for unemployment.[118]

"The coronavirus pandemic created an unprecedented crisis for American workers, many of whom struggled to stay in their jobs while keeping themselves and their families safe. This crisis had a particularly devastating impact on historically marginalized groups, including hourly workers, women, workers of color, and older workers, who were more likely to suffer worse outcomes and less likely to have access to the benefits needed to protect themselves and their families."[119]

When the crisis ended, the US had over one million deaths in the worst pandemic since the Spanish Flu outbreak of 1918–1919.[120] As with West Virginia's coal mine disasters, the pandemic sparked a revitalization for unions. Amid this disaster, protesting nurses, fast food clerks, factory workers, and delivery persons took to the streets to bring national attention to the crucial role they played in the nation's survival. Their protests educated the public, changed hearts, and enlightened minds about the need for organized labor. Workers from various sectors united around issues of fair pay and safe working conditions. Despite the increased desire by workers to form unions, their efforts to organize have been undermined by employers that use their economic weight to exploit weaknesses in labor laws, allowing them to legally and illegally defeat union organizing.[121]

CHRISTIAN SMALLS VS. AMAZON

Christian Smalls and other workers at the Staten Island, New York, Amazon facility walked off the job in 2020 to protest low wages and an unsafe working environment. Under his leadership, they had to navigate a labyrinth of intimidation, paperwork, and votes, but in March 2022, they successfully formed the first Amazon union, a victory that made international news. Since this herculean accomplishment, Amazon has refused to meet with this new union at the negotiation table.

On May 5, 2022, the Senate Budget Committee held a hearing on companies' anti-union activities in one of the Capitol's hallowed marble and oak hearing rooms. Christian Smalls, as the Amazon Labor Union's president, testified with a steady gaze as he looked up at Senator Lindsey Graham. The South Carolina senator, known for his icy conservatism, had just given an opening statement as minority leader of the committee. From his seat at the long table, facing Senator Graham, the union leader, sporting a nicely trimmed beard, looked up from under his black New York Yankees baseball cap. Instead of a business suit, Smalls wore a red and black letterman jacket.

Christian Smalls became a media star. Amazon's massive Staten Island facility is nearly a million square feet and employs eight thousand workers. In this gray, windowless facility and the others that comprise Amazon's complex network of warehouses and hubs across the United States, countless items are processed and distributed twenty-four hours a day, seven days a week, through the labor of human beings and machines. Founded in 1994, Amazon is the brainchild of Jeff Bezos, who began this online "store" from his garage, focused on selling books, and has grown it into a global clearinghouse valued at $1.85 trillion. Amazon employs over 1.5 million workers, whose grievances in this behemoth go largely unheeded.

Smalls testified that workers at the Staten Island facility were facing unsafe conditions, repetitive motions that led to carpal tunnel syndrome, unrealistic requirements in how fast they performed tasks, and rigid time clocks controlling every minute of their workday, including how long they could spend in the bathroom. His description hearkened back a century. As had laborers of past generations, from the textile mills to the railroads and the coal mines, the Amazon workers believed that as a union, they would be a more powerful force and their voices would be heard. After a year of organizing, Staten Island voted to unionize and Christian Smalls became the leader of the union, and he spoke of paying the price with the loss of his job and intimidation.

When Smalls spoke before the Senate Budget Committee in May 2022, he made clear that the motivation to organize was "not a left or right thing. It's not a Democrat or Republican thing. It's a workers' thing, a workers' issue. And we are the ones that are suffering in the corporations."[122] Christian spoke openly about the vulnerability of workers in need of federal protections. "Our victory in Staten Island was lauded as newsworthy and inspirational for the thousands of workers across the country, hundreds of thousands of workers," he said. "And, even though we may have won, we did everything right pressuring Amazon to recognize a victory and comply with legal obligation to meet us at the bargaining table. But Amazon is refusing to do so. They are going to stall. They filed 25 objections, and they got the NLRB to move the hearing to a whole other location."[123]

Smalls's testimony before Graham and the committee about how Bezos and Amazon have used their power, influence, and immense wealth to flout the laws hearkened back to the criticism leveled at Rockefeller and railroad, steel, and coal mine magnates. "They control whatever they want," Smalls said. "They break the law. They get away with it. They know that breaking the law during election campaigns won't be resolved during election campaigns. So, they purposely continue to break the law."[124]

He asked Congress to pass the Protecting the Right to Organize Act (also known as the PRO Act).[125] In that ornate but soulless Senate hearing room, Christian Smalls spoke truth to power with the impatient tone of a man who had seen too much and the passion of one who has many more battles to fight for workers' rights. He was a combination of Mother Jones and A. Philip Randolph. In response, Senator Graham could only sit and nod in agreement.

CONCLUSION

Workers are the backbone of any nation. In the United States, workers have shown the power to fight for fair wages, safer conditions, equal treatment, and the right for an organization to speak on their behalf at the negotiation table. For nearly a century and a half, the power of union membership has opened opportunities, provided employment security, and advanced the dreams of workers of color, immigrants, women, and workers in general.

When a union membership helps guarantee a steady paycheck and safe working conditions, that stable economic foundation allows one to make better choices with respect to education, housing, health, and political representation. In the ongoing battle against the working class, allegiance with or concern about workers is largely absent. People are only consumers, and what is paramount is corporate profit and return on investment (any investment).

The twenty-first-century Gilded Age is reminiscent of the era of the mill systems and coal mines of the nineteenth and twentieth centuries.

Once again, the battle between the American ideal of working hard to earn an honest living is pitted against the US desire for profit at any cost. This nation failed to learn the lessons from the original Gilded Age, so we now have to learn them all over again, while the people pay for painful consequences as too many corporate oligarchs build enterprises without conscience and spread their controlling reach across the country and into every aspect of life.

With advances in artificial intelligence, corporations may soon find a way to fully automate our lives, with AI working the jobs, healing our bodies, creating our laws, and writing our books. Not all forms of AI are bad, but since human minds thought of the machine in the first place, and human beings keep the national economy moving, they should be respected; paid fairly; provided safe, adequate housing; and kept healthy—not just because it is the right thing to do but because maintaining the profit motive above all else is an unsustainable model of capitalism. Profit by any means necessary produced slavery, provoked genocide against the Indigenous, triggered bloody labor battles, and led to a civil war. The oppressed worker will not remain crushed under the boot of trillionaires, billionaires, or their less wealthy minions. Protest, rebellion, and resistance will be the human choice.

What would Eliza say to workers fighting for their rights against twenty-first-century corporate barons? Keep the faith, perhaps, do not give up. In scorching summers, icy winters, pouring rain and miserable humidity, my thoughts turn to her and the years of her laboring in all seasons, under all conditions, for free, on threat of death. She did so much more with so little. The photo of her sitting serenely, loved by Mattie, and living gently, does not reveal the time stolen from her, the physical scars from that beating from Harriet Christian, or the emotional wounds that may have haunted her. The era of slavery revealed the debauched social and economic code of those who worshipped profit above all, leaving a slimy trail their heirs wish to cover with myths.

I am not naïve to the fact that many workers who have challenged serf-based economies, indentured servitude, peonage, unfair conditions, wage theft, and modern slavery by another name often pay for it with their livelihoods, future opportunities, and some with their freedom and very lives. Some rose victorious, but many were replaced, shunned, forced to find work in other towns, and suffered for their stance with little to show for it. Having experienced the backlash from taking a stand in the workplace, I still prefer my soul intact despite hardships and only wish I had done more to make Eliza proud.

ANTI-WAR MARCHES
AND CONSCIENTIOUS OBJECTORS

My family has seen its share of military veterans. I remember Uncle Wayne, my father's younger brother, a veteran of the Korean War, sitting at our dining room table, staring ahead at nothing, his back rigid as if he were being judged by an invisible sergeant. I pretended he was listening to me, during his Fourth of July visit and family gatherings. Relatives would walk outside, eat barbeque and potato salad, tell stories, crack stale jokes, pass heaping plates to each other, but he would sit alone in the kitchen or on the porch. Auntie, who was an older cousin, would place food in front of Uncle Wayne, and wait.

Uncle Wayne smiled and turned away, distracted by some conversation taking place in the distance where no one stood, nodding in response to questions only he could hear. I would sit at his feet, watching this harmless adult with childish wonder, as his soft brown eyes said "thank you" and "I love you" after pills were placed in his shaking palms. This was the man my father said was made different by going to the war. That he had been handsome once, not bloated and sad. That he had had a bright, quick smile and enviable brawny muscles. But that part of him must have been left in Korea.

Throughout my life, when war was imminent (and in the United States, a war is always imminent), I recall ministers saying, "Pray for peace, but if war comes, then pray for God to grant victory." There was no discussion of right or wrong. But I don't recall prayers for civil rights protesters, who were soldiers in a form of war, or prayers for Black people trying to stay alive in a nation fomenting genocide. In grade school, upon the warning bell, I walked hand-in-hand with my classmates to our designated bomb shelter, in the basement of Frances Willard Elementary School. I sat quietly on the dusty concrete, covering my head, as instructed, until the horn blew again, signaling no nuclear bomb had been dropped, this time. I didn't fully grasp the destruction in the films we watched of nuclear tests. Nor did I understand how people could kill strangers in war in another country at the same time that the United States was using the criminal system of injustice to decimate our families. I am fighting battles to survive racism, to thrive as a female amid misogyny, and to stay a loving human being in a race war that has been going on since enslavement ended.

I wondered what my uncle Wayne had experienced as a soldier in the United States Army. In 1951, the NAACP sent Thurgood Marshall, the preeminent civil rights attorney, to investigate the treatment of African American soldiers in Korea, America's first fully racially integrated war. Marshall found racial discrimination in the treatment and punishment of soldiers, and with those soldiers dishonorably discharged, according to Carl Rowan in his biography of Marshall, *Dream Makers, Dream Breakers*. If such investigations have continued, I want to be a part of shedding light on the treatment of African American, Brown, Indigenous, and immigrant service members. Considering racial attacks that have gone unabated in civilian life, it seems naive to believe discrimination based on color, gender, or race in the military is no longer an issue. Although legal or de jure racism had ended early in the armed forces, the fact or tradition of discrimination has clung to each succeeding generation.

But there have always been those who decide to defy the barriers of prejudice by proving their patriotism. African Americans have fought in nearly every war at least since the arrival of Africans into the Virginia Colony in 1619. As early as 1680, after Bacon's Rebellion, most Africans in Virginia were prohibited, by law, from carrying weapons or acting in self-defense. But when the colonists were under attack, they armed Africans out of desperation. There was a sense of pride in fighting and of rage knowing only perilous circumstances led to an enslaved person fighting to protect a colony of oppressors.

Leonard Bradshaw lived on a farm in Kansas and dreamed of becoming a pilot. That's what he wrote in his high school yearbook even before the start of World War II. He scored first in his class on the test required for pilots' school and looked forward to being a Tuskegee Airman, but his White commanding officers transferred him overseas to England, where he missed a chance for flight school, discovering his excellent exam scores while researching his military files in Washington, DC. By that point he was in Alabama, retired and living with liver cancer. Yet, he only spoke with great pride about military life and the friends made in those decades of service.

Leonard had retired to Montgomery, Alabama, when I landed a job there as a civil rights attorney. He was my staunch supporter, having gone to law school later in life. We were geeks sitting together in the front row at law conferences and he surprised me by attending my first oral argument. The Iraq War moved me to protest. We were a group of about twenty loosely knit friends, all African American women of various backgrounds who agreed the war was wrong and someone needed to say it. We decided to hold an anti-war march in downtown Montgomery. Little did I know, the march I led there was the first in Montgomery's history.

A month later, I traveled with a group from Montgomery to Washington, DC, via a yellow school bus, to protest the US conflict in the Persian Gulf. My actions were broadcast on the local television news, but I avoided discussing any of it with Leonard. He was a proud veteran, a member of Kappa Alpha Psi Fraternity, and a thirty-third-degree Freemason. I loved and admired him, even his curmudgeonly ways, but I felt it my duty to protest. Although he knew my thoughts about war (it was, after all, broadcast on the local news), we kept an unspoken and respectful truce.

Since war is hell, anti-war protests have centered on preventing the escalation of conflict before it rises to a declaration of war, demanding and end to the wars that are ongoing and dismantling the weapons of war. However, given this book's expanded examination of protest, although I have no intention of inflaming pacifists, enlistment in war also needs to be included in a discussion of anti-war protest. For some, participation in the military challenges racist and gender stereotypes that cast people of color and women as unpatriotic, or incapable of the courage needed to be a soldier. Traditionally, anti-war protests rally against armed conflict and its human carnage, whether it is a civil war or one fought on foreign soil, and whether the tragic toll is in military lives or the so-called collateral damage of civilians. In all cases, there is hell to pay—famine, disease, amputations, rape, the loss of homes, the rise in refugees, strains on infrastructure, generational trauma, and untold effects that ripple worldwide.

REFUSING TO KILL

War is our refined art, a unique talent of the United States of America cultivated over centuries. This nation has remained in constant battles, military conflicts, skirmishes, and declared wars since its founding as a colony. War, as practiced in the United States, should be an officially acknowledged national export, employer, and area of expertise. The secretary of war was an original cabinet position and only transitioned into the secretary of defense in 1947, following World War II.[1] War has become integral to this nation's identity, and solving personal or political disputes with gun violence is an accepted and respected first option. The United States' relationship with war represents yet another source of deep hypocrisy, in that the country's brutal aggression is at odds with its benevolence in times of global disasters.

Pacifists in the US have entered a lion's den, because opposing violence to settle disputes, refusing to engage in armed combat, and bravely facing social shaming runs counter to the nation's bluster. Yet, those same warmongers tout "Blessed are the peacemakers," which is a core belief for many pacifists, who oppose all wars, for any reason. This is distinguished from some anti-war protesters who oppose war on the basis of a particular rationale or because it uses a certain type of weapon.[2] Protests were based on personal, political, or religious values, but either way there have always been those who have refused to fight. George Fox, a Protestant, broke from the Church of England and began a new religion called Quakerism; its adherents were known as the Religious Society of Friends, or Quakers. Fox believed the presence of God was found within people rather than in churches. Quakers maintain a commitment to nonviolence and conscientious objection to participating in war.

In colonial Pennsylvania, named for the Quaker William Penn, having a high position did not shield a Quaker from persecution when their religion forbade them from defending the new colonies.[3] Although Quakers have a commitment to nonviolence and conscientious objection to participating in war, some Quakers have served in the military.[4] Shakers, the Amish, and Quakers had been jailed, tortured, and whipped in Europe for their religious beliefs. Persecution of religious pacifists would continue for hundreds of years. A refusal to engage in military violence, despite the consequences, shaped early religion-based anti-war protests.

Later, followers of the Jehovah's Witnesses faith would oppose war and refuse to be drafted into military service. All followers of these faiths would be subject to abuse and have their right to oppose war litigated before the US Supreme Court. Many who refused to engage in war were abolitionists as well. Mennonites were conscientious objectors and early abolitionists, and the Unitarians established crucial components of the Underground Railroad. For example, Quakers in Indiana provided food and shelter to enslaved persons escaping to freedom in the North from Kentucky, facilitating their travel through the Underground Railroad to safety.[5]

For people of African descent, being anti-war raises conflicting historical narratives. During colonial years of enslavement, the government prohibited Africans from carrying weapons or engaging in any acts of self-protection. An African could be lawfully killed for resisting the orders of any White person to labor, cook, or clean and had no legal right to self-defense. Fear of rebellion led White colonists to enact laws restricting African self-defense, gatherings, and meetings, assuming treachery of the free as well as the enslaved, and dispensing sadistic punishments, at will.

> WHEREAS the frequent meeting of considerable numbers of negroe slaves under pretence of feasts and burialls is judged of dangerous consequence; for prevention whereof for the future, Bee it enacted by the kings most excellent majestie by and with the consent of the generall assembly, and it is hereby enacted by the authority aforesaid, that from and after the publication of this law, it shall not be lawfull for any negroe or other slave to carry or arme himselfe with any club, staffe, gunn, sword or any other weapon of defence or offence, nor to goe or depart from of his masters ground without a certificate from

his master, mistris or overseer, and such permission not to be granted but upon perticuler and necessary occasions; and every negroe or slave soe offending not haveing a certificate as aforesaid shalbe sent to the next constable, who is hereby enjoyned and required to give the said negroe twenty lashes on his bare back well layd on, and soe sent home to his said master, mistris or overseer. And it is further enacted by the authority aforesaid that if any negroe or other slave shall presume to lift up his hand in opposition against any christian, shall for every such offence, upon due proofe made thereof by the oath of the party before a magistrate, have and receive thirty lashes on his bare back well laid on. And it is hereby further enacted by the authority aforesaid that if any negroe or other slave shall absent himself from his masters service and lye hid. [6]

In spite of the limitations imposed by such laws, that did not stop African men, women, and children from fighting back, mounting slave revolts, and escaping.

CIVIL WAR

The war was about slavery and states' rights. When the Civil War began, requests by African Americans in the US to join the battle were forcefully rejected and often maligned. Abraham Lincoln and the Republican leadership feared the prospect of freeing and arming African Americans to fight against the Confederate army. In 1863, Frederick Douglass delivered a speech entitled "Men of Color, to Arms!" to motivate African American men to continue their push for inclusion in the military. In the words of Douglass, "Action! action! not criticism, is the plain duty of this hour."[7]

Enlistment in the military represented patriotism and belonging, an act of rebellion given the deep hostilities toward free African American men and women. In January 1863, Governor John Andrew of Massachusetts obtained authorization from Secretary of War Edwin Stanton to form an African American regiment.[8] This was an extraordinary development, given that the majority of Africans in America were in bondage and the Indigenous had been stripped of millions of acres of their sovereign land. The men of the Fifty-Fourth Massachusetts Volunteers were the first military regiment of African American soldiers in America. Here, people of African descent responded to slavery by fighting in the military to show their courage and claim their freedom and rightful place as citizens.

Along with fighting voluntarily for the Union, some enslaved African Americans were forced to fight for the Confederacy by their slaveholder. A small number of free Creoles fought willingly for the Confederacy. Asians fought on both the Union and Confederate sides, as did more than twenty-eight thousand Indigenous soldiers.[9]

Under the Emancipation Proclamation, those who escaped slavery were deemed "contraband of war" and could become Union soldiers. The Union forces recruited African American troops from around the country, and Asians served as well. In 1863, William Ah Hang became the first Asian to serve in the military. Hang, like many others, representing all ethnicities, used enlistment in the military to prove their rightful place as a US citizen. He was among the first of many waves of Asians and Asian Americans to serve in the military.

However, fearing the reaction of Whites to the prospect of African American military officers, commissioned officer positions of the Fifty-Fourth and other African American regiments were restricted to Whites. Although promised equal pay by President Lincoln, African American soldiers received less pay than White soldiers and performed manual labor. The Militia Act of 1862 provided White soldiers with thirteen dollars per month plus an extra three dollars and fifty cents for a clothing allowance, whereas African American soldiers received ten dollars per month and had three dollars deducted for clothing, an insult that African American soldiers protested.

Democrats and Republicans both believed that equal pay for soldiers of different races was an insult to the White soldier.[10] The US Congress hesitated in supporting this stance—the Union army relied on African American soldiers in the North and South. In 1864, at the insistence of abolitionists, Congress enacted legislation granting equal pay to African American soldiers, to be paid retroactively. Unfortunately, the pay was differentiated based on the soldier's former status, either free or enslaved, at the time of his recruitment.

African Americans in the United States expanded the war over slavery into their battle for freedom. They were a liberating army—fighting to liberate themselves. The contraband law was the brainchild of Major General Benjamin Butler of the Union Army.[11] Butler had witnessed desperate escapes by fugitives who risked all in seeking sanctuary among Union camps and at Fort Monroe in Virginia. Butler, a lawyer who had fought on the side of the Lowell mill girls in New England and other oppressed workers, initially had tried to stop the flow of fugitives from the battlefields and bondage in the South but found their determination was unbounded. He then realized that if, in war, property seized from the opposing side could be considered contraband and seized, that would also apply to Confederate property, even human property.

Slavery was abolished in part because of the bravery shown by African American soldiers fighting for their freedom through service in the Union Army. During the congressional debate on the passage of the Thirteenth Amendment, African Americans' bravery was recognized, with Sergeant William H. Carney becoming the first African American to be awarded the Congressional Medal of Honor. US congressman Henry Wilson, a Republican, pointed to the feats of sacrifice and heroism of African American soldiers who had convinced many skeptics that winning the war against the Confederacy, and thus abolishing slavery, provided African American soldiers with an inducement to fight. Men who could not show their courage to insecure Whites had feigned physical timidity, to appease slave masters, but could display their true nature on the battlefield and should have, then and there, proved themselves brave in battle.

Henry Wilson said: "We owe it to the course of the country, to liberty, to justice, and to patriotism to offer every inducement to every African American man who can fight the battle of the country to join our armies."[12] On January 31, 1865, the Thirteenth Amendment, which abolished slavery, was passed by Congress and later signed into law by President Lincoln. After the war, in 1866, Congress reorganized the African American troops into the Ninth and Tenth Cavalries and then, in 1869, it created the African American Twenty-Fourth and Twenty-Fifth Infantries.[13] Those African American men who desired a military career were met with simmering animosity in the newly reconstructed country and were thus assigned to the frontier in order to fight the Indigenous, who were still defending their land rights. (These men became known as the Buffalo Soldiers.) Elsewhere, military conflict would place African American soldiers at bloody oppositional odds against other people of color in the wars in Cuba, during the Spanish-American War of 1898, and in the conflict in the Philippines.[14]

African American soldiers fought in these overseas conflicts only to return to Jim Crow racism in the United States. Segregationist laws, fear of competition for jobs, and deep White resentment of their status as military heroes or "uppity" met them behind the golden door of liberty but not before they had experienced a certain freedom overseas, "where that race line which the Anglo-Saxon insists on does not exist."[15] Still, the murder of African American soldiers returning home from foreign war persisted without arrest or trial for the perpetrators. The first acknowledged global conflict was World War I.

WORLD WAR I

Germany's attacks on US ships in the early months of 1917 resulted in President Woodrow Wilson asking Congress for a declaration of war on April 6. Wilson, a segregationist who aired the racist propagandist film *Birth of a Nation* at the White House and directed the segregation of the Capitol building, delegated the most menial positions within the government and in the war effort to African American men and women. Once again, patriotism was partially the reason African Americans fought, but it was not their only motive.

The United States entered World War I for what was called a sacrifice for global freedom, even as African Americans faced segregation and violence by White mobs at home. Charles Hamilton Houston, the NAACP's first general counsel and the brilliant architect of the organization's legal strategies, faced the harsh realities of racism as a first lieutenant in the segregated US Army during World War I. This motivated him to pledge his lifetime to striking blows against *Plessy v. Ferguson*'s doctrine of racial apartheid. When Houston died in 1950, he left behind a mighty legacy, having claimed significant ground against Jim Crow, creating inroads through crucial cases and mentoring dozens of civil rights attorneys.

On August 29, 1914, fifteen thousand women assembled for the Women's Peace March in Manhattan. It was the confluence of peace activism and women's suffrage. The United States was on the brink of entering the European conflict that would become World War I. The New York march demanded the vote for women; if women could vote, went the activists' argument, the anti-war contingent would have enough electoral power to prevent elected leaders from entering the war. It was New York City's first anti-war protest, and the fact that it was organized by women made it dangerous because their stance was associated with socialism or communism, both unpopular and suspect by many, and women were maligned for voicing strong opinions in public because their assumed place was as silent homemakers during the war.[16] Yet, those women involved in anti-war rallies chose to bring attention to their cause by dressing as if in a funeral procession while others wore white as a symbol of peacetime.

The government crushed anti-war efforts. In the 1919 decision *Schenck v. United States*, the Supreme Court ruled that protest of the military draft was a violation of the Espionage Act, passed in 1917. Charles Schenck, a slightly built, mustached man with dark-blond hair, believed he was exercising his First Amendment right to free speech when he mailed and handed out flyers to young men in Philadelphia asking them to resist induction into the war. The court upheld his conviction of ten years in federal prison, stating that Schenck's words were a clear and present danger to society and not protected by the Constitution.[17]

POST-WAR PROTESTS

The fight at home was as segregated as the battlefield. In 1919, as the world emerged from the Spanish Flu pandemic, White mobs attacked and murdered hundreds of African Americans. It was called the "Red Summer," so named for the blood that was shed during that period. W. E. B. Du Bois wrote in *The Crisis* magazine:

> Tens of thousands of African American men were drafted into a great struggle. For bleeding France and what she means and has meant and will mean to us and humanity and against the threat of German race arrogance. . . .
>
> But by the God of heaven, we are cowards and jackasses if now that the war is over, we do not marshal every ounce of our brain and brawn to fight a sterner, longer, more unbending battle against the forces of hell in our own land.[18]

That year, veterans of color used their military training to create organizations, civil rights strategies, and protest movements.

World War I had been long over, but in the summer of 1932, there was unfinished business. More than seventeen thousand World War I veterans gathered in Washington, DC, to demand early payment of their "bonus" money. Their bonus was not scheduled to be paid until 1945, but many veterans were struggling financially during the Great Depression and wanted payment for their service to be made immediately. Calling themselves the Bonus Army, the veterans set up shantytowns in the US capital and conducted daily protests and rallies.

The government was initially supportive of the veterans' cause, but as the protest continued, tensions escalated. On July 28, 1932, President Herbert Hoover ordered the US Army to clear the encampments, and the troops used tear gas, bayonets, and tanks to force the veterans and their families out of the city. "If the Army must be called out to make war on unarmed citizens, this is no longer America," said the *Washington Daily News*.[19] Government-sanctioned violence against the protesting veterans caused public outrage. Americans became sympathetic to the Bonus Army's cause. The incident damaged Hoover's reputation, and a few months later he lost the presidential election to Franklin D. Roosevelt. The bonus was eventually paid in 1936, but the incident remains an unforgettable reminder of America's ill-treatment of veterans.

Also in the 1930s, a contingent of African Americans protested racism by leaving the country to be repatriated to Africa or by becoming expats in Europe and Canada. They also joined the military of other nations to fight on behalf of Africa and the Philippines. In 1935, the fascist and racist dictator Benito Mussolini's Italian forces attacked Ethiopia. African Americans in the United States rose to Ethiopia's defense against this invasion. Marches took place in New York City, and some African American civilians even signed up to fight on behalf of Ethiopia.

WORLD WAR II

Bayard Rustin was deeply affected by the carnage of World War I. The war at home and abroad was part of his African American community in West Chester, Pennsylvania, a segregated township but surrounded by a Quaker stronghold. Born in 1912, Rustin was tall and thin, with a remarkably quick mind, and would have been considered a child prodigy, if an African American boy could have been so honored at that time. He was an intellectually curious child who began to study the Quaker religion and embrace its anti-war tenets while challenging its prejudiced contradictions. Rustin also explored communism and other avenues for change outside of the African American Church.

In 1941, Rustin was hired by the Fellowship of Reconciliation (FOR), founded by Reverend A. J. Muste, a White minister who had known the brutality of World War I, and other pacifists, who did not want to see it repeated. He also opposed racial segregation. Rustin was nearly thirty, draft age, and although Europe's war had not touched the isolationist United States when he started working at FOR, in December 1941, the Empire of Japan attacked Pearl Harbor. In response, Rustin traveled across the United States, lecturing on nonviolence and pacifism to diverse audiences, the "Negro and white, Jew and Gentile," telling all who would listen that violence was not the answer to end national conflicts, international attacks, or racial segregation.[20]

Rustin's pacifism had come from studying the great Mahatma Gandhi's philosophy of nonviolent direct action to create social change. By the time Rustin joined King as an adviser in the 1955 Montgomery bus boycott, Rustin had long been an opponent to war. His objection to war could have gotten him killed when his pacifism resulted in jail time, considering the fever pitch of patriotism surrounding World War II. It is said he organized students to boycott businesses that refused to serve African American people. Rustin was using the sit-in and the boycott as economic strategies for social change some two decades before the activists in the 1960s movement used them. Rustin was charismatic, and Muste thought him a born leader. It was Rustin who brokered a relationship between FOR and the integrated Congress of Racial Equality around the Gandhian principles of nonviolence.

Also in 1941, Rustin met A. Philip Randolph, the head of the Brotherhood of Sleeping Car Porters, the largest labor union of African Americans in the United States. Rustin convinced Randolph to use nonviolence as a strategy to gain needed traction for the men and women shut out of good-paying defense jobs. As war waged in Europe, the military's segregation policy forced soldiers of color into menial labor, at best. The military defense plants manufacturing the clothes, weapons, and artillery for the war prohibited most people of color from those jobs. As a response, Rustin and Randolph threatened President Roosevelt with a mass demonstration in Washington, DC, to protest the segregation of African American workers and the denial of defense plant jobs to them. The activists' victory came in the form of Roosevelt's Executive Order 8802, issued on June 25, 1941, prohibiting discrimination in the defense industry and creating the Fair Employment Practices Committee to monitor hiring practices.

Another historic development affecting African Americans at this time was the construction of Moton Field, in Tuskegee, Alabama, which was completed in 1942. It was the training ground and flight academy for a group of African American pilots known as the Tuskegee Airmen; however, they were precluded by federal policy and local traditions from interacting with White pilots or White civilians.[21] At another facility, Freeman Field Air Base in Indiana, more than one hundred African American officers, fed up with segregation, were arrested in April 1945 for leading a protest. The hypocrisy at the air base was so deep a soldier decided he would rather "fight and die here for our rights as to do it on some foreign battlefield."[22] Ironically, it was the military that led America's racial desegregation beginning on July 26, 1948, with an executive order by President Harry Truman.[23]

Order 9981 stated that "there shall be equality of treatment and opportunity for all persons in the armed services without regard to race, color, religion or national origin." It also added that the order "shall be put into effect as rapidly as possible, having due regard to the time required to effectuate any necessary changes without impairing efficiency or morale." But answering the call was a Sisyphean struggle, as African American servicemen were assigned the most dangerous and labor-intensive work, such as loading munitions at Port Chicago on the Sacramento River near San Francisco, California, which on July 17, 1944, exploded, shaking the earth, spewing fire, shrapnel, and bodies. In what was the worst domestic loss of life during World War II, 320 naval personnel and civilians died, 202 of them African American servicemen. Hundreds more people were injured.[24] Additionally, African Americans were denied the usual thirty-day leave that had been provided to their White peers after the explosion.

African American servicemen protested the dangerous and unfair conditions by walking off the job, and the African American press closely followed the protest. But, within weeks of the Port Chicago explosion, the survivors were ordered back to work loading ammunition, without any improvement in safety conditions. Fearing for their lives, 258 men rebelled, refusing to return, and were arrested. Fifty of the men who had refused to load any more ammunition were tried and found guilty of mutiny by naval court-martial.[25] They were dishonorably discharged and given sentences of five to fifteen years of hard labor. After many years of protests in Black communities and NAACP lobbying and litigation, forty-seven of the men were released from prison. Although the dishonorable discharge was removed for some, felony convictions remained on their records, until decades of protests by their families and African American naval veterans finally moved President Bill Clinton to respond. However, there was only one lone survivor for him to pardon.

THE BOMB

The US wanted prompt and utter destruction while America spoke of peace. One of the great historical ironies in the story of American protest is that the architect of the world's most powerful weapon turned against war. After Franklin Delano Roosevelt died in office in 1945, it became the responsibility of his vice president, Harry Truman, to lead the US war effort. The end of World War II on the European front was in sight with the surrender of Germany after Adolf Hitler's suicide and crushing defeats but only after massive civilian deaths, the destruction of swaths of homes and sacred buildings, and the systematic murder of millions of Jewish people, gays, ethnic minorities, political opponents, disabled people, and their allies in concentration camps across Europe.[26] However, in the Pacific, the continuing war with Japan, a nation crippled but still fighting, led President Truman to make a fateful decision to bring "prompt and utter destruction."[27]

The project to build the atomic bomb had begun under President Roosevelt, but it was Truman who ordered the world's first atomic bomb attack, with a weapon that had been built secretly under the leadership of Dr. J. Robert Oppenheimer, director of the Manhattan Project.[28] It was an escalation of the US firebombing air raids of Tokyo, which ended in an estimated one hundred thousand civilians dead, just as Hitler's regime had bombed London, and England, in tandem with the US, had bombed Dresden and other German cities. On the clear morning of August 6, 1945, at 8:15 a.m., the United States detonated an atomic bomb over Hiroshima, Japan, that had the force of fifteen thousand tons of dynamite.[29]

The bomb produced a "bubbling mass of purple-gray smoke with a red core in it and fires springing up like flames shooting up on a bed of coals."[30] Unlike the firebombing attacks, the atomic bomb killed eighty thousand in minutes, with a possible one hundred forty thousand deaths in total from radiation, and over one hundred thousand injured.[31] On August 9, a slightly larger plutonium bomb was detonated at 11:02 a.m. over Nagasaki, killing seventy-four thousand and causing severe injuries to seventy-five thousand.[32] At the initial bombing test, Oppenheimer recited a line from the Bhagavad Gita in which Vishnu says, "Now I am become Death, destroyer of worlds," but by October of 1945, beset by the murderous power of nuclear weapons, he confessed to having blood on his hands to Truman.[33]

PROTESTERS AND THE VIETNAM WAR

Activists played a complex role in a complicated war. A little over two decades later, young American men were being drafted into a steadily escalating war in Southeast Asia. The number of US soldiers went from twenty-three thousand three hundred in 1964 to over one hundred eighty thousand the next year.[34] At this time, students at the University of Michigan had made their campus a stronghold of intellectual discussion and political activism against the war in Vietnam. They carried banners that said "Bring the Boys Home" and "Stop the War," walking through the streets and halting traffic. Students, as well as faculty and the school's administration, played roles in advocating for political change.[35]

A major figure in student activism was Tom Hayden, of the University of Michigan, who would decades later rise to the California Senate. While a student in 1960, Hayden cofounded Students for a Democratic Society (SDS).[36] He was raised in a White middle-class home but believed privilege brought a responsibility to social justice. While a student, he published the highly regarded Port Huron Statement in which he explained the need to participate in righting America's racial injustice. Hayden wrote: "We are people of this generation, bred in at least modest comfort, housed now in universities, looking uncomfortably to the world we inherit."[37]

Segregationist practices remained on interstate transportation despite laws to the contrary. Hayden risked his life as a Freedom Rider during the Civil Rights Movement when buses were attacked and burned by White mobs opposing the integrated activists protesting racist practices. He was a community organizer in Newark, New Jersey, through SDS's Economic Research and Action Project, or ERAP, living in the Clinton Hill neighborhood and mobilizing protests against substandard housing.[38]

Protest leaders who apply their strategies on the ground are rare. From 1964 to 1968, when Newark was segregated and wrestling with poverty, Tom Hayden and other ERAP members lived in the city, working with the Newark Community Union Project, a local community group that assisted the residents. He was in Newark during the 1967 uprising caused by police brutality and wrote about what he witnessed in the book *Rebellion in Newark: Official Violence and Ghetto Response*.[39]

But it was his activism regarding the Vietnam War while on the campus of the University of Michigan that made Tom Hayden a national figure and the U of M the anti-war epicenter. He organized anti–Vietnam War marches and sit-ins. Hayden is also credited with assisting in the release of three American POWs in Hanoi. He was one of the leaders of the 1968 Democratic National Convention protests in Chicago, where he was arrested and tried as one of the Chicago 8.[40]

In December 1964, the University of Michigan SDS chapter began plans for a national demonstration against the Vietnam War. They agreed to a three-pronged manifesto: "SDS advocates that the U.S. get out of Vietnam for the following reasons: (a) the war hurts the Vietnamese people; (b) the war hurts the American people; (c) SDS is concerned about the Vietnamese and American people."[41] On October 16, 1965, the National Coordinating Committee to End the War in Vietnam, founded in Washington, DC, earlier that year in August, coordinated with the Berkeley Vietnam Day Committee and other groups to stage the International Days of Protest. Over two days, protests of various sizes against US involvement in Vietnam took place in dozens of American and several European cities.

The Vietnam War was the largest and most protested in US history.[42] Hundreds of thousands participated in total, and the SDS March on Washington to End the War in Vietnam, held on April 17, 1965, was the largest peace protest to that point in American history, drawing between fifteen thousand and twenty-five thousand college students and others to the nation's capital.[43] Protests took place across the country, on college campuses and in cities from San Francisco to New York City, with good reason: by the end of the war there were more than fifty-eight thousand casualties, with over forty thousand dying in military action.[44] Folk music conveyed the heartache of anti-war protest.

The nexus between civil rights and the peace movements during the Vietnam War revealed fissures of race, class, patriotism, and the strategy of embattled people of color in clashes with one another as the result of a divide-and-conquer strategy. The Vietnam War divided the entire country, and the African American community was no exception. It was turmoil between those who felt loyalty to the US and its involvement in Vietnam, and those who saw the war as an extension of the war against people of color, and that young men of color were being drafted to serve as cannon fodder on the front lines for a nation that hated them. Given the Civil Rights Movement's embrace of pacifism, its role within the anti-war movement seemed logical at face value, but many who had marched with Dr. Martin Luther King Jr. for civil rights spoke against his opposition to the Vietnam War. Pacifism did not sit well with American patriotism, even in the African American community, which had historically shown its worthiness to a racist nation through enlistment in the military.

The war in Southeast Asia had become another staging ground in the fight for American freedoms that African Americans had yet to fully enjoy. It was also a conflict between the West and the East, with the Republic of Vietnam (South Vietnam), an ally of the West, warring with the Democratic Republic of Vietnam (North Vietnam), an ally of the Soviet Union. During the Cold War, the United States first became a military presence in this war-torn nation under President Dwight Eisenhower. Later, President John F. Kennedy steadily increased America's presence in Vietnam through military force, advisers, and economic aid. Whistleblower Daniel Ellsberg, as well as Ben Bradlee and Ben Bagdikian of the *Washington Post*, and Neil Sheehan of the *New York Times*, among others, would make history by releasing the Pentagon Papers. Commissioned in 1967 by Secretary of Defense Robert McNamara and officially known as the *Report of the Office of the Secretary of Defense Vietnam Task Force*, the Pentagon Papers revealed the government's knowledge that the Vietnam War was unwinnable and showed how thousands of conscripted men from communities all over the US were merely serving as pawns for a powerful and unaccountable Congress.[45]

Fire may have spiritual powers, but suicide is not a viable method of protest, even in the famous case of the monk who died by self-immolation during the war. On June 11, 1963, Thích Quảng Đức, a South Vietnamese Mahayana Buddhist monk, as he was calmly sitting cross-legged on the ground near a traffic intersection in Saigon, lit himself on fire. *Time* photographer Malcolm Browne was on hand and took the tragic photos of Quảng Đức's self-immolation. Browne recounted, "Two young monks . . . poured [gasoline] all over him. He got out a matchbook, lighted it, and dropped it in his lap and was immediately engulfed in flames." Quảng Đức died without screaming in pain or changing expression.[46] When watchful monks had determined he was dead, they brought up a coffin.[47] Ray Boomhower's *The Ultimate Protest: Malcolm W. Browne, Thich Quảng Đức, and the News Photograph That Stunned the World* argues that Browne's photographs changed US foreign policy in Vietnam and caused a coup there in November 1963 that resulted in the assassination of South Vietnam president Ngo Dinh Diem.[48] But there is a debate as to whether this act of protest—whether one calls it self-sacrifice or suicide—did indeed have that effect on subsequent events.

President Kennedy was assassinated in 1963. Vice President Lyndon B. Johnson, upon becoming president, escalated the level of aggression and number of American personnel in Vietnam. Bombing raids in Southeast Asia had considerable implications in America. More troops were needed. Costs rose. The government's strategies for victory appeared unworkable. As the death toll increased, college students kept protesting America's continued involvement in the war. The war continued amid a complex web of cultures, political conflicts, and human loss.

Politicians can protest too. However, not everyone agrees with that assertion, and in 1966, amid America's anti-war protests, the US Supreme Court sought to resolve the dispute in the case of *Bond v. Floyd*.[49] Julian Bond, a young African American activist, was elected to the White supremacist–led Georgia House of Representatives in 1965. Bond opposed the Vietnam War, and, as communications director for the Student Nonviolent Coordinating Committee, or SNCC, he was responsible for a press release denouncing the murder of civil rights activist Samuel Younge in January 1966. The statement compared Younge's lynching by gunshot to the United States' invasion of Vietnam:

> The murder of Samuel Young [sic] in Tuskegee, Alabama, is no different than the murder of peasants in Vietnam, for both Young and the Vietnamese sought, and are seeking, to secure the rights guaranteed them by law. In each case, the United States government bears a great part of the responsibility for these deaths.[50]

The Georgia House of Representatives accused Bond of treason and voted 184 to 12 to block him from assuming his seat in government, denying him the right to take the oath of office.[51]

Bond argued that, as a pacifist, he was not required to support the war and, as an African American who was mistreated in the United States, he would still be able to uphold the Constitution even if it was not upheld for him. Moreover, the Constitution did not require allegiance to war. The US District Court for the Northern District of Georgia ruled against Bond, then the House filled Bond's seat with a White politician while the case was on appeal to the Supreme Court. But Bond would not relent and ran against the person in his seat, winning the race a second time by an overwhelming majority. It was the second denial of his seat, resulting in the US Supreme Court ruling based on *New York Times v. Sullivan*, that allowed Julian Bond the freedom to complain about the government as freedom of speech and a right to speak against the war and racial prejudice.

THE YOUTH AND ANTI-WAR PROTESTS

As the Vietnam War escalated, with televised bomb raids, rising body counts, and the conscription of thousands of young men, younger people became more involved, demonstrating nationally out of their empathy for the loss of life in the United States and abroad. Two of those protesters were fifteen-year-old John F. Tinker and sixteen-year-old Christopher Eckhardt, both from Des Moines, Iowa. Tinker went to North High School, and Eckhardt went to Roosevelt High School. Mary Beth Tinker, John's younger sister by three years, attended Harding Junior High School. On December 16, 1965, the three youths decided to protest the Vietnam War. After a meeting in the home of Eckhardt, in which they debated how to express their demand for peace, they fasted over the holiday and decided they would wear plain black armbands to school. Principals at the Des Moines schools learned of the plan and quickly created a policy making wearing the armbands cause for suspension.

Mary Beth Tinker and Christopher Eckhardt did not make disruptions in their respective schools, but they grew nervous as students began whispering, spreading word about the armbands. The school administrators sent both of them home. The next day, on December 17, John Tinker wore his black armband to school and met the same fate—told to go home and not to return until after the new year. The Tinker and Eckhardt families responded by suing the Des Moines School District, arguing that the policy violated their First Amendment right to free expression.[52] The students lost. Their parents appealed, taking the case to the US Supreme Court, again arguing that wearing the black armbands was a form of symbolic protest protected by the First Amendment.[53]

Young people had protested in the 1903 March of the Mill Children led by Mother Jones, bringing attention to child labor abuses. In his book *The Young Crusaders*, historian V. P. Franklin details the student protests of the Civil Rights Movement, in which some student activists walked out of school en masse to protest poor conditions at the schools: no heat or hot water, a leaking roof, and few learning resources.[54] Some twenty years earlier, the highest court of the land ruled that two Jehovah's Witnesses students in West Virginia were within their religious rights to refuse to salute the American flag in their high school.[55] But the Tinker and Eckhardt case was one of the first involving an anti-war, in-school student protest. By the time the Court heard the case, on a cold November day in 1968, a negative wind was blowing against the war as the Court jabbed questions at attorneys for the Des Moines Independent School District. More than five hundred thousand soldiers were now overseas, casualties were mounting, and protests were tearing the nation apart.

The Tet Offensive and protests surrounding this brutal battle changed public sentiment and became a turning point in the war. Shortly after midnight on January 30, 1968, on Tet, the Vietnamese Lunar New Year, the North Vietnamese and Viet Cong crossed into South Vietnam and attacked civilians and US and South Vietnamese troops.[56] After the Tet Offensive, Americans realized the Vietnam War was far from over, with the casualties of both soldiers and civilians in the tens of thousands, in spite of the glowing propaganda coming from high-ranking officials.

In February of 1969, the Supreme Court ruled in favor of the Tinkers and Eckhardt, and free speech. High school students had gained the right to protest, in school, if they did it in a manner that was not aggressive or disruptive.

Young people had carved out a role in the anti-war movement, but the Vietnam War would take many more lives. By 1969, millions were participating in mass demonstrations, the largest of which was the Moratorium to End the War in Vietnam. There were two moratorium days. The first took place on October 15, a protest that according to estimates involved over two million people nationwide in a weekday stoppage of work and school. The second was held on November 15 with demonstrations in Washington, DC.[57]

INTERNAL AND EXTERNAL STRIFE

Some believed the nation was coming apart as assassinations, protests, and riots rocked the foundation of a segregated patriarchal society, pulling it into a true democracy. The relationship between communities of color and the US military was evolving in the face of murderous backlashes against civil rights leaders and continued racism faced by soldiers within the military.

Anti-war protests took place across the country, dividing families by generation and political affiliation. Some protests were merging with urban uprisings and the Black Power movement's confrontation with police violence. Others were merging with the women's movement. There were college take-overs demanding broader educational curricula, while some environmentalists chained themselves to redwood trees and others fought for the oceans. Protest begat protests.

All of these developments at this time were unknown to Norman Alexander McDaniel, who was in Vietnam trying to stay alive as a prisoner of war and fending off being used as a propagandist tool. McDaniel grew up in the farmland of Fayetteville, North Carolina, wanting to fly, and found a career in the air force. On July 20, 1966, the cruel chapter of Captain McDaniel's life as a prisoner of war began when his *Skywarrior* aircraft was shot down over Quang Bac Thai Province, North Vietnam. He suffered burns across his body, a sprained ankle, and a gunshot wound, and he was taken prisoner, starved, beaten, interrogated, and tortured for nearly seven years.[58]

Because McDaniel was Black, in April of 1968, after the assassination of Dr. Martin Luther King Jr., his captors ordered him to broadcast a message telling "African American soldiers not to fight because the United States is waging a war of genocide, using dark-skinned people against dark-skinned people."[59] Instead, McDaniel, who would not allow his community's pain to be used for propagandist warfare, responded, "We deal with our problems within our country," which resulted in harsher treatment and a reduction in his food rations. Later, as a survivor of war, McDaniel said, "If a person's values, priorities, commitment, and faith are right and strong, that person could endure as I did."[60]

But it was the story of a boxing champion and his rebuke of the Vietnam War that revealed the tension over the conflict within the African American community, lifting the debate about pacifism to the world stage and the highest court in the land. Muhammad Ali, born Cassius Marcellus Clay Jr. in Kentucky, was the renowned world heavyweight champion and a convert to Islam. In 1966, although he was twenty-four years old and past the traditional draft age, Ali was called for military service. Some people believe that Ali was drafted because the government was singling him out for his religion. When he requested an exemption as a conscientious objector based on his religious beliefs, the US Army threatened prison and denied all his appeals. The World Boxing Association also stripped him of his title and prohibited him from boxing. Leaning on his faith in the Qur'an, the Nation of Islam, and his political beliefs, Ali said, according to some reports, "I ain't got no quarrel with them Vietcong; no Vietcong ever called me a nigger."[61]

Ali was convicted of willfully refusing to submit to induction and sentenced to five years in prison for draft evasion, though he appealed the case to the Supreme Court. Ali's anti-war protest meant the loss of vital years at the height of his athletic prowess. Mounting demonstration marches, religious pronouncements, and political indictments of a failing war combined with criticism of the country's double standard. Black Americans, once again, were expected to silently fight for a nation that denied them full citizenship rights. In 1971, the US Supreme Court reversed Ali's conviction, ruling that, indeed, as a pacifist his rights as a conscientious objector were protected under the Constitution. His stance was protest, and it came at a price over the prime years of his boxing career.

EVEN VETERANS PROTESTED

Those who had witnessed firsthand the dead and dying, the mental and physical injuries of the Vietnam War, could not remain silent. In April 1971, Vietnam veterans organized Operation Dewey Canyon III, a national protest to draw attention to the atrocities committed by American soldiers in Vietnam. The protest was named after a military operation that took place in Indochina in 1969. Hundreds of veterans marched from Arlington National Cemetery to the US Capitol in Washington, DC, where they staged a five-day protest. The veterans threw their medals, ribbons, and other military decorations over a fence on the steps of the Capitol building, symbolically rejecting the war.

The protest included testimonies from veterans who spoke about the brutality and senselessness of the war. Operation Dewey Canyon III was one of the most high-profile protests organized by Vietnam War veterans, and it helped to galvanize the anti-war movement in the United States.[62] The protest was part of a larger effort by veterans to challenge the sanitized narrative of the Vietnam War and to push for a more honest and critical assessment of the conflict.

A 1970 Chicano protest in Los Angeles was among many instances of ethnic groups challenging the disproportionate number of casualties among service personnel of color, especially drafted soldiers. Mexican American leaders believed the US military was using Chicanos as cannon fodder in the war. Furthermore, the Chicano Movement also saw war as a distraction from pressing domestic issues affecting the Chicano community, such as police brutality, housing discrimination, and poor educational opportunities. On August 29, 1970, thirty thousand people, mainly of Mexican descent, marched through the streets of East Los Angeles, demanding a withdrawal from Vietnam and the return of US soldiers.[63] But the police attacked, resulting in three deaths, including that of journalist Ruben Salazar. Despite the police suppression, the Chicano Movement played a significant role in raising awareness of Chicano identity and the inequalities faced by minority groups drafted by the US military.

IT IS NOT WINNABLE

A different kind of protest leader can be found in the story of Daniel Ellsberg. He was raised in Detroit and experienced a life of both privilege and trauma. When he was fifteen years old, both his mother and sister died in a car accident, on the Fourth of July 1946, caused by his father's reckless driving. His father, a structural engineer, remained emotionally aloof. Ellsberg channeled his grief into studying, attending Harvard College on scholarship (during which he studied at Cambridge University for a yearlong fellowship) and graduating summa cum laude in economics, eventually obtaining his doctorate. He then became a military analyst, working for the RAND Corporation, which led to him writing reports on the Vietnam War and finding a place in protest history.

With each trip Ellsberg made to Southeast Asia, he became more troubled by the US government speaking to the public about winning a war that the country was, in fact, losing. In 1971, following an epiphany he had at an anti-war conference while listening to a pacifist awaiting prison for refusing induction, Ellsberg decided to act. "He was going to jail as a very deliberate choice—because he thought it was the right thing to do," Ellsberg recalled. "There was at this time no question in my mind that my government was involved in an unjust war that was going to continue and get larger. Thousands of young men were dying each year."[64]

While employed by the RAND Corporation, he chose to disclose seven thousand pages of top-secret documents to the *New York Times* and *Washington Post*. These documents, referred to as the Pentagon Papers, proved the Vietnam War was a military debacle. The disclosure set a vindictive President Richard Nixon against the newspapers, the man who leaked the documents, and Beacon Press, which published the entire Pentagon Papers.[65] In publishing the papers, the *Washington Post* and *New York Times* caused an upheaval over the deaths of American soldiers who had been sent to fight a war that five administrations of presidents knew the United States could not win. Their act of protest became a battle between the First Amendment and presidential executive powers.

The US Supreme Court upheld the newspapers' right to publish the controversial report.[66] In 1973, Ellsberg was charged under the

Espionage Act of 1917, which carried a maximum sentence of 115 years, and was tried in federal court in Los Angeles. But near the end of the trial, even before issuing a decision, the judge determined the case could not be tried due to government misconduct, including illegal wiretapping, a break-in at the office of Ellsberg's former psychiatrist, and an offer by President Nixon to appoint the judge himself as director of the FBI.[67] The arrest of the Watergate burglars in 1972 began an unraveling that led to Nixon's resignation in 1974. Daniel Ellsberg then turned his prodigious talents to the anti-war movement.

The Vietnam War had always been a conflict ignited by arrogance and fueled by pride, but it was a failure, marking the downfall of Western colonialism. When the Pentagon Papers were leaked to the press in June of 1971, they revealed the war as unwinnable. But losing in Vietnam did not bring an end to the United States' involvement in declared and undeclared wars or end the work of anti-war activists. Champions of the anti-war effort found camaraderie in protesting police violence, which extended to advocating for prison abolition.[68]

Howard Morland joined the air force with plans of becoming an astronaut, but he quickly found his stride protesting war and the military's ultimate weapon, the hydrogen bomb.[69] At eighty-one, Morland is known for his prowess in water sports and the court case in which he divulged that knowing how to make the hydrogen bomb was an anti-war tactic.[70] Morland began protesting while attending college at segregated Emory University, in Atlanta, before the Civil Rights Act was signed by President Lyndon Johnson and the nation had broken out in calls for freedom. One day, when Morland and several of his White college friends saw Black students protesting downtown, outside Rich's Department Store, Morland was bold enough to go into the store and talk with Rich's management about ending its segregation and hiring policies. But he admits he was too intimidated to talk to the well-known activist Frank Smith and other protesters picketing those segregationist policies outside the store.

The combination of protests inside and outside led to Rich's Department Store changing its policies. Activism was not much on Morland's mind at that point, however. From the age of six he had longed to be an astronaut, but disillusionment came soon after enlisting in the air force. Even though President Lyndon Johnson had portrayed himself as the peace candidate, Morland had learned that Johnson was planning to escalate the war as soon as he won the presidential election in 1964.

It was in his travels that Howard Morland met draft dodgers and read about American veterans condemning the Vietnam War and throwing their military medals across the wall into the White House yard. In 1971, when Morland was twenty-nine, four students were shot at Kent State, and Morland protested with the University of Hawaii's students. But he drew the line when some within this massive demonstration turned their rage on the air force ROTC building on campus, burning it to the ground. From there, he chose the path of full-time activist in the antinuclear movement.

He was arrested in the Clamshell Alliance demonstrations, waged against the construction of the Seabrook nuclear power plant in New Hampshire. He was pushed to act by his awareness of the risks of nuclear power. "It was the requirement of perfection in plumbing for nuclear power that concerned me," he said. "Because you've got to keep cooling water going to the reactor no matter what happens in the world, whether disaster or military attack. The Fukushima reactors in Japan melted down, in 2011, and blew up not because of an earthquake or tsunami, but electricity died."[71] Morland's arrest, along with fourteen hundred others, on May Day 1977, in Groton, Connecticut, while protesting nuclear weapons and the construction of submarines armed with nuclear warheads, was the biggest mass arrest in US history since the start of the Vietnam War.

But it was an article he wrote for *The Progressive* in 1979, titled "The H-Bomb Secret: How We Got It and Why We're Telling It," that led to the federal government issuing an injunction against the magazine on publishing the article. What followed was a Supreme Court case reminiscent of *Schenck v. United States*. Morland knows how to construct and detonate a hydrogen bomb.[72] *The Progressive* had Morland tour nuclear bomb factories because he was well informed, having read highly redacted congressional reports. From there, he learned enough of the basics and then learned more as a reporter on a tour of the plants, especially the Y-12 plant in Oak Ridge, Tennessee, where components for hydrogen bombs were made. On a chance trip to Tennessee, Morland was driving when he saw a valley packed wall to wall with buildings and realized it was a hydrogen bomb factory.

H-bomb plants started closing as a result of protests, first at Seabrook, then at nuclear power plants all over the country, especially the ones in California situated right on the ocean and vulnerable to tsunamis. "Our protest movement stopped a plant from being built in Nashville," Morland said. "And the ones in California that were [built] ran for a while, and now they've been shut down." The government will flex its muscles, protecting itself through propaganda and attacking anyone who comes too close to secrets, or who does not share the government's belief in the bomb as a necessary evil, Morland says. He speaks of the "Father of the Atomic Bomb" Dr. J. Robert Oppenheimer's federal hearing in 1954 and clarifies that "Oppenheimer wasn't arrested or charged with treason; they took his security clearance and discredited him" because he no longer embraced the propaganda of the bomb.[73] After the civilian deaths and destruction in Hiroshima and Nagasaki, Oppenheimer became a complex figure who expressed reluctance about the hydrogen bomb, and some have interpreted his later actions as anti-war protests.[74]

By 1978, how to make a hydrogen bomb was an open secret because the information was available to the smart and curious if they read the unclassified government documents, did other research, and used their common sense. It is through this process that Morland and *The Progressive's* editors settled on the plan for the hydrogen bomb article. They asked an MIT professor, George Rathjens, to review the draft article and accompanying drawings. Rathjens then informed the government, at which point federal agents halted publication of *The Progressive*. The magazine's editor, Sam Day, argued it was a violation of the freedom of speech and freedom of the press, telling the government that if the information in the article was accurate, they would ignore the injunction and publish it.

The United States argued that Morland's article contained state secrets, which led to a federal case, which the magazine lost at trial and appealed before the US Circuit Court in Chicago. Morland was nervous at first about losing again on appeal but later realized that the lawsuit would only help build the anti-nuke movement. The *New York*

Times, which had won a battle over publishing the Pentagon Papers, joined the fray and gave credibility to Morland and *The Progressive*.

Once the government realized Morland's information on the bomb was, indeed, in the public domain, it withdrew the threat of injunction, fearing a high-level loss. Publicity from the court case helped fuel the movement against MX missiles and Trident submarine missiles, which Catholic pacifist groups had been protesting for decades. "Nuclear weapons are suicidal because they harm us more than they harm our enemies," he said. "If we're attacked by Russian nuclear weapons, the only thing we can do is murder the civilian population of Russia." Howard Morland and Daniel Ellsberg remained anti-war speakers on the lecture circuit until attention faded on nuclear war.

Iconic films such as *Dr. Strangelove or: How I Learned to Stop Worrying and Love the Bomb* (1964), *Apocalypse Now* (1979), and *Born on the Fourth of July* (1989) protest war by providing a harsh reality of armed conflict, while *Top Gun* (1986), video games, and gaming apps depict war as adventure. Perhaps for the US both are true, and this dualism fits neatly within the conflicting personality of a nation at war with itself. However, possession of nuclear bombs has taken war to a point of no return. "Nuclear weapons are like slavery," Morland says, shaking his head in disbelief that there are some who would argue in support of such weaponry in the twenty-first century. His argument is simple: "You can't say, 'I'm against slavery' but then can't figure out how to end it. Emancipate them!"

CONCLUSION

"Burning cities like Dresden and Hamburg, Tokyo, and Hiroshima, and Nagasaki is pointless, gratuitous cruelty," wrote Daniel Ellsberg in his 2017 book *The Doomsday Machine*. In it, he reveals that the United States never had a plan to wait for the Russians to fire first and then retaliate against them.[75] The US plan had always been to disarm Russia with a first strike, meaning Russia would have had to launch all its missiles when it got the warning of an incoming attack. Ellsberg, known for leaking the Pentagon Papers, had been a marine and a military analyst who became an anti-war activist. Today, even though the Soviet Union no longer exists, Russia remains a nuclear threat. Both it and the United States have weapons considered doomsday machines that, according to the late Ellsberg, are "susceptible to being triggered on a false alarm, a terrorist action, unauthorized launch, or a desperate decision to escalate."[76] He advised action on the part of all government officials, at all levels, in all nations—merely hoping for peace is not enough. "Don't do what I did," Ellsberg wrote. "Don't wait to tell the truth to the public and legislatures, with documents, until you've lost your access or (in my case) the documents themselves."[77] There is no failsafe. "The President has the codes and can say a few magic words and missiles will go off and the world will end."

Most people are against war and especially the use of nuclear weapons. But they can't figure out how to get rid of them. That is why Morland says that we should take the fission material out of the weapons and put it in nuclear power plants to generate electricity. Young people who work on environmental issues and climate change issues must also see the importance of anti-war and anti-nuclear protests. Nuclear war is an existential threat to the climate and all life on this planet.

War remains hell in any of its forms or pieces of machinery. The risk of nuclear war is more imminent than we think. All it takes is a despot with a short fuse and long-standing political vendettas, a miscommunicated threat, a short circuit in technology triggering a false alarm, or a natural disaster such as an earthquake. My contribution to the anti-war movement is quite small, but movements require efforts of all sizes. I have participated in many marches. But, back in 1991, when I led Montgomery's first anti-war protest, it was cold and near sundown. We were walking with signs calling for the end of the Iraq War when a pickup truck containing two White men drove up close and stopped. The passenger rolled down his window. We braced ourselves. It was too late to run, and there was nowhere to hide. Montgomery's brutal history flashed across my mind. The youngest man leaned out the window and yelled "Communist!" before speeding away. We laughed, knowing it could have been a lot worse. Hours later, the cold chilling us deep in our bones, our small group celebrated our bravery at a friend's home. Later that night, I suspected the Alabama police or local FBI had been in my home while I was at the march. Unsettled,

I reflected on a long day and wrestled with the creepy sense of being watched. That night, the local PBS station broadcast the march, and me, carrying my anti-war sign, with legal experts debating if the march was treasonous or protected under the First Amendment.

––––––––––––

The United States counts the large conflicts and forgets the smaller ones. But people in the small conflicts and wars are not any less dead than in the large ones. Our violence, whether waged on or among civilians, or waged in constant wars overseas, has created a nightmarish reality in which the country's guns outnumber its people. Yet, the guns and wars have not brought this nation a sense of security. Our militarized police force has not made the country safer. Ingrid Washinawatok El-Issa, an activist, said the "roots of war and violence go deep, into the earth herself. As an indigenous woman, I wish to simply state that until we make peace with earth, there will be no peace in the human community."[78]

Eliza and other African Americans trekked from Kentucky to Kansas and fought in battles from Buffalo Soldier campaigns to world wars, and yet there remains a failure to accept people of color as first-class citizens, able to live in peace under a flag of a united nation that allegedly represents liberty and justice for all. To live in the United States is to be as conflicted as this nation, embracing an uncomfortable quiet that at any moment will be broken by a war abroad or a police shooting at home. Blessed are the peacemakers wherever they may be. But no justice, no peace.

CHAPTER FIVE

REBELLIONS IN
THE TWENTIETH-CENTURY

Eliza Bradshaw bore her scars of slavery into the twentieth century, living to witness the automobile replace the horse, her grandchildren attend college, and legalized racial segregation burn away America's democratic pretenses. But she persevered, found joy, and told her story. I wonder if Eliza was pragmatic about her country's ability to change without challenge and if she fully expected the recalcitrance of the White supremacy myth. Perhaps she understood that some elites would trade a true democracy for a guarantee of power once given the opportunity. When racial segregation became the law of the land, through the infamous *Plessy v. Ferguson* decision, democratic principles became secondary to racism.

The *Plessy* ruling, more than any other measure, set the stage for the next one hundred years of protests. What the US Supreme Court had planted, American people of good will sought to pull up, root and branch, before it so poisoned the soil that the possibility of redemption died on the vine. Eliza's grandson, William Bradshaw, became a civil rights attorney in Kansas who brought desegregation cases. He graduated from Washburn Law School in 1920, and as an attorney devoted himself to civil rights. William, and his sister, Mattie Leatha Bradshaw, who was born in 1888, about ten years after Reconstruction ended, witnessed the erosion of constitutional rights and the continuing failure of America's promise to people of color.[1]

Exodusters might have found less hostility in their new home because of the remoteness of the Kansas plains, but it was no heaven and offered little protection from segregation or lynching.[2] When Eliza died at age eighty-six, in 1913, the National Association for the Advancement of Colored People (NAACP) was deepening its foothold as an organization. It had been formed four years earlier, in 1909, after White mobs in Springfield, Illinois, home of Abraham Lincoln, attacked and lynched African Americans, torching dozens of homes and businesses. The shocking Springfield race riots sparked action by African Americans, as well as those White Northern progressives who had been shaken from their belief that the barbarity of lynching was purely a Southern sickness. As a fighter herself, Eliza must have been proud to have lived long enough to witness the rise of these advocacy groups. Perseverance was protest, and Eliza's story of striking back at her enslavers and living to tell the story to her granddaughter Mattie has inspired me to push forward.

Mattie wrote Eliza's story while in college and lived until 1956, long enough to witness the desegregation of the military during World War II and the momentous *Brown v. Board of Education* decision in 1954, finding segregated public schools to be inherently unequal.[3] Her brother William, who had laid some of the legal groundwork for the *Brown* case, had died in 1948 in Kansas without witnessing *Brown*, the fruit of his years of labor. There was no talk in my family about who would follow in William's footsteps as a civil rights attorney. Although we had joyful family reunions and visited the Kansas homeland for funerals, the family members who remained on the farms in Kansas grew up exploring newly desegregated America, in separate silos.

In college, my dream was to become either a writer or a lawyer. Back then, one only had the choice of a single profession, and it had to be a "real job." But, secretly, I wanted both and took the GREs, hoping to attend the University of Iowa's writing program, and took the LSAT, the law school exam, for entry into Iowa's law school (as well as eight other schools). After staying up two days straight writing essays and completing graduate school applications, I was elated as the sun rose on my potential new life as a graduate student. Sleep-deprived and ecstatic, I handed my stamped envelopes (this was before the internet) to the new mailman, a tall, youngish, brown-haired White man, sharing my joy about graduate school. He smiled, took them, and I went to bed.

By April, I was worried. Not a single graduate school had contacted me. I nervously began calling the offices of admission. My heart still races when I recall contacting the University of Iowa law school and then its writing program. The response was similar—they checked several times but had received no application. Not one of the ten graduate programs knew of my application because, we must assume, that smiling young White mailman had thrown them away. I went through many stages of grief and, over the years, inevitably wondered about the possible life paths I may have taken. But then I come back to reality. Like Eliza, and all those who survived their own form of slaveholding, I survived this and other malevolent acts, by faith and forward motion, because keeping a dream alive is a form of protest.

Entering the twentieth century, protesters had a daunting task in a nation of purported liberty where race laws filled a 746-page book.[4] However, challengers would not be denied. They broke stereotypes and pushed against what appeared to be the impenetrable walls of political power, law, and history by achieving excellence, participating in marches, litigating cases, writing and organizing, engaging in civil disobedience, and lobbying Congress. Civil rights leaders—both those known today and others who have faded into obscurity—along with unsung women, men, and children, played a role in the herculean effort to uproot a system of legal oppression based in a nineteenth-century feudal mindset, thus securing freedoms in the twentieth century and beyond.

THE COST OF HEAVEN

American idealism was legendary long before Emma Lazarus's words were engraved on a plaque at the base of the Statue of Liberty in 1903: "Give me your tired, your poor, your huddled masses yearning to breathe free, The wretched refuse of your teeming shore. Send these, the homeless, tempest-tost to me, I lift my lamp beside the golden door."

However, for some of the new arrivals, that promise led them to a nation where Asians lived amid a Chinese Exclusion Act, the US military invasion of the Philippines, the shooting of three striking transit workers in cold blood by wealthy anti-union merchants in St. Louis, and the denial of basic rights to most women. Reaching the golden door was paramount for those who, as an act of protest, left their home nations, hungry for the freedom and opportunity promised by our Constitution and the Statue of Liberty. The gulf between the

American promise and the reality of the United States drove some to crime, others to despair, but a rare handful took a stand against the nation's hypocrisy.

But the immigrants found a young nation with an inherited caste system, as evidenced by wealthy elites so disconnected from their own humanity that they collected dead human beings of color for display in museums and live ones for zoo exhibits.[5] Protest was a necessary tool with which to pry away layers of injustice and build a life worthy of a million dreams, and that accorded with that towering symbol of freedom standing with an upheld torch in New York Harbor. The new century would bring explosive change, forcing back the racism and xenophobia unleashed by the US Supreme Court, the terrorists' torches burning down homes and businesses, and the lynching of people of color as well as European immigrants with such regularity that these heinous murders became acceptable parts of American justice.[6]

Not all US founders were slaveholders. It is worth noting, especially for those who rely on originalism, that there were signatories to the Declaration of Independence and Constitution who opposed slavery or chose to cut their ties to human bondage for profit. John Jay, the first chief justice of the Supreme Court and governor of New York, set free his enslaved servants after realizing that slavery did not align with his Christian beliefs. As an American founder, his belief in the new country was conflicted. In 1777, Jay is quoted as saying, "The Americans are the first people whom heaven has favoured with an opportunity of deliberating upon, and choosing the forms of government under which they should live."[7] John Jay did not address the cost of heaven's alleged favor on America: slavery. But even during slavery, there were protests and petitions, speeches and demonstrations, by free people of color against slavery and the romantic notion of the United States as a heaven, as long as one was a White landowner and not concerned about equality.

The tradition of protest in America dates back to England's Magna Carta in 1215, and, like that document, the Declaration of Independence was a protest document. Africans were protesting then, too. Whether as a result of Manifest Destiny or sheer will, the myth of White supremacy as a sacred right has been upheld by law and violence. However, rebellions seeking to make this country a heaven on earth have taken the form of demonstrations, marches, urban uprisings, sit-ins, legal challenges, lobbying efforts, and millions of unwritten personal conquests.

The 1896 *Plessy* decision ruled that even a Black passenger who had paid for a first-class train ticket and could pass for White must sit in the segregated car designated for Black people. It was this "separate but equal" decision that unmoored the United States from the ideals of an America that Union soldiers fought for and lost their lives to protect in the Civil War. With the nation divided by color, once again, an immoral code of conduct justified any sort of barbaric behavior in the name of White superiority and profit. To combat this commitment to segregation, the National Association for the Advancement of Colored People was formed in 1909. That was a year after race riots and lynch mobs overwhelmed Springfield, Illinois, the home of Abraham Lincoln. Shocked Northerners were appalled at the lynching that was rampant in the South but did nothing. The Springfield riot brought the mob north. The NAACP arose, as had many groups at that time, to address the political, economic, and social rights of African American citizens. It grew to be one of the largest protest and advocacy organizations in the nation.

Racial and ethnic oppression was constant during this era, with White mobs attacking communities of color across the country. The consensus was that African Americans ought to work and suffer derision silently; leaders who chose to resist emerged among them. Educator and journalist Ida B. Wells-Barnett, of Memphis, refused to allow the lynching of her friends to take place without bringing attention to these barbaric acts. Another leader was Harvard-educated William Monroe Trotter, an activist and newspaper publisher who made crusading against lynching his vocation.

Trotter traveled to the White House and confronted the segregationist president Woodrow Wilson. Wilson, who had a celebratory screening of the propagandist Klan film *Birth of a Nation* at the White House and segregated all federal jobs in Washington, DC, intimidated most of the African American leaders but not Trotter. He traveled to the White House and demanded a meeting to discuss the film and Wilson's race policies. This was at a time when White reformers within the NAACP still assumed a certain submissiveness from Black people, even activists. Trotter would not be brought to heel.[8] Movements often require strong personalities and egos to drive them.

Trotter was a "race man," proud to be African American. He was overshadowed by better-known people such as W. E. B. Du Bois and Booker T. Washington, who were less confrontational with White moderates and racists alike. Speaking truth to power, on all levels, is necessary, which also means refusing to curry favor with the White elite and moderates at a time of abject racism and violence. This was the stance of both Trotter and Wells-Barnett, as well as Marcus Garvey and Daisy Bates. Their refusal to be obsequious may explain why they and other very deserving protest leaders are missing from mainstream histories about this era.

LOOK FOR ME IN THE WHIRLWIND

Pride despite the denigration of law and society is protest. Marcus Garvey, founder of the Universal Negro Improvement Association (UNIA), was the personal and political leader of millions worldwide. He stirred the masses of tormented Black humanity into action against the segregation, abuse, and discrimination that were the common experience of all Black people. His Black pride and certainty were a salve to the injured spirit of those who had endured a life of race-based brutality by White America and European colonialism in Africa and the Caribbean. John Henrik Clarke wrote of Garvey's complexities as a leader revered by the Black masses worldwide, rejected by the Black elite and a troublesome figure for Whites who feared his power.[9] Garvey was more than his confidence and soldier-like uniforms with admiral's headgear; he held a place in the hearts of thousands of people who lined the streets of New York City for him or stood hours to hear his speeches, because he stirred the dying embers of cultural pride and hope.[10]

Marcus Mosiah Garvey was born in St. Ann's Bay, Jamaica, in 1887, to Marcus, a stonemason, and Sarah, a domestic. Although not formally educated, Marcus Garvey was promoted through the ranks as a printer, involving himself in union activities, and took elocution lessons to fine-tune what would become a prodigious aptitude for public speaking. From 1910 to 1914, Garvey traveled extensively. In the West Indies, Europe, and Central and South America, he witnessed firsthand the dismal burdens placed on people of African descent by colonial powers and racial oppression. Garvey sought a unification of Black people around the world. On July 20, 1914, he founded the UNIA in Jamaica. Its bold motto was "One God! One Aim! One Destiny!" The very existence of the UNIA was itself a protest of the ill-treatment of African people worldwide and a rejection of their depiction as lesser humans.

Garvey was a leader who could spark a sense of destiny in the humblest of his followers. Domestic workers, sharecroppers, train porters, longshoremen, and teachers joined the UNIA. A seamstress named Rosa Parks, in Montgomery, Alabama, found the courage to take a stand against segregated transportation because of the inspiration she took from Marcus Garvey. Earl and Louise Little, the parents of Black Muslim leader Malcolm X, were both followers of Marcus Garvey.[11] Earl Little was a leader of a UNIA division in Omaha, Nebraska, while Louise Little was the division's secretary and contributed articles to the UNIA's official weekly newspaper, the *Negro World*.[12]

Garvey's organizations, the UNIA and the African Communities League, became the largest Black membership organizations in the world. He boasted of a God who was Black and a people who must take their place as the New Negro, a proud people willing to use their economic power and intellectual strength to create the United States of Africa. His back-to-Africa movement galvanized the masses and gave courage to the timid. With a commanding speaking voice, strategic mind, and a clothing style featuring epaulet-studded military uniforms, Garvey evinced pride and power.[13]

Garvey's commanding spirit and vision of African Americans above a place of subservience captured the imagination of millions of oppressed people. His fiery eloquence spread through Black communities through radio and recorded speeches. He reached into crowded city slums and desperate sharecropping farms, all parched from oppression, and was able to rekindle spirits that Jim Crow had tried to smother, creating grassroots organizations with branches in forty nations. In one of his speeches, he declared:

> If the white man has the idea of a white God, let him worship his God as he desires. [. . .] We, as Negroes, have found a new ideal. Whilst our God has no color, yet it is human to see everything through one's own spectacles, and since the white people have seen their God through white spectacles, we have only now started out (late though it be) to see our God through our own spectacles.[14]

Garvey fiercely believed that a people without knowledge of their history, their origin, and their culture was like a tree without roots. This was at a time when most White historians dismissed the notion that people of African descent had any significant history, origin, or culture, and had said the same regarding the history and contributions of all people of color. His belief was echoed by Carter G. Woodson, the founder of Black History Week, which expanded to Black History Month; Arturo Schomburg, historian and bibliophile; Mary McLeod Bethune, an educator and founder of a girls' school that became a college; and many others who helped people to better understand Garvey's appeal. Although he was not formally educated beyond high school, he understood the importance of Black people having knowledge of their history, and he worked with Woodson and the Black intellectual Hubert Harrison to write the materials instrumental in the intellectual growth of UNIA members.[15]

He believed in the arming of African Americans against lynch mobs, as well as arming them intellectually. White publishers refused to print books by Black historians, and schools taught nothing but derisive propaganda about African peoples. In 1918, Garvey created the weekly *Negro World*, which was printed in Harlem and distributed in North and South America, the West Indies, Europe, and Australia. Although most White-owned newspapers carried stories of Black men, women, and children murdered with impunity across the country, they did so without addressing the lack of legal consequences. In turn, Garvey called out this callousness in his speeches. He also derided Europeans and people of European descent as brutes while chiding those Black elites, like Du Bois, for putting their full faith in integration.

Garvey's leadership and vision of Black self-determination in Africa ran counter to the integrationist views of the Harvard-educated Du Bois and other Black elites. To Du Bois, the Garvey movement of Black self-segregation undermined efforts to end legal segregation, and Garvey was a self-proclaimed demigod and a negative influence. As with many leaders of mass movements, the federal government became alarmed with Garvey's global power, particularly when he started planning a coordinated migration to Liberia by ship. The ships of the Black Star Line were meant to carry passengers to Africa. They were purchased from unscrupulous White businessmen, through the sale of shares of stock to thousands of people. Unfortunately, Garvey relied on White businessmen to negotiate the sale of vessels that would prove to be unseaworthy.

In 1922, negative sentiment in the African American community grew against Garvey after it was discovered that he secretly met with the Imperial Wizard of the Ku Klux Klan, the symbol and probable perpetrator of racial murders. Opponents launched "Garvey Must Go" campaigns, which combined with the application of pressure by Whites in the highest levels of government, all of whom were searching for ways to undermine the leader's immense power. Garvey was soon arrested after a governmental investigation into UNIA businesses showed that the advertising for the sale of Black Star Line stock was questionable. He was charged with mail fraud, a federal crime in New York City, for selling stock in an undercapitalized company and its unseaworthy ships. Intelligent and headstrong, Marcus Garvey represented himself at trial after dismissing his attorney, which proved a calamitous decision.

Garvey was found guilty and sentenced to five years in prison and fined $1,000, the maximum sentence. The appellate court's decision showed its disdain for him and his philosophy of racial pride. The judge wrote:

> It may be true that Garvey fancied himself a Moses, if not a Messiah; that he deemed himself a man with a message to deliver, and believed that he needed ships for the deliverance of his people; but . . . if his gospel consisted in part of exhortations to buy worthless stock . . . he was guilty of a scheme . . . no matter how uplifting, philanthropic, or altruistic his larger outlook may have been.[16]

Garvey appealed his case to the US Supreme Court, but it was denied. In 1924, he promised "with God's grace, I shall come and bring with me countless millions of black slaves who have died in America and the West Indies and the millions in Africa to aid you in the fight for Liberty, Freedom, and Life."[17]

In 1927, his sentence was commuted, and he was released and deported back to Jamaica. Thousands of supporters bade him farewell as his ship carried him from New Orleans to Panama and Jamaica. However, Marcus Garvey maintained his leadership role as the religious founder of what would become the Rastafarian movement. In 1928, he traveled to Switzerland and presented "A Petition of the Negro

Race" to the League of Nations, detailing race-based crimes against African peoples worldwide. He died in London in 1940. That year, jazz artist Billie Holiday, known as "Lady Day," was in New York City, singing a blues repertoire in which her protest song "Strange Fruit" left audiences with the eerie imagery of a Black body hanging from a tree after a lynching. It was written by Abel Meeropol, a White, Jewish high school teacher from the Bronx and a member of the Communist Party, as a protest poem, exposing American racism, particularly the lynching of African Americans.

ACTIVISM HAS A HEARTBEAT

Uprisings have a life, a spirit, in that they can grow, mutate, gather others, and split, only to have each disjointed piece die, or begin another life cycle. People of different races, religions, and backgrounds find solace and power on the basis of common ground. However, White moderates were consistently a point of disappointment for Dr. King and other protest leaders who chastised those who had been in the group oppressing others so long that they could not appreciate the pain of the oppressed and take action.

America extols its Constitution and its freedom fighters. Along with the promise of liberty under a democratic government is the right under the First Amendment "to petition the Government for a redress of grievances." Civil rights groups used the law as well as the art of protest to force the US Supreme Court to face many of its legal hypocrisies regarding liberty for people of color.

After the *Plessy v. Ferguson* case of 1896, states in the North and South enacted laws segregating the races. These "Jim Crow" laws were passed with racialized fervor after *Plessy* in nearly every state. Criminal laws discriminated against Blacks by providing harsher punishments than those given to Whites who committed the same crimes. Homer Plessy's decision to sit in the car designated for Whites only was an act of protest against the Jim Crow laws. Ida B. Wells-Barnett and W. E. B. Du Bois participated in similar protests against racial segregation in public accommodations. History has largely focused on the Supreme Court's decision in *Plessy*, which helped cement inequality, as opposed to the constant efforts of Blacks to end it.

African Americans, acting individually and within formal associations, planned the defeat of the *Plessy* doctrine of racial separation and the hundreds of segregation laws that mandated separate treatment. Blacks protested America's racial caste system using a myriad of methods. They lobbied Congress and presidents for change through legislative action as civil rights litigation continued; they protested unequal treatment across America, holding fast to their demand for full citizenship, including the freedom to protest against governmental wrongs. On July 28, 1917, thousands of African Americans participated in a silent march in New York City. That year, Blacks were murdered with impunity by lynch mobs in Waco, Texas; East St. Louis, Illinois; and Memphis, Tennessee. In five other American cities, Blacks were maimed and murdered. The silent march protested this national wave of violence against Blacks, as well as the abject failure of law enforcement and the courts to provide protection against such lawlessness.

Protest marches served to bring attention to racial injustice and to demonstrate the unity and power of the masses. During World War II, segregated defense plants refused to employ Blacks. A. Philip Randolph, leader of the first Black labor union, planned a demonstration march in Washington, DC. In the event that President Franklin D. Roosevelt did not desegregate US defense plants for Black workers, one hundred thousand African American protesters would have marched in front of the White House. After negotiations led by Randolph and his threats of the protest march, Roosevelt chose to sign Executive Order 8802, desegregating the defense industry.

After the sudden death of Franklin Roosevelt in the spring of 1945, President Harry Truman faced a world war and a nation divided by racism. Randolph had already been successful in his campaign against segregation in the defense plants under Roosevelt. With respect to integrating the US military, there was little time to debate the matter. The United States realized the nation needed every soldier as it grew to a place of global dominance militarily and could not tout liberty to communist nations with its shameful racial segregation. Though it happened after the war ended, on July 26, 1948, Truman issued Executive Order 9981, banning segregation in the military, predating all twentieth-century civil rights legislation. The US post-war economic boom lifted millions of Whites into the middle classes; however, rural White communities and people of color languished.

CIVIL DISOBEDIENCE

Defying unjust laws for just reasons is a core tenet of the American psyche, unless, of course, one is protesting the powers of White supremacy, commerce, or patriarchy. Civil disobedience is a nonviolent strategy that remains an effective tool of direct action when utilized skillfully. Randolph and Bayard Rustin would go on to organize the 1963 March on Washington for Jobs and Freedom. The government never really fully heeded the march's demand for jobs, as African Americans remain unemployed at a rate twice that of Whites and the national average. Marching without a permit has long been used as a form of civil disobedience. Many consider the father of civil disobedience to be Mohandas Gandhi, known by the title Mahatma. Born in 1869, Gandhi organized thousands of protesters across India in sit-ins, work stoppages, and other nonviolent protests that eventually led to independence from Great Britain.

Rev. James Lawson made his commitment to the ministry and to nonviolence early in life. At age eighteen he was ordained into the clergy. Rev. Lawson urged others to resist violence and come together as "the beloved community," based on the values of love and solidarity Dr. King envisioned.[18] He remained steadfast to those lessons learned from Dr. King and Gandhi, passing on the philosophy to young people at Vanderbilt University in Tennessee, the college that once expelled him for civil rights activism.

Rev. Lawson was opposed to war. When the military tried to draft him to fight in the Korean War, Lawson refused based on his religious beliefs. He was imprisoned for his stance. After completing his prison sentence, Rev. Lawson traveled to India to study Gandhian principles of nonviolence, or satyagraha. He was also involved in Dr. Martin Luther King's Poor People's Campaign, conceived in November 1967 at a meeting of the Southern Christian Leadership Conference. That year, African Americans who were frustrated with debilitating living conditions, economic struggles, and racism, coupled with blatant police abuse, took their anger to the streets in urban uprisings. Dr. King understood that poverty, as well as racial discrimination, was at the core of these rebellions. The Poor People's Campaign was a mechanism of protest to bring attention, education, and better jobs to the country's hidden poor. The campaign continued after Dr. King's murder on April 4, 1968, while he was in Memphis to stage protests with the striking sanitation workers.

When other members of the civil rights leadership, those with the Student Nonviolent Coordinating Committee (SNCC) and the Big Five of civil rights groups walked away, Rev. Lawson remained part of a loyal few who supported Dr. King's expansion of the traditional civil rights strategy to include economic rights: a path that would lead to the Poor People's Campaign. Lawson also supported King's stance against the Vietnam War, a decision that was unpopular among many in civil rights leadership. Rev. Lawson marched with Dr. King in 1968 when Memphis sanitation workers appealed to Dr. King for help in forming a labor union, after two men were crushed to death in a sanitation truck. The Memphis sanitation workers' strike became a symbol of Dr. King's Poor People's Campaign for economic justice.

THE SIT-INS BEGIN

The student protesters appeared calm, having been trained to wait, without any sudden movements, for the verbal or physical assault that would likely come. A sit-in is an organized protest in which activists remain seated, refusing to act with any force in the face of insults, assault, or physical violence by the police or other civilians. It takes great effort to suppress one's instinct for self-defense, so making this form of protest is an act of courage. Those who participate in sit-ins typically receive extensive training and education on the philosophy of nonviolence. Throughout history, the United States has boasted of conquest through violence, though it has only been reserved for the oppressor. For oppressed people, in and outside of the country, the mere thought of acting with violence is grounds for annihilation. Yet, at the same time, America applauds the quiet of civil disobedience, though it mistakes its lack of violent action for a lack of nerve.

Sit-ins were used by Gandhi in India and were a tool of protest for NAACP youth in the United States, who played a pivotal but largely overshadowed role in social justice movements, as explored in V. P. Franklin's *The Young Crusaders*.[19] In 1960, in Greensboro, North Carolina, African American college students attending North Carolina A&T State University led protests at the segregated F. W. Woolworth

Company lunch counter. Joseph McNeil, Franklin McCain, David Richmond, and Ezell Blair Jr. sat down at the counter and refused to leave after being denied service. They remained seated despite being taunted and insulted by the White customers in the diner, disrupting service with their presence and thus causing a loss of income for the company.

The civil rights organizations Congress of Racial Equality (CORE) and the Southern Christian Leadership Conference (SCLC), hesitant at first to get involved, soon joined the young people's protests. Activist Bayard Rustin persuaded Martin Luther King Jr. to confront the oppressor's violence using Gandhi's philosophy of civil disobedience. King, collaborating with other civil rights leaders, further developed the modern sit-in by applying nonviolent and economic principles to the protest strategy. King understood that neither America's economy nor its international image could afford the disruptions caused by civil rights protesters in stores and restaurants.

Sit-ins took place in Alabama; Louisiana; Kansas City, Missouri; and Northern cities such as New York. They resulted in the arrest of hundreds of nonviolent protesters, who refused to post bail. As with Gandhi, the arrests overwhelmed law enforcement and created havoc for a criminal justice system that relied (and still relies) on 90 percent of defendants pleading guilty or refusing jury trials.[20] The arrest of dozens of protesters overburdened the jails and brought media attention to the struggle against apartheid in the United States.

Young protesters were essential to the movement because, while their parents likely needed to be at work or would have been fired for participating in a demonstration, the young people did not face those circumstances.[21] The young people in the movement were smart, dedicated, organized, and, unlike their parents, they could be arrested without endangering the family's source of income. Still, for people of all ages, participating in acts of civil disobedience posed the risk of great physical harm to themselves and their families.[22] White people's reactions to civil disobedience in the South as well as in the North were often violent.

Young people continued their sit-ins despite beatings and arrests. States were determined to maintain the racial segregation sanctioned by the Supreme Court in *Plessy*. However, the change in the composition of the recent Supreme Court had given rise to the *Brown* decision and meant that the states no longer held carte blanche power to discriminate based on race or to prohibit protest against that discrimination. Protesters now heavily relied on the Supreme Court to address their demands for civil rights and American liberties.

Lombard v. Louisiana, a case involving a dispute over a segregated restaurant in New Orleans, was decided in favor of the student protesters.[23] They had been convicted of criminal mischief because it was the tradition in New Orleans to serve people of color outdoors, instead of inside the restaurant. When the White manager told them, "We have to sell to you at the rear of the store where we have a colored counter," the students sat at the Whites-only counter until police arrested them, leading to their convictions and sentences of sixty days in prison and a fine of $350 ($3,535 in today's dollars). Leading to this incident, other New Orleans students had protested until the mayor "directed the superintendent of police that no additional sit-in demonstrations will be permitted . . . regardless of the avowed purpose or intent of the participants," which was an unconstitutional order.[24] Lawyers helped the arrested students appeal their convictions to the US Supreme Court, which reversed their convictions, finding the mayor's edict had violated the Fourteenth Amendment of the US Constitution.

In 1961, Black high school and college students protested at the South Carolina State House. The student protesters expressed their dissatisfaction with discriminatory actions "against Negroes," stating that they "would like for the laws which prohibited Negro privileges in this State to be removed."[25] The students sang "The Star-Spangled Banner" while walking peaceably around the State House grounds. They carried signs with messages such as "I am proud to be a Negro" and "Down with segregation." When they refused to comply with the city manager's order to disperse, the students were arrested for breach of the peace.

Their criminal sentences ranged from a fine of ten dollars or five days in jail to a fine of one hundred dollars or thirty days in jail. Since the students had not blocked traffic and there was no violence on their part or on the part of any member of the crowd, the Supreme Court ruled that protesting injustice is not cause for arrest and that arresting them was a violation of the student protesters' freedom of speech, freedom of assembly, and freedom to petition for redress of their grievances. South Carolina could not criminalize the peaceful expression of unpopular views.

These victories were momentous steps forward because it meant protests could now shine a bright light on local and national injustices and the many concerns involving race, gender, religion, class, housing, voter suppression, poverty, and police brutality. Progress would not have occurred but for the countless protesters who placed themselves in harm's way for a greater good.

The culmination of that work was seen on August 28, 1963, when tens of thousands came in buses, cars, and on foot to protest peacefully in front of the Lincoln Memorial in Washington, DC. An estimated two hundred fifty thousand people made the March on Washington for Jobs and Freedom the largest protest demonstration in the United States at that time. They came bearing signs for voting rights and affordable housing, demanding an end to segregation in all its ugly forms. The military had tanks and soldiers on standby, but they were not needed as no one posed any sort of threat. They only listened as speakers such as Dr. Martin Luther King, Bayard Rustin, and A. Philip Randolph derided America's racism and enjoined the country to let freedom ring, to let African Americans live as first-class citizens of their country.

The March on Washington was such a shining success that, in this instance, the one step backward accompanying the customary two steps forward was total backlash and even murder. That year had seen the killing of Medgar Evers, on June 12, 1963, shot down in front of his home. Then, four little girls were killed and another maimed when Klansmen bombed the Sixteenth Street Baptist Church on September 15, 1963, in Birmingham, Alabama. Assaults against African Americans were daily occurrences.

When President John F. Kennedy was assassinated in Dallas, Texas, on a sunny November afternoon, his vice president, Lyndon Johnson, inherited a nation in chaos.

Lobbying is an effective means of protest, so while the NAACP had members protesting in the streets, they were also lobbying in the halls of Congress for federal legislation to end discrimination in public accommodations.[26] On July 2, 1964, President Lyndon Johnson signed the Civil Rights Act, the most extensive civil rights legislation since the end of the Civil War a century earlier.[27] The 1964 Civil Rights Act prohibits discrimination based on race, color, religion, sex, and national origin, striking a near fatal blow to private segregation.

However, even though the Civil Rights Act ended de jure (by law) discrimination, it did not end the vestiges of de facto (by tradition) discrimination. In 1965, the Supreme Court decided the case of *Cox v. Louisiana*, in which the Reverend Ben Elton Cox challenged the tradition of segregation that remained even after racist laws were repealed. In 1961, Cox (who went by Elton back then) joined the Freedom Riders, who rode interstate buses throughout the South in mixed groups to protest segregation policies. Born in the farm town of Whiteville, Tennessee, he was the seventh of sixteen children and became an NAACP youth organizer when he was sixteen. In 1961, Cox, at nearly thirty years old, was leading a church as well as non-violent voting rights protests when he accepted the national call to action from activist James Farmer to be a Freedom Rider.

After a week of training in Washington, DC, he learned how to take the abuse that typically accompanies civil disobedience and even wrote his will the night before his first Freedom Ride. On May 4, 1961, Cox was among the earliest Freedom Riders, African American and White, who rode across state lines into the South pressing their constitutional rights. It would be ten days later when the Freedom Riders were badly beaten and the bus was burned—luckily, the passengers were able to escape before succumbing to the fire. The attack made international news, with photos showing the charred bus and the nonviolent Freedom Riders blood-soaked from their blows. Cox was undeterred, however.

Rev. Cox brought these experiences with him as field secretary of the local chapter of CORE. In December 1961, Cox and two thousand students from Southern University, a historically Black college, assembled at the state capital of Baton Rouge, Louisiana, to protest the arrest and detainment of some of their fellow students. The group walked toward the courthouse carrying signs reading, "Don't buy discrimination for Christmas," which spoke to the racial segregation practiced by Baton Rouge stores and restaurants. An orderly group sang "God Bless America" and "We Shall Overcome."[28] Suddenly, tear gas exploded, and police rushed the choking women, men, and children, who stumbled home, sickened. The next day Cox was arrested and soon after convicted of breach of the peace and unlawfully obstructing public passages.

The laws for which Cox was convicted were enacted to prevent protesters from marching or holding sit-ins. After his criminal trial, the judge ruled that the very presence of so many African Americans

Rebellions in the Twentieth-Century **191**

in a White business district created such an inflammatory situation as to be illegal:

> [It] must be recognized to be inherently dangerous and a breach of the peace to bring 1,500 people, colored people, down in the predominantly white business district . . . and congregate across the street from the courthouse and sing songs . . . such as "black and white together" and to urge those 1,500 people to descend upon our lunch counters and sit until they are served. That has to be an inherent breach of the peace.[29]

Cox was convicted and sentenced to serve four months and pay a $200 fine for disturbing the peace, five months and a $500 fine for obstructing public passages, and one year and a $5,000 fine for picketing before the courthouse. He appealed his conviction to the US Supreme Court, which had a progressive majority. The court reversed the conviction, finding that Louisiana had violated freedom of speech and freedom of assembly, both First Amendment rights.

Not all protests in this era found favor with the Supreme Court. This includes the African American protesters in the 1966 case of *Adderley v. Florida*, which involved Harriett Adderley and thirty-one students from Florida A&M University in Tallahassee, who were found guilty of "trespass[ing] with a malicious and mischievous intent" after demonstrating in front of the Leon County jail.[30] The students were protesting the jail's segregated facilities. The high court upheld their convictions in a 5–4 decision, ruling that the protesters could not hold a sit-in on the jail's driveway because they were blocking nonpublic property. Among the four dissenters were Chief Justice Earl Warren and William O. Douglas. In the dissenting opinion, Douglas wrote:

> The jailhouse, like an executive mansion, a legislative chamber, a courthouse, or the statehouse itself . . . is one of the seats of government, whether it be the Tower of London, the Bastille, or a small county jail. And when it houses political prisoners or those who many think are unjustly held, it is an obvious center for protest.[31]

It remains uncertain whether the rights of protesters who demonstrate on government property are protected.

URBAN UPRISINGS

Uprisings are a form of protest, as controversial as coal mine gun fights, Indigenous battles, and slave revolts. But protests have not all been nonviolent or organized with strategies designed to achieve particular outcomes. Upheavals and rebellions in urban spaces can be triggered by years of harm: economic stressors, frustration, and the unrepentant use of force by corporations and governments. Poor communities under siege may lack access to conventional channels of protest such as recourse through the courts or lobbying, finding their power instead in the size of the crowds and the destabilization with which they can bring attention to their righteous cause. The ignited rage of the masses is, too often, the most direct way they can be heard by the power elite.

The US has ignored the lynch mobs that intentionally murder people of color and destroy their progress but finds urban uprisings to be merely illegal riots by the ignorant used only to loot stores. In the 1960s and over subsequent decades, the fires set by urban rebels brought light to the pressing issues in dismal ghettos. Families could no longer struggle in silence with unfair housing, police harassment, and high unemployment. Racial discrimination faced them at every turn. Oppression causes revolts, be they urban uprisings or coal mine strikes. On August 11, 1965, in the Watts section of Los Angeles, the questionable arrest of three African Americans by White police officers led to the neighborhood's Black community (already frustrated with police brutality, the recent assassination of Malcolm X, and racial injustice) unleashing its fury on South Central Los Angeles. The Watts Riots lasted six days and cost the lives of thirty-four people and injured over a thousand.[32] Fire swept through city blocks, eating through homes, belongings, and precious memories. Thousands were arrested in the Watts urban uprising.

With justice routinely denied in state courts, uprisings became a common response to manifest injustice. Violent uprisings have typically followed the deaths of Blacks at the hands of White police officers. Miami, Seattle, Detroit, Chicago, New York City, and Los Angeles have all been the sites of urban uprisings against police brutality. In 1991, Rodney King, a Black motorist, was beaten by members of the Los Angeles Police Department following a high-speed chase on the Foothill Freeway in a suburban neighborhood in the San Fernando

Valley region.[33] Officers beat King with clubs, stomped on him, and shocked him with electric tasers. The brutality was captured by an amateur videographer.

In April 1992, when the White police officers charged with the brutal beating were acquitted, Los Angeles's Black community erupted in a mass uprising. Property damage resulting from the uprisings exceeded $1 billion; there were over fifty fatalities and more than two thousand people injured, with over thirteen thousand arrests made.[34] Mayor Tom Bradley, Los Angeles's first Black mayor, needed the California National Guard. President George H. W. Bush sent federalized troops to Los Angeles. Later, the US Justice Department brought an action alleging violation of King's civil rights in federal court, which found in favor of King. However, the communities affected have yet to fully recover. A commission, chaired by attorney Warren Christopher and formed to investigate police abuse in Los Angeles in the wake of the King beating, found widespread evidence of racism and a failure to reprimand officers who used excessive force. For urban Blacks impatient with the pacifying rhetoric of Whites and the Black elite, the LA uprising and those that have followed it have all but replaced civil disobedience as the primary method of protest.

On the other hand, some experts argue that violent movements are counterproductive and that nonviolent protests are more effective in achieving social change. They base these conclusions not on a subjective philosophy but on hard data.[35] Some believe nonviolence is rooted in a moral imperative that can change hearts, while others see it in pragmatic terms: a minority of activists, even when well-armed, cannot defeat a better-armed majority. There have been activists, such as Dr. King, who follow a nonviolent philosophy as an extension of their faith. Those who have practiced nonviolence in life as well as in their social justice activism, such as Bayard Rustin, a Quaker, had learned from Mahatma Gandhi that anger, when controlled, can be transmuted into a power that can move the world.[36]

Called "satyagraha," meaning "holding on to the truth," the Gandhian philosophy is based on the premise that social change and racial justice occur through persuasion, by appealing to the reason and conscience of the oppressors, "ending the evil by converting the evil-doer."[37] Gandhi used this method in India's independence movement, which ended Great Britain's colonial rule of the country. But like King, he was a victim of violence, assassinated on January 30, 1948, in New Delhi, India, at age seventy-eight.

Not all leaders of protest movements meet violent ends, but we do well to remember those who do, from the Indigenous who died fighting settler colonialism to Dr. King, Medgar Evers, schoolteachers Harry and Harriette Moore, Fred Hampton of the Black Panthers, and el-Hajj Malik el-Shabazz (Malcolm X). Reading, remembering, and writing about them is a form of protest, and their lives can inspire one to carry out their own great works of individual protest, whatever their place in this world. Writing about injustice can be protest, as can writing about those who are marginalized in the mainstream narrative, as Margo Jefferson eloquently demonstrated.

PROTEST IN THE PRESS

Media brings the outside world to the battle because journalists can make a person who is quite consumed with their own troubles care about injustices happening to others. In large and small ways, the media can be informed and inform others about pressing issues of injustice. As a feminist and an African American aware of gender and racial exclusion, Margo Jefferson, a former *New York Times* journalist and Pulitzer Prize recipient, intentionally chose to include women and people of color, whenever possible, in her internationally read columns.[38] Stories in the media that would otherwise go untold can be used to protest the silences that allow injustice to flourish. Also, readers can place their grievances with the government in the form of advertisements, owing to the legal precedent set by *New York Times Co. v. Sullivan*, a 1964 case involving the newspaper and a group of civil rights activists. The dispute stemmed from an advertisement, paid for by civil rights activists, that recounted abuses against Dr. Martin Luther King Jr. and college students at Alabama State College in Montgomery. The libel case *New York Times Co. v. Sullivan* was brought by four African American ministers who sought to bring national attention to police harassment and racial discrimination in Alabama. They bought a full-page advertisement in the *New York Times* titled "Heed Their Rising Voices."[39]

Although he was not named in the *Times* ad, L. B. Sullivan, police commissioner of Montgomery, filed a libel action against the ministers and the *New York Times*, alleging that false statements in the ad caused damage to his reputation as a public official. The ad, for example, stated that Dr. King was arrested seven times when he had only been arrested four times by that point. Defamation laws were passed during the Civil Rights Movement era to silence social justice protesters by subjecting them to a fear of costly, protracted litigation and financial damages for defaming public officials. Sullivan won the initial case before the Alabama state court and was awarded $500,000 in damages, more than $5 million today.

The *New York Times* and the ministers then appealed to the US Supreme Court and won. It was a victory over public officials who sought to be protected from the people's protest. In the decision, the Court ruled that in a libel case, there must be proof of actual malice against the offended party. The Court also ruled that commercial advertisements were protected under the First Amendment. This civil rights case expanded freedom of the press and gave the public clearer protections to protest governmental entities. As past movements had shown—from anti-slavery campaigns to union struggles and anti-war protests—when the people are united, they can defeat even well-financed government-supported oppressors.

A wide swath of America—from college students, to ministers, lawyers, and those across the country from all backgrounds, citizen and non-citizen, who chose to push America forward—worked together to give meaning to the Constitution and the words etched on the Statue of Liberty. Their effectiveness can be judged by the backlash many of them would suffer, much of it through the passage of undemocratic legislation.

JUST REFUSE

Disrupt by saying no is a simple adage that has also been known to trigger assaults, arrests, and death. For too long, it was the law, and then a violently enforced tradition, for people of color to acquiesce to the whim of any White man, woman, or child. This may seem absurd, but placating White people was a tradition dating from colonialism and running through slavery and *Plessy v. Ferguson*. It required a socio-racial hierarchy of pure domination that was maintained by arrest, assault, or death if necessary.[40] As this hierarchy related to public transportation in the era of segregation, it meant that when seats became scarce on a bus, a person of color, without question, would relinquish their seat to any White passenger and be relegated to the back of the bus.[41] In Alabama, arrest and a fine of $500 awaited anyone who refused to do this. In 1955, Rosa Parks refused to give up her seat because she was still furious over the tragedy of Emmett Till, the fourteen-year-old boy who had been brutally murdered in August while visiting relatives in Money, Mississippi. A White male passenger on the crowded bus wanted Parks's seat, and when she did not rise, even after the beefy White driver stopped the bus and ordered her to get up, she was arrested.

Parks was an African American seamstress who served as secretary of the NAACP in Montgomery. A petite frame and round glasses belied the courage and fortitude of this follower of Marcus Garvey, with experience conducting intrepid investigations of racial violence, especially the rape of Black women by White perpetrators. One notable case Parks investigated was that of Recy Taylor, a wife and mother abducted by six men on her way home from church near Abbeville, Alabama. Parks was herself a survivor of an attempted rape by a White male neighbor in 1931.

Recalling the attack years later, Rosa Parks, who barely escaped the sexual attack, described her thoughts at the time: "I was ready to die but give my consent never. Never, never."[42] Parks worked for years on the Taylor case, which, along with the gruesomeness of the attack, was notable because Taylor dared to speak publicly about her White attackers. Although one of the men confessed and named the others who were involved, none were indicted. Taylor's outspokenness was a protest against all assaults on Black women and the silence surrounding them.

As with anyone who makes history, Parks was not the first person to defy an oppressor's command, but she took her stand at a pivotal time in the Civil Rights Movement. Fred Gray, a young and brilliant attorney who represented Parks in her protest case, and Rev. Martin Luther King Jr. in his cases, saw Parks's case as a means to end segregation in intra-state public transportation.

The Women's Political Council was mobilized immediately after Parks's arrest. From the beginning, and as part of an intentional strategy, the Montgomery bus boycott was led by women, not the Black male ministers of the movement. Rosa Parks was one of hundreds of African American female passengers struggling with financial insecurity and tired of being accosted, receiving racist insults, and living with the threat of being thrown off the public bus by White drivers.[43] The women at the core of the bus boycott rarely receive credit for organizing the cars to transport Black people to work, create signs, prepare meals, supervise volunteers, call meetings, and maintain momentum for a protest involving thousands of people over 381 days.[44] Pressure from all sides weighed on twenty-six-year-old Rev. Martin Luther King Jr. and other leaders of the protest, as well the regular men and women, domestics, mechanics, teachers, students—all foot soldiers for justice.[45]

While protesting African Americans walked to work, took private cars, and pooled rides, Fred Gray challenged the bus segregation law in court. Gray sued William Gayle, mayor of Montgomery, born the year of the *Plessy* decision. Gray represented other women besides Parks: Aurelia Browder, forty years old, had refused to give up her seat eight months earlier, and a month before that, teenaged Claudette Colvin had screamed about her constitutional rights as police took her away for refusing to give up her seat.[46] These women were part of a case Gray presented to the US Supreme Court. In November 1956, the Court ruled in *Gayle v. Browder* that racially segregated public transportation violated the Constitution.[47]

Successful protests will typically generate a backlash, and after the Montgomery boycott, Alabama attorney general John Patterson retaliated in 1956 by barring the NAACP from doing business in the state unless it provided a list of all of its members. Although the Alabama chapter of the NAACP was granted a charter in 1918, it was revoked without a hearing.[48] Patterson contended that since the Supreme Court had forced the Buffalo, New York, chapter of the Knights of the Ku Klux Klan to provide its membership list in *Bryant v. Zimmerman*, in 1928, the NAACP should do so as well. In what seemed to be a case of Southern governments sharing strategies against protest and progress, an Arkansas city brought a similar case, *Bates v. Little Rock*, against the NAACP. In the case, decided in 1960, Daisy Bates and Birdie Williams took a Rosa Parks–like stance. They were convicted for refusing to disclose the names of the members of the Little Rock branch of the NAACP.[49]

Daisy Bates was president of the NAACP of Little Rock, and Williams was president of the North Little Rock NAACP. In 1957, Daisy Bates had led the campaign to desegregate Central High School, famously known as the Little Rock Nine. During the campaign, Bates's home was firebombed, and its windows were smashed. She also received death threats and her newspaper business was undermined when advertisers turned away and readership fell. But she had no intention of capitulating to the demand to release the member list of the NAACP chapter. Despite relentless threats, she and Williams both refused. The Supreme Court ruled in *NAACP v. Alabama* (1958) and *Bates v. Little Rock* (1960) that the zealots left over from Senator Joseph McCarthy's Communist Red Scare investigations would not rule the day. Contrary to the Red Scare myths, the NAACP was not a Communist front; it simply sought equality under the law. Litigation nearly drained the NAACP's budget, but the organization survived, and survival is protest.

Daisy Bates, Rosa Parks, and the social justice foot soldiers who held the line were courageous and human, placed often in frightening situations but stepping out on faith. The spirit of demonstrators was captured in protest songs that uplifted souls in fearful times and brought joy in jailhouses. Musicians like jazz drummer Max Roach, saxophonist Jackie McLean, dancer/choreographer Alvin Ailey, and singer Nina Simone captured the frustration and cultural affirmation of people within an oppressive society. Protest songs spoke to action, justice, and emotion.

Roach composed an album, appropriately titled *We Insist! Max Roach's Freedom Now Suite*, with a cover image of a sit-in at a segregated lunch counter. Mahalia Jackson's songs inspired Dr. King and touched all who heard the internationally renowned gospel singer. Amiri Baraka (LeRoi Jones), of Newark, New Jersey, was a key figure in the development of the Black Arts Movement, which was a force for change in theater, music, and dance, that began during the Civil Rights Movement of 1960s. Embracing one's culture was an act of protesting forced assimilation, and the arts exemplified this stance.

BATTLE ON THE BRIDGE

The battle for voting rights protections reached its climax at Selma, Alabama's Edmund Pettus Bridge, site of the Bloody Sunday attack.[50] On March 7, 1965, hundreds of protesters were assaulted while walking across the bridge. It took place in front of reporters and photographers who filmed the mayhem—tear gas, falling bodies, and police on horseback swinging clubs and whips. Several days earlier in Selma, on

February 18, Jimmie Lee Jackson had been summarily gunned down while leading a peaceful protest. He died several days later. Killing him was an Alabama state trooper named James Bonard Fowler. John Lewis, at twenty-five years old, led the march across the Edmund Pettus Bridge to protest Jackson's murder and call attention to Alabama's notorious violence, especially against African Americans.

After the Bloody Sunday attack on the bridge named for a deceased leader of the Ku Klux Klan, Dr. Martin Luther King planned another march, which was halted due to pending litigation. On March 9, while King awaited a ruling, James Reeb, a White minister and social worker who had come to Selma to support the movement for civil rights, was beaten by White supremacist thugs. He died of his wounds on March 11. At his eulogy, an angry Dr. King refused to only lay blame on the killers, declaring that others had a hand in Reeb's death. He admonished religious leaders for their indifference, rebuked fearful politicians, castigated the lack of courage of Black people who had accepted second-class citizenship, criticized a corrupt criminal justice system, and saved a special reproach for a White majority hiding silently in the shadows. When a third protest march to Montgomery was held a few weeks later, on March 21, thousands joined the fifty-four mile walk to the capital.

Selma is a tiny town. Once known for cotton, today it is more likely known for its outsized place in brutal battles for civil rights. Selma is in Dallas County, which is adjacent to "Bloody Lowndes County," where the Rev. C. T. Vivian, one of Dr. King's most trusted advisers, organized voting rights protests and was beaten by the sheriff while leading residents to register to vote.[51] Just as with the miners in the coal country of West Virginia in an earlier era, Black farmers in Southern company towns owned by textile mills, and sharecroppers working on modern slave-like plantations were unceremoniously evicted for attempting to vote. The power of protest and bravery shown on the Edmund Pettus and elsewhere—in the face of murderous opposition that included the killing of voting rights leader Medgar Evers, who was gunned down in front of his home in Jackson, Mississippi; the Birmingham church bombing that killed four little girls; lawsuits before the US Supreme Court; and death threats against Dr. King and all of the activists demonstrating for full citizenship—were all that was needed to force the United States to accept the inalienable truth that all citizens have the right to vote. The Voting Rights Act of 1965 did not give the right to vote to people of color—they already had it—but it was a necessary legal shield of protection.[52]

John Hope Franklin, the renowned African American historian whose father, a lawyer, survived Oklahoma's Tulsa Race Massacre of 1921, wrote about the remarkable struggles, sacrifices, and courage of activists in the seminal book *From Slavery to Freedom*. The beloved Greenwood community of Tulsa, called Black Wall Street due to its wealth, was attacked by a White mob of thousands who left hundreds buried in mass graves and a mile of burned homes and businesses. Resilient, Greenwood was rebuilt only to be destroyed again as told in *Built from the Fire: The Epic Story of Tulsa's Greenwood District, America's Black Wall Street*.[53] They showed unfathomable bravery and generous grace. John Lewis's memoir, *Walking with the Wind*, charts the man's trajectory as a leader of nonviolent protest, taking him from activist teenager to elder statesmen of the movement.[54]

FIRST, KILL ALL THE LAWYERS

Social justice law is a calling, a passion to use the law as a tool of liberation. From Robert Morris, who led the 1849 school desegregation case in Boston, to A.W. Tourgee, Clarence Darrow, Thurgood Marshall, and Constance Baker Motley, protesting for social progress relies on legal professionals imbued with an activist spirit. When the states could not stop the NAACP protesters, the legislatures went after the lawyers. Virginia passed a law to prevent organizations from hiring an attorney from another state: if a resident hired an out-of-state attorney, the attorney was not allowed to collect any fees. Since the NAACP was headquartered in New York and represented clients around the country, especially in the Deep South, if the case was upheld other states would replicate it, jeopardizing the organization's core mission and victims of discrimination, and upending the Civil Rights Movement. It would also damage fundraising, the lifeblood of any nonprofit. Virginia's high court upheld their law. The outcome of *NAACP v. Button* benefited all those in the legal profession and their clients.[55] Yet, little attribution is given to the lawyers and protesters, foot soldiers, and NAACP members behind the legal victory.

One cannot legislate or litigate the heart. Protests, together with lawyers, grassroots organizations, and politicians, are a proven weapon in the struggle for equal rights. During wartime or peacetime, the right to exercise civil liberties must be fundamental to any democracy. The United States has described itself as a shining light on the hill of democracy. That light was made bright by the sacrifice of protesters in the Civil Rights Movement using methods honed in the labor movement.

AFRICAN AMERICANS AND CIVIL LIBERTIES

African American protests have benefitted the entire country because the victories inure not just to the parties involved but to all of America's disenfranchised yearning to breathe free. The proliferation across this country of advocacy and civil liberty organizations in the areas of civil rights, gay rights, immigrant rights, and women's rights demonstrates the impact of court decisions in which Blacks, more than any other racial group, challenged societal racism and discrimination. Their victories and sacrifices have deepened fundamental rights for all people in America.

Unfortunately, the efficacy of civil disobedience, outside of a larger strategy for change, is now questionable. "Protest marches are largely seen as ineffective because deeply rooted racial practices continue despite one hundred years of protest. Ironically, past successful strategies of the Civil Rights Movement have been replicated to defeat further progress in civil rights," as protecting the progress of the "Black Elite" has become the focus of most civil rights litigation.[56] Class divisions have undermined the credibility of racial justice movements. Race discrimination flourishes while mass incarceration, racial profiling, housing discrimination, poor educational opportunities, and limited employment are silently devastating certain communities.

That destruction is all but ignored by lawmakers as they fight for their own political survival. Frustration with the status quo can lead to violent revolts and uprisings, which can become the dominant trend if other methods are forgotten or viewed unfairly as ineffective. Tools for change must be used strategically and with a vision for the end goal, because no single method is going to cure any socially created problem with a deep-rooted history, nor will it defeat opponents willing to throw all of their legitimate and illegitimate resources behind maintaining the status quo.

Nonviolent demonstrations and acts of civil disobedience have a decreased impact today. "Violence has become a popular tool for social change for those who remain outside the 'talented tenth' or any mainstream channels through which people can effect change" and be heard. Bayard Rustin stated that "the tragedy is that those who are in deepest revolt are responding not only to [the] frustrations of their objective situation, but more fundamentally to the morality of a society which is teaching them that violence is the only effective force for social change."[57] Dr. King's "Letter from Birmingham Jail," published on April 16, 1963, reiterated the frustration of Black America. African Americans were tired of promises unkept and the government's reticence in protecting the rights of its citizens of color.

Dr. King knew that violence becomes a tool for change when other mechanisms are not working. The struggle is against not just racism but impatience. Many in the struggle have grown tired of embracing a nonviolent philosophy in a nation that has more guns than people. Dr. King was not blind to the armed regiment of African Americans scattered around the country. He was also aware of the artillery amassed by White supremacists, and under these circumstances, nonviolent protest was a brilliant strategy. King spoke of loving one's neighbor, but he was wise enough to know that that although love is a powerful weapon, history has shown the US will murder its own with impunity, making victory by any minority fighting alone unlikely.[58]

He had always been willing to give his life for truth. But such a bargain assumed that the United States was worth that level of investment, and that there was enough love in humanity to overtake hatred. I believe that one should try to love one's neighbor as one loves oneself, but that assumes that the individual loves themselves, which may be why the core principle of the Black Power movement was self-love first, because then, there is affection to give your enemies, bless them who curse you, love those who spitefully use and persecute you.[59] In their study *The Negro Revolution in America*, William Brink and Louis Harris explore the conventions of love and other nontraditional weapons of protest.[60]

The twentieth century witnessed the ascent of the United States as an economic and military superpower. John Jay, who died in 1829, invoked the old spiritual by saying Americans were the first people whom heaven has favored. If Jay and John Brown could see this nation, they might recognize the dream but also sense the simmering tensions of those who refuse to acknowledge any other than a White-controlled nation and a thin democracy in which people of color remain second-class laborers, silent and miserable, forever waiting for crumbs from a patriarchal feast. This was the message sent to the world by track and field athletes Tommie Smith and John Carlos, gold and bronze medalists, respectively, when they raised black-gloved fists and bowed their heads to protest US segregation, at the Mexico City Olympics, on October 16, 1968.

When the United States declared it had chosen democracy, it constructed a golden door representing the opportunity to live free. But that door was slammed shut when the wealthy and powerful decided to use the law and the nation's bounty of natural resources to engorge themselves and force the poor and people of color to stand outside and watch the feast as they starved. Rebellions occur when dissatisfaction rises to the point that fear of physical reprisals is outweighed by the mere possibility of better days. African Americans rebuilt lives and communities after slavery—and, having endured every cruelty that can be imagined and those that can't, they rebuilt not with hatred and bitterness but with hope.

Yet, the guilt of slavery, the sin of Jim Crow segregation, and continued greed have twisted the tormentors into believing in a self-righteousness beyond logic. Protest was and continues to be a mirror of society's ills. The late historian John Hope Franklin titled his autobiography *Mirror to America*.[61] Franklin was brilliant. Yet, this Harvard graduate consistently faced racism and lived with the threat of White violence, as other people of color do. He wrote of America's twentieth-century transformation into an empire. An empire built on slavery and subjugation.

America had promised a New Colossus, and holding her to that promise were protesters, like Fannie Lou Hamer, who was a share-cropper, a voting rights champion, and an extraordinary grassroots organizer. She was a plainspoken warrioress for the Southern Black laborer. Rebellions behind the elusive golden door made the nation a better place, even if those who are arriving just to take advantage of others and those who have deep roots here give no attribution or reparation. Parents of color have waged a century-long legal battle to provide a proper education for their children. Yet, most children of color today receive their education in segregated and underfunded public schools. Teachers as well as students protested.[62] By the end of the twentieth century, public schools had enacted policies to prevent student protests and colleges threatened expulsion as well as criminal charges in response to campus protests. Educators who protest risk their jobs. A majority of US public school children are of color attending segregated schools with primarily White teachers. Social media is a method of communicating grievances as well as propaganda. This situation will affect the future struggle for equality on many levels and the creation of successful strategies. The movement for human rights and social justice must produce new leaders who have a vision for the twenty-first century's unique obstacles while carrying the wisdom gleaned from past leaders who were tested by the crucible of activism.

His college plans did not involve protesting discrimination or changing the lives of hundreds of farmers in Mississippi. But Frank Smith's life in activism began at Morehouse College, marching in front of an Atlanta department store until they hired African American workers, before he moved on to community activism in Mississippi, where he worked with Fannie Lou Hamer. Today, he is a retired Washington, DC, politician and the founder and executive director of the city's African American Civil War Museum.

As a college student as Morehouse, Frank Smith was called to be an early leader in SNCC, and he chose to protest for civil rights over completing college. He served four terms on the Council of the District of Columbia and jokes about having the scars to prove it. At eighty-two years old, Frank Smith is overseeing the expansion of the African American Civil War Museum, as well as an upcoming installation on voting rights. His Georgia accent remains with him, as does his unique blend of optimistic pragmatism concerning social change in the United States and the role of protest in making Dr. King's dream a reality.

But he took a stand during the days when civil rights for African Americans was far from an assured victory and murder was a fact of life. He began first, on his own initiative, protesting in front of segregated Rich's Department Store, the jewel in the crown of Atlanta's shopping district. The store had a deep legacy beginning in 1867. Morris Rich, a Jewish-Hungarian immigrant, built the store with $500 borrowed from his brother. It grew from a dry goods store on Whitehall Street in Atlanta to a flourishing downtown business that expanded into the greater metropolitan area.[63]

Frank Smith, who grew up on a farm outside Atlanta that had no indoor plumbing, was thrilled to become a freshman in 1959 and an enviable "Morehouse Man," as was Dr. Martin Luther King Jr. Smith's story of protest and voting rights work in the Deep South represents the countless lieutenants and admirable foot soldiers for justice. He recounts the terrors and triumphs surrounding the work for social justice and racial equality, without which the United States would have remained mired in a feudal labor system, racism, and broken American promises.

Smith was called to the cause in the spring of 1960, when he heard about Black student sit-ins and demonstrations in Greensboro, North Carolina. Since Atlanta was as segregated as Mississippi and Alabama, Smith began picketing, demonstrating, making demands, and boycotting Rich's Department Store. He had no idea that, at the same time, Howard Morland, from Emory College, and his friends had decided to pressure the store into hiring Black workers. Morland walked right past Smith's protest to go inside and challenge management.

As the protest gained news coverage, SNCC members asked Smith to join their efforts in Mississippi. In 1962, he left Morehouse to become a full-time SNCC organizer. To Dr. Noam Chomsky, one of the intellectual giants of the twentieth and twenty-first centuries, "my heroes are people who were working with S.N.C.C. . . . people who day after day faced very harsh conditions and suffered badly, some of them were even killed."[64]

For the young Frank Smith, the most memorable event in his time as a voting rights organizer in Mississippi was when he helped get Fannie Lou Hamer released from jail. "I want to tell you that they beat her and two other women really badly," he said. "Because the US attorney was not in town, I had to come back a third day. When we finally got them out, her eyes were all puffed up and she could barely walk. It's hard to talk about it."[65] Frank Smith bent his head for a moment, overcome with emotion. "I'm a Black man. And I was supposed to protect them. We knew it was part of activism, getting arrested." But jail was particularly bad for women. Law enforcement and their appointed deputies attacked Black women. "They risked being raped, beaten, mutilated while they were in jail. . . . And that's what happened."

After Smith composed himself, he continued with difficulty. "But the most striking thing for me was that after getting out, about ten people [and] Ms. Hamer stopped in front of the jailhouse, and . . . locked arms and started singing 'We Shall Overcome.'" After sixty years, Smith is still amazed by what he witnessed. Fannie Lou Hamer was going to have the last word. His voice cracked as he said, "Through our tears of sorrow, we stood there singing two verses of 'We Shall Overcome.'" Then Hamer said, to whomever could hear inside of the jail, "God is on our side."

Smith had seen horrible things as a SNCC activist, including assaults, mutilations, and the funerals of other protesters. But it was that moment outside the jail, with a beaten but not defeated Fannie Lou Hamer, that stays with him. "Those women were so badly mistreated that some of those scars they carried with them the rest of their lives. And there was nothing we could do about it. We were never going to get justice for them."

Smith recalled the frustration of organizing the hardworking Black farmers in Mississippi who farmed from sunup to sundown but remained poor. "They suffered, with the prayer that next year, praying things would be better, despite the weather, or the boll weevils getting into the cotton, or corn not growing, or being cheated, but next year, by God, 'we're gonna be better off.'" But prosperity never came. They lived in perpetual poverty. They were mistreated by the White population. "Sharecroppers did not even get paid in cash, only scrips, a piece of paper where the White employer writes his name and says 'ten dollars' and it can only be used at the company store," a story so similar to the coal miners' struggle in West Virginia. Smith was determined to "break the back of this thing to help save our people."

Smith focused on Holly Springs, Mississippi, where SNCC was working hard to get the vote for African American farmers who had been working the same land there since Reconstruction but had never been allowed to vote. Holly Springs is a town on the Tennessee-Mississippi border in north Mississippi, and the county seat of Marshall County, known back then for sharecropping, cotton fields, a small HBCU attended by Ida B. Wells (now known as Rust College), and racism. "We knew if we could get these people registered to vote, they could take over the political machinery there. They could stop the abject violence from the police." So, he led protests, registered voters, picketed, and made a success of it, one person at a time, meeting

---

people where they were, going to their homes and churches. "We were working on it for a long time and finally had a little success in 1964."

Success took time, Smith said and smiled, but, he quickly added, not nearly as long as it took to oppress the people in the first place.

CONCLUSION

The century began with race riots, segregation, and lynching but ended with urban rebellions, as activists found their voices and regular people chose to stand up against a tradition of oppression. Protesters need not agree on all issues, because some will not allow Philadelphia to forget the 1985 firebombing of the MOVE house, killing all but two of its residents and destroying a city block, while others will not let the world ignore the issues of workers' rights when in 1999 anti-globalization protests brought more than forty thousand demonstrators to Seattle's World Trade Organization ministerial meeting.

A prominent social justice issue sparking protest is the nation's ravenous prison system, which has created dozens of crucial issues, catastrophic damage, and millions of victims, making the US criminal justice system a priority for activism for the twenty-first century. To tackle any social justice issue, knowledge of the strategies, defeats, and victories from centuries past can only benefit any struggle for progress.

———

Rest when the struggle becomes overwhelming and recall your ancestors when motivation wanes. As a teacher and a civil rights attorney, respectively, Mattie Bradshaw and William Bradshaw honored their grandmother Eliza's legacy through their personal accomplishments. Their educational feats were personal and family achievements that occurred during legal segregation, instituted by *Plessy v. Fergusion* in 1896. Mattie wrote about Eliza Bradshaw for the *State Normal Bulletin*, using her student newspaper to remind the world of Eliza's existence and her fearless protest of her slave masters.

Neither Mattie nor William wrote of their experiences with segregation or racial violence, but they almost certainly had them, given the twenty lynchings that took place in Kansas during their lifetimes.[66] Lynchings were sometimes called "neck-tie parties," and the town's sheriff would feign justice by presenting "evidence" in the courthouse before members of the community, who would vote and then execute the suspect, White, Indigenous, or Black, all in a single day.

In the midst of this, William Bradshaw still sought the opportunity America promised. He worked on early desegregation cases in Kansas and sought a position with the Department of Justice, but his race and political affiliation as a Lincoln Republican held him back.[67] "My Grandmother's Story," by Mattie Bradshaw, appeared in the October 18, 1907, edition of the *State Normal Bulletin*, and nearly one hundred years later, Dr. Sam Dicks, a history professor at Emporia State University, found Mattie's article about Eliza and researched her story of migration as an Exoduster.[68] As the writer Ishmael Reed astutely observed and as Mattie demonstrated, writing is fighting, and life has made me a fighting writer.

CHAPTER SIX

HER BODY. HER BALLOT. HER PROTEST.

My mother lay dying. Her youthful dreams of a career as a classical pianist had passed away seventy years earlier and were quietly buried beneath the piano she kept but rarely played. Even in her frail and dependent state, Ardythe Bradshaw, who enjoyed the title "Lady Bradshaw," had a haughty bearing that irritated White medical staff and bemused people of color. She had grown up on the plains of Kansas, a farmer's daughter who detested farmwork and had shown such a strong interest in playing the piano that her father, Levi Bradshaw, my grandfather, purchased an upright piano, along with the services of a White music tutor.

Grandfather Levi had enjoyed a short-lived position as a local schoolteacher, until the colored school was closed and farming was forced upon him. Perhaps listening to his classically trained daughter play Rachmaninoff's Concerto No. 2 soothed his frustrated mind while confirming his belief that talent within the Black community was artificially limited by insecure and less talented White people. Voting was difficult but not impossible for most people of color in Kansas, and Grandfather Levi and Grandmother Hazel so deeply instilled the importance of voting in my mother that, as an adult, she prided herself on being the first person in line on election day.

Levi Bradshaw was the grandson of Eliza, whose survival as an abused enslaved woman and Exoduster in Kansas was protest.[1] George, one of Eliza's sons, married Sarah Freeman on a hot August day in 1885, and that surname, taken by Sarah's father, the formerly enslaved Jeremiah Freeman, was a proclamation of his independence and yet another protest.[2]

Just as Grandfather Levi had few options other than farming, Mattie may have had a passion for history, journalism, or writing, but in Kansas in the 1900s, teaching was the only acceptable area of education for women, especially African American women. Mattie's essay about Eliza's painful and courageous path from enslavement to freedom, "My Grandmother's Story," was published in her college's journal.[3] After graduation, when Eliza became ill, Mattie left teaching to care for her, holding her grandmother's hand when she passed away on July 26, 1913. No other stories have been found, but I imagine Mattie sitting at the kitchen table, writing, while Eliza slept.

This was a time before women could vote, of racial segregation, with rumblings of an imminent war in Europe. Perhaps Mattie read of suffragists putting their lives on the line for women's rights and the Woman Suffrage Procession in March of 1913. Or of how, in Surrey, England, suffragist Emily Davison died from wounds she suffered after she ran onto the track of the Epsom Derby in protest, reaching for the reins of King George V's racehorse.

My grandfather Levi's sister, Great-Aunt Cora Bradshaw, had to move to the city to become a teacher. Birdia Haller—who later became Birdia Haller Bradshaw—traveled one thousand miles away to Atlanta to attend Spelman Seminary, now Spelman College, in 1917.[4] Birdia had to take a horse and buggy to a train depot and then ride to Union Station, a major train hub, in Kansas City, Missouri, where she was forced to ride in racially segregated cars into the Deep South. Despite widespread lynching, Birdia, and later her sister-in-law, Cora, attended Spelman, the nation's first college for women of African descent. Spelman's location in a state with widespread lynching made it a courageous move for both sisters.

Birdia arrived in Atlanta during a time when severed pieces of lynched African Americans were displayed as souvenirs. The NAACP reports that Georgia was second in lynchings only to Mississippi, and that, of the 4,743 recorded murders by White mobs in US history, at least 531 had been committed in Georgia.[5] Gang rapes of women of color by White men were pervasive, as were assaults on Black men. But Atlanta was a rising mecca for African American intellectualism and was the recent home of the Harvard-educated intellectual W. E. B. Du Bois.[6]

Spelman Seminary, one of six colleges in Atlanta for African Americans, was founded in 1881 by two White Bostonians, Sophia Packard and Harriet Giles, but the college was renamed for Laura Spelman, wife of industrialist-cum-philanthropist John D. Rockefeller, a major funder of the college.[7] In 1920, after Birdia graduated from Spelman with honors, she returned to Kansas to work as a teacher and marry Ralph Bradshaw. But for Birdia and for all women teachers during this time, there were many obstacles. The US Supreme Court had ruled in 1908 that "female frailty" meant employers could restrict the hours women, particularly White women, could work, while women earned less for the same work.[8] No married woman, of any race, by law and tradition, could work as a teacher.

Birdia Haller Bradshaw wisely kept the fact that she was married a secret—up until she became pregnant and then had to reveal her marriage. She was forced to leave teaching, forever. Basically, the only options for work available to most married Black women were as domestic workers, sharecroppers, or hotel maids, but Birdia, instead, chose to give her immense talents to her church. Eliza, Birdia, and my mother faced gender restrictions by law and tradition, against which each generation protested and resisted, finding progress and persistent barriers. Gaining the vote was crucial to maintain women's control of their bodies, their lives, and their futures, and it required protest campaigns, petitions, pamphlets, conventions, demonstration marches, lobbying, soapbox speeches, and litigation to abolish the gender oppression embedded in US laws and traditions.

FEMALE FERTILITY WAS WEAPONIZED

Female reproduction is a power that has for too long been controlled by men. For much of history, whether they were in positions of authority, servitude, or bondage, women were focused on reproduction, because wombs build empires.[9] Women's independence and control of their bodies signified the removal of a central weapon from the hands of men. Men had used this weapon for thousands of years in order to expand territory, sustain nations, become wealthy, inflict cruelty, and reproduce, thereby making workers, soldiers, heirs. In colonial America and later the United States, White women were expected to produce a population to sustain this nation. Their White wombs were commercial and political investments, weaponized to give birth to the dominators of this stolen land.

Indigenous women were targeted for sterilization, starvation, and massacres, while enslaved African women were forced to produce children to further European, and then American, empires.[10] This process began when women, along with men, were kidnapped from Angola and brought to the newly settled Virginia Colony. Angela, or Angelo, was the first recorded African woman in the colony.[11] Indigenous and African women variously endured, resisted, challenged, and fought the laws and violence subjugating them and their wombs.[12] Under less repressive conditions but still contending with misogyny, the upper-class European and American wives of tycoons were expected to produce male heirs to carry on the family pedigree. To supply the workforce and the military, women on both sides of the Atlantic were expected to have multiple births, while suffering the heavy burden of high infant mortality rates.

By 1620, when the *Mayflower* landed in Massachusetts, England was shipping European women to Virginia to fend off the threat of miscegenation between colonial men and Indigenous and African women. White women were recruited to marry the men of the colonies and build families, which meant taking more Indigenous land and stamping it a conquest of the king. Given the commercial nature of the Virginia Colony, sending English women to the colony was purely a business decision. In *Encyclopedia Virginia*, Brendan Wolfe writes:

> In the summer of 1620, the Virginia Company of London announced that it would send . . . "eight hundred choise persons," half of whom were assigned to be tenants of company land. One hundred "yong Maides" were sent to "make wives for these Tenants," and one hundred boys to serve as apprentices. Finally, "one hundred servants [were] to be disposed amongst the old Planters, which they greatly desire, and have offered to defray their charges with very great thankes."[13]

The exportation of brides-to-be was replicated throughout the colonies to populate and entrench the power of European monarchies.

But as early as 1648, at a time when a woman was considered to have the mind of a child, Margaret Brent demanded the right to vote in the colony of Maryland. Brent, forty-seven years old, boldly told the all-male Maryland Assembly that she deserved the right to vote in her name as well as that of her client, the late governor Leonard Calvert. Calvert, a prosperous landowner, had named Brent executor of his will. Unfortunately, Brent was denied both, supposedly because the late governor's brother was unhappy with her administrative duties, but even in making the attempt at suffrage, Margaret had set the precedent that women had intelligence and sought the right to vote.[14]

There were noteworthy cases during this period in history, when women in positions of power distinguished themselves as iconic figures, such as Queen Mary I of England, coronated in 1553, followed by Elizabeth I, coronated six years later. Princess Njinga of Ndongo (present-day Angola) negotiated a peace treaty with the Portuguese invaders of her land in 1622 and later became a warrior queen of military forces, primarily male, in Ndongo and Matamba. However, the exalted status of these queens did not extend to the masses of women.

The wombs of African women in Virginia became profit-making machines by law when the offspring of enslaved women became slaves. Elizabeth Key (also known as "Black Bess"), who had a European father and an African mother, marked a rare moment in history when an enslaved woman sued for her freedom and won. Key presented her case in 1655. She lost in court, but a special committee of the Virginia legislature ruled that, owing to her lineage through her father, she was a free woman. Key died in 1660. The ruling that had given Key her freedom was reversed by a 1662 act passed by the Assembly of Virginia, which shifted status of the African child to that of the mother.[15] The law stated:

> Whereas some doubts have arrisen whether children got by any Englishman upon a Negro woman should be slave or ffree, Be it therefore enacted and declared by this present grand assembly, that all children borne in this country shalbe held bond or free only according to the condition of the mother, And that if any christian shall committ ffornication with a Negro man or woman, hee or shee soe offending shall pay double the ffines imposed by the former act.[16]

It would take centuries for African women to gain control of their wombs, as they were expected to be both laborers and supply children to be laborers, working perpetually for free, without any rights, on penalty of death.[17]

American colonies protested English rule in 1776 with the Declaration of Independence, then guaranteed certain freedoms with the drafting of the Constitution in 1787. Neither document mentioned or guaranteed the rights of women, Africans, other people of color, or immigrants. Enslaved Africans continued to be legally kidnapped until 1808 when the importation of people into the US ended, but the assault on enslaved African women continued, fueled by the barbaric breeding practiced by White men in North and South America as well as in the Caribbean islands.[18]

Enslaved women were expected to give birth, willingly or by rape, and, in the manner of a factory, increase the population of enslaved workers and thus the profitability of slaveholders and the nation.[19] The high incidence of death in childbirth, often the result of women having multiple pregnancies, led White enslavers to attend conventions and educate themselves on how to breed African women without killing them.[20] African women were subjected to torturous forms of experiments by physicians such as Dr. J. Marion Sims, considered the "Father of Modern Gynecology," who conducted barbaric surgeries on three enslaved women, Anarcha, Lucy, and Betsy, all without anesthesia.[21]

WHITE FEMALE ABOLITIONISTS

Landholding slave masters, tradesmen, merchants, and other bourgeois Whites held power over laws from which, by maintaining perpetual servitude and a high birthrate of enslaved Africans, they made fortunes and built the foundation for an American empire. However, the wife of a slave owner rarely felt gender solidarity with the abused enslaved mother or girl; instead, any venom she had for her rapist husband was likely spewed on the African women of their plantation. Yet, there was a small but committed force of allied women, such as the wealthy Grimké sisters, who, as Southern women abolitionists, utilized their status and privilege to shine a light on the injustice of slavery. Sarah Grimké, born in 1792, and her sister, Angelina Grimké Weld, born in 1805, were siblings in a family of fourteen children headed by Judge John Fauchereaud Grimké, a powerful South Carolina slaveholder filled with racial hatred.[22]

French philosopher Jean-Jacques Rousseau summed up the social obstacle facing women, writing,

> Thus the whole education of women ought to be relative to men. To please them, to be useful to them, to make themselves loved and honored by them, to educate them when young, to care for them when grown, to council [sic] them, to console them, and to make life agreeable and sweet to them—these are the duties of women at all times, and what should be taught them from their infancy.[23]

Raised on a sprawling plantation, Sarah Grimké was tasked by her father with watching over enslaved workers. She later observed, "Perhaps I am indebted partially to this for my life-long detestation of slavery, as it brought me in close contact with these unpaid toilers."[24] She moved to Philadelphia, where African Americans were free, and upon returning to South Carolina, she noted: "After being for many months in Pennsylvania when I went back it seemed as if the sight of [the slaves'] condition was insupportable . . . [and] can compare . . . only with a canker incessantly gnawing. . . . I was as one in bonds looking on their sufferings I could not soothe or lessen."[25]

Influenced by the kindness of Quakers in Philadelphia, Sarah and Angelina converted to Quakerism and made permanent moves to Philadelphia in 1821 and 1829, respectively. Enflamed with outrage over human bondage, the Grimké sisters waged war against the evils of slavery, especially the enslavement of women. When the Grimké sisters discovered an enslaved woman had given birth to two boys, and that the father was their slaveholding brother, the sisters educated their nephews as family members and financially provided for them. The boys, Archibald and Francis Grimké, would go on to become African American activists and help found the NAACP.[26]

Educating those forced to the periphery of society is a protest against the system of oppression. While in Canterbury, Connecticut, Prudence Crandall, a Quaker and an abolitionist, placed her resources in creating education for free women of color. In 1833, she opened a school advertised as "Miss Crandall's School for Young Ladies and Little Misses of Color." Crandall next faced the rage of White violence and racist laws. Her school violated a Connecticut criminal statute prohibiting out-of-state African Americans from attending school without the local town's permission. After she won an appeal before the Connecticut Supreme Court, with the charges against her dismissed, mobs attacked the school, smashed windows, destroyed furniture, and forced Crandall to leave the town. She moved to Illinois, where she later became a suffragist for women's voting rights.[27]

SENECA FALLS

Over two days in July of 1848, about three hundred women and a handful of men met in Seneca Falls, New York, near the pristine Finger Lakes district. It was a diverse population of four thousand people with an unabashed pride in their anti-slavery activism. The American fight for gender equality was launched here in this relatively secluded town with advertisements in the abolitionist newspapers, including Frederick Douglass's the *North Star*.[28] The Seneca Falls Convention was a daring protest in which Lucretia Mott, a Philadelphia Quaker, known for a fiery intellect and a fearlessness in using it, and Elizabeth Cady Stanton, a brilliant orator in her own right, distinguished themselves as the progenitors of the women's rights movement.[29]

These women came together to discuss a document known as the Declaration of Sentiments, modeled after the Declaration of Independence. Mott, born in 1793, began as an abolitionist and in 1833 formed the Philadelphia Female Anti-Slavery Society, which served as an auxiliary organization to the male-only American Anti-Slavery Society. In 1840, she traveled to the World Anti-Slavery Convention in London, England, only to confront raw sexism at this male-dominated meeting of abolitionists.[30] Although she was a respected abolitionist in the United States, the men at that anti-slavery convention turned her away because of her gender, and this rebuff, along with discovering that female educators were paid half the salary of male teachers, kindled Mott's determination to act. The 1848 meeting in Seneca Falls, New York, had no women of color present. Frederick Douglass, who was the only person of African descent at the convention, urged the convention's leaders to include the demand for women's suffrage in their Declaration of Sentiments.[31]

Movements can splinter from within, causing internal protests and heated divisions over issues and strategies, and though the movement for women's rights was the principal platform in the minds of many, other issues emerged. Carrie Nation, leader of the temperance movement, focused on a national prohibition on alcohol, blaming it for crime and divorce. At the same time, moderate temperance adherents protested the free access to alcohol but did not support banning it. Other women protested on behalf of immigrant women and child laborers, while many women of African ancestry were determined to bring attention to the evils of slavery and racial discrimination.

Certain factions of the movement had once been abolitionists and even supported voting rights for African Americans. African American female suffragettes protested for the vote and against White female segregation within the movement, as perhaps best exemplified by Sojourner Truth's powerful extemporaneous speech in 1851 at the segregated Ohio Women's Rights Convention in Akron, Ohio, which became known as the "Ain't I a Woman?" speech.[32] Truth spoke eloquently of the labor she was forced to do as an enslaved person that was equal to that of a man, yet, as a Black woman, she still lacked the same recognition that White women received at the suffragists' convention.

Poet and orator Frances Ellen Watkins Harper was clear in chastising the White segregationists who denied equality to women of color while demanding equality for themselves. Speaking at an 1866 suffrage convention, she said, "You white women here speak of rights, I speak of wrongs."[33] During Reconstruction, as conflicts in the South continued after the Civil War, Harper drew attention to racism African Americans experienced in her book of poems *Sketches of a Southern Life* and her novel *Iola Leroy*.[34]

When the Civil War ended, in 1865, it caused division within the movement, exacerbated for White suffragists when Black men in 1870 gained the vote, through the Fifteenth Amendment, ahead of women. Frederick Douglass believed that Black men, who had fought in the Civil War and turned the tide to victory for the North, deserved to have the vote first. Among White women who protested for the right to vote, there remained deep-seated prejudices about men of color; many embraced long-standing myths of marauding Black, Asian, and Indigenous males lurking after White women.

No attention was paid to the actual marauding White men who had raped and murdered women of color for centuries. This lopsided propaganda within the White suffragist movement caused further friction between White suffragists and women of color, including African

American newspaper editor Ida B. Wells-Barnett. She could personally attest to the lynching of her friends by jealous White store owners competing for the money of Black shoppers while disrespecting them at every turn, or to murders triggered by Whites who cheated laborers out of their pay and killed them for arguing the point by spreading lies of rape. Wells knew there were no White women involved and alleged that the rape of White women was used to cover mob violence and terrorize Black communities.[35]

After her newspaper offices were burned and her life was threatened, Wells-Barnett had to leave her home in Memphis.[36] She continued her anti-lynching work, joined by sister activist Mary Church Terrell, cofounder, in 1869, of the National Association of Colored Women. Terrell's favorite phrase, "Lifting as we climb," became the organization's motto.[37] However, White suffragists, such as Alice Paul and Frances Willard, continued to spread myths to curry political support for White female voting rights from reticent Southern women.

BEYOND THE VOTE

Suffragists wanted an equality that began with voting, but they were also marching for greater pay, access to birth control, freedom from domestic violence, and property rights. During this time, a woman was still expected to have multiple pregnancies even if they were a danger to her health. Secretly, women sought medically safe birth control and forms of contraception beyond the rhythm method. Anthony Comstock was determined never to allow them to have it, however. A devout Christian born in 1844 to a farming family in New Canaan, Connecticut, Comstock fought in the Civil War. When he moved to New York City after the war, he felt surrounded by sin, so, in the late 1860s, he assisted the police by giving them information about brothels and obscene materials. The police used Comstock as an informant to conduct raids, and his religion-fueled crusade escalated to politics and a focus on birth control.

Comstock decided that contraceptives were evil and set to curtail their availability and ban advertisements for them. Appealing to the American Puritan standards that were prevalent in the Victorian era, Anthony Comstock successfully lobbied Congress for a federal anti-obscenity law. The Comstock Act, as it came to be known, was enacted on March 3, 1873, labeling contraceptives as obscene and illicit and making it a federal crime to disseminate birth control through the mail or across state lines. The battle lines were drawn on a woman's body. Without a right to vote, women could only lobby men to effect political change, and with laws like the Comstock Act, they could only seek out illegal forms of abortion. A few decades later, nurse and activist Margaret Sanger would take on the formidable cause of helping women in New York City's poverty-stricken Lower East Side whose lives were endangered by multiple pregnancies. Sanger is associated with the invention of contraception. But it was her role in the distribution and advocacy of contraceptive devices that placed her in the crosshairs of society, history, and the law.

VOTING RIGHTS ABOVE ALL OTHERS

Protesting patriarchy was not pretty or socially acceptable to most men and many women of the early twentieth century. It had been Frederick Douglass who warned women at the Seneca Falls meeting that without voting rights, their other rights would be meaningless. With the death of Douglass in 1895, Booker T. Washington rose to prominence as the most famous Black person in America. In 1908, Washington wrote a letter to the *New York Times* in which he opposed a woman's right to vote.[38]

In 1913, suffragists Alice Paul and Lucy Burns took their march for the vote, picketing at the White House. It continued until Woodrow Wilson took office, when these women, along with dozens of others of the National Woman's Party, were berated and beaten, arrested, and put in jail. Some went on hunger strikes, but the jailers force-fed them. They were tied down while matrons pried open their mouths and stuck a thick hose down their throats, pumping gruel into the women, these gagging victims of Wilson's revenge. Sympathetic newspapers ran stories that led to their release, and their march galvanized the movement. Congress passed the Nineteenth Amendment in 1919, and the following year the required number of states, thirty-six, ratified the change to the Constitution, with Tennessee serving as the deciding state.

Suffragists had seen a Civil War, violence, decades of disappointment, arrest, struggle, and division. In 1920, over seventy years after the fateful meeting in Seneca Falls, women gained the right to vote. Getting the Nineteenth Amendment ratified took political savvy and determination fueled by the rage felt by women in every unequal aspect of American life. The amendment provides: "The right of citizens of the United States to vote shall not be denied or abridged by the United States or by any State on account of sex. Congress shall have power to enforce this article by appropriate legislation."

Women had successfully protested and obtained their right to vote, but their full equality as first-class citizens in the United States was still an elusive dream within American life. The next step was the Equal Rights Amendment (ERA), which was drafted in 1923 and would be passed by both houses of Congress fifty years later but could not pass without the states' support.[39] In each era since the amendment was drafted, women have made ratification of the ERA their life's dream, and many have died without achieving it. Protest, litigation, and legislation would be needed to break the patriarchy in its firm stance against sharing power with women. Female life was being changed by female hands and minds, even though their bodies were still controlled by males. A woman's control over if and when to grow a fetus in her body and give birth meant being reliant on unreliable options or prophylactics that were primarily under male control. The battle over contraceptives involved married as well as single women, and activists had a plan.

FIGHTING FOR CONTRACEPTIVES

Women were to be chaste while men were free to have sex and, as teenagers, encouraged to practice on prostitutes or sow wild oats with girls until they met the virgin worthy of marriage. Pregnancy was the evidence of female sexual independence or assault. She was to accept the condition as if pregnancy were an apt punishment and consequence for her to bear. Hastily made marriages were the social compromise, more to place a bridle on her than to provide security for the child.

Contraceptives provided a choice and freedom from society's hypocritical standards, but using them was against the law. Comstock's "chastity" laws haunted the lives of single and married women alike. Protests by female voters, led by Margaret Sanger, were influencing laws. After the ruling in the 1936 case *United States v. One Package*, doctors were finally able to distribute contraceptives across state lines.

In *United States v. One Package*, a female gynecologist working at one of Sanger's clinics had received a device to block pregnancy, known as a pessary, from a Japanese company.[40] Federal law prohibited the mailing and receiving of any contraceptives across state lines or from outside of the country.[41] Sanger had been instrumental in maneuvering behind the scenes to bring the matter before the Court. In the end, the case successfully challenged a New York State law that held a prison sentence and a fine as the price for the use of contraceptives. *People v. Sanger* allowed physicians to prescribe medications to prevent pregnancy to save the lives of women.[42] It took a case involving a foreign country to remove an oppressive law and give legal permission to American doctors to mail contraceptives and birth control information inside the United States. But some Black women protested Sanger's reproductive advocacy targeted at the African American community as a form of eugenics to limit the birth of Black babies as well as other babies of color.

FEDERAL GENDER PROTECTIONS

It took the martyred deaths of activists, televised assaults, street protests, international pressure, and bipartisan compromises between political giants, with decades of the NAACP lobbying Congress, to enact the 1964 Civil Rights Act.[43] This momentous civil rights legislation outlawed discrimination based on race, color, religion, sex, and national origin, and although sex had been placed in the bill with hopes of undermining its passage, this ground-breaking legislation was signed by President Lyndon Johnson on July 2, 1964, amid celebrations for all oppressed people in the United States, especially women.[44] Often hailed as the most important law of the past century, the Civil Rights Act prohibits discrimination in private employment. In order to rise above being a symbolic gesture, this important legislation required protest to ensure it would deliver on the protections it promised.

However, the right to vote was still beyond the reach of people of color in the South because of White terrorism. Women placed themselves in danger across the South, teaching freedom classes, registering voters on isolated farms, being jailed and beaten, doing sit-ins at lunch counters, working in the NAACP offices, creating activist strategies, marching in street protests, being supporters of and parties in lawsuits, and practicing nonviolence. Some women were active with SNCC, while others joined CORE, the Black Panthers, nationalist groups, and other organizations. All of these entities worked for the liberation of people of African descent and to force the United States to honor its constitutional guarantees. But it was the brutal assault on peaceful marchers at Edmund Pettus Bridge on March 5, 1965, that was most pivotal in bringing about the passage of the Voting Rights Act of 1965, a second historic legislative feat.

WOMEN OF THE MOVEMENT

In contrast to the White women who pretended not to see the crimes and used the specter of the Black rapist to violent and deadly effect were other White women like Virginia Foster Durr and Viola Liuzzo, who risked their societal status, ostracization, and even their lives in the fight for civil rights.[45] In December 1955, Durr, born a Southern belle in 1903, threw aside convention when she and her husband, Clifford, an attorney, posted the $100 bond to bail out Mrs. Rosa Parks, a local seamstress and friend. Parks was in jail for refusing to give up her seat on the bus to a White man.[46] Stepping in to help Parks was not an impulsive act; Durr realized that if Southern Whites did not speak up for African Americans, especially enjoining White women to support Black women, no real progress would be made.[47]

Those with the resources to financially support social progress, and with a position to speak up in the elite environments where members of oppressed groups are rarely found, have a role to play in protest. The Durrs joined the NAACP, organized Black and White women, and opened their home to civil rights workers, journalists, and like-minded individuals.[48] Virginia and Clifford had been involved in politics and social issues for nearly twenty years, taking on causes that were unpopular in their circles, such as the abolition of high poll taxes levied by Southern states to keep African American people from voting.

Like Virginia Durr, Viola Liuzzo, the thirty-nine-year-old White middle-class mother of five from Detroit, was sympathetic to the Civil Rights Movement.[49] When, in 1965, she saw the images of Bloody Sunday on Edmund Pettus Bridge, she declared that the battle for civil rights was "everybody's fight."[50] Liuzzo traveled to Alabama to be among the thousands of marchers crossing the bridge for a third time, and volunteered to shuttle protesters between Montgomery and Selma. On her way to Montgomery to pick up the final group of the day, a carful of Ku Klux Klan members, one of whom was an FBI operative, pulled up beside Liuzzo and shot her and Leroy Moton, a nineteen-year-old local African American activist who was also in the car. He managed to survive by playing dead. Three of the four men indicted for Liuzzo's murder were convicted in federal court of violating her civil rights instead of cold-blooded murder. The informant was granted immunity for testifying for the prosecution, although he had done nothing to stop the murder.

Fearful of backlash, the notorious civil rights opponent and FBI director J. Edgar Hoover initiated a smear campaign against Liuzzo, spreading rumors that she had abandoned her family (she called them every one of the five nights she was in Alabama) to have sex with Black men, and other damaging lies. Though she was seen as a martyr by some, her reputation was still damaged, and the lies about her would persist until her family was able to open her FBI file in 1977, revealing the truth. She had merely been a kind-hearted woman seeking to lend her support to the cause of voting rights. Viola Liuzzo's death spurred an investigation into the KKK and increased support in Congress for the Voting Rights Act, which was signed into law on August 5, 1965.[51]

———

Angela Davis was born into the movement in 1944 and grew up in tumultuous Birmingham, Alabama. This was during the era when the city was known as "Bombingham" due to the Klan-led terrorist bombing of Black homes and the Sixteenth Street Church, which killed four little girls. She is the Frederick Douglass of our time, given her appeal with students as a professor at University of California and with general audiences who have been drawn to Davis's ideas on social justice, such as the abolition of all prisons, her steadfast feminism, optimism, and decades of belief that change is possible. She has lectured on a philosophy of advocacy whereby one is to believe every day that it is possible to radically transform the world.

Davis was unfairly incarcerated during 1971–1972 as an alleged accomplice in an August 7, 1970, attack on a Marin County courthouse where several people were shot and three killed, including Judge Harold J. Haley. She was not at the courthouse at the time of the attack, but some of the weapons were registered in her name. At twenty-six, Angela Davis was a professor and only the third woman in US history to be placed on the FBI's Top 10 Most Wanted list when she fled after being indicted for murder and kidnapping in connection with the courthouse attack. While in hiding, and during her trial and incarceration, she became an international figure and her large round Afro an iconic symbol of Black resistance.

It was while incarcerated and witnessing the abuse of inmates by guards and the dehumanizing treatment in prisons that Davis took on anti-prison advocacy, which she has continued through her career. Angela Y. Davis was a candidate for vice president of the United States for the Communist Party in 1980 and 1984. Writer Zadie Smith recalled that Davis has protested for causes of critical concern for over fifty years, especially women's issues, racial justice, and policing.[52] "She has the ability to deal with very complex academic ideas and also make those ideas popular and present to ordinary people all around the world."[53] Davis has engaged in the full spectrum of activism, from advocating for prisoners while in jail to supporting the Black Panthers, in television appearances and as a distinguished professor at the University of California, Santa Cruz, as well as on the street with common people and at conferences in Africa and Europe. "You can't ask for more than that," says Smith. Angela Davis was an honorary co-chair of the January 21, 2017, Women's March.

———

Movements need witnesses like Margo Jefferson. She has protested for the creation of a Black Studies program on her college campus, for voting rights in the 1960s, to end racialized police violence during the urban uprisings, to free political prisoners, and to end apartheid, but throughout all of this activism, she has also consistently protested for women's rights.[54] Jefferson, a feminist, witnessed the confluence of events that ignited America's twentieth-century movement for gender equality. Protesters like Jefferson were foot soldiers in the streets while bridging the movement for civil rights with the movement for gender rights, participating wherever possible and feeling the energy of change. As a cultural critic, Jefferson was able to chronicle in newspapers the evolution of the United States from mid-century into the twenty-first century, pushed into progress by protests.

The energy of anti-war demonstrations and struggle for racial justice movements stirred protests by immigrants forced into menial jobs and spurred many White middle-class women to rattle the chains binding them to patriarchy. Access to a college education, the assassination of President John F. Kennedy, financial affluence, access to

political power, affirmative action for women, and advances in broadcast journalism were all elements that combined to bring women into
the streets pushing for equal rights, first in fits and starts and then
as a full-fledged women's movement.[55] There were a few luminaries
whose accomplishments as feminists paved the way for others. One
of them was US Supreme Court justice Ruth Bader Ginsberg, who
faced gender discrimination as a lawyer and used her legal expertise
and passion to fight sex discrimination.[56]

Millions of women realized their courage to strike against social
confines after heeding the message of writer and activist Betty Friedan.
Revealing that the nation's facade of the idyllic post–World War II
White middle-class life was hiding a prison, she was at the forefront of
launching a second wave of the women's movement, adding "feminist"
to the national lexicon.[57]

Unfortunately, painful racial divisions, vestiges from enslavement
and Jim Crow segregation, burdened the feminist movement. Women
of color, believing that White feminists—much like their forebears—
were ignoring racism, poverty, and police violence, set off on their
own feminist or womanist path. These women of color, as in the time
of Sojourner Truth, protested men for denying women's rights and
challenged the racism of White women.[58]

PROTESTING MISS AMERICA

Rebelling against objectification became an important strategy of feminist organizations, which struck at symbols of discrimination that
brought attention to sexism and raised female consciousness while
pressing for societal change. In 1968, the Miss America Pageant, an
annual event held in Atlantic City, New Jersey, and broadcast to millions
of homes in the United States and abroad, became the target of women's
groups protesting the pageant's objectification of the female body. It was
organized by the group New York Radical Women, with support from
the Jeannette Rankin Brigade, the National Organization for Women
(NOW), and the American Civil Liberties Union. The "Miss America"
protest is remembered as a landmark event in the feminist movement.

Writing about the protest fifty years later, Roxane Gay noted that
the Miss America protesters "were responding not only to the pageant
and its antiquated, misogynistic attitudes toward women and beauty,
but also to how the United States, as a whole, treated women."[59]

Carol Hanisch, who popularized the phrase "the personal is political," believed disrupting the Miss America pageant was necessary.[60] The women's movement, like many movements at that time, was losing traction, and protesting a high-level event helped re-ignite national attention and bring the "fledgling Women's Liberation Movement into the public arena."[61] Gloria Steinem, a vocal feminist and journalist, recounted gender-based bias and discrimination in magazines and on television when few women were afforded the platform to do so.[62]

In 1970, on the fiftieth anniversary of ratification of the Nineteenth Amendment, NOW organized protests in New York City and across the country demanding equal pay, equal employment, and equal treatment under the law, as well as greater educational opportunities for women, affordable childcare services, and the legal right to abortion.[63] The action, known as the Women's Strike for Equality, influenced the passage of Title IX in 1972, a federal law that prohibits gender discrimination in education. Protest and litigation had led to Title IX becoming a valuable tool in the fight for equal funding for sports in K–12 schools and colleges. Today, women's achievements in college, professional sports, and the Olympics can be traced to Title IX funding in high schools.

HER BODY. HER CHOICE.

Laws, like shackles, bound women as male-dominated legislatures and courtrooms controlled female sexual freedom and reproduction. Protests had called for the repeal of state laws that criminalized abortion, and the momentum was spreading. But it was the case of *Roe v. Wade* that would make history. In 1973, the US Supreme Court found women had a constitutional right to terminate a pregnancy. Attorney Sarah R. Weddington argued the case on behalf of Jane Roe; Jay Floyd and Robert C. Flowers represented Henry Wade. Jane Roe (a fictional name used in court documents to protect the plaintiff's identity) had filed the lawsuit in 1970, suing Henry Wade, the district attorney of Dallas County, Texas, where she resided. She challenged the Texas law stating that any woman seeking an abortion had to have orders from her doctor saying the procedure was required to save her life.

Before the Court, Weddington argued that the state laws were unconstitutionally vague and abridged the right to personal privacy, protected by the First, Fourth, Fifth, Ninth, and Fourteenth Amendments. The court juggled the controversial question of whether the

Constitution recognized a woman's right to terminate her pregnancy by abortion.[64] In the end, the Court ruled in favor of Roe, giving women autonomy over their own bodies for the first time in US history.

Justice Harry Blackmun delivered the opinion of the Court, supported by seven of the nine justices. The argument centered on a "right to privacy," but it also stated that this right, along with the government's interest in protecting women's health, is balanced against its interest in protecting "the potentiality of human life."[65]

GROWING INTO ACTIVISTS FOR WOMEN'S RIGHTS

It was a natural organic process, says Gloria Steinem, feminist icon and journalist, who believes that if you write about what you care about, and other people care about it, too, suddenly, it is activism.[66] Born in Toledo, Ohio, in 1934, Steinem attended Smith College, graduating magna cum laude and a member of Phi Beta Kappa. She was initially reticent to take an outspoken role in social justice movements, but she realized that as a reporter, she could listen to others and use her pen as a weapon to bring stories of injustice to life. Abortion rights became an issue for Steinem and other women of her generation. She cofounded *Ms.* magazine in 1971 with the transformative community activist Dorothy Pitman-Hughes.[67] Along with political luminaries and activists, including Shirley Chisholm, Bella Abzug, Fannie Lou Hamer, and LaDonna Harris, Steinem also cofounded the National Women's Political Caucus in 1971. Steinem is a crucial part of the fight for women's equality and abortion rights that drove the feminist second wave, whose demonstrations, started in 1970 from a church basement in Manhattan, made the evening news as their numbers grew into the thousands.

Steinem was introduced to protest in that church basement, and the issue was a clear lack of access to a safe, legal abortion. "The first march was an exhilarating and a huge demonstration on Fifth Avenue," she remembered, "but as we proceeded down Fifth Avenue, and we were shouting, 'Join us, join us,' then women would flood out of the office buildings and restaurants and cleaning women came out. It was very spontaneous and was covered by *Time* and *Newsweek*. . . . That began our ability to be acknowledged by the media."[68]

Steinem recalls Eleanor Holmes Norton standing on the platform with politician Bella Abzug and the first Black US congresswoman,

Shirley Chisholm. Seeing herself as an activist took time, however. "This did not happen while I was in college," Steinem says. It took a two-year-long stay in India after graduating college, during the movement for independence led by Gandhi, Kamaladevi Chattopadhyay, and many others, that made her realize "it was possible to have effective activism that was not from the top down, but from the bottom up."

It was also violence against women and girls that drove Steinem into activism. She saw "sexual assault, rape and violence, as gendered weapons of power, lust, and social control." Women protested to end police abuse and the methods for prosecuting rape and other forms of sexual assault. She notes that each step in the prosecutorial process needed to be protested, beginning with the rape survivor's painful task of reporting the assault. At that time, prosecutors frequently retraumatized victims in their questioning, and police and attorneys typically questioned a rape victim about her reputation, behavior, and actions in a way that presumed she was partly responsible for the assault.

Evidence-collection boxes known as "rape kits" were often not readily available in all towns or required in hospitals, and compounding the trauma, some facilities required assault victims to pay for their own rape kits. Hospitals also often failed to provide a change of clothes to replace those the woman was wearing, as those needed to be taken as evidence. The victim left the emergency room burdened with physical pain, trauma, a loathsome fear of communicable disease, and even pregnancy. The media broadcasted her name and sometimes her address. Police lost the rape-kit evidence. Women and girls were publicly shamed when their names appeared in newspapers and on television news. Protests changed these things.

Too often, women cannot safely walk alone at night, a fact that inspired what we know today as "Take Back the Night" marches and rallies. Fueled by the activism of Women Organized Against Rape and other groups, feminists took back the night as early as 1972. In 1975, women and men in Philadelphia took to the streets for a night protest after the murder of Susan Alexander Speeth.[69] Such protests eventually forced police departments and politicians to provide resources for rape victims, free of charge. "Take Back the Night" rallies are still routinely held in the United States and other countries. Pauli Murray, activist, legal scholar, and a founder of NOW, delivered a powerful speech on June 19, 1970, titled "Extending Protection Against Sex-Based

Discrimination," in which she advocated for expanding legal protections for women and focused on the intersectionality of race and gender. Murray said, if someone were to ask any Black woman in America what her greatest achievement has been, her honest answer would be "I survived."[70] Far too many women find that survival is their protest.

GENDERED VIOLENCE

Audre Lorde was a self-described "Black, lesbian, feminist, mother, warrior, poet" who would take to the pavement for action when necessary. On October 14, 1979, Lorde addressed a crowd of more than seventy-five thousand at the first National March on Washington for Lesbian and Gay Rights.[71] The march was in response to intolerance toward LGBTQ people, the imminent election of Republican Ronald Reagan to the presidency, and the recent assassination of popular gay California politician Harvey Milk. "Thirty years ago, the first time I came to Washington, my family and I couldn't eat ice cream in a drugstore here because we were Black," said Lorde. "I am proud to raise my voice here this day as a Black lesbian feminist committed to struggle for a world where all our children can grow free from the diseases of racism, of sexism, of classism, and of homophobia, for those oppressions are inseparable."[72]

Gender-based violence and intimate partner violent crimes are most often inflicted on women and LGBTQ people. Violence against women remains a constant threat across economic and racial lines. The tragic case of Jessica Gonzales and her children is but one example of what violence against women looks like. Gonzales's children did not survive the brutal violence of their father. In the 2005 Supreme Court case *Castle Rock v. Gonzales*, the police failed in their duty to a woman and her children.[73] Jessica Gonzales sued the city of Castle Rock, Colorado, because the police there refused to take action to enforce a court-issued restraining order against her violent husband. The court order required Simon Gonzales to stay away from her home and her children, stating, "Police shall use all reasonable means to protect her and her children." In 1999, Simon Gonzales abducted their three daughters, Rebecca, Katheryn, and Leslie, from their home and, several hours later, shot and killed them.

When Jessica Gonzales realized her daughters were missing, she immediately called the Castle Rock Police Department. She showed the officers the court's restraining order and requested help. Colorado law requires the police to arrest anyone who violates a restraining order. Mrs. Gonzales stated that the police officers did not seem very concerned. They told her to call back in a few hours if the girls had not returned home.

Simon finally called Jessica to tell her he was with the girls at a well-known amusement park. Jessica then called the police and asked them to please get the girls and bring them home. She was told they could not because the park was not in their jurisdiction. They refused her request to call the police in that jurisdiction. After her third call, the police asked her to call again at midnight if the girls still were not home. She drove to the police station after her fourth call and again told the officers about the restraining order and again asked for help before going home.

At 3:20 in the morning, Simon drove his car to the Castle Rock Police Station and began shooting at the building with a semi-automatic pistol that he had just purchased. Police officers shot and killed him and found the dead bodies of the three girls in his truck. The Women's Legal Defense and Education Fund wrote an amicus brief in 2005 arguing that the US government violated Jessica's human rights by failing to protect her and her children. In 2007, New York congressman Jerry Nadler spoke in Congress about securing new funding for special victim assistants to act as liaisons between law enforcement agencies and victims of domestic violence.[74] These and other measures fell under the Violence Against Women Act, enacted in 1994 to create comprehensive, cost-effective responses to domestic violence and sexual assault.[75]

MORE THAN A BLOODY WEDDING DRESS

All the women wear white at the Annual Brides' March that honors Gladys Ricart, who was shot to death by her ex-boyfriend, Agustin Garcia, on her wedding day. After their breakup, Garcia had stalked her for months. She was at home in New Jersey on September 26, 1999, excitedly preparing to marry her fiancé, when Garcia walked in as Ricart was handing out flowers to her bridesmaids.[76] He pulled a .38-caliber handgun from his briefcase and shot the bride-to-be three times in front of her family and members of the wedding party.[77]

In 2001, Josie Ashton, a Dominican woman from Florida, turned her outrage over Ricart's death into action by walking 1,600 miles from

Miami to Queens, New York, wearing a wedding gown with Ricart's picture pinned to the front. Since then, a march has been held annually in New York on the anniversary of Ricart's death to draw attention to domestic violence. Thousands of women, men, and youth—including members of the Ricart family and other families affected by domestic violence, as well as elected officials, civic leaders, clergy, students, and scores of domestic violence advocates and survivors—gather every September 26, rain or shine, to memorialize Gladys and the many other victims who have lost their lives to domestic violence.[78]

As the Supreme Court whittled away at *Roe v. Wade*, women continued to protest. In 2004, a March for Women's Lives, composed of hundreds of women's organizations, demonstrated in Washington, DC. With over one million protesters taking part, it was one of the biggest demonstrations up to that point in American history. That record was broken in 2017 with the Women's March, the largest single-day protest in US history since the 1963 March on Washington, part of a worldwide series of marches to protest the inauguration of Donald Trump, who had run his 2016 campaign on a platform challenging progress for women, people of color, and immigrants. Over four million people protested in Washington, DC, alone.

Signs at the Women's March demanded that the government take its hands off a woman's body. Millions took to the streets in major cities and small towns around the country. These protests took place before the *Dobbs v. Jackson Women's Health Organization* decision in 2022, when the US Supreme Court overturned *Roe v. Wade*.[79] For fifty years, conservative groups had chipped away at the decision that constitutionally protected a woman's decision to have or end a pregnancy. Attacks on women's clinics and the murder of physicians who terminated pregnancies had escalated. Through political machinations, the US Supreme Court was packed to create a supermajority of preselected conservative justices who had marked the overturning of *Roe v. Wade* as part of their judicial agenda.

The credibility of the US Supreme Court suffered mightily by the political nature of the *Dobbs* decision. Although the response of the Court's conservative majority and their allies was to cynically advise women to take their grievances to the ballot box in their states, the problem was that conservative governors and legislators had already begun passing anti-choice laws, some states outlawing the termination of pregnancies even in cases of rape and incest. The court stated that no right to terminate a pregnancy can be found in the Constitution, ignoring the fact that thousands of rights are not written in the document and it would be impossible to include all of them. The dissents articulated made clear that the Dobbs decision had unjustly taken away 150 years of work toward gender equality, relegating women to second-class status. Protests continue in the streets, in the voting booths, in the halls of legislatures, in courtrooms, classrooms, and at the dinner table.

DON'T GIVE UP

Protest takes a toll, emotionally and physically, with no paid vacation days or sick leave. For protesters working by passion and not pay, it can be a hardship felt in isolation. Friends who are enjoying their weekends question a commitment to a cause that seems doomed, because the effort invested in activism rarely takes a quick, direct path from hard work to victory. But do not despair. Like Gloria Steinem, Christian F. Nunes, the president of the National Organization for Women, charted a circuitous route in her life of activism on behalf of women. Nunes, who grew up in Arizona, became the national president of NOW, headquartered in Washington, DC, in August 2020 and is the organization's youngest president in over forty years. She is the second African American to lead the most prestigious activist organization for women in the United States. Her earliest memory of participating in protest was in high school, fighting for the observance of Martin Luther King Jr. Day.

In 1983, President Ronald Reagan signed a law creating a national holiday honoring Dr. Martin Luther King Jr. The brilliant musical artist Stevie Wonder, a leading advocate for the holiday, had recorded a special birthday song on his 1980 album *Hotter Than July* to spur the public to contact their local politicians about the day (artists can be activists). But certain states refused to recognize the national holiday. Arizona was one of them.

Nunes was part of a Black student group that brought attention to King Day at her school. Corporations joined the protest, deciding not to hold their conventions in Arizona.[80] As more and more states passed bills making the holiday official, Arizona governor Bruce Babbitt decided to sign his own executive order to create an MLK Day.

But later, Babbitt's successor, Evan Mecham, rescinded the order, abandoning the holiday.[81] For refusing to recognize the holiday, Arizona lost the chance to host the 1993 Super Bowl and became a national laughingstock. Finally, in 1993, after a state referendum was held, Arizona and Nunes could celebrate Dr. King Day, the third Monday in January. There is still work to be done as some states allow employees to choose to take off work on King Day *and* the day commemorating General Robert E. Lee, commander of the Confederate Army during the Civil War.

Christian Nunes was in graduate school at Columbia when she began to take on the issues of women's rights. Although she had never identified as a feminist until then, she grew up in a very strong Black matriarchal family structure that set her path. "We knew we were leaders and were supportive of each other," Nunes says. "But we didn't see it as feminism." She believed she was equal to any other person and could do anything she needed to do. But it was going to a NOW meeting that introduced her to feminist theory and led her to "the belief that women have the right to be treated as equal and valued in society. The right to live their lives with the same autonomy and equality as men."

Since women's equality has never been fully enshrined as a constitutional protection with the Equal Rights Amendment, she believes "we've never really been fully protected under law. The little progress we make is always taken away. These cases and situations keep happening, pulling us back, restarting because we are not fully recognized as first-class citizens." Nunes is a social worker by profession, which she takes to heart as an activist. Social work "means activism is embedded in what you do. I think I've always been an activist. I am trained to understand and look at the problem of injustice."

She also believes that as a woman of color, "we've carried this double burden, fighting against sexism but also against racism; that's the heavy burden to carry." However, it is not enough in her estimation to just feel the burden; Nunes uses her experiences of race and gender to stand up, refuse, and fight back. Women of color have had to be activists. "We had to create activism, educate, and speak up, talk, negotiate and to protest. We had to learn to collaborate and form coalitions. We've learned to do this for survival." She believes feminism should come easy for most women of color. But there is a history of distrust to overcome. "From being a Black girl to a Black woman, the things I've experienced are used to help me to be strategic, to get my message across as an organizer, a leader, finding solutions, getting my voice heard in rooms that didn't want to hear my voice and tried to silence me. Being a Black woman helped me to become a very effective activist."

Her first major march was the first Women's March, in 2017, after the presidential election of Donald Trump. She was in Arizona at the time, passing out signs, registering people to vote, signing up members, handing out information and telling them why it was important to be a part of a march. Many were protesting for the first time. "We cannot sit quietly about this. It was so powerful to see." The hugely attended Women's March showed the power of women coming together in solidarity because, Nunes says, "women can't allow oppression to be our destiny."

She recalls the time she participated in the annual march across Edmund Pettus Bridge to mark the brutal attack on peaceful voting rights protesters in Selma, Alabama, that took place in March, 1965. "I heard stories of actual foot soldiers, most of them women, whose stories you don't hear because of the sexism and racism at that time. They still have scars." These women were willing to put their lives on the line even if they were not recognized as walking across that bridge. "It was so emotional, impactful, knowing they are facing cops on the side of the bridge. The people who are supposed to keep us safe are attacking women."

In terms of where women are currently, she sees "our rights rolled back with the end of affirmative action, voter suppression, overturning reproductive rights" with the Supreme Court's decision in *Dobbs*, "which is essentially saying women have no right to make these decisions for themselves. It's a human rights violation." Nunes believes the oppression we see with respect to the Supreme Court is deeply a matter of racism. "Who's impacted by affirmative action decisions? The same group—BIPOC communities, those of immigrant status, with limited incomes, and those women who stand at the intersection and will be highly impacted."

According to Nunes, the Constitution was not intended to give rights to women, especially women of color. "It was never meant for immigrants, a disabled person or for any person outside of a White man. Legislators at the state and federal level want to maintain power and control. Activism has been at the heart of any change. Continually pushing. Those women in Selma walked fifty-four miles from Selma to Montgomery for voting rights, facing possible death, bludgeoning, for the possibility of a better future. We need that collective pressure, solidarity in equality or equity." From the suffragist movement to #MeToo, there are women of color who feel left out when the conversation is dominated by White feminists. Nunes says, "It's time to move forward in trust, invested in the same issues, for true gender justice."

Nunes advocates for a holistic, multi-strategy approach. "Protest is one part, but we need to negotiate, inform, and educate using social media so we are hitting different angles for different learners, every person, and meet them where they are." When protesters are united, carrying signs, shouting, and chanting together, there is empowerment, a motivation to keep going and not give up. Nunes repeats this message to women. "Keep going. Don't give up."

CONCLUSION

The journey for women's rights was a complex one based on not only gender but class, race, and religion. In the end, a woman's body was the battlefield. Manifest Destiny—the concept that Americans were divinely empowered to settle, and eventually rule, the North American continent—could be applied to women. Controlling her life was akin to ruling over the land. There is a religious fervor that places men in a position of dominion over her. She is the missing rib of Adam, and that rib belongs to the man even if she stands apart from him.

Two steps forward and one back is the dance of protest. Patience and persistence are the cornerstone of all social justice victories. The fight for women's rights is intergenerational. Adversaries know this, as well. The ground for the vulnerable is forever unsteady.

My mother could not fulfill her dream of attending Juilliard and having a career as a concert pianist. It is a form of protest for me to desire more than what the world offers me as an African American woman, and to create the freedom necessary for walking my unique path as an activist and artist. For women, our freedom and progress are incremental. I wonder if Eliza lived a life better than the one her mother lived.

CHAPTER SEVEN

PROTESTING VIOLENT POLICING

When Eliza and Lewis Bradshaw protested terrorism by leaving the school-burning nightriders of Kentucky to start anew in Kansas, there was no investigation, no prosecution of the White arsonists or arrests for terrorizing and assaulting African Americans. For people of color, the lack of protection by local, state, and federal law enforcement, along with being vulnerable to arrest, harassment, and incarceration by those same forces, is a daily reality in the United States. Yet, Eliza and Lewis survived, along with Mattie, William, Grandfather Levi, my mother, and those ancestors known and unknown. I need to make them proud with each book, lecture, stage play, legal case, and public appearance involving issues of justice.

Since the struggle requires all types of talent and service, my contribution to activism encompasses many different pursuits—being a playwright as well as a professor and nonfiction writer, a social justice attorney and novelist, and a constitutional law commentator on television programs, rendering an opinion on legal issues involving the US Supreme Court or police-involved civilian shootings. Not being quiet about racial injustice in any of these roles is my protest, and it is difficult because many people mumble complaints in corners while pretending there are no real problems in hopes of staying in their comfortable place of noncommitment. Choosing one's battles is a wise strategy, but pretending there is no war at all to be fought is based on fear and probably selfishness. My courage to speak up came from reading the biographies of hundreds of activists and being in the rooms with some of them or watching others from afar.

James Baldwin entered my life in sixth grade. I was at home, sitting cross-legged on a shag carpet in my living room with our family dog, Lobo, when Baldwin appeared on a television talk show. Watching him moved me to make a silent vow. I decided to be like him—a writer, a playwright, and an activist, one day giving words to my swirling thoughts on prejudice and gender, race, and class with Baldwin's fearlessness and now hoping others do the same. Years later, after completing dozens of interviews on national and international news programs, taking the opportunities to discuss complex issues of law, I have observed how the criminal justice system manifests itself in every aspect of life in the United States and is intricately woven into its empire building.

Yet, even though the criminal justice system is a vestige of settler colonialism, slavery, state-sanctioned racial terror, xenophobia, and classism, it continues to reveal itself as a profit-making scam, a death machine, it a mechanism for social control and racial oppression. This is rarely addressed head-on without being challenged by protesters. They send a message that the United States, as a capitalist machine of White supremacy, remains in control despite incremental reforms and the continual protest of some groups, especially people of color.

The knowledge that this country suffers over a thousand deaths yearly at the hands of police has a numbing effect.[1] Without channels for action, people's despair and rage can become apathy, depression, and a desire for self-harm.

When I get the media call asking for my perspective on yet another African American shot or choked or found dead in police custody, it can leave me feeling physically and emotionally drained.[2] But the ancestors and community need me to push forward, as part of my lesson from Baldwin, even though no one appears to be listening. During one of those media interviews, on a live call-in public radio show, a listener powerfully articulated the reason why the police kill us.

It was during a discussion of another shooting of a Black man by police and the ensuing protests; we were debating the issue of increased police training as a solution when the host took the call.[3] After identifying himself as a White male, the listener said plainly, "It's not about training." His next words haunt me: "They kill Black people because they know they can get away with it." They know they can get away with murder. It is a crime with so few prosecutions that death by police is as inconsequential an act today as it was during colonial times, slavery, and Jim Crow.

On a building across the street from my apartment someone had painted the word BREONNA. It appeared one morning in thick, twelve-foot-high white letters after she was murdered and a grand jury decided not to charge the police officers who shot and killed Breonna Taylor, a young Black woman in Louisville, Kentucky. Taylor was killed as she slept, which left her grieving family now forced into activism on behalf of their deceased loved one. In one barbaric episode after another, government-sanctioned weapons and death are accepted by the highest US courts.

Police kill and then say they feared for their lives if the person they killed was a person of color. Meanwhile, the same fate doesn't befall heavily armed White men after they commit mass murder, standing in a carnage of bodies and blood. They are left alive when they are apprehended, so they can later stand trial and plead not guilty, because the White officers had no fear that required them to use deadly force.

Only in the rarest instances, perhaps 1 percent of the time, is a White officer indicted and tried in a court of law if they gun down a man, woman, or child of color. An acquittal is usually the outcome, after which people debate the solutions of better officer training, civil rights lawsuits, the hiring of more officers of color, and cultural sensitivity classes. After much deliberation and historical research, that man who called into the radio show had excavated the core of the country, the buried truth of calculated sin that belied the rosy pictures of American idealism. Some police simply kill "because they can."

Protesting law enforcement abuses, whatever form they take, is as old as the abuses themselves, for as long as the ideals of America have cowered before the conquest-driven United States, her bullying twin. This void in the US system of justice creates the need for full-throated outrage and protest, for acknowledgment of sin, and for a demand for change in this recalcitrant nation. Shining light on all the victims, families, activists, allies, lawmakers, and acts of protest on the local, state, and federal levels, over generations, that have wrestled with this country's tangled and multifarious web of criminal justice is an impossible task, but perhaps providing the following instances will spark a disruption of this barbaric bloodletting.

During the era of enslavement, laws restricted the travel of free and enslaved men and women, in the North as well as in the South.[4] Free Africans had to carry freedom papers, while those in bondage walking public streets had to present tickets from their masters detailing the route and dates of their travel. Then, after the Civil War, segregationist laws and unwritten edicts allowed White militia groups to create havoc in communities of color, attacking those who dared embrace their citizenship rights and those who had no protection from law enforcement. Too often, law enforcement officers were members of a mob or a militia group, and the badge of law enforcement had the town's insignia on the front and the Ku Klux Klan membership number etched into the back. Whether on horseback in a slave patrol, as bounty hunters, or in police departments—up north or down south—members of law enforcement have killed because they could, and those who protested police violence risked everything. But they did it anyway.

THE KILLING BEGAN EARLY

Colonial laws allowed the murder of Africans with impunity. In 1669, the House of Burgesses in Virginia passed a law permitting the casual killing of the enslaved: "If any slave resist his master (or other by his master's order correcting him) and by the extremity of the correction should chance to die, that his death shall not be accompted felony."[5]

For nearly four hundred years, Europeans and their descendants have been killing Africans and the Indigenous with legalized impunity. Even though Europeans and, later, White Americans have killed, kidnapped, tortured, raped, maimed, or otherwise caused the death of countless Black people, it is the Black person who is considered violent. In colonial times, the cruel punishments of the enslaved were deemed necessary because the African was suspected of "mischief." In the Georgia colony, the militia received special orders to "disperse, suppress, kill, destroy . . . any Company of Slaves, who shall be met together, or who shall be lurking in any suspected places, where they may do Mischief or who shall have absented themselves from the Service of their Owners."[6]

Laws required Africans to possess a signed note from a White person granting permission to be away from the master's presence.[7] Defiant, the enslaved met in secret at risk of death, beatings, and torture, knowing slave catchers were ever present. Africans resisted the less-than-human status assigned to them by Whites and the corrective beatings meant to force them into submission.

In 1680, the Virginia Colony passed a statute prohibiting acts of self-defense by Africans. From this law, one deduces that Africans were fighting back, plotting escapes, securing weapons, and acting with agency. It stated:

> Whereas the frequent meetings of considerable numbers of Negro slaves under the pretense of feast and burials is judged of dangerous consequences [it is] enacted that no Negro or slave may carry arms, such as any club, staff, gun, sword, or other weapons, nor go from his owner's plantation without a certificate and then only on necessary occasions; the punishment twenty lashes on the bare back, well laid on. And further, if any Negro lift his hand against any Christian he shall receive thirty lashes, and if he absent himself or lie out from his master's service and resist lawful apprehension, he may be killed and this law shall be published every six months.[8]

The person rendering the twenty lashes on the bare back presaged the police officer and corrections officer of the modern era. But the enslaved were valuable to the US economy, so bounty hunters brought fugitives back alive whenever possible.

In 1787, the slaveholders were given a constitutional right to use bounty hunters to reclaim their human property:

> No person held to Service or Labour in one State, under the Laws thereof, escaping into another, shall, in Consequence of any Law or Regulation therein, be discharged from such Service or Labour, but shall be delivered up on Claim of the Party to whom such Service or Labour may be due.[9]

Yet, at this time, the rise of Haitians against their French enslavers sent a resounding protest message to Europe that Africans would not accept subjugation.

When the Haitian leader Toussaint L'Ouverture defeated Napoleon Bonaparte's army, routing the French and expelling them from Haiti in 1803, forming the first Black republic in the New World, it set an example of protest that triumphantly echoed worldwide, giving spiritual marching orders to Africans to fight bondage and forever fueling the paranoia and indignation of those within the United States fixated on White superiority. The success of Toussaint's uprising gave the nascent United States a fear that it would lose its African commodity, which formed the foundation of its economy: free labor, enforced on penalty of death. The threat of torture or even murder did not deter escape.

HUNTED BOUNTY

Slaveholders hired bounty hunters and paid them to travel to distant states in search of escaped human property. Africans, however, continued to challenge their condition through word and deed. Free Africans, who were susceptible to bounty hunters capturing them and selling them into slavery, petitioned the government with grievances on behalf of their enslaved brethren and themselves. The word of a free Black man in a Southern court meant nothing under the law, while free Africans in the North lived with the constant fear that while walking alone at night, they may be attacked, dragged away, and sold at auction to a plantation owner in the Caribbean.

As early as 1777, Prince Hall, an activist and the first African Freemason, spoke boldly against slavery by invoking human and divine law, referring to the Masonic creed that all men are equal. Prince Hall would present several petitions to the Massachusetts legislature protesting on behalf of free Africans kidnapped from the streets of Boston.

Hall reproached White leaders in business and government for allowing the arrest of free Black men on trumped-up charges. These free men were in short order sold into bondage in Southern states, with undisclosed payments made to those complicit in these lucrative plots. Hall wrote: "What then are our lives and Lebeties worth if they may be taken away in [such] a cruel & unjust manner as these?"[10] Justice in the courts was circumscribed. Lawsuits were not an option. As early as 1717, the law prohibited Africans from testifying in court against any White person.

COLONIAL POLICING

From the beginning, wealthy people in colonial North America relied on bounty hunters. Poor Europeans and kidnapped Africans were bound in their service to landholders and tradesmen. European-born indentured servants were under contract to work for a specified number of years as a way to pay off the expenses incurred traveling to North America. Some Africans were forced to work under indenture as well. Free labor, whether for the enslaved or the indentured, meant brutal work, little food, and severe reprisals by the masters who made it a crime to break the contract or defy the master.

Escape was protest.

The bounty hunter was hired to bring back the laborer, servant, or enslaved to the landholder and did not receive full payment unless successful. Once the fugitive was returned, after a public hearing, punishment could be thirty or more lashes on their bare back, "well laid on"; time in the public stockade with their hands or feet held in wooden blocks; or even death. Laws were enacted by the powerful elite but enforced by a different social tier beneath them, which maintained order based on the elite's will. Someone had to be the human face of consequence for failing to adhere to law. This was the nebulous beginning of modern law enforcement.

The laws governing the indentured and enslaved required policing by those who continuously watched laborers and meted out punishments. In the case involving John Punch, an African who ran away with two European indentured servants, the White servants received thirty lashes. Punch was given perpetual servitude as his punishment. Thus, the racial disparity between the criminal penalties was the poison in the nation's roots and would remain in the tree as it fully bloomed. The fruit that the tree bears is still poisonous.

Black men, women, and children were tied down nude and whipped nearly to death with rawhide straps because Africans were thought to not feel pain. The malevolence of White people twisted popular belief to such an extent that those formally or informally acting as enforcers believed, or numbed themselves into believing, that "the thickness of [Africans'] skulls . . . [enabled] them to bear without injury the blows afflicted in sudden rage by their masters," requiring brutal force beyond what Whites themselves could bear.[11] Unfortunately, vestiges of this depraved thinking about people of African descent and their missing threshold for pain remain, leading some to use brutal force as practice in law enforcement and even the medical profession.

Africans and African Americans fought back against this regime. Black women, in particular, were pivotal—from Queen Njinga of Ndongo (Angola) to Elizabeth Key, Sojourner Truth, Elizabeth Freeman, and countless women I cover in my book *She Took Justice: The Black Woman, Law, and Power*—resisting through nonviolent protest, diplomacy, legal challenges, the arts, escape, and even violent means, as in the case of Celia and Margaret Garner.[12] In response to this resistance, Congress only strengthened the existing fugitive slave laws in 1850, creating criminal consequences for anyone who assisted a person fleeing bondage or who had knowledge of their escape and did not report it. Thus, the law made *everyone* a bounty hunter. The fugitive slave laws further divided the United States over slavery and states' rights, precipitating a war. Colonial laws were drafted and enacted specifically to subjugate Black people in North America, both free and those in bondage. Slave catchers culled the woods in search of Africans who dared escape. They became nightriders assaulting Black citizens with abandon.

HATED FOR BEING FREE

Enslavement ended, finally, in 1865. War was the protest that led to freedom. Africans made themselves African Americans through enlistment and battle. The Fourteenth Amendment, enacted in 1868, provided citizenship at birth, rebuffing the Supreme Court's decision in *Dred Scott v. Sandford* in 1857. Privileges and immunities, due process rights, and equal protection were gained under the amendment. Voting rights for Black men soon followed in 1870 with the ratification of the Fifteenth Amendment, but America's embrace of these new citizens was short-lived. The United States enacted laws criminalizing the behavior of people of color for the purpose of using their incarcerated labor for free, obstructing their economic progress, and undermining their voting rights. These "Black Codes" marked the beginning of criminalizing people of African descent.

These criminal laws cruelly turned African American livelihoods into a liability. Any display of freedom, from playing cards to taking a moment to rest, was made a crime. Discriminatory on its face and in its application, the Black Codes were intended to incarcerate African

American men, women, and children for White commercial benefit as indicated by the Constitution of Mississippi in "An Act to Confer Civil Rights on Freedmen, and for other Purposes": "An Act to Amend the Vagrant Laws of the State":

> Section 2. . . . all freedmen, free negroes and mulattoes in this State, over the age of eighteen years . . . with no lawful employment or business . . . shall be deemed vagrants. . . .
>
> "An Act to punish certain offenses therein named, and for other purposes"
>
> Section 1. . . . no freedman, free negro or mulatto, not in the military service of the United States Government, and not licensed so to do by the board of police of his or her county, shall keep or carry fire-arms of any kind, or any ammunition, dirk or bowie knife.[13]

The punishment for vagrancy was forced labor for people of color.

Convictions under the Black Codes came quickly, especially during the planting and harvest seasons, when labor was desperately needed. The convicted person was leased out as free labor to the highest bidder. This system of criminal exploitation, which some refer to as "slavery by another name," existed from 1865 into the second half of the next century.

Once again, survival was itself a protest. African Americans had suffered soul-crushing brutality and emerged seeking a new day. They entered the economy as laborers for hire, business owners, farmers, and professionals. But their rise was met with bloodshed once federal troops were removed from the South in 1877. The former Confederate states, once at war with the Union, now began a war against African Americans. The United States' response was to turn its back, again. It was the end of the postwar Reconstruction era and the beginning of lynching.

The heinous murders were intended to send a message to people of color. Without the protection of troops or local law enforcement, people of color defended themselves as best as they could while petitioning presidents and Congress for justice and the prosecution of murder suspects under federal civil rights law. Since criminal cases rely on the government to bring charges against suspects, state and local prosecutors ignored the crimes and some, frankly, likely participated in them.

DISINVITED IMMIGRANTS

In the early part of the nineteenth century, America beckoned foreigners to its shores, and among the immigrants who arrived were the Chinese, as well as European nationalities such as the Italian and Irish. They were greeted eagerly, only to be later disinvited, propagandized, and terrorized by law enforcement when the US economy fell on hard times. Competition for jobs and societal xenophobia gave law enforcement the power to assault immigrants with impunity and treat them with general disdain, as a way to make living in the United States untenable for immigrants. The country hereafter would follow a pattern of opening its borders, using the labor of immigrants, and, when they were no longer needed, enacting laws to criminalize them, which made them fodder for police violence at the hands of those willing to criminally debase themselves to feel superior.

Brutal extrajudicial violence awaited outsiders: lynching.

Lynching is extrajudicial punishment, meaning it does not occur within the established judicial code of rights. It is believed that lynching may have originated with Judge Charles Lynch of Virginia, who presided during the Revolutionary War. Judge Lynch was known for detaining British loyalists without trial, and he condoned communities taking the law into their own hands with immigrants when the courts were unavailable or too far removed from the community to deliver justice swiftly. After the Civil War, the practice of lynching—of suspected criminals or any vulnerable person who went afoul of social dictates—turned its ugly face toward freed Black people.

Lynching was just one of many tools employed in a racial and economic hierarchy that thrived on dividing racial and ethnic groups of the working class. By paying Blacks, immigrant workers of color, and certain European immigrants less than most Western European and White American workers, the employers not only drove down wages but also fomented hostilities that resulted in mob violence. Factory owners applied race-based divide-and-conquer tactics passed down from Bacon's Rebellion in 1676. By abusing the vulnerable, police did the bidding of the wealthy elite and politicians. In the end, law enforcement, prosecutors, and judges did little to enforce laws against murderous mobs or to protect those under attack.

PROTEST SAVED PINK FRANKLIN

The White sheriff was armed and so was the Black man asleep in his own home when the law tore at the door, determined to make an unlawful arrest. Pink Franklin, a twenty-two-year-old Black man, shot Constable Henry Valentine, a White man, on a dark, hot July night in Orangeburg, South Carolina, in 1907.[14] When Valentine arrived at the door of Franklin and his wife, Patsy, at 3 a.m., the couple was asleep. Sheriff Valentine was there to arrest Franklin for failing to return to the job he reportedly held as a fieldworker. His contract was for peonage labor in nearly slave-like conditions, as he was forced to live on the property of White landholder Jake Thomas, but Franklin did not even have a bed.[15] He had been tricked into the onerous labor contract by Thomas. The sheriff arrived to the house carrying an arrest warrant signed by Magistrate Henry Valentine, his brother, for the crime of "breach of an agricultural contract."[16]

Without announcing himself, Sheriff Valentine kicked Franklin's door open. Then he shot into the dark house. Franklin returned fire in self-defense, to protect himself and his wife. Both men were wounded, but only Valentine died of his wounds. Franklin and his wife, Patsy, were beaten by deputies and then charged with murder.[17] The deputies claimed Patsy leveled an axe at the intruder. A lynch mob wanted vigilante justice. Rumors spread that Valentine had been ambushed while peacefully serving a warrant for the arrest of a thief, and that the thief's wounds were self-inflicted.

Protests came from the venerable Booker T. Washington. The fledgling National Association for the Advancement of Colored People took Franklin's murder charge as its first criminal case. Established in 1909, the organization's founding mission was to advocate for the African American community, as the NAACP recounts in its history:

> In 1908, a deadly race riot rocked the city of Springfield [Illinois], eruptions of anti-black violence—particularly lynching—were horrifically commonplace, but the Springfield riot was the final tipping point that led to the creation of the NAACP. Appalled at this rampant violence, a group of white liberals that included Mary White

Ovington and Oswald Garrison Villard (both the descendants of famous abolitionists), William English Walling and Dr. Henry Moscowitz issued a call for a meeting to discuss racial justice. Some 60 people, seven of whom were African American (including W. E. B. Du Bois, Ida B. Wells-Barnett, and Mary Church Terrell), signed the call, which was released on the centennial of Lincoln's birth.[18]

The NAACP lawyers challenged Black voter suppression, which resulted in all-White juries because potential jurors were culled from the voting rolls.[19]

Pink and Patsy Franklin were tried for murder in a one-day trial. Patsy was acquitted but Pink Franklin was found guilty by an all-White jury and sentenced to death by hanging. The Black community sent letters stating Franklin would not have been convicted under the same facts if he had been White. This and other forms of protest accomplished what the lawyers could not: after strategic lobbying and the gathering of more than one thousand signed petitions, along with a personal letter from President William Howard Taft pushing for Franklin's freedom, Franklin was taken off death row. He remained in custody, however, tormented by guards as he labored on a South Carolina chain gang until his sentence was commuted by Governor Martin Frederick Ansel. NAACP lawyers Jacob Moorer and John Adams, both African American, had appealed Franklin's case to the US Supreme Court. Although the high court turned its back and refused to change his sentence, the people refused to give up on Pink Franklin. They demanded justice. Even Washington powerbrokers, pushed by the NAACP and their constituents, used their influence.

Perhaps they understood the double standard in the case—that a White man would not have been convicted for protecting his own home. When Governor Martin Frederick Ansel commuted Franklin's sentence to imprisonment, it was an act of generosity rare for the era. Protests continued for years until Governor Richard Manning handed Franklin a full pardon in 1919. The protests had freed Franklin, and upon his release from prison, he and Patsy moved to Blackville, South Carolina, where he lived under the name Mack Rockingham until his passing in 1949.[20] However, consider this: Constable Henry Valentine was dubbed a hero and is listed in the South Carolina Law Enforcement Officers Hall of Fame.[21]

WITHOUT POLICE PROTECTION

Murders by police, vigilantes, and lynch mobs occurred more frequently and became normalized, as much a part of life in the United States then as police-involved civilian deaths are today. As Margaret Burnham argues in *By Hands Now Known*, killings by police, "like lynching, were a form of marketing, selling whites on why Jim Crow had to be sustained."[22] Lynching was considered low-class, extrajudicial, and distasteful by the White elite, whereas death at the hands of police provided a semblance of law and civilized judgment. It gave towns a reason to boast, because they could use the killings by police as proof of a safe environment for White families.

On the other side of town, Black residents paid their taxes, knowing that that money was going toward the salaries and pensions of law enforcement officers who abused their power through violence against people of color, or who stood by as vigilante groups attacked people of color. But through petitions, lobbying, and civil and violent demonstrations, communities of color challenged the United States to prosecute those police officers who took the lives of civilians. Burnham notes, "The resistance reminded whites of the need to square their actions with their law's purported neutrality. The total system was illegitimate; resistance was meant to remind whites, who had a monopoly on law, that it was for them to prove otherwise. Resistance also stripped law of its false majesty."[23]

Whether the product of jealousy, fear, or vindictiveness, lynching was, as Ida B. Wells stated in *Southern Horrors: Lynch Law in All Its Phases*, the "last relic of barbarism and slavery."[24] Since the foundation of the United States some four hundred years ago, this means of control has meant the killing of Africans and the Indigenous with legalized impunity. Protests ensued to bring attention to the lack of protection by law enforcement, the refusal of government attorneys to prosecute racial violence, and the failure of Congress to enact federal anti-lynching legislation.

In the United States, mobs of hundreds, sometimes thousands, of enraged White men would converge on a community of color, burning homes and businesses, shooting anyone they encountered, lynching men from streetlights until smoke and fire and screams filled the night. On July 28, 1917, such a mob had attacked the Black community of East St. Louis, Illinois. Bewilderment and anguish led the NAACP to protest in silence. Over ten thousand African Americans marched in what is now known as the "Silent Protest Parade," a demonstration against lynching and the failure of the government to protect its citizens from racial violence.[25]

A drum corps led the way. No one spoke. They carried signs. The children wore white. All marched side by side, in silence, down Fifth Avenue in New York City. Only the sound of the soles of their shoes hitting the sidewalk could be heard. One sign stated, "The first blood for American independence was shed by a Negro—Crispus Attucks." They marched to protest the East St. Louis, Illinois, riots that began because White factory workers so resented the hiring of Blacks that they attacked them with clubs and burned Black homes and businesses, leaving six thousand homeless and at least forty Blacks and eight Whites dead. No one was prosecuted. Despite the protests that would follow riots like these, police and prosecutors were rarely held accountable by White voters or politicians for failing to prosecute mob violence.

POLICE DEFY THE SUPREME COURT

The sheriff allowed a mob to lynch a man who was supposed to be protected by an order from the US Supreme Court. In *U.S. v. Shipp*, the Supreme Court attempted to intervene in a local justice matter to save the life of Ed Johnson, a Black man falsely accused of raping a White woman in Chattanooga, Tennessee, in 1906.[26] The sheriff, Joseph Shipp, allowed a vigilante crowd to enter the jail housing Ed Johnson. Shipp had an obligation to protect Johnson as a federal prisoner, but at that time, once a person of color had been deemed a suspect in an offense against whiteness, the consequence was either murder by lynching or an expedited execution by the state. Even though the Supreme Court had delayed the execution, Shipp ignored the order, allowing the lynch mob to enter the jail and drag Johnson down the street to a bridge to be hanged. Before he was murdered, Johnson told the bloodthirsty mob, "I am not guilty and that is all I have to say. God bless you all. I am innocent." Then Johnson was executed—twice—because the rope broke, after which the executioners resorted to shooting him multiple times.

These malevolent murderers were so brazen, they pinned a note to Johnson's corpse addressed to Supreme Court justice John M. Harlan, who was the only dissenting opinion in the *Plessy v. Ferguson* case. It read, "To Justice Harlan: Come get your nigger now."[27] These facts were recounted in the 1909 US Supreme Court case in which Shipp was charged with contempt of court "in that Sheriff Shipp, with full knowledge of the court's ruling, chose to ignore his duties to protect a prisoner in his care." His deputies, Matthew Galloway and Jeremiah Gibson, were charged with aiding and abetting a crime. Nick Nolan, Luther Williams, Bart Justice, Henry Padgett, William Mayse, and Frank Ward were charged as accessories to murder.

There have been over four thousand reported lynchings throughout US history—the specific total is uncertain because of a lack of official reporting—but each death epitomizes the criminal neglect of law enforcement as well as the courage of protesters who dared challenge White supremacy.[28] The US sanctioned such heinous public murders, and the silence emboldened the criminals and spectators to take photographs of themselves at the scene of the crime and mail them via the US Postal Service as postcards, which people proudly sent to family and friends. Much as Nat Turner's skull was kept as a relic, the severed fingers and ears and other body parts of lynching victims were taken as souvenirs, displayed in store windows as sickening heirlooms.

Without prosecutions, the murders became an American tradition, sending a message to reinforce racial boundaries: *Thou shalt not trespass*. It wasn't just the fact that people were murdered, but that they were murdered in the most vile fashion, with castration, amputation, rape, and other forms of torture preceding the final deed, all accompanied by a frenzied crowd shooting rounds of bullets into the victim.

Sam Hose was burned alive in 1899, and pieces of his charred body were saved as souvenirs or sold to the highest bidder. As the *New York Tribune* reported, "those unable to obtain the ghastly relics directly, paid more fortunate possessors extravagant sums for them."[29] Mr. Hose's only "crime" was that he had demanded full payment for his work, and then defended himself when the White man who had cheated him began assaulting him, at which point it became a fight to the death. Alfred Cranford died in the encounter because he had tried to kill Sam Hose, but the right of self-defense for people of color had been taken centuries ago. Criminal justice was a White person's domain, not one for people of color. Therefore, Sam Hose was killed without legal consequences for anyone.

The message from law enforcement was to stay oppressed and in one's racially defined place, because the government would not protect you and may even be the instrument of your death, whether extrajudicially or through an expedited capital proceeding. In 1931, nine boys were riding a freight car on the Southern Railroad through Alabama to Tennessee, and, as trouble would have it, two White men and two White women were also in the boxcar. The men provoked a fight, and the boys threw them off the train. To the boys' surprise, a lynch mob was waiting when the train arrived at a stop in Scottsboro, Alabama, where they were falsely accused of rape.

Rape was a capital offense at the time, and when applied to Black men accused of assaulting a White woman, there was no pretense of justice. A one-day trial of the boys, without lawyers and with no evidence of a rape, led to capital convictions, while it was a hung jury for one of the nine, twelve-year-old Roy Wright. Alabama's appellate courts would have allowed the boys to die, expeditiously, as a lynch mob intimidated even White jurors with lynching, and no African Americans were allowed to serve on juries. Such was the state of criminal justice when the Supreme Court overturned the boys' death sentences in 1932, ruling that all defendants on trial facing the possibility of a death sentence must have assistance of counsel.[30]

SHE SAID NO TO THE POLICE

As more African Americans protested, police pushed back to control the growing urban populations and unrest over discrimination and police brutality. State law enforcement officers regularly searched homes and offices without a warrant, despite clear legal protections against unreasonable searches and seizures. Unlike with federal police, whose evidence from illegal searches would be excluded in criminal hearings, state and local police would search illegally as a regular practice because judges allowed it. When Dollree Mapp said no to this practice, it was a protest.

Dollree Mapp earned the title of the "Rosa Parks of the Fourth Amendment."[31] She refused to relinquish her rights when police broke into her home without a warrant while searching for a suspect. Believed to be born on October 30, 1923, Mapp knew her rights as early as 1957, several years before the landmark civil rights legislation of the 1960s. Born in the Deep South, Mapp had found her way from the isolated farming town of Forest, Mississippi, to create a life as a single mother in Cleveland, Ohio.[32] She liked to dress well and had a penchant for the raucous world of boxers and dating its athletes, who could keep her well dressed. She had been married to the boxer Jimmy Bivins, whom Mapp accused of domestic violence. She divorced him, and later became engaged to Archie Moore, the light heavyweight, until they parted ways.

Mapp was in her thirties when Ohio police arrived at her home, looking for a suspect involved in the bombing of a home belonging to a man named Don King.[33] King, who was a rough character, would later serve prison time for assault and then gain fame as a garrulous, mega-rich boxing promoter. Three officers, all White, arrived at Mapp's home and asked to search it. She called her lawyer, who advised her not to let them conduct a search without a search warrant. When she refused to open the door, they returned hours later with additional officers. This time the police waved a piece of white paper as if it were a warrant. But they did not let Mapp read it.[34]

The officers broke into Mapp's house, and when she took the paper that was supposed to be a warrant and put it down her blouse, the officers dragged her to the floor and tore open her blouse to get the paper. They then handcuffed her to a chair as they searched every room, rifling through her drawers and closets, until they found a trunk with magazines, belonging to Mapp's former tenant, that in that era were considered pornographic. Possession of pornographic materials at that time was against Ohio law, so the police officers chose to arrest her as punishment for exercising her Fourth Amendment right to refuse a warrantless search of her home. No warrant was ever produced in court.

Mapp was convicted by an all-White jury and sentenced to seven years in prison. It did not matter that the Fourth Amendment protects against unreasonable police searches: "The right of the people to be secure in their persons, houses, papers, and effects, against unreasonable searches and seizures, shall not be violated, and no warrants shall issue, but upon probable cause, supported by oath or affirmation, and particularly describing the place to be searched, and the persons or things to be seized."[35]

She appealed.

It was the first major criminal case for the Warren Court.[36] In 1961, the US Supreme Court decided in Mapp's favor.[37] The facts so shocked the Court that it decided that all state courts must exclude evidence, such as pornography, if no warrant is provided. The ruling of *Mapp v. Ohio* placed controls on local policing across the country, which led to a decrease in police abuses. The court had delivered decisions requiring poor defendants to have access to free legal representation and ensuring that arrestees were provided a warning explaining their constitutional rights.

KILLING PROTESTERS

He was unarmed in Selma and had just led a protest for the right to vote when law enforcement beat his parents and gunned him down. In the 1960s, protest demonstrations were as frequent as the murders of protesters and civil rights leaders. Too often, the murderers were police officers. Jimmie Lee Jackson was unarmed when he was murdered by state troopers in Selma, Alabama. Jackson's crime was leading a peaceful protest for the right to vote in that virulently racist small town. It was 1965. Jackson, a farmer and deacon in his church, chose to take the example of Rev. Martin Luther King Jr. and march peacefully to the voting registrar. Black citizens had been refused the registration forms and the access to the literacy tests that were required of them to vote. As evening fell, the streetlights were shut off, leaving the marchers prey to a calculated attack by police with nightsticks.

While trying to protect his mother and his grandfather, who were with him, Jackson was shot by Alabama state trooper James Bonard Fowler, who claimed it was in self-defense and that he had feared for his life. Justice was delayed until 2007, when Fowler was indicted and pled guilty to manslaughter, serving six months for the cold-blooded murder of Jackson. When Rev. King mourned Jackson's death, he asked Black people not to feel bitter toward White people.

A CHANGING TIDE

The red tide of war was turning with calls for equality by women, people of color, labor, and young people combined with the urgency to end the war in Vietnam. By 1968, though, the tide had changed for the worst on the high court as Richard Nixon nominated conservative law-and-order justices to take the place of more liberal justices. Civil disobedience was replaced by urban unrest as rioting captured more television news coverage. Blacks grew tired of accepting police abuse and economic hardship. The 1960s bore witness to the assassinations of President John Kennedy, his brother Robert Kennedy, Malcolm X, and Martin Luther King Jr., and a war in Vietnam.

In Cleveland, the movement for civil rights had changed things for some and hardened the hearts of those who refused to accept a desegregated America. Officer Martin McFadden had been on the police force since the Great Depression. McFadden, who was White, had not risen above a plainclothes pickpocket detail in the downtown area.[38] On October 31, 1963, he saw John W. Terry, who was Black, and two other men in front of a store window. They looked inside and then walked to a street corner to talk. Officer McFadden would later testify that he believed that the men planned to rob the store. Probable cause is required before a person can be seized and searched by police, and *Mapp v. Ohio* established that probable cause must be laid out in a search warrant; otherwise, the evidence obtained in the search is obtained illegally and cannot be used in court.[39] McFadden would tell the Court he had no time to seek out a warrant. He stopped Terry, searched him, and found a gun.

Terry was arrested and convicted of possessing a concealed weapon. Although the *Mapp* case had placed limits on what police could do, the US Supreme Court created a new rule in the 1968 ruling of *Terry v. Ohio*. It decided police could act based on "reasonable suspicion" of imminent danger to the public or police. There did not have to be an actual crime. There was no crime in walking on the sidewalk, looking into a store window, or talking to friends on the corner. As the Black Codes did when they were enacted after slavery, the *Terry v. Ohio* ruling allowed officers to criminalize the actions of people of color once again, extending the power of police in urban communities just as they are demanding full citizenship rights under law.

The court ruled that a stop-and-frisk was allowed by police to search for dangerous weapons, justifying it by noting a stop-and-frisk amounted to a mere "minor inconvenience and petty indignity, which can properly be imposed upon the citizen in the interest of effective law enforcement on the basis of a police officer's suspicion."[40] What the ruling failed to recognize was that being touched by an officer while made to stand or sit on the curb or lie face down is a form of public humiliation beyond a "petty indignity." It is traumatizing. In 1967, nearly sixty years ago, communities of color argued that this power would be abused by police and lead to greater tensions, and it has.

RACIAL PROFILING UNDER LAW

Quoting from the President's Commission on Law Enforcement and Administration of Justice, the *Terry* decision recognized that "in many communities, field interrogations are a major source of friction between the police and minority groups."[41] From slave catchers to bounty hunters and night riders to urban police officers, the enduring tradition has been to arm those who oversee communities of color and let them kill with impunity. The US Supreme Court gave near blanket authority to stop citizens in the street and feel over their bodies. Of course, this has led to abuses that disproportionately affect communities of color, the same communities that have been historically the target of abuse by law enforcement.

With the assassination of Dr. Martin Luther King Jr. on April 4, 1968, the role of nonviolence became overshadowed by violent urban uprisings. Blacks, in pain and shock over King's murder, struck out against the injustice and tragic irony of the murder of a Black man who stood for peace. Their grief and rage led to urban uprisings in every major city in America. With justice routinely denied in state courts, Black uprisings became the response to manifest injustice. Violent uprisings have followed the deaths of Blacks at the hands of White police officers, including in Miami, Cleveland, Seattle, Detroit, Chicago, Harlem, and Los Angeles.

Dr. Martin Luther King Jr. had been drawn to Memphis as part of the Poor People's Campaign for economic development and equality, responding to a request from Rev. James Lawson and others to assist the striking sanitation workers. Dr. King hoped he could redeem the nonviolent movement, having admitted in a recent television interview that his "dream had turned into a nightmare." He was exhausted when he arrived in Memphis to disputes over his presence, dismayed that young people, the police, and instigators had turned a peaceful march into a store window–smashing melee, during which Dr. King had to be rushed away for his safety, opening him to embarrassing media ridicule.

Dr. King returned to Memphis in April 1968 against the advice of those who warned him it was dangerous. He stood on the balcony of the Lorraine Motel, as he was preparing to go to dinner with other SCLC workers, after a terrible night of thunderstorms. He was feeling triumphant from delivering the powerfully inspiring "Mountaintop" speech the previous night when a bullet struck him. The Prince of Peace was dead. As the news of the assassination spread, there was a blaze of riots, rebellions, and protests across the streets of the United States, the country that had taken away nearly everything that African Americans had sought to scratch out over hundreds of years of abuse. African Americans, and many others in the US, were devastated. Though some Black people disagreed with King's stance on Vietnam, they believed in the righteousness of his cause, and they knew that he always believed in them.

Young and old, squeezed into ghettos with limited resources and broken dreams, had decided that they would no longer believe in the laws of the US or in American ideals. Betrayed again by the refusal of America to live up to her promises and despising a Constitution dangled before them as a constant reminder that it never applied to them, Black people's hearts were broken. The rage of the broken-hearted lit the flames that burned neighborhoods for weeks in April 1968—flames the rebellious hoped would pierce the greedy, cold, brutal beasts of commerce and government that oppressed them and murdered their king.

WAR ON PROTESTERS

The war on poverty became a war on the protesting poor. *Mapp v. Ohio* had restricted evidence obtained illegally by police, but the Supreme Court gutted it by finding exceptions. President Richard Nixon rose from the political ashes to defend law and order, fomenting police violence against communities of color. Protests continued to follow acts of police and civilian violence against people of color. Rebellion and the obstacles to full inclusion were broken, one demonstration at a time.

Police officers were then given a shield of protection that would allow them to harm civilians and not be held accountable. Urban uprisings helped trigger the *Terry v. Ohio* decision regarding stop-and-frisk. It was a tacit understanding that this policy of patting down a person to find a weapon without possessing a warrant would harm communities of color. *Terry* opened communities of color to police abuse and violence.

Racial profiling, with few limits, was now allowed by the Court. Case after case and protest after protest, the difference in facts has made little difference in outcome. Police were free to harm or kill. In her book *By Hands Now Known*, Margaret Burnham shows the long pattern and practice of police violence with impunity.[42] Legal contrivances allowed the violence to continue. Civil cases were brought after a death or assault, resulting in possible money damages, which were covered by taxpayer dollars, but prosecutors failed to charge officers. Protests were effectively pushing to demand answers and accountability, but laws worked in favor of the law enforcers, not the victims. Using culture, organizations, and the arts, including a genre that would become hip-hop, people of color protested police violence.

Gang members turned their rage into establishing organizations to protest and protect their communities from wanton police violence. In September 1968, Jose "Cha Cha" Jimenez led the transformation of a street gang known as the Young Lords into an organization focused on demanding political and civil rights. Starting in Chicago, the Young Lords branched out into other cities including New York City. Johanna Fernandez's *The Young Lords: A Radical History* examines this movement led by poor and working-class Puerto Ricans.[43]

COMMUNITIES RISE

Residents of Chinatown protested New York City's police. They had taken abuse, paid unwarranted traffic tickets, and suffered police-involved civilian shootings in silence. But on April 26, 1975, they rose to protect Peter Yew, who had been brutally beaten by police at the Fifth Precinct in Chinatown. The incident began with a traffic accident between two drivers, a Chinese American and a White male. The White driver left the scene, knowing that the all-White precinct officers would be sympathetic to him. Yew, a witness to the incident, and others told the Chinese driver's side. The police reacted angrily, pushing the witnesses around, and when Yew spoke up, they pulled him into the station and beat him mercilessly, then charged him with resisting arrest and assaulting a police officer.[44]

This Chinatown community formed associations to voice their complaints and organized unprecedented protests, the first of which was on May 12, 1975, the day before Yew's preliminary hearing. It drew nearly 2,500 protesters, and the second protest, on May 19, 1975, was the largest Asian American protest in US history with an estimated twenty thousand marchers. Shouting "Minorities Unite!," many had closed their shops, posting signs on the doors that read "Closed to Protest Police Brutality."[45] The protesters demanded that the charges against Yew be dropped, that the offending officers be charged with assault and the others involved be suspended, and that the captain of the Fifth Precinct resign.

Additionally, they demanded the end of harassment tactics and the hiring of Chinese Americans in city government. The power of their unified demands led to the release of Yew, assault charges for two of the officers, the transfer of the Fifth Precinct captain, and a new policy in city government that included Chinese-speaking people and a Chinese interpreter acting as liaisons to the Chinese community.

The power and effectiveness of African American organizations shifted local, state, and federal governments from the negotiation table to suppressive violence as those in power sought to maintain their historic levels of control over people of color. The Black Panther Party was targeted for extermination, as examined in Joshua Bloom and Waldo E. Martin Jr.'s *Black Against Empire: The History and Politics of the Black Panther Party.*[46] Police violence against the Black community was the catalyst for the Black Panthers' decision that members carry arms. That decision, a legal one under California law, became the government's trigger for firing on Black Panthers, now labeled armed and dangerous.[47]

The federal government infiltrated activist organizations and allowed agents provocateurs to foment violence among and against the Black Panthers, the Congress of Racial Equality, the Nation of Islam, and the American Indian Movement, as well as the Young Lords. The 1969 killing of Fred Hampton, a leader of the Panthers' Illinois chapter, was a direct consequence of the government's use of informants (through COINTELPRO, short for Counterintelligence Program) and the fact that it could commit assassinations on US soil with impunity if it was in the name of law enforcement.[48] War and domestic police merged into a militarized force that made a mockery of democracy. This force uses tanks and military weaponry that are rarely revealed outside of urban uprisings and peaceful voting rights protests.[49]

GAY AND FIGHTING BACK

Police harassed gay people because they believed they could do so. Fear of arrest and a police record kept many gay people quiet about police harassment and in the closet because homosexuality was not only a crime in many states; it was also considered a mental illness. The New York Police Department, like police around the country, made a habit of raiding gay bars. The Stonewall Bar at 51 and 53 Christopher Street in Greenwich Village was no exception. The West Village was not the trendy place of high-end shops back on June 28, 1969, when the Stonewall Rebellion took place, changing the course of the LGBTQIA+ movement and the relationship between the police and the gay community.

It was hot in the city and police had already raided the Stonewall Inn on Tuesday, arresting some employees for operating without a liquor license. Early in the morning on Friday, police returned and pulled employees from behind the bar and began filling a police van with patrons, many of whom were arrested for cross-dressing and because failing to conform to societal gender expectations was a crime. Crowds gathered and a scream was heard as police tussled with arrested patrons. Hundreds began pushing back, bottles were thrown, more police arrived, and the rebellion had started. The next day, the crowd was larger, and the police response with tear gas and clubs with confrontations ended July 1.

Fighting back has a healing effect on those who protest and creates momentum for policies to protect the gains created by the uprisings. A year later, thousands took to the streets and marched from the Stonewall Inn to Central Park, chanting gay pride slogans in what became America's first gay pride parade. Inspired by New York's example, activists in other cities, including Los Angeles, San Francisco, Boston, and Chicago, organized gay pride celebrations that same year. The fight for gay rights did not begin with the Stonewall Rebellion, but its impact is immeasurable. Vulnerability to blackmail, loss of child custody, involuntary institutionalization, and termination from employment were consequences of arrest.

Bayard Rustin protested gay oppression by refusing to hide his sexuality and by using the force of personality and intellect that he gave to the civil rights and anti-war movements to the movement for gay rights. However, Rustin's sexuality often overshadowed his contribution to civil rights and assistance to Dr. King as an advisor and community organizer.

No protest leader is perfect. On January 21, 1953, Rustin was arrested in Pasadena, California, along with two White men, and charged with violation of a local public decency law. He pled guilty to lewd vagrancy, and despite all of his good works this impropriety would become leverage to remove him as a leader in the Civil Rights Movement. Rustin was a known advisor and friend to Dr. King, and some may have been jealous of his relationship, opposed to him based on religious dictates, or simply saw this brilliant man as arrogant.[50] But when his Pasadena arrest surfaced, Rustin was ousted from his place among the Big Five groups in civil rights. But Rustin persevered and refused to turn his back on the fight for racial justice.[51] His dedication, vision, and organizational skills resulted in the historic 1963 March on Washington for Jobs and Equality, which, at the time, with an estimated quarter million attendees, was one of America's largest peaceful demonstrations.

MEMPHIS, AGAIN

His father would not allow police to get away with shooting his son in the back while the boy was climbing a fence, trying to get away. In 1974, Memphis police shot a fifteen-year-old unarmed African American boy in the back as he was scaling a fence. The boy, Edward Garner, was running from police, who suspected he was involved in a nonviolent break-in. The teen was getting away, so police shot and killed him. Protests erupted, demanding accountability, and the father of Edward Garner sued to get answers and justice. It seemed a rise in deadly shootings by police accompanied the rise in political, economic, and social standing among African Americans.

Tennessee v. Garner had to be decided by the Supreme Court because the lower courts believed this shooting of an unarmed teen in the back was an acceptable use of force. In its 1985 ruling, the high court ruled that the police use of force was excessive, and that deadly force could only be used when police are facing a "threat of death or serious physical injury."[52] Yet police continue to use lethal force against unarmed civilians because prosecutors refuse to charge officers, zealously exploiting the grand jury system in order to not hold officers accountable.

The impunity of police officers led to the brazen and brutal assault on Rodney King in 1991. The legal system's denial of justice to him and the subsequent riots set the stage for decades of uprisings. Rebellions are the frustrated articulation of people petitioning the government for a redress of grievances; they are expressing the passion of ignored pain. Just as the police have kicked and beaten and clubbed citizens, the community's outrage is kicking the United States into creating remedies to live up to America's constitutional promises.

THIS IS WHAT IMPUNITY LOOKS LIKE

The police beat him with nightsticks dozens of times, kicked, and punched him, amused by his stamina. In the early morning of March 2, 1991, members of the Los Angeles Police Department suspected Rodney King, a Black man, of driving under the influence. Following a high-speed chase on the Altadena highway, King pulled his car over into a parking lot.[53] Upon exiting the car, he initially refused to lie prone on the ground as instructed.

King was checked into a hospital and treated for a fractured leg, multiple facial fractures, and numerous bruises and contusions.[54] One of the officers, Laurence Powell, was at the hospital, and upon learning that King worked at Dodger Stadium, Powell said to him: "We played a little ball tonight, didn't we Rodney? . . . You know, we played a little ball, we played a little hardball tonight, we hit quite a few home runs. . . . Yes, we played a little ball and you lost and we won."[55] Officers Stacey Koon, Ted Briseno, Roland Solano, and Powell were charged with assault with a deadly weapon and excessive use of force by a police officer.

However, even with the videotape evidence of abuse, on April 29, 1992, a jury comprising ten White people, one Latino person, and one Asian American person acquitted the officers. The acquittals were met with outrage from the Black community. Mass uprisings erupted, resulting in more than $1 billion in property damage, at least forty fatalities, over thirteen thousand arrests, and two thousand people injured.[56] On August 4, 1992, a federal grand jury indicted the four officers, charging them with using unreasonable force. Koon was also charged with willfully permitting officers to use unreasonable force.

Once again, the lack of justice for Blacks in state courts required federal intervention and the reliance that the Civil Rights Act would be employed in federal courts. In April 1993, after the trial of the officers in the US District Court for the Central District of California, the verdicts were announced. The jury convicted Koon and Powell but acquitted Timothy Wind and Theodore Briseno. There were no riots. Separate from this trial, Rodney King brought a successful civil action in 1994 that resulted in a monetary settlement of $3.8 million against Los Angeles due to widespread evidence of racism and a failure to reprimand officers who used excessive force.

Officers Koon and Powell were sentenced to thirty months in prison, reduced from a possible seventy to eighty-seven months.[58] There was clear video evidence that this was a brutal, unwarranted beating, along with evidence of officers confessing to excessive force, and yet it took an uprising to secure justice. The Rodney King case remains an extreme example, yet at the same time, the basic circumstances repeat themselves weekly in some form across the United States. Cell phone videos and audio recordings, plainly exposing police abuse, regularly compete against an entrenched tradition of law-ordained violence running centuries deep.

BROKENHEARTED

The following cases were chosen to reflect a few representative instances of police abuse with impunity. I mean no disrespect to the slain and their grieving families whose stories are not told here.

Shortly after midnight on February 4, 1999, four members of New York City's Street Crime Unit knocked on the door of Amadou Diallo's apartment in the Bronx. Diallo, a legal resident of the United States, was born in Liberia, a country in western Africa, to middle-class parents. He moved to the French-speaking country of Guinea and then to New York City.

The officers, all of whom were White, were Sean Carroll, Edward McMellon, Richard Murphy, and Kenneth Boss. They had wanted to question Diallo regarding several rapes, although they had absolutely no evidence against him. Diallo answered the door, and upon seeing the men, he reached inside his jacket to retrieve his ID from his wallet. Without any other provocation, the officers began shooting. They shot at Diallo forty-one times, riddling his body with nineteen bullets. Diallo, only twenty-two, died on the vestibule floor outside his apartment. His murder led to protests in New York and news coverage around the world.

Protesters would not let the case die. Daily, they marched in front of City Hall demanding justice for Diallo. Celebrities and politicians joined the activists in their campaign. They engaged in acts of civil disobedience leading to their arrest, until prosecutors finally took action.[59] A grand jury in Bronx County indicted the officers on two counts of murder in the second degree and reckless endangerment in the first degree. Citing negative pretrial publicity, they requested a change of venue, asserting that it was not possible to receive a fair trial in the Bronx. The request was denied by Patricia Williams, the African American judge appointed to the case.

The White officers appealed Williams's decision. Their request was granted by the New York Appellate Court, moving the case from the Bronx, a New York borough with a diverse population of color, to a predominately White jurisdiction in Albany County, in upstate New York. The case now had a new judge, Joseph Teresi, a White man. Before a jury of four Black women and seven White men, the officers testified that the shooting was an accident and that Diallo contributed to his death by not obeying their orders, despite the evidence to the contrary. After deliberating for three days, the jury affirmed that they believed the officers, delivering twenty-four "not guilty" verdicts on the six charges against each of the four officers.

Diallo's brokenhearted mother, Kadiatou Diallo, wrote of her son's death and the effect it had on her family in *My Heart Will Cross This Ocean: My Story, My Son, Amadou*.[60] The family filed a civil action against the officers and the City of New York. The case was settled before going to trial, with the parties reaching a $3 million settlement. New York City disbanded the Street Crime Unit. The officers returned to law enforcement.[61] Diallo's body was returned to Africa for burial. A commission formed to study the incident found the officers had not overreacted. In other words, the commission deemed forty-one bullets an appropriate response to Diallo reaching into his pocket.

America's history of racial bias and denigration of African Americans continues to play a role in police brutality cases. In particular, the murder of Diallo illustrated the learned assumptions of race, power, and place. First and foremost, there was the assumption that an African man should have known that the unknown White men who appeared in the vestibule of his apartment building in a predominately African American community must be conducting official police business.

Sometimes it seems that White police officers presume African Americans should fall to their knees in the presence of cops. Do they feel they are superior beings vested with the power to decide who lives and who dies, and therefore people of African descent, and other people of color, must fully prostrate themselves whenever police approach them?

While we don't know Diallo's understanding of slavery's legacy or systemic racism in the United States, we know he did not fall to the ground upon seeing White men at his door. He couldn't have known that the officers (allegedly) feared for their lives when confronted with his slender frame and would shoot him nineteen times.

Along with dismantling the Street Crime Unit, the New York Police Department initiated cultural training and mandatory race relations courses. Similar changes were implemented elsewhere, with cities initiating task forces, cultural awareness training, and college classes to address what they considered to be the root causes of police-involved civilian shootings that disproportionately took the lives of people of color. There were efforts to increase the number of Black and Latino police officers and prosecutors. Yet the killings continued and continue still. The number of officers facing prosecution remains minuscule. In a country of eighteen thousand police jurisdictions, modest changes can only have so much reach. National legislation is required to make changes comparable to those brought about by the Civil Rights Act and Voting Rights Act. Protesters demanded national criminal justice reform and received a federal holiday celebrating Juneteenth.[62]

FATHER'S DAY MARCH

On Father's Day in 2012, thousands of New Yorkers from varied racial and ethnic backgrounds and different generations participated in a silent march. Similar to the Silent March of 1917, held to call attention to lynching, these protesters walked from Harlem to Mayor Michael Bloomberg's home on the Upper East Side of Manhattan. They protested the city police department's wanton practice of stopping and frisking citizens, most of whom were predominately Black or Latino and innocent of any crime. The demonstrators charged that the practice violated the Constitution's ban on unreasonable searches and its guarantee of equal protection under the law.

Protests of police tactics are necessary because historical forces are aligned against the average person, allowing law enforcement to inflict sometimes lethal force, with impunity, against one who may or may not be innocent but is not allowed to live long enough to be tried in a court of law. Police kill people of color, prosecutors often fail to bring charges, and despite witnesses, books, litigation, and protesters, no one can definitively state how many people have died in the United States at the hands of law enforcement.[63] According to the *Washington Post*, more than one thousand people die at the hands of the police each year.[64] It is assumed this scathing level of deaths goes back many years. But the Federal Bureau of Investigation, the nation's law enforcement agency, did not keep accurate records. In 2019, the FBI began collecting data on the use of force, but its numbers are questionably low.[65] The *Post* took on the task of maintaining a databank with names, ages, places, and circumstances around police-involved civilian deaths in the United States. An article by the *Washington Post* titled "Fatal Police Shootings Go Unreported" goes into further detail.[66]

BLACK LIVES SHOULD MATTER

He was shot dead by a law enforcement officer. For hours, the corpse of the eighteen-year-old lay in a street in Ferguson, Missouri, while the summer sun baked his body. On this day, August 9, 2014, Michael Brown was shot dead by Officer Darren Wilson. *Michael Brown.* I wept as I learned of this murder, overwhelmed because not only had I been to Ferguson during my college days and knew the simmering heat of the city's asphalt on a Midwestern summer afternoon but also because my oldest brother bore the same name. Brown's body lay in the hot street for hours, just as the police had let the body of another Black man shot in the street near my apartment in Philadelphia lay uncovered in the summer heat for hours, as though death was not punishment enough. Michael Brown, a big boy with a chubby, dark face, reminded me of a large child. As someone who as a girl was tall for my age, I understood being mistaken as an adult. This young man had a look of manliness that he had yet to possess placed on his shoulders.

Protests began. Officer Wilson, after taking days to speak with lawyers and his union, finally gave a statement using the usual adage of law enforcement: he "feared for his life." In Ferguson, fire engulfed a Little Caesars pizza restaurant, its white-tipped flames mixing with screams of rage and sirens amid looting. The city was set ablaze with rage. And so was I. Prosecutors eventually conceded to the will of protesters and convened a grand jury to decide on whether to indict Wilson. It is supposed to be a secret process; however, it was later revealed that the chief prosecuting attorney, Robert P. McCulloch, the people's lawyer, had undermined his own case. It is an old trick of prosecutors to do this, and then refute the arguments that they failed the public. Instead of zealously representing the victim, the actual defendant here was the officer.

Prosecutors are known to overwhelm grand juries with mountains of evidence instead of curating evidence meant to persuade laypeople to indict the officer suspected of a crime, and tradition followed that path in this case. The dumping of excessive evidence on the grand jurors resulted in no charges brought against Officer Wilson. The county prosecutor admitted he was going to be "neutral," which is an appalling abdication of duty for someone whose title is prosecutor and considering that only the judge and jury are supposed to be neutral.[67] It is an act of self-sabotage for a prosecutor to tell jurors to decide for themselves what evidence is important in forming the basis of an indictment, and were a prosecutor to do so in a case involving a civilian suspect, it would be cause for their termination. After the grand jury failed to indict Wilson, it was the ongoing and widely covered protests—in the streets and behind closed doors—that led to the US Justice Department conducting its own investigation of the case.

Prosecutors and police have a close relationship. They are nearly family or, at least, have a co-dependent relationship. Police and prosecutors work together to create the criminal cases taken before the court. By conducting the ballistics tests and gathering other evidence, and by testifying in court, police provide the cornerstone for the case. The victim is a stranger in this scenario, merely a visitor in the house of criminal justice. Yet, the prosecutor's job is to give justice to the victim on behalf of society. As of this writing, there have been only fifty criminal cases against the police for civilian death throughout American history, an embarrassingly low number given that each year there are over one thousand civilian deaths at the hands of police.[68] Over one thousand deaths—now much more in the public consciousness because of protests and advances in cell phones and other technology.

Seventeen-year-old Michael Brown was unarmed and yards away from Darren Wilson, yet the officer said he feared for his own life. Without prosecution, there is no process to force an officer like Wilson to explain why and how he feared for his life. Communities have protested the failure of law enforcement to protect against racial violence, against the lack of prosecution of police when the victim is a person of color, and against the over-policing of communities of color, and must continue to do so.

Protest has a spirit. There is something otherworldly about the bodies of strangers packed close together, chanting "No justice, no peace" or "This is what democracy looks like." The crowd is sharing breath, risking their safety, and anticipating the birth of a new day. Protesting is an altar call for justice and a prayer for healing. For me, protesting the violence of our government against its people is a spiritual and patriotic act, and a call for a better use of the resources designated for a community's protection. Rather than providing for our protection, our tax money is funding death and weaponization against us. We come to the streets with our voices and pleas and hope for a new day, seeking the good news that they have listened and heard our plea. But they are not God or any kind of divine power. They are human beings abusing positions of human power.

UPRISINGS IN NEWARK

He witnessed the fire and smoke, walked through streets of broken glass, and learned at a young age what repressed anger could do to a city. Larry Hamm's story is one of community activism in his hometown of Newark, New Jersey, but it illuminates the many dimensions of protesting police violence.[69] He grew up at a time when New Jersey was segregated. He was a child witness to the Newark Uprising of 1967, which was triggered when Newark police assaulted and brutally beat John William Smith. Throughout that summer, James Brown's "Say it Loud—I'm Black and I'm Proud" was on the radio, and Newark was one of the hubs of the Black Power movement. As a student government president, an athlete on the school's cross-country team, and a member of the National Honor Society, he was trying to stay out of trouble in high school, a dramatic turnaround after being expelled in eighth grade.

But four years later, in 1971, Hamm was drawn to battle and led a march of hundreds of high school students to the luxurious Gateway Hotel. He and the others refused to leave, but then the first Black mayor of Newark, Ken Gibson, agreed to talk to him. The students were young and demonstrating to end the Newark teachers' strike because they wanted to return to school. It was the longest in the history of any major US city and improved facilities at his segregated school, which did not have a gymnasium or athletic field.[70] Gibson did not want to see Hamm and the students arrested by the police eagerly waiting outside. "It was four years after the rebellion, and they thought it was going to be an uprising," Hamm told me. Gibson was impressed enough to invite Hamm, then seventeen years old and unable to vote in US elections, to be a voting member of the Newark Board of Education.

Hamm didn't come from a politically active family. His mother was a seamstress, and his father was a truck driver who died when Hamm was four years old. "They were regular folks who never talked about race around me," he said. "The very first conversation we had about race was the first night of the 1967 rebellion, when fires broke out on Springfield Avenue." Asking his grandfather about the uprising begins with a story about the racial abuse he experienced in the US Army and how much abuse Black men have had to endure. His grandfather served in World War I, and Hamm's father was a veteran of World War II. Regarding Dr. King, Hamm recalls that his grandfather would only say King "should stick to civil rights and stop talking about opposing the Vietnam War."

Hamm says policing was always an issue in his community in Newark's Central Ward, where Black people were redlined into ghettos and it was very hard to receive a mortgage loan from the bank. In 1967, Newark had the highest concentration of Black people per square mile in the country, with huge housing projects, substandard housing, and horrendous poverty. He grew up in an apartment with no hot running water. "My mother had to get one of those big wash pans and put it on the stove and heat the water for baths and wash dishes," Hamm says. Coincidentally, this was when Tom Hayden of the Students for a Democratic Society led a group of University of Michigan students to do work in Newark's Clinton Hills Neighborhood, organizing around housing issues.

Police brutality triggered the 1967 rebellion. On July 12, John William "J. W." Smith, a forty-year-old trumpet player and part-time cab driver in Newark, was pulled over by police near Fifteenth Avenue.[71] He was beaten by the police and taken to the Seventeenth Avenue Police Precinct, which was wedged in between large thirteen-story high-rise housing projects. "People could see police dragging somebody into the police station, and rumors were that Smith had been killed," Hamm said. Members of CORE, the Nation of Islam, and other civil rights organizations in Newark went to the police station and issued calls for more information. Holding police accountable is protest.

There was no information and anxiety grew as did the crowds demanding answers. Then there was a fire, and the smell of fire, everywhere, and late in the evening of July 14, New Jersey governor Richard J. Hughes deployed the National Guard, who arrived by the truckload, marching in formation.[72] Governor Hughes stated to the press, "The line between the jungle and the law might as well be drawn here as any place in America," which basically gave police authority to shoot looters.[73] A half-track tank, half the size of a regular tank but with a long barrel, rolled down the street. Soldiers held Black citizens at checkpoints.

Newark was placed on curfew, with searches conducted on cars coming into and out of the Central Ward. Guards went door to door, looking for contraband from looted stores. Newark was under military occupation. "There was nowhere I could walk without glass crunching under my feet, because almost every store window was broken and only Black-owned businesses that wrote 'Soul Brother' on their door were not looted," Hamm remembered. Governor Hughes deployed about seven hundred state troopers because Newark police couldn't put the rebellion down, and "they shot out all the windows with 'Soul Brother' on the door."

"Amiri Baraka [a famous Newark poet and playwright] called it a rebellion," Hamm said. "It was destructive, physically, with destroyed property, but psychologically, it was constructive. In fact, the rebellion reconstructed Black people's consciousness, because many of us went from 'Negro' and 'Colored' to 'Black' after the 1967 Rebellion."

Before 1967, "Black" was a derogatory term, an insult. But after the rebellion, it became a word signifying pride and dignity. "The rebellion reconstructed our consciousness. Made us proud of ourselves." And that made Black power a manifestation of the community. Hamm believes that Ken Gibson, and other Black mayors, would not have been elected but for the protests, rebellions, and urban uprisings. Hamm believes the working class will not realize its full power until it is able to overcome the racial divide and divisions that include race and sex.

Hamm led anti-apartheid protests on Princeton University's campus his senior year. For sixty-six consecutive days, the group held rallies in front of Nassau Hall, the historic building on campus, culminating in a takeover of the hall in 1978, which resulted in Princeton divesting from several South African companies. Hamm completed two years of a doctoral program there, but he didn't finish and decided to return to Newark.

Several years later, on April 11, 1999, the police killed Earl Faison in the town of Orange, not far from Newark, after pulling him from a cab. They arrested Faison, twenty-seven years old, a father on the way to see his kids, when he was pulled out of the car and badly beaten. "Instead of taking him to the hospital, they took him to the Orange, New Jersey, police headquarters and beat him in the stairwell, dragged him to the jail cell, sprayed pepper spray directly into his mouth, causing his lungs to collapse," Hamm said. "The medical examiner said it was such a violent reaction, that the blood vessels in his ears, eyes, and nose burst."

He was killed on April 11, and within a few days, people were demonstrating. Hamm recalls SWAT teams on the rooftops with automatic rifles pointed at them. "It didn't deter or frighten us," he said. Prosecutors did not bring criminal charges against the officers, but they were found guilty of violating Faison's civil rights. Then, shockingly, the trial judge vacated the guilty verdicts. Undeterred, Hamm and others demonstrated to demand an appeal of the ruling. The appeal was accepted, with the case moving out of New Jersey to the Third Circuit Court of Appeals in Philadelphia, and Hamm reserved two buses.

The buses took the protesters over the Benjamin Franklin Bridge to the Court of Appeals. About a month later, the guilty verdicts on the federal civil rights charges were reinstated. "We consider the case still open because there is no statute of limitation on murder. They killed the man and need to be held accountable for his death. Probably the Earl Faison case was to New Jersey what Amadou Diallo was to New York." The vast numbers of civilian deaths at the hands of police produce waves of grief, shock, and anger that keep communities off-balance. In the face of this scale of death, it's impossible to write fully about these murders within any single book.

BALTIMORE REBELLION

On April 15, 2015, Freddie Gray Jr. was arrested by Baltimore police officers for possessing a knife. He was placed in a police van and taken out in a coma.[74] Gray never recovered. Massive riots ensued for over a week in the city of Baltimore. On September 12, 2017, the Justice Department announced that the independent federal investigation into the death of Freddie Gray found insufficient evidence to support federal criminal civil rights charges against the six Baltimore police officers who were involved.[75]

On May 1, 2015, the Baltimore State's Attorney's Office charged the six individuals—Officers Caesar Goodson, William Porter, Garrett Miller, and Edward Nero; Lieutenant Brian Rice; and Sergeant Alicia White—with criminal offenses related to Gray's arrest and death. The charged offenses included reckless endangerment, involuntary manslaughter, and second-degree murder (specifically depraved-heart murder, in which the individual acts in a way that shows a "depraved indifference" to the life of the person killed). Baltimore exploded into the national news headlines as the state's attorney Marilyn Mosby, an African American, was placed in the untenable position of being the representative of a corrupt criminal justice system.

As more people of color become prosecutors, judges, mayors, and police officers within the criminal justice system, the intractable nature of institutionalized racism becomes more apparent. Ultimately, four out of the six officers took their cases to trial, and in each instance, the prosecution was unable to secure a conviction. The other officers were able to walk away. As far as who was responsible for Freddie Gray's death, it remains a mystery.[76]

SAME AS IT EVER WAS

She was asleep when they shot her. It was a chilly night in Louisville, Kentucky, when Breonna Taylor went to sleep on March 12, 2020, and neither she, nor her boyfriend, Kenneth Walker III, could have known that the Louisville Police Department had obtained a no-knock warrant for their home. Taylor was a few months shy of her twenty-seventh birthday. Her chubby-cheeked smile and bright eyes were trademarks from her mother's side.

A little past midnight, three officers broke open Taylor's door with a battering ram. Walker grabbed his handgun, a weapon he was licensed to possess. The officers, at no point announcing themselves as police, proceeded to fire into the apartment, with five bullets hitting Breonna Taylor as she slept in her bedroom. There was an exchange of gunfire. An officer was wounded. Bullets sprayed the apartment, penetrating the wall of the apartment next door. Taylor was unresponsive, pronounced dead upon arrival at the hospital. An emergency room technician, like her, probably assisted the physicians. Taylor's devastated family called for criminal charges of the officers. Protesters were beaten and arrested as officers and prosecutors delayed justice, hid information from family members, passed laws to limit freedom of assembly, intimidated witnesses, and created obstacles, while devastated parents could only tell their stories on television hoping to receive a public response powerful enough to move prosecutors to stop shielding officers with bureaucratic obfuscation.

Protests erupted the next day as news swept the country about the police's fatal shooting of an African American woman as she lay asleep in her bed. As in the case of Pink Franklin, over one hundred years earlier, the police blamed the homeowner. Walker was arrested and charged with attempted murder for firing his weapon that injured an officer. Two months after Breonna Taylor was killed, Derek Chauvin murdered George Floyd in Minneapolis, Minnesota. Even amid a global pandemic, Black Lives Matter protesters felt they had no option but to take to the streets.[77] Kindled by the 2012 killing of Trayvon Martin in Florida and enflamed by the riotous fires of Ferguson, Missouri, four years later, BLM continued to grow, becoming the premier organization for racial justice protests by the time Floyd was lynched in broad daylight in Minneapolis.[78]

Thousands of people from around the world, of all races, ages, genders, educational backgrounds, and occupations, protested for police reform in the United States. Leaders of the BLM movement have been called anti-American threats, but their actions pale in comparison to the violence of some self-professed patriots who oppose this re-sistance.[79] As with all movements, there have been internal conflicts and groups have splintered off, but BLM has effectively amplified the voices of those seeking justice, igniting dozens of groups, movements, philosophies, and creative paths for advocacy.[80]

Colin Kaepernick's NFL career, which began in 2011, was cut short in 2016 after six seasons. He chose to protest police-involved civilian violence by "taking a knee," meaning kneeling on the football field during the performance of the slavery-inspired "Star-Spangled Banner." Francis Scott Key, a slaveholder himself, wrote a poem on which the national anthem during the War of 1812. Its third verse includes a line about maintaining slavery and killing fugitives from slavery and those who assisted them:

> *And where is that band who so vauntingly swore,*
> *That the havoc of war and the battle's confusion*
> *A home and a Country should leave us no more?*
> *Their blood has wash'd out their foul footstep's pollution.*
> *No refuge could save the hireling and slave*
> *From the terror of flight or the gloom of the grave,*
> *And the star-spangled banner in triumph doth wave*
> *O'er the land of the free and the home of the brave.*

Kaepernick lost a stellar football career as a result of his protest but earned the respect of millions. Since taking a knee in 2016, momentum has gained for changing the national anthem to "America the Beautiful," a song that unlike "The Star-Spangled Banner" contains no insulting lyrics. In the tradition of John Carlos and Tommie Smith, Colin Kaepernick used the platform that sports gave him to bring attention to racial prejudice and demand action from lawmakers. Carlos and Smith paid a price for their stance, and Kaepernick's career ended with the termination of his contract. But the legacy of "taking a knee" remains a historic symbol of protesting race-based police violence.

During the Spanish Flu pandemic, a century earlier, a series of race riots in what was known as the Red Summer of 1919 crushed the progress of African Americans. It was a nadir in this country's history. During the Covid pandemic, as racism continued to drive the murders of African Americans by civilians and police, the NAACP continued its push for the passage of an anti-lynching law. Finally, after 150 years of lobbying, protests, petitions, and obstruction in Congress, President Joe Biden signed into law the Emmett Till Antilynching Act on March 29, 2022.

After the protests surrounding the deaths of Breonna Taylor, George Floyd, and hundreds of others, it seemed that reform of the criminal justice system was possible. Congressional sponsors of the George Floyd Justice in Policing Bill had hopes of a level of national change similar to what had come out of the Civil Rights Act of 1964, the Voting Rights Act of 1965, and the Fair Housing Act of 1968. But it did not happen. Instead, on June 1, 2020, Donald Trump used the power of the White House to tear-gas protesters in Washington, DC, and stage himself as a bringer of peace while holding the Bible (upside down, of course). State and local jurisdictions passed anti-riot laws in Arkansas, Florida, Iowa, Oklahoma, Tennessee, Montana, and Alabama with the intent to chill First Amendment rights. Nonetheless, protests continued even though arrests under these laws became more likely.

CONCLUSION

From colonial America to current times, there has been inordinate legal control of Americans for a land that boasts of liberty and free will. Police surveillance has taken many forms over the centuries, but it continues to adhere to a mission of controlling people of color, the poor, immigrants, those who believe in progress, and their allies. Racial profiling arose from the need to remain aware of the movement of people of color and to systematically restrict their social, political, and economic progress. As people of color compete, ever burdened with discrimination, lower pay, poor educational systems, and fewer opportunities, breaking new ground triggers White insecurities, legal machinations, and violence, which requires protests to bring light and change.

Law enforcement officers, like the bounty hunters, slavecatchers, and night riders before them, are too often used as the pit bulls of White supremacy set upon immigrants and non-White people. Prosecutors and police under-protect those who can least protect themselves, and that is why protest remains an important and powerful instrument for justice. Lynching began three hundred years ago, and "lynching by another name" continues through police-involved civilian deaths and murders by vigilante groups and modern militia.[81] National criminal justice legislation as sweeping as the Civil Rights Act and the Voting Rights Act, and Supreme Court decisions as momentous as *Brown v. Board of Education*, are needed to address the inherent racism of the US criminal justice system.

I propose that the prosecutor's office in every police jurisdiction in the country take responsibility for reporting deaths at the hands of police. Report this information to the Department of Justice within seventy-two hours of a death or face certain penalties for failing to do so. That way, each prosecutor's office would be primed to play a larger role in maintaining the data, acknowledging the incident and thus beholden to its constitutional duty of bringing justice to the victim.

Three hundred Denver protesters who were attacked and detained by police during a rally received an initial $4.7 million settlement, and there are at least twenty-nine pending lawsuits nationwide challenging the police use of force during 2020 protests.[82] The protesters were detained by police for violating an emergency curfew put in place to end demonstrations over the killing of George Floyd in 2020. This remarkable outcome sends a message that should resonate with law enforcement across the US. Excessive force used against protesters violates civil rights, civil liberties, and the Fourth Amendment of the Constitution, a significant message that regular people respect the right of protest and demand change from the government, which police and prosecutors have intentionally undermined.

Guns were pointed into the car as I sat frozen and enraged, with a female friend, wondering what we had done. It was Brooklyn, New York, and, ironically, I had spoken at a police brutality conference earlier that day. Perhaps we "fit the description," but then they casually handed back our identification and mumbled something about a broken taillight and drove away, flashing lights, as quickly as they had swarmed the car, leaving us shaken and changed. This was life in the United States for people of color, especially African Americans. In 2022, I took a trip to Minneapolis and stood at the obelisk that is old and anchors the roundabout in the center of the intersection of East Thirty-Eighth Street and Chicago Avenue, a fitting marker for George Floyd, murdered May 25, 2020.

The site is surrounded by weathered signs from mourners, where the aggrieved and the curious, like me, stand awkwardly taking photos of where a Black man was lynched in the twenty-first century. I stared at the memorial image spray-painted on the side of the building, a portrait of Floyd with sad eyes, a face made famous around the world because he epitomizes both police brutality as well as protest. I could not bring myself to enter the store where an alleged counterfeit twenty-dollar bill, the contraband in an alleged crime over which local police had no jurisdiction, led to Office Derek Chauvin asphyxiating Floyd in a public execution, recorded for all to see, while his police trainees did nothing to stop the murder.[83] Uprisings in response to police-involved civilian deaths are a recognition of a life lost, injustice done, grief, and a frustration with a racist, recalcitrant nation.

Each morning I look out to see if the word BREONNA is still there, in bold, thick white paint, across the street above a small park and below the Manhattan skyline featuring a gleaming financial district. In the distance, an American flag flies atop the Manhattan Bridge straightened by strong winds from the East River. Elders on the park benches below watch teenagers on the basketball court, concentrating on jump shots, their laughter mixes with trash talk and hip-hop blasts nearly as loudly as police sirens.

BREONNA— the letters, and my refusal to forget the crime committed against her, are acts of protest. The basketball, laughter, music, and trash talk rises from the playground. Unfortunately, my fear for these young men is constant. I worry about the militarized police just as people of color worried about the militia in colonial days and the sheriffs during Jim Crow. None of us is safe, but perhaps that is the point. Eliza kept the faith, and she fought the good fight, against greater foes, with worse odds. So, we must push forward. Living is protest.

CHAPTER EIGHT

CONTESTING CLIMATE DENIAL AND ENVIRONMENTAL RACISM

The climate change struggle returns to the story of stewards of the land, as the Indigenous believe we all are. Early in my social justice career, I was an attorney at the Southern Poverty Law Center (SPLC), in Montgomery, Alabama. One day, a call came from an attorney in the Choctaw Nation, located in Mississippi, and the litigation director gave me the phone. Members of the Choctaw tribe had turmoil of their own. They needed an attorney to oversee a bitterly contested vote. A toxic waste plant wanted to construct a dumping site on Native land, even though Mississippi laws prohibit such a site. Located within central Mississippi, the Choctaw reservation is sovereign territory. The reservation is sprawling land along Highway 16 and, back then, was dotted with small wood houses and rusty trailer park homes.

This was my first encounter with environmental racism as a civil rights attorney, but in my personal life I had seen that communities of color and low-income neighborhoods were targeted for or made vulnerable to toxic manufacturing plants, electromagnetic radiation from transformer towers, lead paint, terminals where idling buses spew fumes, contaminated water, factory waste, and pollution from highways. The term "environmental racism" presented the problem and the manner of suffering, while "environmental justice" was minted to appease donors, broaden the activist tent, and remove any triggers caused by the word "racism." It also downplayed the powerful connection between race-based subjugation and zoning policies, forged over many decades.

The Choctaw were hoping that former president Jimmy Carter, a federal government mediator, or Morris Dees, founder of the SPLC, would assist them, but what they received was me and an older White female paralegal. When we arrived at a motel in Philadelphia, Mississippi, about five miles from the Choctaw Nation, the motel manager and his wife were in a small gravel parking lot hanging out white sheets on a clothesline. The image kept me seated in my car with the doors locked. Philadelphia was the site of the infamous June 1964 murders of James Chaney, age twenty-one; Michael "Mickey" Schwerner, age twenty-four; and Andrew "Andy" Goodman, age twenty.

Chaney had become engaged in voting rights activism in high school as a youth member of the NAACP, and then went on to become an organizer for the Congress of Racial Equality (CORE) in Meridian, Mississippi. Goodman and Schwerner were students from New York City. Schwerner was a CORE activist in New York City and was assigned by civil rights activist Bob Moses to work in Meridian.[1] Goodman was a student at Queens College but had participated in a youth march in Washington, DC, to desegregate public schools. He lived in a coal mining town to bring attention to poor working conditions in West Virginia.[2]

Goodman wrote in a school paper, "The Senators [in Congress] could not persist in this polite debate over the future dignity of a human race if the white Northerners were not so shockingly apathetic."[3] He joined the Freedom Summer of 1964, registering African Americans to vote in Mississippi. On Goodman's first day, all three men were murdered by the Ku Klux Klan, setting off national calls for voting rights legislation, action against racial attacks, and an investigation into these murders. The bodies were found weeks later. The story of these three martyred activists, along with the murder of Medgar Evers and the killing of the four little girls in the Sixteenth Street Church bombing in Birmingham, contributed to enacting the Voting Rights Act of 1965.[4]

The iconic photo of Chaney, Goodman, and Schwerner that was used in the search for their bodies played in my mind, emboldening me. After all, they fought in the bloodiest of times and died for Black people like me to freely travel across this state. I spent four days with Choctaw leadership, mainly powerful women, who showed me a community in chaos due to lack of resources and opportunities. Greenpeace, the environmental group, had reported on how desperation forced some Indigenous people into selling acres of the land they'd long been devoted to.[5]

I was in the room when discussions broke down over the promise of jobs in exchange for allowing a major waste company to place its facility on their beloved, sacred land. A toxic waste facility was marketed to them as a project that would create employment for a community suffering from high poverty, alcoholism, and despair.[6] In 1983, a waste disposal company tried to build a plant in the town of Shuqualak in Noxubee County, Mississippi, and was defeated.[7] The moratorium that emerged from the community's fight over building that waste facility had expired in 1991. This was another attempt to build a hazardous waste disposal plant.

The issue of environmental protection has gathered momentum among the general population, while Indigenous peoples have stood as guardians of the earth and her resources from time immemorial. Still, many people believe that climate change is nonexistent and the fears about global warming are simply mass hysteria. Environmental activism attacks the very core of commerce and thus is dangerous work for those who engage in it. Lives are lost, threats are made, and assaults are a reality. Winona LaDuke's environmental battles for Indigenous land rights as a climate change activist and organizer have taken her around the world. Her friend and activist, Ingrid Washinawatok El-Issa of Menominee People, was kidnapped and murdered, along with Hawaiian activist Lahe'ena'e Gay and Terence Freitas, in Colombia while building a school and defending the land rights of the U'wa People in the department of Arauca.[8]

Protests, petitions, lawsuits, demonstrations, conferences, books, organizations, and public education have placed climate change, environmental racism, and other essential concerns for our earth at the forefront. The impacts of floods, droughts, earthquakes, tornadoes, hurricanes, and disappearing glaciers present an imbalance that is too prevalent to ignore. So many activists, educators, scientists, politicians, meteorologists, and everyday people are part of this protest history. Below are a handful of representative examples.

A HISTORY OF WARNING SIGNS

They knew it would harm us. According to NASA, scientists were aware of the damage that could create a climate change crisis as early as 1824. During the time of slavery and Indigenous battles to protect their land, French mathematician and physicist Joseph Fourier was calculating the warming of Earth. In 1824, he figured out that, given our distance from the sun, our planet should be colder than it was and theorized that there was an insulating blanket keeping it warm.[9] Then, in 1856, as suffragists in the United States were fighting for the right to vote, scientist and inventor Eunice Newton Foote delivered a paper in London, showing that an insulating blanket in the form of carbon dioxide and water vapor was trapping heat in Earth's atmosphere.[10]

This greenhouse effect was experimentally proven in the 1860s by physicist John Tyndall, while America was fighting a civil war.[11] In 1896, the same year the US Supreme Court legalized race hatred through forced segregation, Svante Arrhenius of the Royal Swedish Academy of Sciences published a paper that predicted carbon dioxide levels in the atmosphere could affect Earth's surface temperature. "On the Influence of Carbonic Acid in the Air upon the Temperature of the ground" was published in the *London, Edinburgh, and Dublin Philosophical Magazine and Journal of Science.*[12]

It was in 1938 that an English steam engineer, Guy Callendar, developed a theory connecting carbon dioxide increases in Earth's atmosphere to global warming.[13] Callendar understood the correlation through his exposure to thermodynamics from his physicist father. In a paper titled "The Artificial Production of Carbon Dioxide and Its Influence on Temperature," Callendar wrote: "By fuel combustion man has added about 150,000 million tons of carbon dioxide to the air during the past half century. The author estimates from the best available data that approximately three quarters of this has remained in the atmosphere."[14]

In 1941, Serbian mathematician and astronomer Milutin Milanković linked the ice ages in Earth's history to its orbital characteristics. The Canadian physicist Gilbert Plass next formulated the "Carbon Dioxide Theory of Climate Change"—in 1956. In short, we had been warned. Repeatedly. But attention in the United States was given instead to Jim Crow segregation, empire building, and maintaining the American veneer of global superiority.

President Theodore Roosevelt feared the loss of America's wildlands. What he called "the lavish use of our resources" would result in depleted soil, polluted rivers, and denuded fields. Although he was a big game hunter throughout his entire adult life, Roosevelt, spurred on by Sierra Club founder and visionary environmentalist John Muir, became the "Conservationist President."[15] Roosevelt established 150 national forests, fifty-one federal bird reserves, four national game preserves, five national parks, and eighteen national monuments by signing the 1906 American Antiquities Act, and founded efforts to preserve 230 million acres of public lands.[16]

Activists began to speak not just for the people affected by climate change, pollution, and contaminated water but for the whales and tuna caught in fishing trawlers, and redwood forests that were being cut down. They placed their lives on the line to speak on behalf of the mountains, streams, and valleys, and on behalf of the inanimate objects that could not speak for themselves. The environmental movement became dangerous work as companies fought back with their tractors and propaganda, lobbying state and federal governments to protect their property interests and profits.

The lure of jobs or the threat of company operations shutting down, with its shadow of unemployment, weighed heavily on the side of business interests, creating community division. "America the Beautiful" was positioned in competition against the image of US progress. Corporate greed and irresponsibility have challenged the future health of the people, wildlife, waterways, and flora. The environment is now finally taken seriously as a political, economic, and social issue of concern to millions.

EARTH'S MONTH

The earth had early allies to speak, march, and write in defense of the environment. Rachel Carson's book *Silent Spring*, published in 1962, was part of the tidal change of activism on behalf of the planet.[17] Carson wrote, "The pollution of the environment by the profligate use of toxic chemicals was the ultimate act of human hubris, a product of ignorance and greed," and it was something she felt compelled to bear witness against.[18]

Carson spoke out about the danger of the things science had conceived, and technology made possible, being foisted on society without those things first being assessed for their safety and benefit to the whole stream of life. "There would be no peace for me," she wrote to a friend, "if I kept silent."[19] *Silent Spring* challenged the government policies that would permit toxic chemicals to be placed in our air, land, and water without fully understanding the long-term consequences on people, animals, and the environment.

The need to address the harm of oil and gas emissions, oil spills, and factory pollution on the health of all living beings reached beyond mere conservation. People began to pay attention and ask questions about toxins in their food, water, and air. As is often the case, young people were at the heart of the movement. Senator Gaylord Nelson, who had learned from his experience organizing anti-war protests, recruited environmentalist Denis Hayes to organize college students to demonstrate.[20] A Wisconsin native, Nelson lost his bid for reelection in 1980 but is known there for his work with the Wilderness Society, ensuring that millions of acres were set aside as preserved land. He went on to become counselor for the Wilderness Society and would be honored with the Medal of Freedom by President Clinton.

As early as 1969, the connection between greenhouse gases, fossil fuels, and climate change was put in writing and placed on the desk of the president of the United States. It was placed there by Daniel P. Moynihan, an adviser to President Richard Nixon. In a memo dated September 17, 1969, Moynihan reported to Nixon that "carbon dioxide in the atmosphere has the effect of a pane of glass in a greenhouse. The CO_2 content is normally in a stable cycle, but recently man has begun to introduce instability through the burning of fossil fuels."[21] (The oil and fossil fuel industries would later wage a counteroffensive to deny this information.) Moynihan's memo predicted the effect of burning fossil fuels on the earth: "CO_2 content will rise 25% by 2000. This could increase the average temperature near the earth's surface by 7 degrees Fahrenheit. This in turn could raise the level of the sea by 10 feet. Goodbye New York. Goodbye Washington, for that matter."[22]

But it was an oil spill on January 28, 1969, near the beautiful beaches of Southern California, that prompted Gaylord Nelson to begin holding teach-ins on the environment.[23] That spill, with over nine thousand gallons of crude oil per hour pouring into the Pacific Ocean, became the third worst environmental hazard in our history.

Young people, with the men in suit jackets, arrived in Southern California and held sit-ins on the sidewalks near the beach while officers stood by. Those teach-ins that raised awareness of environmental issues were the genesis of what we now celebrate as Earth Day, established on April 22, 1970, to recognize the negative effects of humans on the planet. It has become a global event, with over 200 million people in nearly 150 countries participating in some form of Earth Day protest, rally, petition, or community project. Earth Day marks the anniversary of the modern environmental movement. The date of April 22 was selected with college students in mind, as it falls between spring break and final exams for most colleges.

Organizations joined demonstrations against smoke and toxins spewing from the factories built by Industrial Age tycoons that had been harming millions of Americans for a century and a half. The opposing sides of the conflict, the commercial United States and the American idealists who held sit-ins, teach-ins, conferences, and demonstrations, were clearly delineated, with groups lobbying politicians and protesting corporations until Congress was forced to create government agencies to prevent the abuse of the environment. The result was President Nixon's establishment of the Environmental Protection Agency within the Department of the Interior in 1970. Subsequent federal legislation created the Endangered Species Act, Marine Mammal Protection Act, Toxic Substances Control Act, Resource Conservation and Recovery Act, Clean Air Act, Clean Water Act, and an initiative for environmental remediation known as the Superfund Program.

The momentum ebbed and flowed with the political times. Some environmental activists believed in confrontation, while others protested using civil disobedience with planned arrests but no violence. Pressure remained on government officials as heatwaves, floods, and fires from droughts devastated the country. The twentieth century logged the hottest days in the recorded history of the planet. National borders cannot contain a nation's pollution. Climate change affects the world. Over fifty years ago, the United Nations Environment Programme (UNEP) was founded to work with governments, civil society, the private sector, and other UN entities to address environmental challenges, from restoring the ozone layer to protecting the world's seas and promoting a green, inclusive economy. In 2016, the United Nations chose Earth Day as the day for the signing of the Paris Agreement on climate change, which has 175 signatory nations as of this writing.

Headquartered in Nairobi, Kenya, UNEP is the leading global environmental authority that sets the environmental agenda for the planet, promotes the prudent implementation of the environmental dimension of sustainable development within all the member states of the United Nations, and serves as an authoritative advocate for the global environment. Its mission is to provide leadership and encourage partnership in caring for the environment by inspiring, informing, and enabling nations and peoples to improve their quality of life without compromising that of future generations.

The United States is a member of the UNEP and signatory of the Paris Agreement. Although this type of document is a legal agreement, enforcement, as with other such agreements, happens through peer pressure from other nations, domestic protest, and political pressure in Congress. The Paris Agreement has become a political platform issue for presidents and a source of global criticism of the United States for falling short of its promises in the agreement. On November 4, 2020, the Trump administration withdrew the US from the Paris climate pact, sending a troubling message and triggering protests.[24] On his first day in office, January 20, 2020, President Joseph Biden signed the agreement, recommitting America to the Paris Agreement.[25]

GONE TOO FAR

The greenhouse effect would burn us all alive was the message behind his suicide by self-immolation. On April 14, 2018, David Buckel, an environmentalist and a civil rights lawyer, poured gasoline on himself and set himself on fire, taking his life by self-immolation. This drastic measure was meant to be his final act of protest, to use his death to bring attention to what was happening to the planet. "My early death by fossil fuel," he wrote in an email, "reflects what we are doing to ourselves."[26] This email was sent at 5:55 a.m. At 6:08 a.m., an emergency call was received by the New York City Police Department that a man was on fire. Buckel's death was considered the first known case in the United States of self-immolation to bring attention to climate change.

His climate change activism had included developing a small compost site in Brooklyn into one of the largest private such sites on the East Coast. But, as in his prior work for same-sex marriage, Buckel struggled with the sense of endlessly pushing for change and seeing no progress—and often seeing reversals. The Trump administration had called for an end to federal vehicle emissions policies, and conservatives planned to gut the Environmental Protection Agency.

There were no signs revealing the depth of Buckel's despair or why, despite its symbolic meaning, he would turn to such a horrifically painful measure as burning himself alive to send his climate change message. Neither Buckel's husband and partner of thirty-four years, Terry Kaelber, nor any family members, could recall what had caused him to reach a point of hopelessness about climate change that could lead to his suicide.[27]

He decided to die for the cause. It is unclear if Buckel knew the extent of pain he would sustain in choosing death by fire. But he was known as a meticulous and deliberate man. Perhaps he knew that if he had survived the fire, his self-inflicted burn wounds would have destroyed his flesh, causing hyperemia and then suppression of his immune system, which would predispose him to sepsis and multiple organ failure, all while experiencing excruciating pain.[28] He doused himself with enough gasoline to ensure death.

Perhaps the protest suicide of Thích Quang Duc, the Buddhist monk, who is said to have set himself afire to protest the Vietnam War, inspired Buckel's own self-immolation protest. Buckel had a deep interest in Buddhism, and he and Kaelber had traveled to Asia together. He also had two brothers who served tours in the Vietnam War. But Kaelber said there were no signs that Buckel was distraught.

Buckel's suicide letter shows a desperation simmering beneath the surface, a man frustrated by the lack of attention the environment received, especially climate change and the growing greenhouse effect. "Pollution ravages our planet," he wrote. "Most humans on the planet now breathe air made unhealthy by fossil fuels, and many die early deaths as a result."[29]

On Earth Day 2022, four years after Buckel's death, there was another protest suicide by self-immolation.[30] This time a man took his life by fire on the stairs of the US Supreme Court. His name was Wynn Bruce, a photographer and environmental activist. Two months earlier, the high court had heard *West Virginia v. Environmental Protection Agency*.[31] In the case, the Court was asked to limit the authority of the EPA to control pollution from power plants under the Clean Air Act. The existence of a conservative supermajority on the Court essentially assured a ruling in which limits would be placed on the agency.

Climate despair is affecting activists who are wrestling with making a difference during a time of wildfires, rising water levels, and unnatural weather conditions, and in many respects this is affecting the entire nation. This despair may have moved Wynn Bruce, who had suffered a brain injury as a teenager, to take his life. His Buddhist practice should not be seen as playing a role in his suicide. This incident is included because climate despair is said to have caused, on April 22, Wynn Bruce to join Buckel in becoming a sad part of climate change history.

Despite the message that Bruce's and Buckel's deaths sent, on May 25, 2023, the Supreme Court again ruled against the Environmental Protection Agency, this time in the case of *Sackett v. Environmental Protection Agency*. It was a decision with wide-ranging consequences. Michael and Chantell Sackett purchased property near Priest Lake, Idaho, in 2004, and began backfilling a lot in order to build their home. The EPA told the Sacketts that, because their property contained wetlands, backfilling the lot violated the Clean Water Act. In *Sackett v. EPA*, the Court ruled that the agency no longer had the power to regulate the pollution of bodies of water beyond those that have a "continuous surface connection" to adjacent bodies of water.[32]

The EPA had been able to regulate not just navigable waters but adjacent wetlands like marshes, berms, and swamps. The decision left environmentalists deeply disappointed, while shoring up the power of corporations to pollute waterways. *Sackett v. EPA* and *West Virginia v. EPA*, a 2022 case about the Clean Air Act, were dual losses for climate change advocates. Nevertheless, protesters must find ways to sustain their fighting spirit and hope for the future, because history teaches that progress is inevitably followed by retrenchment.

THE FUTURE SPEAKS

Nature proved willing to provide a beautiful September day for an international climate protest in Manhattan. On September 20, 2019, the largest climate demonstration in world history took place. Winona LaDuke was among the millions of adults, college students, and children who participated in the strike for climate change action. Some students received permission from their schools to miss school in order to hold or attend rallies; others who didn't receive permission boldly walked out of their classes. Between September 20 and 27, an estimated six million people across 150 countries demonstrated against climate change. Greta Thunberg, the sixteen-year-old Swedish climate activist phenom, led this global demonstration from New York City.[33]

Media around the world heralded the massive size of the strike and the young people who championed it. It came a few days before the United Nations Climate Action Summit held at the UN headquarters. Across the United States, tens of thousands of demonstrators participated in a wave of strikes in more than one thousand locations, with rallies in New York, Washington, DC, Boston, Chicago, San Francisco, and Miami.[34] Young people have taken an active stand to protect their futures.

YOUNG PERSPECTIVES ON CLIMATE ACTIVISM

He was frightened at first, but as a high school student Michael Waxman led his own climate strike in 2019 in Scarsdale, a suburb of New York City. The twenty-one-year-old climate activist, now at Harvard University, helped create an organization at the school that brought dozens of climate activists together. He said in an interview that climate crisis issues were brought to his attention during a school icebreaker activity that predicted the end of the world. He was shocked but decided that rather than wallow in climate despair, he would take a role in making change happen. Waxman believes that every single action matters and every single ton of carbon that is prevented from entering the atmosphere makes a difference, which gives him hope—a sense that the glass is half full.[35]

He also believes that scare tactics in the climate movement can create a sense of hopelessness and stifle action. "My first protest wasn't the climate one," he said. "It was the March for Our Lives, in my freshman year of high school, after the Parkland school mass shooting. It was part of a National Day of Action, specifically through strikes." Waxman was given an opportunity to speak on behalf of a student who had been killed in the Parkland shooting. "Representing a kid my age in this way was challenging, but it was empowering to see all these students going out on strike."

Waxman found going to different climate strikes exciting and empowering. "Hundreds of people from different universities and residents from Boston came together with great music, speeches and big emotions, ending with a march to City Hall, holding posters, and chanting." He has participated in dozens of protests, each of which has had a unique mix of music and speeches from community leaders, faith leaders, and young people, some of whom have become his dear friends. At Harvard, he did not see a vibrant climate change scene and decided to be proactive, taking a job as a climate awareness educator.

A demonstration march represents a unique gathering of human beings, but Waxman knows activism needs all talents and personalities. His personality befits a speaker and organizer; he is aware that not everyone will take to the street for a demonstration. He suggests that if you like the written word, then "write about what you're feeling, write about what's going on around you. Draw and paint about it. Some museums are so incredibly moving in terms of social justice. There's always a way to intersect your passions." He finds protests and rallies empowering because they demonstrate the power of community and are opportunities to meet people with similar views and feelings. "It leaves you with something special." Activism only requires one to see a problem and to decide to act and not acquiesce. Protest means not only being discontented, but acting on that discontentment and voicing it, whether in anger, frustration, or sadness. "Doing it with other people is a feeling of being part of something greater than yourself. And doing nothing is easy, but living with the regret of doing nothing is hard."

CONCLUSION

Opposition to climate policy and climate denial can be legal, political, or personal. The conservatives who make up the Supreme Court's supermajority have not shown themselves to be neutral on environmental issues. Associate Justice Amy Coney Barrett, who was nominated by Donald Trump, wrote her first majority opinion assailing the Sierra Club, a Colorado-based environmentalist group, weakening the Freedom of Information Act, an investigative tool relied on by journalists, writers, lawyers, and activists who wish to gain access to government documents. However, Noam Chomsky, the elder statesman of public intellectualism who has used his international platform and brilliance to advocate for the working people, wrote a plan, with renowned economist Robert Pollin, that is not just a road map of catastrophic consequences of unchecked climate change but a practical blueprint for change known as the Global Green New Deal. There must be a balance of plans, because the geopolitical concerns and obstacles are multilayered.

It will take generations of activists, broadly varied in age, working together worldwide for us to avert further damage to our planet and, ultimately, ourselves. Unity is, and remains, the most powerful tool against the naysayers, politically connected polluters, and conservative-dominated courts. History has shown that there is power within one's personal span of influence. It is an intergenerational struggle, but the protection of our land, water, air, and wildlife is worthy of all who are willing to step forward for the greater good—the future.

They persevered. After my meeting with the Choctaw, as I was driving away under the crystal-blue skies of Mississippi, I felt dismayed. It was my first environmental racism case, and I was deeply disappointed about the options left for the Choctaw. But, in the end, they held out against the plans for the toxic waste site, despite conflicts that took years to resolve and a desperate need for economic assistance. They stayed true to their beliefs and their spiritual connection to the natural world. A report titled *The Toxic Threat to Indian Lands* exposed corporate attempts to place waste facilities on Indigenous lands, but it was inspiring to read "Choctaw Tribe in Mississippi recently rejected a hazardous waste dump on their land."[36]

Although the tribal chairman had supported the proposed incinerator, tribal members voted the project down."[37] Today, instead of a toxic waste dump on Choctaw land, the community has a thriving gaming industry that has attracted hotels and jobs. It has helped the Choctaws advance their economy without them selling out future generations by contaminating their land. These types of struggles need to be fought endlessly, because the forces of earth's destruction for profit will not yield without resistance. The original stewards of the land and the young who are trying their best to correct generations of damage must come together.

Meanwhile, just as in Greenwood in Tulsa, Oklahoma, and many other communities across America, in Kansas City, Missouri, highways were constructed in predominately African American communities. In

Kansas City, a ten-mile highway now facilitates White-flight suburbanites commuting to their offices downtown. Plans were first made in 1951. There were protests and objections, but powerbrokers, politicians, and legal manipulations finally achieved their objective in 2001. The highway, with its eighty thousand cars per day, tore apart a community, and today drivers speed along US Highway 71, leaving in their wake exhaust fumes and other carcinogens, tire dust, noise, litter, destroyed businesses, accidents at the three intersections that allow cars to connect to the other side of the highway, and disrupted families. It is another instance of urban renewal, or "racial removal," but protests continue against this development and its negative consequences, in terms of environmental and health impacts, damage to businesses, and declining home values.

And, on the plains of Kansas, my cousin, the one who held the photo between the gravestones of Eliza's Kentucky enslavers, is teaching her two daughters traditional Indigenous customs—in particular, how to care for their land. My cousin is the daughter of a Bradshaw and of an Indigenous mother. She has kept the family history alive, updating research on Eliza, Mattie, Birdia, Cora, and William Bradshaw while learning about her own roots as a Haliwa-Saponi member of the Saponi Nation of Ohio, working with local Indigenous communities, raising five sheep on her homestead, and planting ancestral corn.

Her little girls are being taught the history of both their Bradshaw and Indigenous grandparents. We have to invest in our children, give them a sense of history, freedom, and choices beyond any we have experienced. Unselfishly, we must all work to give America's children a nation better than the one we have, as our ancestors did for us.

The United States of America has come far. July 4, 2026, marks the two-hundred-and-fiftieth anniversary of a conflicted nation. Throughout US history there have been protests that have compelled this country into being a more perfect union despite its commercial nature. Protesters made the words "equal justice under law" more than a hollow slogan and challenged those who led the US empire to give substance to American idealism. Protesters will not rest until liberty rings for all people in the United States of America. Progress in the United States of America was made by regular people using resistance, rebellion, and activism.

Obstacles may shift and forces form to seemingly block the sun, but history shows that while these obstacles may be formidable, they are not intractable. Progress will continue as long as voices rise and people stand shoulder to shoulder as part of a cause bigger than themselves, using creativity and tenacity, envisioning the change they wish to have, and then pushing for it. Faith is protest. Hope in one's ability to make the world a better place is protest. Because protest, in large and small ways, can change the world.

ACKNOWLEDGMENTS

I am so pleased to have had the assistance of family, friends, colleagues, librarians, and scholars from across the country. Since a project that intertwines history with memoir relies on hundreds of people, I ask for forgiveness in advance for any omissions here. My cousins tirelessly clarified centuries of family history and legacy as descendants of Exodusters. I am grateful to my Bradshaw family. Thank you, Kim E. Andrews; Gerri Harvey; Susan Bradshaw, MD; Rev. Terry Bradshaw; Paula Thompson; and Crystal Bradshaw-Gonzalez.

Thank you, Dr. Andrew Smallwood, for your encouragement, wise feedback, and historical insights throughout this project. Friendships and kind words of support are invaluable with a project as lengthy as this one, spent in solitary rooms, traveling to libraries, researching in archives, and rewriting. Thank you, Jawan Finley, Denise Davis-Cotton, and the REACH/PAInT scholars, Jesse Holland, Nadia Fattah, Mary Sims, Barbara Spencer-Dunn (and the entire Dunn family), Lisa Galloway, Gail Garfield, Bobby Field, Brenda McLaughin, Wayne Dawkins, Michelle James, Sharifa Sena, Vivian Fisher, Kim Westcott, Audrey Peterson, Angela Dodson, Brian Baughan, and the wonderfully talented Cinelle Barnes. Thank you to my interviewees for giving their time, insights, and decades of activism: Gloria Steinem, Judith LeBlanc, Frank Smith, Christian F. Nunes, Howard Morland, Margo Jefferson, Michael Greenberg, Zadie Smith, and Lawrence Hamm. I am grateful to my agent, Jennifer Lyons, and to Gayatri Patnaik and managing editor Susan Lumenello, my brilliant, gracious, and patient editors, as well as all the hardworking and gifted members of Beacon Press.

Thank you, Lighthouse Writers Workshop (Denver), for supporting an interdisciplinary writer of nonfiction, fiction, and theater. My deep gratitude is extended to William Haywood Henderson, Andrea

Dupree, Shana Kelly, Amitava Kumar, and my 2023 writing cohort: Kate Livingston, Tochukwu Okafor, James Miller, Sally Rainey, and Maria St. Louis-Sanchez. A writer is guided by a spiritual mentor, and mine is James Baldwin, a light traveling along my path as a writer, activist, and artist. My elders Dr. Adelaide Sanford and Betty Dopson are North Stars. It is a gift to be able to engage in the worlds of writing, law, education, theater, media, and journalism as a proud African American and woman. To God be the glory.

I appreciate the Office for the Advancement of Research at John Jay College (CUNY) for the funding and encouragement of my scholarly goals, books, and research travel. Assistance from librarians, archivists, and docents is essential to any nonfiction writer, and excellent care was given to me at the National Museum of African American History and Culture, the National Archives, the Library of Congress, and the African American Civil War Museum in Washington, DC; the National Civil Rights Museum in Memphis; the National Archives of Angola; the Mine Wars Museum and the Harpers Ferry National Historical Park in West Virginia; the Schomburg Center for Research in Black Culture and the John Brown Farm Historic Site and Museum in New York; the Enoch Pratt Free Library in Baltimore; the Essex County Courthouse in New Jersey; and the Little Bighorn Battlefield National Monument in Montana. My work was supported by writing residencies at Craigardan and John Brown Lives! in New York, and La Baldi and Bread Loaf (Sicily) in Italy.

NOTES

AUTHOR'S NOTE

1. See Gloria J. Browne-Marshall, *Race, Law, and American Society: 1607 to Present* (New York: Routledge, 2013); Gloria J. Browne-Marshall, *The Voting Rights War: The NAACP and the Ongoing Struggle for Justice* (New York: Rowman & Littlefield, 2016); Gloria J. Browne-Marshall, *She Took Justice: The Black Woman, Law, and Power* (New York: Routledge, 2021); Gloria J. Browne-Marshall, *SHOT: Caught A Soul* (New York: TRW, 2023).

2. 2 Timothy 4:7 (New King James Version).

INTRODUCTION

3. From Martin Luther King Jr., from "I've Been to the Mountaintop," address delivered at Bishop Charles Mason Temple, Apr. 3, 1968, available at https://kinginstitute.stanford.edu/.

CHAPTER ONE: INDIGENOUS DEFENSE OF LAND, LIFE, AND CULTURE

1. This translation of the Mohawk version of the Haudenosaunee Thanksgiving Address was published in 1993 and provided courtesy of the Six Nations Indian Museum and the Tracking Project. All rights reserved. "Thanksgiving Address: Greetings to the Natural World," https://americanindian.si.edu/environment/pdf/01_02_Thanksgiving_Address.pdf. English version: John Stokes and Kanawahienton (David Benedict, Turtle Clan/Mohawk); Mohawk version: Rokwaho (Dan Thompson, Wolf Clan/Mohawk); original inspiration: Tekaronianekon (Jake Swamp, Wolf Clan/Mohawk).

2. Winona LaDuke is an Anishinaabekwe (Ojibwe) enrolled member of the Mississippi Band Anishinaabeg. Winona LaDuke, *All Our Relations: Native Struggles for Land and Life* (Chicago: Haymarket Books, 2016); Winona LaDuke, *The Winona LaDuke Chronicles: Stories from the Front Line* (Ponsford, MN: Spotted Horse Press, 2016).

3. Ned Blackhawk, *The Rediscovery of America: Native Peoples and the Unmaking of U.S. History* (New Haven, CT: Yale Univ. Press, 2023), 345–46.

4. Eric Foner, *Free Soil, Free Labor, Free Men: The Ideology of the Republican Party Before the Civil War* (New York: Oxford Univ. Press, 1995).

5. Blackhawk, *The Rediscovery of America*.

6. Kyle T. Mays, *Afro-Indigenous History of the United States* (Boston: Beacon Press, 2021).

7. Blackhawk, *The Rediscovery of America.*

8. See Lindsay G. Robertson, *Conquest of Law: How the Discovery of America Dispossessed Indigenous Peoples of their Lands* (New York: Oxford Univ. Press, 2007).

9. Blackhawk, *The Rediscovery of America.*

10. Roxanne Dunbar-Ortiz, *An Indigenous Peoples' History of the United States* (Boston: Beacon Press, 2014), 3.

11. For examples of Indigenous enslavement, see Blackhawk, *The Rediscovery of America*, 70–71, 123; Alan Gallay, *The Indian Slave Trade: The Rise of the English Empire in the American South, 1670–1717* (New Haven, CT: Yale Univ. Press, 2002).

12. David J. Hacker and Michael R. Haines, "American Indian Mortality in the Late Nineteenth Century: The Impact of Federal Assimilation Policies on a Vulnerable Population," *Annales de démographie historique* 2, no. 110 (2005): 17–29. https://www.cairn.info/revue-annales-de-demographie-historique-2005 -2-page-17.htm.

13. "Indians A.D. 1600-1800," Virginia Department of Historic Resources, Jan. 17, 2017, https://www.dhr.virginia.gov/blog-posts/indians-a-d-1600-1800/.

14. Mark Cartwright, "James I of England," *World History Encyclopedia*, Apr. 28, 2021, https://www.worldhistory.org/James_I_of_England/.

15. "Columbus Reports on His First Voyage, 1493," available at the Gilder Lehrman Institute of American History website, www.gilderlehrman.org.

16. James Horn, *A Land as God Made It: Jamestown and the Birth of America* (New York: Basic Books, 2006).

17. "The Bull Romanus Pontifex (Nicholas V), January 8, 1455," https:// www.papalencyclicals.net/nicholo5/romanus-pontifex.htm; Pope Alexander VI's Demarcation Bull, May 4, 1493, Gilder Lehrman Collection, GLC04093, accessed June 20, 2024.

18. His name has also been spelled Wahunsenacawh and Wahunsenacock.

19. Martha W. McCartney, "Chapter 4: Narrative History," in *Colonial: A Study of Virginia Indians and Jamestown: The First Century,* National Park Service, https://www.nps.gov/parkhistory/online_books/jame1/moretti-langholtz /chap4.htm, accessed July 3, 2024.

20. See Dunbar-Ortiz, *An Indigenous Peoples' History of the United States.*

21. Virginia Center for Digital History, "Monacans: Documentary Evidence," http://www.vcdh.virginia.edu/lewisandclark/students/projects/monacans /Documentary_Evidence/jsmap.html, accessed June 29, 2024.

22. *John Smith's Map of Virginia: A Closer Look.* Captain John Smith Chesapeake National Historic Trail, https://www.nps.gov/articles/000/smith -map-of-virginia.htm, accessed June 30, 2024. "This map of Virginia, made in 1608 by John Smith, is one of the earliest known maps of the area. Oriented with north towards the right of the map, much of Virginia west of the fall line through Richmond was drawn based entirely on reports of Powhatan Indians, rather than travels of Smith himself."

23. Alden T. Vaughan, "'Expulsion of the Savages': English Policy and the Virginia Massacre of 1622," *William and Mary Quarterly* 35, no. 1 (Jan. 1978): 57–84.

24. Joseph Stromberg, "Starving Settlers in Jamestown Colony Resorted to Cannibalism," *Smithsonian Magazine*, Apr. 30, 2013, https://www.smithsonian mag.com/history/starving-settlers-in-jamestown-colony-resorted-to-cannibalism -46000815/.

25. James Horn, *Jane: Starvation, Cannibalism, and Endurance at Jamestown* (Williamsburg: Colonial Williamsburg Foundation/Preservation Virginia, 2013), 53.

26. John Smith, "Video Transcript: Quotes from the Jamestown Settlers," https://naturalhistory.si.edu/sites/default/files/media/file/videotranscriptquotes fromthejamestownsettlersfinal.pdf, accessed May 12, 2023.

27. Smith, "Video Transcript."

28. George Percy, "Video Transcript: Quotes from the Jamestown Settlers," https://naturalhistory.si.edu/sites/default/files/media/file/videotranscriptquotes fromthejamestownsettlersfinal.pdf, accessed May 12, 2023.

29. Camilla Townsend, *Pocahontas and the Powhatan Dilemma* (New York: Hill and Wang, 2005); Jackie Mansky, "The True Story of Pocahontas Is More Complicated Than You Might Think," *Smithsonian Magazine*, originally published Mar. 23, 2017, updated Feb. 20, 2024, https://www.smithsonianmag .com/history/true-story-pocahontas-more-complicated-than-you-might-think -180962649.

30. Townsend, *Pocahontas and the Powhatan Dilemma*.

31. Martha W. McCartney, "The Draft of York River in Virginia: An Artifact of the Seventeenth Century," *Southeastern Archaeology* 3 (Winter 1984): 97–110; McCartney, "Chapter 4: Narrative History."

32. "First Africans in Virginia," Fort Monroe National Monument, National Park Service, https://www.nps.gov/places/first-africans-in-virginia.htm.

33. Entry from April 4, 1623, in Susan Myra Kingsbury, ed., *Records of the Virginia Company, 1606–26*, vol. 4, *Miscellaneous Records*, Thomas Jefferson Papers, Series 8, Virginia Records Manuscripts, 1606–1737, http://hdl.loc.gov /loc.mss/mtj.mtjbib026606.

34. Aaryn Urell, "Mass Killings of Native Americans," Equal Justice Initiative, https://eji.org/news/history-racial-injustice-mass-killings-of-native-americans/, accessed June 8, 2023.

35. David Dixon, *Never Come to Peace Again: Pontiac's Uprising and the Fate of the British Empire in North America* (Norman: Univ. of Oklahoma Press, 2005).

36. Dunbar-Ortiz, *An Indigenous Peoples' History of the United States*.

37. Howard H. Peckham, *Pontiac and the Indian Uprising* (Princeton, NJ: Princeton Univ. Press, 1947).

38. Dixon, *Never Come to Peace Again*.

39. Peckham, *Pontiac and the Indian Uprising*; Detroit Historical Society, https://detroithistorical.org/, accessed June 20, 2024; see also Dunbar-Ortiz, *An Indigenous Peoples' History of the United States*.

40. City of Pontiac, "About Chief Pontiac," https://www.pontiac.mi.us/about /history/about_chief_pontiac.php, accessed May 17, 2023.

41. 5 Geo. 3c. 12, The Stamp Act of 1765.

42. "Declaration of Independence: A Transcription," https://www.archives .gov/founding-docs/declaration-transcript, accessed May 17, 2023.

43. Declaration of Independence.

44. Mike Lee, *Written Out of History: The Forgotten Founders Who Fought Big Government* (New York: Sentinel/Penguin, 2017).

45. See Stuart Banner, *How the Indians Lost Their Land: Law and Power on the Frontier* (Cambridge, MA: Harvard Univ. Press, 2005).

46. Treaty with the Delawares, 1778, Sept. 17, 1778, 7 Stat., 13.

47. Colin G. Calloway, *The American Revolution in Indian County: Crisis and Diversity in Native Communities*, Cambridge Studies in North American Indian History (New York: Cambridge Univ. Press, 1995).

48. Charles J. Kappler, ed., and comp., *Indian Affairs, Laws and Treaties*, vol. 2, *Treaties* (Washington, DC: Government Printing Office, 1904), https:// americanindian.si.edu/static/nationtonation/pdf/Treaty-with-the-Delawares -1778.pdf.

49. "An Act to Regulate Trade and Intercourse with the Indian Tribes and to Preserve Peace on the Frontiers," in *U.S. Statutes at Large. The Public Statutes at Large of the United States of America . . .*, 17 vols. (Boston: 1848–73), 1:469–74.

50. "To George Washington from the Seneca Chiefs, 1 December 1790," Founders Online, National Archives, https://founders.archives.gov/documents /Washington/05-07-02-0005. (Original source: *The Papers of George Washington*, Presidential Series, vol. 7, *1 December 1790–21 March 1791*, ed. Jack D. Warren, Jr. [Charlottesville: University Press of Virginia, 1998], 7–16), https://founders .archives.gov/documents/Washington/05-07-02-0005, accessed June 20, 2023.

51. This speech is titled "The Reply of the President of the United States, to the Speech of the Cornplanter, Half-town and Great-tree Chiefs and Counsellors of the Seneka Nation of Indians," https://founders.archives.gov/documents /Washington/05-07-02-0080, accessed June 15, 2024.

52. *Eighteenth Annual Report of the Bureau of Ethnology to the Secretary of the Smithsonian Institution 1896–1897* (Washington, DC: Government Printing Office), accessed June 3, 2023.

53. 4th Congress, 1st session: 1795–1796, *An act to regulate trade and intercourse with the Indian Tribes, and to preserve peace on the frontiers* (Philadelphia: Printed by Francis Childs, 1796), https://lccn.loc.gov/2020767673.

54. Johnson & Graham's Lessee v. William McIntosh, 21 U.S. 543 (1823).

55. *Johnson & Graham's Lessee v. McIntosh.*

56. *Johnson & Graham's Lessee v. McIntosh.*

57. See Robertson, *Conquest of Law.*

58. Cherokee Nation v. Georgia, 30 U.S. 1 (1831); Worcester v. Georgia, 31 U.S. 515 (1832).

59. *Cherokee Nation v. Georgia; Worcester v. Georgia.*

60. Ronald N. Satz, *American Indian Policy in the Jacksonian Era* (Norman: Univ. of Oklahoma Press, 2002); Anthony F. C. Wallace, *The Long Bitter Trail: Andrew Jackson and the Indians* (New York: Hill and Wang, 1993).

61. Satz, *American Indian Policy in the Jacksonian Era;* Wallace, *The Long Bitter Trail.*

62. See Harold D. Moser, David R. Hoth, Sharon Macpherson, and John Reinbold, eds., *The Papers of Andrew Jackson*, vol. 3, *1814–1815* (Knoxville: Univ. of Tennessee Press, 1991).

63. Dunbar-Ortiz, *An Indigenous Peoples' History of the United States*.

64. "Indian Removal Act: Primary Documents in American History," Research Guides, Library of Congress, https://guides.loc.gov/indian-removal-act, accessed May 20, 2023.

65. Indian Treaties and the Removal Act of 1830, quoted in "1830—The Indian Removal Act," Nottawaseppi Huron Band of the Potawatomi, https://nhbp-nsn.gov/timeline/the-indian-removal-act, accessed Mar. 29, 2024.

66. Statutes at Large, 21st Congress, 1st Session, Ch. 148, 1830.

67. Dunbar-Ortiz, *An Indigenous Peoples' History of the United States*.

68. Martin Van Buren, "December 3, 1838: Second Annual Message to Congress," Miller Center, University of Virginia, accessed July 3, 2024.

69. R. A. Smith, *Moon of the Popping Tree: The Tragedy at Wounded Knee and the End of the Indian Wars* (Lincoln: Univ. of Nebraska Press, 1981), 160–61.

70. Smith, *Moon of the Popping Tree*, 160–61.

71. Lillian Sparks, "Preserving Native Languages: No Time to Waste," Administration for American Indians, https://www.acf.hhs.gov/archive/ana/preserving-native-languages-article, accessed June 4, 2023.

72. See *Annual Report of the Commissioner of Indian Affairs to the Secretary of the Interior* (Washington, DC: Government Printing Office, 1886).

73. Official Report of the Nineteenth Annual Conference of Charities and Correction (1892), 46–59. Reprinted in Richard H. Pratt, "The Advantages of Mingling Indians with Whites," *Americanizing the American Indians: Writings by the "Friends of the Indian," 1880–1900*, ed. Francis Paul Prucha (Cambridge, MA: Harvard Univ. Press, 1973), 260–71.

74. Repealed by Cal. Stats., c. 737, Sec. 1. 1947.

75. In the matter of the Adoption of John Doe v. Heim, 89 N.M. 606 (1976).

76. Troy Johnson, "The Occupation of Alcatraz Island: Roots of American Indian Activism," *Wicazo Sa Review* 10, no. 2 (1994): 63–79, https://doi.org/10.2307/1409133.

77. See "Alcatraz Island," *Britannica*, last updated June 17, 2024, https://www.britannica.com/place/Alcatraz-Island.

78. Casey Ryan Kelly, "Détournement, Decolonization, and the American Indian Occupation of Alcatraz Island (1969–1971)," *Rhetoric Society Quarterly* 44, no. 2 (2014): 168–90, http://www.jstor.org/stable/24753612.

79. There had been previous attempts on Mar. 9, 1964, and Nov. 9, 1969. Rhiannon Bertaud-Gandar, "Laying Claim: Framing the Occupation of Alcatraz in the Indians of 'All Tribes Alcatraz Newsletter,'" *Australasian Journal of American Studies* 35, no. 1 (2016): 125–42, http://www.jstor.org/stable/44779774.

80. Troy Johnson, "We Hold the Rock: The Alcatraz Indian Occupation," Alcatraz Island, National Park Service, https://www.nps.gov/alca/learn/history culture/we-hold-the-rock.htm, last updated Apr. 10, 2024.

81. Johnson, "We Hold the Rock."

82. Howard Zinn, *A People's History of the United States* (New York: Harper Perennial, 2015), 527–29.

83. Bertaud-Gandar, "Laying Claim," 125–42.

84. Kelly, "Détournement, Decolonization, and the American Indian Occupation of Alcatraz Island," 168–90.

85. Johnson, "The Occupation of Alcatraz Island," 63–79.

86. "The Trail of Broken Treaties, 1972," National Park Service, https://www.nps.gov/articles/000/trail-of-broken-treaties.htm, accessed July 3, 2024.

87. LaDuke, *The Winona LaDuke Chronicles*, 105.

88. See Leonard Peltier, *Prison Writings: My Life Is My Sun Dance* (New York: St. Martin's Griffin, 2000); Peter Matthiessen, *In the Spirit of Crazy Horse: The Story of Leonard Peltier and the FBI's War on the American Indian Movement* (New York: Penguin Books, 1992); Gloria J. Browne-Marshall, *Race, Law, and American Society: 1607–Present* (New York City: Routledge, 2013), 136.

89. American Community Survey, "Poverty Status in the Past 12 Months by Sex by Age," US Census Bureau, https://data.census.gov/table/ACSDT1Y2022.B17001?mode=results, accessed June 2, 2023.

90. United States v. Sandoval, 231 U.S. 31 (1913).

91. Blackhawk, *The Rediscovery of America*; Jake Page, *Uprising: The Pueblo Indians and the First American War for Religious Freedom* (Tucson, AZ: Rio Nuevo Publishers, 2013).

92. *United States v. Sandoval.*

93. "The Start and Growth of Alcoholics Anonymous," Alcoholics Anonymous, https://www.aa.org/the-start-and-growth-of-aa, accessed May 20, 2023.

94. IAIA.edu, accessed July 15, 2024.

95. United States v. Sioux Nation of Indians, 448 U.S. 371, 372 (1980).

96. Fort Laramie Treaty of 1868.

97. *United States v. Sioux Nation of Indians.*

98. *United States v. Sioux Nation of Indians.*

99. Quoting US Army Corps of Engineers, Environmental Assessment: Dakota Access Pipeline Project 6 (2016), https://usace.contentdm.oclc.org/digital/collection/p16021coll7/id/2801.

100. Standing Rock Sioux Tribe v. U.S. Army Corps of Eng'rs (Standing Rock VII), 471 F. Supp. 3d. 71, 77–78 (D.D.C. 2020).

101. Author interview with Judith LeBlanc, May 19, 2023. She agreed to have her interview edited.

102. Quoted in LaDuke, *The Winona LaDuke Chronicles*, 81.

103. "Message from the Peabody Director," Peabody Museum of Archaeology & Ethnology, Harvard University, Nov. 10, 2022, https://peabody.harvard.edu/news/message-peabody-director.

104. "Message from the Peabody Director."

105. Pro-Football, Inc. v. Harjo, 415 F. 3d. 44 (D.C. Cir. 2005).

106. LaDuke, *The Winona LaDuke Chronicles*, 253.

107. For an exemplary examination of Indigenous resistance, see Dunbar-Ortiz, *An Indigenous Peoples' History of the United States.*

CHAPTER TWO: "WHAT TO THE SLAVE IS THE FOURTH OF JULY?"

1. F. G. Adams, "The Hodgeman Colored Colony," *Hodgeman Agitator*, Hodgeman Center, May 17, 1879, quoted in *Kansas History: A Journal of the Central Plains* 26 (Summer 2003): 108–13.

2. Gregory D. Smithers, *Slave Breeding: Sex, Violence, and Memory in African American History* (Gainesville: Univ. of Florida Press, 2013).

3. Bailey v. Poindexter, 55 Va. 132 (Va. 1858).

4. Mattie Bradshaw and Sam Dicks, "Eliza Bradshaw: An Exoduster Grandmother," *Kansas History* 26, no. 2 (Summer 2003): 106–11, Missouri Valley Special Collections, Kansas City Public Library, Kansas City, MO.

5. Adams, "The Hodgeman Colored Colony." This article originally appeared in the *Boston Journal* and elsewhere, variously titled, in the *Topeka Daily Commonwealth*, May 7, 1879; *Fordham Republican*, June 11 and 18, 1879; and in other Kansas newspapers. Adams provides March 24, 1878, as the date that a party of 107 from Harrodsburg and Lexington, Kentucky, arrived in Kinsley, Kansas. A few years earlier, in 1877, a small advance party had been selected to choose a location, and "additions have since been made in the number of about 60." The Bradshaw family most likely was among these sixty, because Mattie's article suggests early 1879 as the time of their arrival. Another source gives April 1879 as the date that George Washington Bradshaw (Mattie's uncle) and several others arrived. (H. C. Norman, "History of Hodgeman County Kansas," manuscript, Library and Archives Division, Kansas State Historical Society, 1941, p. 3). The listings of ages and places of birth of the children in the 1880, 1885, and later censuses also corroborate 1879 as the year of arrival. See US Census, 1880, Hodgeman County, Center Township; Kansas State Census, 1885, Hodgeman County, Center Township.

6. C. Robert Haywood, "The Hodgeman County Colony," *Kansas History* (Winter 1989): 210–22, https://www.kshs.org.

7. Haywood, "The Hodgeman County Colony," 210.

8. "Articles, Laws, and Orders, Divine, Politique, and Martiall . . . ," *Lawes Divine, Morall and Martiall for the Colony of Virginea*, http://moglen.law .columbia.edu/ALH/lawesdivine.pdf, accessed May 15, 2023.

9. William Waller Hening, *Statutes at Large; Being a Collection of All of the Laws of Virginia*, vol. 1 (Richmond, VA: Samuel Pleasants, 1809–23).

10. William Waller Hening, *Statutes at Large; Being a Collection of All of the Laws of Virginia*, vol. 2 (New York: R. & W. & G. Bartow, 1823), 170, 260, 266, 270.

11. Chapter XXIII (1705) in William Waller Hening, *Statutes at Large; Being a Collection of All of the Laws of Virginia*, vol. 3, sec. 34 (New York: R. & W. & G. Bartow, 1823), 459; A. Leon Higginbotham, *In the Matter of Color: Race and the American Legal Process* (New York: Oxford Univ. Press, 1978), 55.

12. Nathaniel Bacon, "Declaration of Nathaniel Bacon in the Name of the People of Virginia, July 30, 1676," Massachusetts Historical Society Collections, 4th ser., 1871, vol. 9: 184–87.

13. Herbert Aptheker, *American Negro Slave Revolts*, 5th ed. (New York: International Publishers, 2021).

14. Frederick Douglass, speech at the 23rd West India Emancipation celebration, Canandaigua, New York, Aug. 3, 1857.

15. Frederick Douglass, *The Life and Times of Frederick Douglass* (Hartford, CT: Park, 1881).

16. David Blight, *Frederick Douglass: Prophet of Freedom* (New York: Simon and Schuster, 2018), 13.

17. Frederick Douglass, *Narrative of the Life of Frederick Douglass, an American Slave* (1845; repr., Chapel Hill: Univ. of North Carolina, 1999), 33.

18. Douglass, *Narrative of the Life of Frederick Douglass*.

19. Higginbotham, *In the Matter of Color*, 258.

20. Higginbotham, *In the Matter of Color*, 10.

21. "A Nation's Story: 'What to the Slave Is the Fourth of July?'" National Museum of African American History and Culture, https://nmaahc.si.edu /explore/stories/nations-story-what-slave-fourth-july, accessed July 12, 2024.

22. "A Nation's Story: 'What to the Slave Is the Fourth of July?'" National Museum of African American History and Culture.

23. Francis Ellen Watkins, "Bury Me in a Free Land," *Anti-Slavery Bugle*, Nov. 20, 1858.

24. Dorothy B. Porter, "The Organized Education Activities of Negro Literary Societies," *Journal of Negro Education* 5, no. 4 (Oct. 1936): 555–76.

25. Nikki Taylor, *Brooding over Bloody Revenge: Enslaved Women's Lethal Resistance* (New York City: Cambridge Univ. Press, 2023), 50–51.

26. David W. Blight, *A Slave No More: Two Men Who Escaped to Freedom* (New York: Amistad, 2009).

27. Thomas Cooper and David V. McCord, eds., *The Statutes at Large of South Carolina*, vol. 7 (Columbia, SC: A. S. Johnson, 1830–41), 357, 359–60; Higginbotham, *In the Matter of Color*, 177.

28. Cooper and McCord, *Statutes at Large of South Carolina*, vol. 7, 360; Higginbotham, *In the Matter of Color*, 177.

29. "The New York Conspiracy of 1741," Gilder Lehrman Institute of American History, 2013, https://www.gilderlehrman.org/sites/default/files/inline -pdfs/fin.04205_FPS.pdf, accessed July 1, 2023.

30. Peter Linebaugh and Marcus Rediker, "The Outcasts of the Earth," in Linebaugh and Rediker, *The Many-Headed Hydra: The Hidden History of the Revolutionary Atlantic* (Boston: Beacon Press, 2000).

31. Linebaugh and Rediker, "The Outcasts of the Earth."

32. "The New York Conspiracy of 1741."

33. "The New York Conspiracy of 1741."

34. Herbert Aptheker, *A Documentary History of the Negro People in the United States: From Colonial Times Through the Civil War* (New York: Citadel, 1951), 194.

35. For more information on Toussaint L'Ouverture, see C. L. R. James, *The African American Jacobins: Toussaint L'Ouverture and the San Domingo Revolution* (New York: Vintage Books, 1963).

36. Higginbotham, *In the Matter of Color*, 192–95; Herbert Aptheker, *American Negro Slave Revolts* (New York: International Publishers, 1943).

37. Albert Thrasher, *"On to New Orleans!" Louisiana's Heroic 1811 Slave Revolt* (New Orleans: Cypress Press, 1996); Daniel Rasmussen, *American Uprising: The Untold Story of America's Largest Slave Revolt* (New York: Harper Perennial, 2012); Rebecca Hall, *Wake: The Hidden History of Women-Led Slave Revolts* (New York: Penguin/Particular Books, 2021).

38. Negro Act of 1740, in Cooper and McCord, *Statutes at Large of South Carolina*.

39. Higginbotham, *In the Matter of Color*, 192–95.

40. Edward A. Pearson, *Designs Against Charleston: The Trial Record of the Denmark Vesey Slave Conspiracy of 1822* (Chapel Hill: Univ. of North Carolina, 1999), 23.

41. E. Franklin Frazier, *The Negro in the United States* (New York: Macmillan, 1957), 88.

42. Frazier, *The Negro in the United States*, 88.

43. Edward A. Pearson, *Designs Against Charleston: The Trial Record of the Denmark Vesey Slave Conspiracy of 1822* (Chapel Hill: Univ. of North Carolina, 1999), 135.

44. Pearson, *Designs Against Charleston*, 17–18.

45. See John Killens, introduction to *The Trial Record of Denmark Vesey* (Boston: Beacon Press, 1970); Aptheker, *American Negro Slave Revolts*.

46. Frazier, *The Negro in the United States*, 88.

47. Pearson, *Designs Against Charleston*, 134–35.

48. See *The Trial Record of Denmark Vesey*, 135–37; Aptheker, *American Negro Slave Revolts*.

49. Pearson, *Designs Against Charleston*, 165.

50. Pearson, *Designs Against Charleston*, 165.

51. Pearson, *Designs Against Charleston*, 165.

52. Pearson, *Designs Against Charleston*, 279.

53. Frazier, *The Negro in the United States*, 88.

54. See *The Trial Record of Denmark Vesey*; Frazier, *The Negro in the United States*, 88. The number of co-conspirators has varied.

55. Frazier, *The Negro in the United States*, 88.

56. See Nat Turner, *The Confessions of Nat Turner, the Leader of the Late Insurrection in Southampton, Va. as Fully and Voluntarily Made to Thomas R. Gray* (Baltimore: Thomas R. Gray, 1831), https://docsouth.unc.edu/neh/turner/turner.html.

57. Turner, *Confessions of Nat Turner*.

58. Turner, *Confessions of Nat Turner*.

59. Turner, *Confessions of Nat Turner*.

60. Turner, *Confessions of Nat Turner*.

61. Turner, *Confessions of Nat Turner*.

62. Turner, *Confessions of Nat Turner*.

63. Turner, *Confessions of Nat Turner*.

64. *New York Evening Post*, Nov. 19, 1831; Aptheker, *American Negro Slave Revolts*, 302; Turner, *Confessions of Nat Turner*.

65. Daina Ramey Berry, "Nat Turner's Skull and My Student's Purse of Skin," op-ed, *New York Times*, Oct. 18, 2016; Daina Ramey Berry, *The Price for Their Pound of Flesh: The Value of the Enslaved, from Womb to Grave, in the Building of a Nation* (Boston: Beacon Press, 2017).

66. *New York Times*, July 21, 1860, https://www.nytimes.com/1860/07/21/archives/obituary.html.

67. Aptheker, *American Negro Slave Revolts*, 302.

68. General Assembly of the State of Maryland, Annapolis, 1832, chapters 281, 325; see also Aptheker, *American Slave Negro Revolts*, 313.

69. *Acts Passed at a General Assembly of the Commonwealth of Virginia, Begun and Held at the Capitol, in the City of Richmond* (Richmond: Thomas Ritchie, 1832), 20.

70. General Assembly of the State of Maryland, Annapolis, 1832, chapters 281, 325.

71. *Acts Passed at a General Assembly of the Commonwealth of Virginia*, 20.

72. Frazier, *The Negro in the United States*, 90–91; *State of Missouri v. Celia, a Slave*, File 4496, Callaway County Court, October Term, 1855; DeNeen L. Brown, "*Missouri v. Celia*, a Slave: She Killed the White Master Raping Her, Then Claimed Self-Defense," *Washington Post*, Oct. 19, 2017.

73. Eugene L. Meyer, *Five for Freedom: The African American Soldiers in John Brown's Army* (Chicago: Lawrence Hill Books, 2018).

74. Taken from John Brown's statement at sentencing, Nov. 2, 1859. John Brown, "Address of John Brown to the Virginia Court . . . " Gilder Lehrman Collection, GLC05508.051, Dec. 1859.

75. Charles J. Poland Jr., *America's Good Terrorist: John Brown and the Harpers Ferry Raid* (Havertown, PA: Casemate Publishers, 2020), 182–83.

76. Tony Horwitz, *Midnight Rising: John Brown and the Raid That Sparked the Civil War* (New York: Picador, 2011), 252–55.

77. Poland, *America's Good Terrorist*, 254–55.

78. John Brown, "Final Words," John Brown Papers, Chicago Historical Society, box 1, folder 19, Related Papers, Franklin Benjamin Sanborn, 1857, lecture notes on John Brown, http://chsmedia.org/media/fa/fa/M-B/BrownJohn-inv.htm.

79. *Liberator*, Oct. 11, 1859; David S. Reynolds, *John Brown, Abolitionist: The Man Who Killed Slavery, Sparked the Civil War, and Seeded Civil Rights* (New York: Vintage, 2005), 339–40.

80. *New-York Tribune*, Oct. 28, 1859; Reynolds, *John Brown, Abolitionist*, 340.

81. Horwitz, *Midnight Rising*, 210.

82. "John Brown Lives!," https://johnbrownlives.org, accessed June 11, 2023.

83. Horwitz, *Midnight Rising*, 238–39.

84. Frances Ellen Watkins Harper, *Sketches of Southern Life* (Philadelphia: Ferguson Bros. & Co., 1888), available at Smithsonian Libraries and Archives, https://library.si.edu/donate/adopt-a-book/sketches-southern-life, accessed Apr. 2, 2024.

85. "William Lloyd Garrison," Boston National Historical Park, Boston African American National Historic Site, National Park Service, https://www.nps.gov/people/william-lloyd-garrison.htm, accessed Nov. 14, 2023.

86. "William Lloyd Garrison."

87. Douglass spoke at the 23rd West India Emancipation celebration at Canandaigua, New York, Aug. 3, 1857.

88. *Slave Bible* (London: Law and Gilbert Publishing House, 1807); Anthony Schmidt interview "Slave Bible from the 1800s Omitted Key Passages That Could Incite Rebellion," NPR, Dec. 9, 2018, https://www.npr.org/2018/12 /09/674995075/slave-bible-from-the-1800s-omitted-key-passages-that-could -incite-rebellion; Va. Stat. 1682. Act III; Hening, *Statutes at Large*, vol. 2, 18.

89. Arthur Diamond, *European Masonic Congress Says Distinctions Between Races in Masonry Is Wrong* (New York: Livingston Library, 1912), 99.

90. Cécille Révauger, *Black Freemasonry: From Prince Hall to the Giants of Jazz* (Rochester, VT: Inner Traditions Publications, 2016).

91. Prince Hall et al., "Documents Relating to Negro Masonry in America," *Journal of Negro History* 21, no. 4 (1936): 411–32.

92. Révauger, *Black Freemasonry*.

93. Révauger, *Black Freemasonry*.

94. Révauger, *Black Freemasonry*, 242–43.

95. "Belinda Sutton's 1783 Petition," Royall House & Slave Quarters, https:// royallhouse.org/belinda-suttons-1783-petition-full-text, accessed Oct. 29, 2023.

96. "Belinda Sutton's 1783 Petition."

97. Petition to the Massachusetts Legislature, 1787; "Massachusetts Slavery and Segregation," Primary Research, https://primaryresearch.org/massachusetts -slavery-segregation/, accessed June 29, 2024.

98. "Massachusetts Slavery and Segregation."

99. Howard Zinn, *A People's History of the United States* (New York: Harper Perennial, 1999), 180.

100. J. N. Mars, John B. Smith, and B. B. Young, "Liberty or Death!" *The Liberator*, Oct. 4, 1850.

101. Zinn, *A People's History of the United States*, 24.

102. Aptheker, *American Negro Slave Revolts*, 75.

103. Proceedings and Acts of the General Assembly, 1717–April 1720, vol. 33, p. 111.

104. Dred Scott v. Sandford, 60 U.S. 393, 406 (1856).

105. Jon Meacham, *And There Was Light: Abraham Lincoln and the American Struggle* (New York: Random House, 2022).

106. General Order #3, Headquarters, District of Texas, Galveston, Texas, June 19, 1865, Issued by Order of Major General Granger, Juneteenth Order. https://catalog.archives.gov/id/182778372?objectPanel=transcription, accessed June 20, 2024. Emphasis added.

107. 39th Congress, 1st session, 14 Stat. 27 (1866).

108. US Const., Am. 14 (1868).

109. For further discussion of the debates leading to passage of the Fifteenth Amendment, see Daniel A. Farber and Suzanna Sherry, *A History of the American Constitution* (St. Paul, MN: Thomson/West, 2005), 455–87.

110. US Const., Am. 15 (1870).

111. Ku Klux Klan Act of April 20, 1871 (17 Stat. 13).

112. Civil Rights Cases, 109 U.S. 1 (1883).

113. Ida B. Wells-Barnett, *Crusade for Justice: The Autobiography of Ida B. Wells*, ed. Alfreda M. Duster (Chicago: Univ. of Chicago Press, 1970), 18–19.

114. Chesapeake & Ohio & Southwestern Railroad Company v. Wells, Tennessee Reports: Supreme Court of Tennessee for the Western Division, Jackson, April Term, 1887.

115. Wells-Barnett, *Crusade for Justice*, 20.

116. Wells-Barnett, *Crusade for Justice*, 20.

117. Charles Vincent, *Black Legislators in Louisiana During Reconstruction* (Urbana-Champaign: Southern Illinois Univ. Press, 2011).

118. Otto Olsen, *Carpetbagger's Crusade: The Life of Albion Winegar Tourgee* (Baltimore: Johns Hopkins University Press, 1965).

119. Plessy v. Ferguson, 163 U.S. 537, 560, 562 (1896).

120. *Kansas History* 26, no. 2 (Summer 2003): 108–13, citing F. G. Adams, "The Hodgeman Colored Colony," *Hodgeman Agitator* (Hodgeman Center), (May 17, 1879). This article originally appeared in the *Boston Journal* and with various titles in the *Topeka Daily Commonwealth*, May 7, 1879; *Fordham Republican*, June 11, 18; and in other Kansas newspapers. H. C. Norman, "History of Hodgeman County Kansas," manuscript, Library and Archives Division, Kansas State Historical Society, 1941, 3, gives April 1879 as the date that George Washington Bradshaw (Mattie's uncle) and several others arrived. See US Census, 1880, Hodgeman County, Center Township; Kansas State Census, 1885, Hodgeman County, Center Township.

121. *Kansas History* 26 (Summer 2003): 108–13.

122. Nell Painter, *Exodusters: Black Migration to Kansas After Reconstruction* (New York: Knopf, 1977).

CHAPTER THREE: LABOR RIGHTS AND UNION STRIKES

1. Walter F. Peterson, *An Industrial Heritage: Allis-Chalmers Corporation* (Milwaukee: Milwaukee County Historical Society, 1978); "Long Strike Ended at Allis-Chalmers; Workers Ratify New Contract Which Grants 18-Cent Rise and One-Week Vacations," *New York Times*, Oct. 18, 1946; "Allis-Chalmers Corporation," Encyclopedia of Milwaukee, https://emke.uwm.edu/entry/allis-chalmers-corporation, accessed Dec. 10, 2023.

2. Ron Chernow, *Titan: The Life of John D. Rockefeller Sr.* (New York: Random House, 1998).

3. Charles R. Morris, *The Tycoons: How Andrew Carnegie, John D. Rockefeller, Jay Gould, and J. P. Morgan Invented the American Supereconomy* (New York: Holt Books, 2006).

4. Chernow, *Titan*.

5. Walter Licht, *Industrializing America: The Nineteenth Century* (Baltimore: Johns Hopkins Univ. Press, 1995).

6. Mark Twain and Charles Dudley Warner, *The Gilded Age: A Tale of Today* (1873; repr., New York: Oxford Univ. Press, 1996).

7. Howard Zinn, *A People's History of the United States: 1492–Present*, rev. ed. (New York: New Press, 2003); Sean Dennis Cashman, *America in the Gilded Age: From the Death of Lincoln to the Rise of Theodore Roosevelt*, 3rd ed. (New York: New York Univ. Press, 1993).

8. John Smith apprenticeship indenture, August 3, 1799, box 524, MS 2014.7, John D. Rockefeller Jr. Library, Colonial Williamsburg Foundation, Williamsburg, VA.

9. Philip S. Foner, ed., *The Factory Girls: A Collection of Writings on Life and Struggles in the New England Factories of the 1840's* (Urbana: Univ. of Illinois Press, 1977); Daniel Walker Howe, *What Hath God Wrought: The Transformation of America, 1815–1845* (New York: Oxford Univ. Press, 2009).

10. Lori Merish, *Archives of Labor: Working-Class Women and Literary Culture in the Antebellum United States* (Durham, NC: Duke Univ. Press, 2017), 33–72.

11. Erik Loomis, *A History of America in Ten Strikes* (New York: The New Press, 2018), 19.

12. "Labor Reform: Early Strikes," Lowell (Massachusetts) National Historical Park, National Park Service, https://www.nps.gov/lowe/learn/history culture/earlystrikes.htm, accessed June 29, 2023.

13. "Labor Reform: Early Strikes."

14. "Labor Reform: Early Strikes."

15. Loomis, *A History of America in Ten Strikes*, 20.

16. "Preamble & Constitution of the Lowell Female Labor Reform Association History of Lowell," History of Lowell: Voice of Industry, Center for Lowell History, University of Massachusetts Lowell Library, https://libguides.uml.edu/c .php?g=528655&p=3615580, accessed June 29, 2023.

17. *Voice of Industry*, UML MICROFILM: May 1845–April 1848 scattered #5 7, Center for Lowell History, UMass Lowell Archives and Special Collections, University of Massachusetts Lowell Library; *Voice of Industry* (Fitchburg, Mass.) 1845–1848, vol. 1, no. 1 (May 29, 1845), v. 3, no. 40 (Apr. 14, 1848), published in Lowell, Mass., Nov. 7, 1845–Sept. 3, 1847; Boston, Mass., and Lowell, Mass: Sept. 10–Nov. 19, 1847; and Boston, Mass., Nov. 26, 1847–1848, https://www.loc.gov/item/sn84023802/, accessed June 20, 2024.

18. *Voice of Industry* masthead, Apr. 9, 1847, Center for Lowell History, University of Massachusetts Lowell Library.

19. "Lowell Female Industrial Reform and Mutual Aid Society," *Voice of Industry*, Jan. 8, 1847, History of Lowell: Voice of Industry, Center for Lowell History, University of Massachusetts Lowell Library, https://libguides.uml.edu/c .php?g=528655&p=3615703.

20. Benita Eisler, ed., *The Lowell Offering: Writings by New England Mill Women, 1840–1845* (Philadelphia: J. B. Lippincott, 1977); Thomas Dublin, "The Lowell Mills and the Countryside: The Social Origins of Women Factory Workers, 1830–1850," in *Essays from the Lowell Conference on Industrial History, 1980 and 1981*, ed. Robert Weible, Oliver Ford, and Paul Marion (Lowell, MA: Lowell Conference on Industrial History, 1981).

21. Ulysses S. Grant, "Proclamation Establishing Eight Hour Workday," May 19, 1869, https://millercenter.org/the-presidency/presidential-speeches /may-19-1869-proclamation-establishing-eight-hour-workday, accessed Nov. 1, 2023.

22. Grant, "Proclamation Establishing Eight Hour Workday."

23. Manu Karuka, *Empire's Tracks: Indigenous Nations, Chinese Workers, and the Transcontinental Railroad* (Oakland: Univ. of California Press, 2019), 72.

24. "Chinese-Americans 1785–: Demographics," Buley Library, Southern Connecticut State University, https://libguides.southernct.edu/c.php?g=15048 &p=81577, accessed July 9, 2024.

25. Chinese Exclusion Act, Chap. 220, Section 13, HeinOnline–23 Stat. 118, 1881–1885, 118 Forty-Eighth Congress. Sess. I., chs. 220, 221, 1884.

26. "An Act to Execute Certain Treaty Stipulations Relating to the Chinese," May 6, 1882, Enrolled Acts and Resolutions of Congress, 1789–1996, General Records of the United States Government, Record Group 11, National Archives.

27. Chinese Exclusion Act, Title 8—Aliens and Nationality, Chapter 7—Exclusion of Chinese, May 6, 1882, ch. 126, 22, Stat. 58, https://www.archives .gov/milestone-documents/chinese-exclusion-act.

28. Forty-Eighth Congress, Sess. I., Chs. 219, 220, 1884, https://www .congress.gov/48/plaws/statute/c48s1ch221.pdf.

29. "Exclusion of Chinese Immigrants, 1923–1947," Government of Canada, https://parks.canada.ca/culture/designation/evenement-event/exclusion -chinois-chinese, accessed Nov. 12, 2023.

30. Yick Wo v. Hopkins, 118 U.S. 356 (1886).

31. "The People of Pullman," Pullman State Historic Site, https://pullman -museum.org/thePeople, accessed Nov. 2, 2023.

32. "Pullman, George Mortimer," Pullman State Historic Site, https:// pullman-museum.org/theMan/, accessed June 29, 2024.

33. Larry Tye, *Rising from the Rails: Pullman Porters and the Making of the Black Middle Class* (New York: Henry Holt, 2004), 172.

34. Tye, *Rising from the Rails*, 72.

35. Tye, *Rising from the Rails*, 70.

36. See Jack Kelly, *The Edge of Anarchy: The Railroad Barons, the Gilded Age, and the Greatest Labor Uprising in America* (New York: St. Martin's Press, 2019).

37. Tye, *Rising from the Rails*, 72.

38. See *Records of the Brotherhood of Sleeping Car Porters, Series A, Holdings of the Chicago Historical Society and the Newberry Library, 1925–1969*, microform, ed. William H. Harris (Bethesda, MD: University Publications of America, c. 1990–c. 1994).

39. Tye, *Rising from the Rails*, 131.

40. Tye, *Rising from the Rails*, 158.

41. Paula Giddings, *A Sword Among Lions: Ida B. Wells and the Campaign Against Lynching* (New York: Amistad, 2009).

42. Ida B. Wells, *Crusade for Justice: The Autobiography of Ida B. Wells* (Chicago: Univ. of Chicago Press, 2020).

43. Beth Tompkins Bates, *Pullman Porters and Rise of Protest Politics in Black America: 1925–1945* (Chapel Hill: Univ. of North Carolina Press, 2001), 78–80.

44. Mother Jones (Mary Harris Jones), *Autobiography of Mother Jones* (1925; repr., New York: Dover Edition, 2004); "Pray for the Dead and Fight Like Hell for the Living: Mother Jones, 1902," photograph, Library of Congress, https://www.loc.gov/item/2015649968/.

45. Elliott J. Gorn, *Mother Jones: The Most Dangerous Woman in America* (New York: Hill and Wang, 2001).

46. See Mary Harris Jones, *Autobiography of Mother Jones* (1925; repr., New York: Dover Edition, 2004); Phillip S. Foner, *Mother Jones Speaks: Speeches and Writings of a Working-Class Fighter* (New York: Pathfinder Books, 1983).

47. See Foner, *Mother Jones Speaks*; Jones, *Autobiography of Mother Jones*, 1.

48. Jones, *Autobiography of Mother Jones*, 7–8; Gorn, *Mother Jones*, 51–52.

49. James Green, *Death in the Haymarket: A Story of Chicago, the First Labor Movement and the Bombing that Divided Gilded Age America* (New York: Anchor Books, 2006), 28–31; "The Eight-Hour Day," University Libraries, University of Maryland, https://exhibitions.lib.umd.edu/unions/labor/eight-hour
-day, accessed June 22, 2024.

50. Green, *Death in the Haymarket*, 144–45, 160–61.

51. Haymarket Square meeting poster, Chicago, May 4, 1886, portfolio 337, folder 4, Library of Congress, Washington, DC, https://www.loc.gov/item/97165248.

52. Green, *Death in the Haymarket*.

53. Jones, *Autobiography of Mother Jones*, 8.

54. James Green, *Death in the Haymarket: A Story of Chicago, the First Labor Movement and the Bombing That Divided Gilded Age America* (New York: Pantheon, 2006).

55. Gorn, *Mother Jones*, 51.

56. Paul Avrich, *The Haymarket Tragedy* (Princeton, NJ: Princeton Univ. Press, 1984); Green, *Death in the Haymarket*.

57. Robert A. Ferguson, "Traitors in Name Only: The Haymarket Defendants," in *The Trial in American Life* (Chicago: Univ. of Chicago Press, 2007).

58. Green, *Death in the Haymarket* (Anchor Books, 2006), 263–64; Jones, *Autobiography of Mother Jones*, 8.

59. Jones, *Autobiography of Mother Jones*, 8.

60. Jones, *Autobiography of Mother Jones*, 8.

61. Ferguson, "Traitors in Name Only."

62. William H. Turner, *The Harlan Renaissance: Stories of Black Life in Appalachian Coal Towns* (Morgantown: West Virginia Univ. Press, 2021).

63. Lochner v. New York, 198 U.S. 45 (1905).

64. "Remembering the Triangle Shirtwaist Fire of 1911," *New York Times*, Mar. 26, 1911.

65. "The Triangle Shirtwaist Factory Fire," OSHA, US Department of Labor, https://www.osha.gov/aboutosha/40-years/trianglefactoryfire, accessed June 26, 2024.

66. "Remembering the Triangle Shirtwaist Fire of 1911."

67. People of the State of New York v. Isaac Harris and Max Blanck, trial transcript, Kheel Center for Labor-Management Documentation Center, Catherwood Library, ILR School at Cornell University, Ithaca, NY; "Remembering the Triangle Shirtwaist Fire of 1911."

68. *People of the State of New York v. Isaac Harris and Max Blanck.*

69. David Von Drehle, *In Triangle: The Fire That Changed America* (New York: Grove Press, 2004).

70. "Remembering: The 1911 Triangle Factory Fire," Kheel Center, Cornell University, https://trianglefire.ilr.cornell.edu/primary/reports/FourthReport OfFIC.html, accessed on Mar. 1, 2024; Laws Enacted as a Result of the Commission's First Year's Work.

71. Bruce Mouser explores the extraordinary life of this union organizer and presidential candidate in *For Labor, Race, and Liberty: George Edwin Taylor, His Historic Run for the White House, and the Making of Independent Politics* (Madison: Univ. of Wisconsin Press, 2011).

72. J. Davitt McAteer, *Monongah: The Tragic Story of the 1907 Monongah Mine Disaster* (Morgantown: West Virginia Univ. Press, 2007).

73. "Dead May Reach 500 in Mine Explosion. Terrible Catastrophe in West Virginia Coal Pitts—Hundreds Buried and Mine Officials Say Chances of Getting Out Alive Are Remote," *Fitchburg (MA) Sentinel*, Dec. 6, 1907.

74. Itemized Pay Envelope, dated Oct. 31, 1933, West Virginia Mine Wars Museum, McDowell Coal & Coke Co., folder 59, Matewan, WV, accessed Nov. 11, 2023.

75. Contract between Bailey-Wood Coal Co. and James Pritchard, dated Feb. 12, 1924, West Virginia Mine Wars Museum, folder 3, Matewan, WV, accessed Nov. 11, 2023.

76. See Robert Shogun, *The Battle of Blair Mountain: The Story of America's Largest Labor Uprising* (New York: Basic Books, 2004); author interview with Lloyd Tomlinson, PhD candidate, West Virginia University, docent at the West Virginia Mine Wars Museum, Nov. 11, 2023.

77. Lon Savage, *Thunder in the Mountains: The West Virginia Mine War, 1920–21* (Pittsburgh: Univ. of Pittsburgh Press, 1990), 48–51.

78. Shogun, *The Battle of Blair Mountain*, 17.

79. Robert Shogun, *The Battle of Blair Mountain: The Story of America's Largest Labor Uprising* (New York: Perseus Book Group, 2006), 45.

80. Tomlinson interview.

81. Tomlinson interview.

82. Tomlinson interview.

83. Savage, *Thunder in the Mountains*, 24.

84. Shogun, *The Battle of Blair Mountain* (New York: Perseus Book Group, 2006), 43; Savage, *Thunder in the Mountains*, 24–25.

85. Tomlinson interview.

86. Tomlinson interview.

87. "A Proclamation by the President of the United States," Aug. 30, 1921, West Virginia Mine Wars Museum, folder 57, Matewan, WV, accessed Nov. 11, 2023.

88. John Hope Franklin, *Mirror to America: The Autobiography of John Hope Franklin* (New York: Farrar, Straus and Giroux, 2005); TulsaHistory.org, accessed Nov. 1, 2023; Sean Murphy, "Oklahoma Supreme Court Dismisses Lawsuit of Last Tulsa Race Massacre Survivors Seeking Reparations," AP, June 12, 2024, https://apnews.com/article/1921-race-massacre-tulsa-black-survivors -b7a4c83514ce79640a8490d49efb9006.

89. See Douglas A. Blackmon, *Slavery by Another Name: The Re-enslavement of Black Americans from the Civil War to World War II* (New York: Anchor Press, 2008).

90. Booker T. Washington, *Up from Slavery* (1901; repr., Mineola, NY: Dover Publications, 1995).

91. Blackmon, *Slavery by Another Name*, 160–61.

92. Clarissa Olds Keeler, *The Crime of Crimes; or, The Convict System Unmasked* (Washington, DC: Pentecostal Era Co., 1907), 16, HV8988. K3.E185.A254, container K, no. 151, African American Pamphlet Collection, Library of Congress, https://hdl.loc.gov/loc.rbc/rbaapc.15100.

93. Keeler, *The Crime of Crimes*.

94. Quoted in Keeler, *The Crime of Crimes*.

95. Sarah Haley, *No Mercy Here: Gender, Punishment, and the Making of Jim Crow Modernity* (Chapel Hill: Univ. of North Carolina Press, 2016).

96. "1938: Pecan Shellers Strike," A Latinx Resource Guide: Civil Rights Cases and Events in the United States, Research Guides, Library of Congress, https://guides.loc.gov/latinx-civil-rights/pecan-shellers-strike, accessed Oct. 26, 2023.

97. Catherine Ceniza Choy, *Empire of Care: Nursing and Migration in Filipino American History* (Durham, NC: Duke Univ. Press, 2003), 121–65; United States v. Filipina Narciso and Leonora Perez, 446 F. Supp. 252 (1977).

98. *United States v. Filipina Narciso and Leonora Perez*, 252–62, 310–12.

99. "U.S. Dismisses Charges Against Narciso-Perez," *Pacific Citizen* 86, no. 5 (Feb. 10, 1978): 1.

100. Catherine Ceniza Choy, *Asian American Histories of the United States* (Boston: Beacon Press, 2022), 139–40.

101. President William McKinley, "Executive Order," Dec. 21, 1898, American Presidency Project, https://www.presidency.ucsb.edu/documents/executive-order-132.

102. Kevin Leo Yabut Nadal, Allyson Tintiangco-Cubales, and E. J. R. David, *The SAGE Encyclopedia of Filipina/x/o American Studies* (Thousand Oaks, CA: Sage, 2022).

103. Choy, *Asian American Histories of the United States*.

104. Akemi Tamanaha, "Why All Americans Should Know About Larry Itliong," *AsAm News*, October 23, 2019, https://asamnews.com/2019/10/23/why-all-americans-should-know-about-larry-itliong, accessed Oct. 23, 2023.

105. Michael Honey, *Going Down Jericho Road: The Memphis Strike, Martin Luther King's Last Campaign* (New York: W. W. Norton, 2008).

106. Robert Curvin, *Inside New Newark: Decline, Rebellion, and the Search for Transformation* (New Brunswick, NJ: Rutgers Univ. Press, 2014).

107. Airline Deregulation Act of 1978. Pub. Law 95-504—Oct. 24, 1978.

108. "August 3, 1981: Remarks on the Air Traffic Controllers Strike," https://millercenter.org/the-presidency/presidential-speeches/august-3-1981-remarks-air-traffic-controllers-strike, accessed June 27, 2024 (Pub. L. 89-554, Sept. 6, 1966, 80 Stat. 524); 5 U.S. Code § 7311, sec. 3—Loyalty and Striking (January 5, 1999).

109. "August 3, 1981: Remarks on the Air Traffic Controllers Strike."

110. Noam Chomsky, *Requiem for the American Dream: The 10 Principles of Concentration of Wealth & Power* (New York: Seven Stories Press, 2017).

111. Chomsky, *Requiem for the American Dream.*

112. Barbara Ehrenreich, *Nickel and Dimed: On (Not) Getting By in America* (New York: Metropolitan Books, 2001).

113. Franklin, *Mirror to America.*

114. Bethany McLean and Joe Nocera, *All the Devils Are Here: The Hidden History of the Financial Crisis* (New York: Portfolio/Penguin Press, 2010).

115. Michael Lewis, *The Big Short: Inside the Doomsday Machine* (New York: W. W. Norton, 2010); Andrew S. Sorkin, *Too Big to Fail: The Inside Story of How Wall Street and Washington Fought to Save the Financial System—and Themselves* (New York: Viking Press, 2009).

116. Arindrajit Dube and Ethan Kaplan, "Occupy Wall Street and the Political Economy of Inequality," *The Economists' Voice* 9, no. 3 (2012), https://people.umass.edu/adube/DubeKaplan_EV_OWS_2012.pdf.

117. Bob Hennelly, "As COVID-19 Deaths Hit Record Numbers, Trump Oversees a Historic Wealth Transfer to the Super-Rich," *Salon,* July 7, 2020, https://www.salon.com/2020/07/03/as-covid-19-deaths-hit-record-numbers-trump-oversees-a-historic-wealth-transfer-to-the-super-rich/. Bob Hennelly, "NYC's EMS Union: Move the Virus Fight into Neighborhoods That Need It Most," *Salon,* Apr. 20, 2020, https://www.salon.com/2020/04/20/nycs-ems-union-move-the-virus-fight-into-neighborhoods-that-need-it-most.

118. Jeremy Reynolds and Reilly Kincaid, "Gig Work and the Pandemic: Looking for Good Pay from Bad Jobs During the COVID-19 Crisis," *Work and Occupations* 50, no. 1 (2023): 60–96, doi: 10.1177/07308884221128511; "How the Pandemic Has Affected NYC's Public Services, Activities, and Residents," *CBCNY Blog,* Citizens Budget Commission, Oct. 20, 2020, https://cbcny.org/research/how-pandemic-has-affected-nycs-public-services-activities-and-residents; Benjamin Mueller and Eleanor Lutz, "U.S. Has Far Higher Covid Death Rate Than Other Wealthy Countries," *New York Times,* Feb. 1, 2022, https://www.nytimes.com/interactive/2022/02/01/science/covid-deaths-united-states.html.

119. "New Select Subcommittee Report Reveals Workplace Disparities Have Persisted Throughout Pandemic, Highlights Need to Address Inequality," press release, House Select Subcommittee on the Coronavirus Crisis, Oct. 25, 2022, https://coronavirus-democrats-oversight.house.gov/news/press-releases/clyburn-pandemic-workforce-gender-fortune.

120. COVID Data Tracker, "United States COVID-19 Deaths, Emergency Department (ED) Visits, and Test Positivity by Geographic Area," Centers for Disease Control and Prevention, https://covid.cdc.gov/covid-data-tracker/#maps_deaths-total, accessed June 23, 2024.

121. Heidi Shierholz, Celine McNicholas, Margaret Poydock, and Jennifer Sherer, *Workers Want Unions, but the Latest Data Point to Obstacles in Their Path,* Economic Policy Institute, Jan. 23, 2024, https://www.epi.org/publication/union-membership-data/.

122. Christian Smalls, Testimony Before the US Senate, Committee on the Budget, May 5, 2022, https://www.budget.senate.gov/imo/media/doc/Christian

%20Smalls%20-%20Witness%20Testimony%20-%20US%20Senate%20
Budget%20Committee1.pdf.

123. Christian Smalls testimony.

124. Christian Smalls testimony.

125. "H.R. 842—117th Congress (2021–2022): Protecting the Right to Organize Act of 2021," Congress.gov, Mar. 11, 2021, https://www.congress.gov
/bill/117th-congress/house-bill/842.

CHAPTER FOUR: ANTI-WAR MARCHES AND CONSCIENTIOUS OBJECTORS

1. National Security Act of 1947 (Pub. L. 80–253, 61 Stat. 495, enacted July 26, 1947).

2. Matthew 5:9 (King James version).

3. "About Quakers," Friends General Conference, https://www.fgcquaker
.org/quakerism, accessed Oct. 11, 2023.

4. Jacquelyn S. Nelson, "Military and Civilian Support of the Civil War by the Society of Friends in Indiana," *Quaker History* 76, no. 1 (1987): 50–61, https://doi.org/10.1353/qkh.1987.0020.

5. Cheryl Janifer LaRoche, *Free Black Communities and the Underground Railroad: The Geography of Resistance* (Urbana: Univ. of Illinois Press, 2014); US Forest Service, "Underground Railroad in Indiana: Lick Creek, Hoosier National Forest," https://www.fs.usda.gov/recarea/hoosier/recreation/camping
-cabins/recarea/?recid=81892&actid=119.

6. "An Act for Preventing Negroes Insurrection" (1680), Encyclopedia of Virginia, *Transcription Source:* William Waller Hening, ed., *The Statutes at Large: Being a Collection of All Laws of Virginia, from the First Session of the Legislature, in the Year 1619, vol. 2* (New York: R. & W. & G. Bartow, 1823), https://encyclopediavirginia.org/primary-documents/an-act-for-preventing
-negroes-insurrections-1680/.

7. David Blight, *Frederick Douglass: Prophet of Freedom* (New York: Simon and Schuster, 2020).

8. Noah Andre Trudeau, *Like Men of War: Black Troops in the Civil War, 1862–1865* (Boston: Back Bay Books, 1999).

9. Jim Percoco, "The United States Colored Troops," American Battlefield Trust, https://www.battlefields.org/learn/articles/united-states-colored-troops, accessed July 4, 2024; Ned Blackhawk, *The Rediscovery of America: Native Peoples and the Unmaking of U.S. History* (New Haven, CT: Yale Univ. Press, 2023).

10. Martin Binkin and Mark J. Eitelberg with Alvin J. Schexnider and Marvin M. Smith, *Blacks and the Military* (Washington, DC: Brookings Institution Press, 1982), 12, 14.

11. Elizabeth D. Leonard, *Benjamin Franklin Butler: A Noisy, Fearless Life* (Chapel Hill: Univ. of North Carolina Press, 2022).

12. Mary Frances Berry, "Toward Freedom and Civil Rights for the Freedman: Military Policy Origins of the Thirteenth Amendment and Civil Rights Act of 1866," unpublished manuscript, Department of History, Howard Univ., 1975.

13. Martin Binkin and Mark J. Eitelberg, *Blacks and the Military* (New York: Brookings Institution, 1982).

14. Gail Buckley, *American Patriots: The Story of Blacks in the Military from the Revolution to Desert Storm* (New York: Random House, 2001), 113.

15. W. Hilary Coston, *Spanish-American War Volunteer: Ninth United States Volunteer Infantry Roster and Muster*, 2d. ed. (Middletown, PA: Published by the Author, 1899).

16. Jill Lepore, *These Truths: A History of the United States* (New York: W. W. Norton, 2018), 393.

17. Schenck v. United States, 249 U.S. 47 (1919).

18. David Levering Lewis, *W. E. B. Du Bois: Biography of a Race, 1868–1918* (New York: Henry Holt, 1993), 578.

19. Paul Dickson and Thomas B. Allen, *The Bonus Army: An American Epic* (New York: Dover, 2020); "Bonus Expeditionary Forces March on Washington," Anacostia Park, National Park Service, https://www.nps.gov/articles /bonus-expeditionary-forces-march-on-washington.htm, accessed Mar. 10, 2023.

20. John D'Emilio, "Before Montgomery: Bayard Rustin and the Fight for Racial Justice During World War II," National WWII Museum, https://www .nationalww2museum.org/war/articles/bayard-rustin-racial-justice-world-war-ii, accessed July 9, 2024.

21. Buckley, *American Patriots*, 84.

22. Alan L. Gropman, *The Air Force Integrates: 1945–1964* (Washington, DC: Office of Airforce History, 1978), 1; Buckley, *American Patriots*, 74.

23. Executive Order 9981, July 26, 1948, General Records of the US Government, Record Group 11, National Archives.

24. Robert L. Allen, *The Port Chicago Mutiny: The Story of the Largest Mass Mutiny Trial in U.S. Naval History* (Berkeley, CA: Heyday, 2006); Buckley, *American Patriots*, 310.

25. Buckley, *American Patriots*, 310–12.

26. Elie Wiesel, *The Night Trilogy: Night, Dawn, Day* (New York: Hill and Wang, 2008).

27. "Decision to Drop the Atomic Bomb," Harry S. Truman Library & Museum, National Archives, https://www.trumanlibrary.gov/education/presidential -inquiries/decision-drop-atomic-bomb, accessed July 5, 2024.

28. Kai Bird and Martin J. Sherwin, *American Prometheus: The Triumph and Tragedy of J. Robert Oppenheimer* (New York: Alfred A. Knopf, 2005).

29. Bird and Sherwin, *American Prometheus*.

30. Peter J. Kuznick, "Defending the Indefensible: A Meditation on the Life of Hiroshima Pilot Paul Tibbets, Jr.," *Asia-Pacific Journal* 6, no. 1 (Jan. 1, 2008), https://apjjf.org/peter-j-kuznick/2642/article.

31. Victor Davis Hanson, *The End of Everything: How Wars Descend into Annihilation* (New York: Basic Books, 2024); "Bombings of Hiroshima and Nagasaki—1945," Atomic Heritage Foundation, June 5, 2014, https://ahf.nuclear museum.org/ahf/history/bombings-hiroshima-and-nagasaki-1945, accessed Mar. 31, 2024.

32. "Atomic Bombing of Nagasaki," Atomic Archive, https://www.atomic archive.com/history/atomic-bombing/index.html.

33. Bird and Sherwin, *American Prometheus*, 331–32.

34. "Vietnam War U.S. Military Fatal Casualty Statistics," Military Records, National Archives, https://www.archives.gov/research/military/vietnam-war /casualty-statistics, accessed Oct. 31, 2023.

35. "Resistance and Revolution: The Anti-Vietnam War Movement at the University of Michigan, 1965–1972," Michigan in the World, https://michigan intheworld.history.lsa.umich.edu/antivietnamwar, accessed Oct. 31, 2023.

36. "Tom Hayden (U of M Student Activist/SDS Leader)," interview, Mar. 29, 2015, "Resistance and Revolution: The Anti-Vietnam War Movement at the University of Michigan, 1965–1972," Michigan in the World, https://michigan intheworld.history.lsa.umich.edu/antivietnamwar/exhibits/show/interviews/tom -hayden, accessed June 29, 2024.

37. "The Port Huron Statement," "Resistance and Revolution: The Anti-Vietnam War Movement at the University of Michigan, 1965–1972," Michigan in the World, https://michiganintheworld.history.lsa.umich.edu/antivietnamwar /items/show/28, accessed June 29, 2024.

38. Robert Curvin, *Inside Newark: Decline, Rebellion, and the Search for Transformation* (New Brunswick, NJ: Rutgers Univ. Press, 2014), 88–90.

39. Tom Hayden, *Rebellion in Newark: Official Violence and Ghetto Response* (New York: Vintage Books, 1967).

40. "Tom Hayden," interview.

41. "Tom Hayden," interview.

42. Ronald B. Frankum Jr., *Historical Dictionary of the War in Vietnam* (Lanham, MD: Rowman and Littlefield, 2011), 306; Melvin Small, *Antiwarriors: The Vietnam War and the Battle for America's Hearts and Minds* (Lanham, MD: Rowman & Littlefield, 2002), 32–33.

43. Penny Lewis, *Hardhats, Hippies, and Hawks: The Vietnam Antiwar Movement as Myth and Memory* (Ithaca, NY: Cornell Univ. Press, 2013), 71, 80; "Resistance and Revolution: The Anti-Vietnam War Movement at the University of Michigan, 1965–1972," Michigan in the World.

44. "Anti-War Protests of the 1960s–1970s," White House Historical Association, https://www.whitehousehistory.org/anti-war-protests-of-the-1960s-70s, accessed Oct. 31, 2023; "Vietnam War U.S. Military Fatal Casualty Statistics." See the "Casualty Category" column in the DCAS Vietnam Conflict Extract File record counts (as of Apr. 29, 2008), https://www.archives.gov/research/military /vietnam-war/casualty-statistics#toc-dcas-vietnam-conflict-extract-file-record -counts-by-casualty-category-as-of-april-29-2008-.

45. Daniel Ellsberg, *Secrets: A Memoir of Vietnam and the Pentagon Papers* (New York: Viking, 2002); Fox Butterfield, Neil Sheehan, Hedrick Smith, and E. W. Kenworthy, *The Pentagon Papers: The Secret History of the Vietnam War* (New York: Racehorse Publishing, 2017).

46. Patrick Witty, "Malcolm Browne: The Story Behind the Burning Monk," *Time*, Aug. 28, 2012, https://time.com/3791176/malcolm-browne-the-story -behind-the-burning-monk, accessed Oct. 31, 2023.

47. Witty, "Malcolm Browne."

48. Ray Boomhower, *The Ultimate Protest: Malcolm W. Browne, Thich Quang Duc, and the News Photograph That Stunned the World* (Santa Fe: Univ. of New Mexico Press/High Road Press, 2024).

49. Bond v. Floyd, 385 U.S. 116 (1966).

50. "SNCC Statement on Vietnam," January 6, 1966, available at Digital SNCC Gateway, https://snccdigital.org/inside-sncc/policy-statements/vietnam/, accessed July 5, 2024.

51. *Bond v. Floyd*, 125.

52. Tinker v. Des Moines Independent Community School District, 393 U.S. 503 (1969) National Constitution Center, https://constitutioncenter.org/the -constitution/supreme-court-case-library/tinker-v-des-moines-independent -community-school-district, accessed Nov. 1, 2023.

53. *Tinker v. Des Moines Community Independent School District*.

54. V. P. Franklin, *The Young Crusaders: The Untold Story of the Children and Teenagers Who Galvanized the Civil Rights Movement* (Boston: Beacon Press, 2021).

55. West Virginia State Board of Education v. Barnette, 319 U.S. 624 (1943).

56. "Tet Offensive at Fifty," Office of the Director of National Intelligence, https://www.intelligence.gov/tet-declassified/tet-at-fifty, accessed Nov. 1, 2023.

57. Daniel Ellsberg, *The Doomsday Machine: Confessions of a Nuclear War Planner* (New York: Bloomsbury, 2017), 313.

58. John G. Hubbell, Andrew Jones, and Kenneth Y. Tomlinson, *P.O.W.: A Definitive History of the American Prisoner-of-War Experience in Vietnam, 1964– 1973* (New York: Thomas Y. Crowell Co., 1976); https://www.pownetwork.org /bios/m/m102.htm.

59. Stuart L. Rochester and Frederick Kiley, *Honor Bound: The History of American Prisoners of War in Southeast Asia, 1961–1973* (Annapolis, MD: Naval Institute Press, 1998); *Vietnam: A POW's Survival Story*; "McDaniel, Norman Alexander," compiled by Homecoming II Project, May 15, 1990, updated by the P.O.W. Network, 2023, https://www.pownetwork.org/bios/m/m102.htm, accessed Mar. 31, 2024; "Hall of Valor: The Military Medals," The Hall of Valor Project, valor.militarytimes.com/hero, accessed June 10, 2024.

60. "McDaniel, Norman Alexander."

61. In Clay, aka Ali v. United States, 403 U.S. 698, 707 (1971); Muhammad Ali with Hama Yasmeen, *Soul of a Butterfly: Reflections on a Life's Journey* (New York: Simon & Schuster, 2004).

62. Vietnam Veterans Against the War, "History: Operation 'Dewey Canyon III,'" *The Veteran* 7, no. 2 (Apr. 1977), http://www.vvaw.org/veteran/article/?id =1656.

63. "1970: National Chicano Moratorium," A Latinx Resource Guide: Civil Rights Cases and Events in the United States, Library of Congress, https://guides .loc.gov/latinx-civil-rights/national-chicano-moratorium, accessed Mar. 17, 2023.

64. Robert McFadden, "Daniel Ellsberg, Who Leaked the Pentagon Papers, Is Dead at 92," *New York Times*, June 17, 2023.

65. "Pentagon Papers," Research Our Records, National Archives, https:// www.archives.gov/research/pentagon-papers, accessed Apr. 2, 2024. Although other trade and university presses were reticent, Beacon Press published the Pentagon Papers, and after doing so was harassed by the federal government under Nixon, with FBI agents attempting to subpoena the publisher's bank records. However, the Nixon administration was unsuccessful in stopping the Pentagon

Papers from being released, and the government's campaign ended with the Watergate break-in. See *The Pentagon Papers: The Defense Department History of the United States Decisionmaking on Vietnam* (Boston: Beacon Press, 1971).

66. New York Times v. United States, 403 U.S. 913 (1971); https://first amendment.mtsu.edu/article/new-york-times-co-v-united-states, accessed Mar. 31, 2024.

67. McFadden, "Daniel Ellsberg, Who Leaked the Pentagon Papers, Is Dead at 92."

68. "Turning the Tide Against Endless War," Dissenters, https://wearedissenters .org, accessed Sept. 12, 2023.

69. Author interview with Howard Morland, Oct. 23, 2023.

70. Alex Wellerstein, *Restricted Data: The History of Nuclear Secrecy in the United States* (Chicago: Univ. of Chicago, 2021).

71. Morland interview.

72. United States v. The Progressive, 476 F. Supp 990 (W.D. Wis. 1979); https://firstamendment.mtsu.edu/article/united-states-v-progressive-inc-w -d-wis.

73. Bird and Sherwin, *American Prometheus*.

74. Bird and Sherwin, *American Prometheus*.

75. Ellsberg, *The Doomsday Machine*.

76. Ellsberg, *The Doomsday Machine*, 339.

77. Ellsberg, *The Doomsday Machine*, 346.

78. Quoted in Winona LaDuke, *The Winona LaDuke Chronicles: Stories from the Front Lines in the Battle for Environmental Justice* (Ponsford, MN: Spotted Horse Press), 262.

CHAPTER FIVE: REBELLIONS IN THE TWENTIETH CENTURY

1. Plessy v. Ferguson, 163 U.S. 537 (1896); Mattie Bradshaw, "Eliza Bradshaw: An Exoduster Grandmother," *Kansas History: A Journal of the Central Plains* 26, no. 2 (Summer 2003): 106–11.

2. Genevieve Yost, "History of Lynchings in Kansas," *Kansas Historical Quarterly* 2, no. 2 (May 1933), https://www.kshs.org/p/kansas-historical-quarterly -history-of-lynchings-in-kansas/12580.

3. Brown v. Board of Education, 347 U.S. 483 (1954).

4. Pauli Murray, *States' Laws on Race and Color* (New York: Women's Division of Christian Service, 1951).

5. *Report of the Steering Committee on Human Remains in University Museum Collections*, Harvard University, Fall 2022; Phillips Verner Bradford and Harvey Blume, *Ota Benga: The Pygmy in the Zoo* (New York: St. Martin's Press, 1992); Ken Smith, *Raw Deal: Horrible and Ironic Stories of Forgotten Americans* (New York: Blast Books, 1998).

6. Jonathan Markovitz, *Legacies of Lynching: Racial Violence and Memory* (Minneapolis: Univ. of Minnesota Press, 2004).

7. John Jay, *The Correspondence and Public Papers of John Jay*, vol. I, ed. Henry P. Johnston (New York: G. P. Putnam's Sons, 1890), 161.

8. Kerri K. Greenidge, *Black Radical: The Life and Times of William Monroe Trotter* (New York: Liveright, 2020).

9. John Henrik Clarke, ed., *Marcus Garvey and the Vision of Africa* (Baltimore: Black Classic Press, 2011).

10. Clarke, *Marcus Garvey and the Vision of Africa.*

11. Les Payne and Tamara Payne, *The Dead Are Arising: The Life of Malcolm X* (New York: Liveright, 2020).

12. Andrew P. Smallwood, *An Afrocentric Study of the Intellectual Development, Leadership Praxis, and Pedagogy of Malcolm X* (Lewiston, NY: Edward Mellen Press, 2001).

13. Clarke, *Marcus Garvey and the Vision of Africa.*

14. Marcus Garvey speech, excerpt from "Look for Me in the Whirlwind," c. 1924, UNIA-ACL website, https://unia-aclgovernment.com/marcus-garvey -look-for-me-in-the-whirlwind-freedom-speech-circa-1924; Clarke, *Marcus Garvey and the Vision of Africa.*

15. *The Negro World* (New York), 1917–33, Library of Congress, https:// www.loc.gov/item/sn84037003, accessed Apr. 10, 2023.

16. Garvey v. United States, 4 F. 2d. 974 (2nd Cir. 1923).

17. Marcus Garvey, "First Message to the Negroes of the World from Atlanta Prison," Feb. 10, 1925, in Marcus M. Garvey, *The Philosophy and Opinions of Marcus Garvey; or, Africa for the Africans*, ed. Amy Jacques Garvey (Baltimore: Black Classics Press, 2022).

18. Robin Lindley, "Why It's Time to Get to Know Black Civil Rights Activist James Lawson: An Interview with Michael K. Honey," History News Network, https://historynewsnetwork.org/article/165542, accessed Oct. 20, 2023.

19. V. P. Franklin, *The Young Crusaders: The Untold Story of the Children and Teenagers Who Galvanized the Civil Rights Movement* (Boston: Beacon Press, 2021).

20. Michelle Alexander, "Go to Trial: Crash the Justice System," *New York Times*, Mar. 11, 2012, http://www.nytimes.com/2012/03/11/opinion/sunday/go -to-trial-crash-the-justice-system.html.

21. Franklin, *The Young Crusaders.*

22. C. T. Vivian, *It's in the Action: Memories of a Nonviolent Warrior* (Montgomery, AL: NewSouth Books, 2021).

23. Lombard v. Louisiana, 373 U.S. 267 (1963).

24. *Lombard v. Louisiana*, 273.

25. Edwards v. South Carolina, 372 U.S. 229 (1963).

26. Gilbert Ware, "Lobbying as a Means of Protest: The NAACP as an Agent of Equality," *Journal of Negro Education* 33, no 2 (1964): 103–10.

27. Civil Rights Act of 1964; Public Law Citation, Public Law 88–352; Congressional Bill Citation, S.1177, 114th Congress.

28. Cox v. Louisiana, 379 U.S. 536 (1965).

29. *Cox v. Louisiana*, 543.

30. Adderley v. Florida, 385 U.S. 39 (1966).

31. *Adderley v. Florida.*

32. Elizabeth Hinton, *From the War on Poverty to the War on Crime: The Making of Mass Incarceration in America* (Cambridge, MA: Harvard University Press, 2016), 68–72; Valerie Reitman and Mitchell Landsberg, "Watts Riots, 40 Years Later," *Los Angeles Times*, Aug. 11, 2005; Watts Riots Records,

Collection No. 0084, Regional History Collection, Special Collections, USC Libraries, University of Southern California, Online Archive of California.

33. Seth Mydans, Richard W. Stevenson, and Timothy Egan, "Seven Minutes in Los Angeles—A Special Report; Videotaped Beating by Officers Puts Full Glare on Brutality Issue," *New York Times*, Mar. 18, 1991, retrieved Mar. 2, 2016.

34. Jeff Wallenfeldt, "Los Angeles Riots of 1992," *Britannica*, last updated June 24, 2024, https://www.britannica.com/event/Los-Angeles-Riots-of-1992.

35. Erica Chenoweth, *Civil Resistance: What Everyone Needs to Know* (New York: Oxford Univ. Press, 2021).

36. More about Rustin can be found in Michael Bronski, *A Queer History of the United States* (Boston: Beacon Press, 2011).

37. Mohandas Karamchand Gandhi, *Non-violent Resistance (Satyagraha)* (1951; repr., Mineola, NY: Dover Books, 2001).

38. Author interview with Margo Jefferson, Mar. 2, 2024; Margo Jefferson, *Constructing a Nervous System: A Memoir* (New York: Vintage, 2023).

39. New York Times Co. v. Sullivan, 376 U.S. 254 (1964).

40. Isabel Wilkerson, *Caste: The Origins of Our Discontents* (New York: Random House, 2020).

41. Alabama General Acts, Title 48, Sec. 301 (31a)(31c).

42. Laura L. Rogers, "National African American History Month: Remembering Rosa Parks' Work to Address Sexual Assault," US Department of Justice, Office on Violence Against Women, Feb. 24, 2020, https://www.justice.gov/archives/ovw/blog/national-african-american-history-month-remembering-rosa-parks-work-address-sexual-assault.

43. Rosa Parks, *Rosa Parks: My Story* (New York: Puffin Books, 1999).

44. Steven Levingston, *Kennedy and King: The President, the Pastor, and the Battle over Civil Rights* (New York: Hachette, 2017), 43–49.

45. Levingston, *Kennedy and King*, 45–49.

46. Gloria J. Browne-Marshall, *She Took Justice: The Black Woman, Law, and Power* (London: Routledge, 2021); Gloria J. Browne-Marshall, *Race, Law, and American Society: 1607–Present* (London: Routledge, 2013), 139–40.

47. Gayle v. Browder, 352 U.S. 903 (1956).

48. NAACP v. Alabama ex rel. Patterson, Attorney General, 357 U.S. 449 (1958).

49. Bates v. City of Little Rock, 229 Ark. 819 (1958); Bates v. Little Rock, 361 U.S. 516 (1960); Bryant v. Zimmerman, 278 U.S. 63 (1928).

50. Vivian, *It's in the Action*.

51. Vivian, *It's in the Action*.

52. Vivian, *It's in the Action*.

53. John H. Franklin, *Mirror to America: The Autobiography of John Hope Franklin* (New York City: Farrar, Straus and Giroux, 2005), 377.

54. John Lewis, *Walking with the Wind: A Memoir of a Movement* (New York: Harcourt Brace, 1998).

55. NAACP v. Button, 371 U.S. 415 (1963).

56. From Browne-Marshall, *Race, Law, and American Society*.

57. "The Anatomy of Frustration," address delivered by Bayard Rustin, 55th National Commission Meeting of the Anti-Defamation League of B'nai B'rith, May 6, 1968, New York, NY; Peter Levine, *What Should We Do? A Theory of Civic Life* (New York: Oxford Univ. Press, 2022).

58. William Brink and Louis Harris, *The Negro Revolution in America* (New York: Simon and Schuster, 1963), 105.

59. Matthew 5:44–46 KJV.

60. Brink and Harris, *The Negro Revolution in America*, 63–77.

61. Franklin, *Mirror to America*.

62. Mark V. Tushnet, *The NAACP's Legal Strategy Against Segregated Education, 1925–1950* (Chapel Hill: Univ. of North Carolina Press, 1987).

63. Matthew Bailey, "Rich's Department Store," *New Georgia Encyclopedia*, https://www.georgiaencyclopedia.org/articles/business-economy/richs -department-store, last modified Aug. 2, 2018.

64. Peter R. Mitchell and John Schoeffel, *Understanding Power: The Indispensable Chomsky* (New York: New Press, 2002), 94.

65. Author interview with Frank Smith, conducted July 12, 2023.

66. Yost, "History of Lynchings in Kansas."

67. Jean Van Delinder, "Early Civil Rights Activism in Topeka, Kansas, Prior to the 1954 Brown Case," *Great Plains Quarterly* 21, no. 1 (2001): 45–61, http://www.jstor.org/stable/23533131.

68. Sam Dicks (1935–2018) received his doctorate from the University of Oklahoma. He was a member of the Emporia State University history faculty from 1965 to 2000 and was also producer and director of Channel 8, the school's television studio. Mr. Dicks served in the US Army and the South Dakota National Guard. He also taught high school in Yankton, South Dakota. Dicks continued as a university historian until retiring in 2003. "Samuel Eugene Dicks," obituary, *Emporia Gazette*, May 12, 2018, http://www.emporiagazette .com/obituaries/article_de26b92d-0808-586d-a69d-a83abd8f1b2d.html.

CHAPTER SIX: HER BODY. HER BALLOT. HER PROTEST.

1. 1940 US Census, Hodgeman County, Kansas.

2. Author interview with Crystal Bradshaw-Gonzalez, Nov. 24, 2023.

3. "History and Traditions," Emporia State University, https://www.emporia .edu/about-emporia-state-university/history-traditions, accessed Mar. 2, 2024.

4. 1930 Hodgeman County, Census Record; Archives, Spelman College, Women's Research & Resource Center; Spelman Archives, Alumnae Record.

5. "History of Lynching in America," NAACP, https://naacp.org/find -resources/history-explained/history-lynching-america, accessed August 23, 2024.

6. David Levering Lewis, *W. E. B. Du Bois: Biography of a Race, 1868–1918* (New York: Henry Holt, 1993).

7. Harry G. Lefever, *Undaunted by the Fight: Spelman College and the Civil Rights Movement, 1957–1967* (Macon, GA: Mercer Univ. Press, 2005).

8. Muller v. Oregon, 208 U.S. 412 (1908).

9. Carrie Chapman Catt and Nettie Rogers, *Woman Suffrage and Politics: The Inner Story of the Suffrage Movement* (New York: Dover Publications, 2020), 6–7.

10. Brianna Theobold, *Reproduction on the Reservation: Pregnancy, Childbirth, and Colonialism in the Long Twentieth Century* (Chapel Hill: Univ. of North Carolina Press, 2019).

11. D. M. Givens et al., "Angela: Jamestown and the First Africans," Jamestown Rediscovery Foundation and Preservation Virginia, 2022, https://historic jamestowne.org/history/the-first-africans/angela; Nichelle Smith, "Meet Angela, the First Named African Woman at Jamestown," *USA Today*, Oct. 16, 2019.

12. Rickie Solinger, *Pregnancy and Power: A Short History of Reproductive Politics in America* (New York: NYU Press, 2007).

13. Brendan Wolfe, "Indentured Servants in Colonial Virginia," *Encyclopedia Virginia*, https://encyclopediavirginia.org/entries/indentured-servants-in -colonial-virginia, accessed Jan. 3, 2023.

14. Lois Green Carr, "Margaret Brent (ca. 1601–1671)," Archives of Maryland, https://msa.maryland.gov/megafile/msa/speccol/sc3500/sc3520/002100 /002177/html/bio.html.

15. "Elizabeth Key," Dictionary of Virginia Biography, Library of Virginia, https://www.lva.virginia.gov/public/dvb/bio.asp?b=Key_Elizabeth_fl_1655-1660, accessed Mar. 19, 2024.

16. Act XII, Laws of Virginia, December 1662 (Hening, Statutes at Large, 2:170).

17. Catherine Lewis and Richard J. Lewis, eds., *Women and Slavery in America: A Documentary History* (Fayetteville: Univ. of Arkansas Press, 2011), 108.

18. Ned Sublette and Constance Sublette, *The American Slave Coast: A History of the Slave-Breeding Industry* (New York: Lawrence Hill Books, 2017); Sasha Turner, *Contested Bodies: Pregnancy, Childrearing and Slavery in Jamaica* (Philadelphia: Univ. of Pennsylvania Press, 2017).

19. Sharon Block, *Rape and Sexual Power in Early America* (Chapel Hill: Univ. of North Carolina Press, 2006).

20. See Richard Sutch, "The Breeding of Slaves for Sale and the Westward Expansion of Slavery 1850–1860," University of California, Berkeley, Institute of Business and Economic Research, 1972.

21. Harriet Washington, *Medical Apartheid: The Dark History of Medical Experimentation on Black Americans from Colonial Times* (New York: Doubleday, 2007); Harriet A. Washington, "A Medical Hell Recounted by Its Victims," *Nature*, Jan. 29, 2019, https://www.nature.com/articles/d41586-019-00340-5.

22. Kerri K. Greenidge, *The Grimkes: The Legacy of Slavery in an American Family* (New York: Liveright, 2022).

23. Jean-Jacques Rousseau, *Emile*, 1762, https://revolution.chnm.org/d/470/.

24. "Grimke Sisters," Women's Rights, National Historical Park, New York, https://www.nps.gov/wori/learn/historyculture/grimke-sisters.htm, accessed Nov. 22, 2023.

25. "Grimke Sisters."

26. Mark Perry, *Lift Up Thy Voice: The Sarah and Angelina Grimké Family's Journey from Slaveholders to Civil Rights Leaders* (New York: Penguin, 2002).

27. Debra Michals, ed., "Prudence Crandall," National Women's History Museum, 2015, https://www.womenshistory.org/education-resources /biographies/prudence-crandall.

28. Sally Roesch Wagner, ed., *The Women's Suffrage Movement* (New York: Penguin Books, 2019).

29. Elizabeth Cady Stanton, "Declaration of Sentiments," Seneca Falls and the Start of Annual Conventions, Library of Congress, https://www.loc.gov /exhibitions/women-fight-for-the-vote/about-this-exhibition/seneca-falls-and -building-a-movement-1776-1890/seneca-falls-and-the-start-of-annual -conventions/declaration-of-sentiments, accessed Nov. 1, 2023.

30. Gail Collins, *America's Women: Four Hundred Years of Dolls, Drudges, Helpmates, and Heroines* (New York: William Morrow, 2003).

31. Gloria J. Browne-Marshall, *The Voting Rights War: The NAACP and the Ongoing Struggle for Justice* (Lanham, MD: Rowman & Littlefield, 2016).

32. Martha S. Jones, *Vanguard: How Black Women Broke Barriers, Won the Vote, and Insisted on Equality for All* (New York: Basic Books, 2020).

33. "Frances Ellen Watkins Harper," Archives of Women's Political Communication, Iowa State University, https://awpc.cattcenter.iastate.edu/directory /frances-ellen-watkins-harper/, accessed Mar. 20, 2024; Frances Ellen Watkins Harper, "Enlightened Motherhood: An Address," Brooklyn Literary Society, 1892, available at https://www.loc.gov/item/91898488/.

34. "Frances Ellen Watkins Harper," Archives of Women's Political Communication.

35. Browne-Marshall, *The Voting Rights War*, 9.

36. "Ida B. Wells-Barnett," National Women's History Museum, https:// www.womenshistory.org/education-resources/biographies/ida-b-wells-barnett, accessed Mar. 19, 2024.

37. "Mary Church Terrell," National Women's History Museum, https:// www.womenshistory.org/education-resources/biographies/mary-church-terrell, accessed Mar. 21, 2024.

38. Booker T. Washington, "Booker T. Washington Questions the Benefit to Women," *New York Times*, Dec. 20, 1908.

39. Alex Cohen and Wilfred U. Codrington III, "The Equal Rights Amendment Explained," Brennan Center for Justice, Jan. 23, 2020, https://www .brennancenter.org/our-work/research-reports/equal-rights-amendment-explained.

40. United States v. One Package, 86 F.2d 737 (2d Cir. 1936).

41. Section 305(a) of the Tariff Act of 1930 (19 U.S.C.A. § 1305(a) provides: "All persons are prohibited from importing into the United States from any foreign country any article whatever for the prevention of conception or for causing unlawful abortion."

42. "The New York Penal Law makes it in general a misdemeanor to sell or give away or to advertise or offer for sale any articles for the prevention of conception except furnishing such articles to physicians who may in good faith

prescribe their use for the cure or prevention of disease." People v. Sanger, 222 N.Y. 192, 118 N.E. 637. New York Penal Law (Consol. Laws, c. 40) § 1145.

43. Todd S. Purdum, *An Idea Whose Time Has Come: Two Presidents, Two Parties, and the Battle for the Civil Rights Act of 1964* (New York: Henry Holt, 2014).

44. Civil Rights Act of 1964, Title VI, 42 U.S.C. § 2000d et seq., July 2, 1964, Enrolled Acts and Resolutions of Congress, 1789–2011, General Records of the United States Government, Record Group 11.

45. "Virginia Foster Durr," *Encyclopedia of Alabama*, https://encyclopedia ofalabama.org/article/virginia-foster-durr, accessed Mar. 30, 2024.

46. "Rosa Parks Arrested in Montgomery and Released on Bail," Martin Luther King Jr. Research and Education Institute, Stanford University, https:// kinginstitute.stanford.edu/rosa-parks-arrested-montgomery-and-released-bail, accessed Apr. 12, 2024.

47. "Durr, Virginia Foster," Martin Luther King Jr. Research and Education Institute, Stanford University, https://kinginstitute.stanford.edu/durr-virginia -foster, accessed Apr. 12, 2024.

48. Patricia Sullivan, *Virginia Foster Durr: Letters from the Civil Rights Years* (New York: Routledge, 2003).

49. "Liuzzo, Viola," *Encyclopedia of Detroit*, Detroit Historical Society, https://detroithistorical.org/learn/encyclopedia-of-detroit/liuzzo-viola-0, accessed Mar. 30, 2024.

50. "Mrs. Liuzzo 'Felt She Had to Help,'" *New York Times*, Mar. 27, 1965.

51. "Viola Gregg Liuzzo," *Encyclopedia of Alabama*, https://encyclopedia ofalabama.org/article/viola-gregg-liuzzo, accessed Apr. 20, 2024.

52. Angela Davis, *Are Prisons Obsolete?* (New York: Seven Stories Press, 2003).

53. Author interview with Zadie Smith, Apr. 2, 2024.

54. Author interview with Margo Jefferson, Mar. 2, 2024.

55. Gail Collins, *When Everything Changed: The Amazing Journey of American Women from 1960 to the Present* (New York: Little, Brown, 2009).

56. Ruth Bader Ginsberg, *My Own Words* (New York: Simon & Schuster, 2016).

57. Betty Friedan, *The Feminine Mystique* (New York: Norton, 1974).

58. Darlene Clark Hine, Wilma King, and Linda Reed, eds., *We Specialize in the Wholly Impossible: A Reader in Black Women's History* (Brooklyn, NY: Carlson Publishing, 1995); Gloria J. Browne-Marshall, *She Took Justice: The Black Woman, Law, and Power* (London: Routledge, 2021).

59. Roxane Gay, "Fifty Years Ago, Protesters Took On the Miss America Pageant and Electrified the Feminist Movement," *Smithsonian*, Jan. 2018, https://www.smithsonianmag.com/history/fifty-years-ago-protestors-took-on -miss-america-pageant-electrified-feminist-movement-180967504.

60. Christopher J. Kelly, "The Personal Is Political," *Britannica*, https:// www.britannica.com/topic/the-personal-is-political, accessed July 7, 2024.

61. Gay, "Fifty Years Ago, Protesters Took On the Miss America Pageant and Electrified the Feminist Movement."

62. Gloria Steinem, *My Life on the Road* (New York: Random House, 2015).

63. "Women's Liberation in New York: The Personal Is Political 1960–1982," Museum of the City of New York, https://www.mcny.org/exhibition/womens -liberation-new-york, accessed Apr. 10, 2024.

64. Oyez, https://www.oyez.org/cases/1971/70–18, accessed Nov. 25, 2023.

65. Roe v. Wade, 410 U.S. 113 (1973).

66. Author interview with Gloria Steinem, July 20, 2023.

67. Gloria Steinem, "We Live as Long as We Are Remembered: Gloria Steinem Remembers Dorothy Pitman Hughes," Women's Media Center, Jan. 5, 2023, https://womensmediacenter.com/news-features/we-live-as-long-as-we-are -remembered-gloria-steinem-remembers-dorothy-pitman-hughes.

68. Steinem interview.

69. "International History of TBTN," Take Back the Night, https://takeback thenight.org/history, accessed Nov. 25, 2023.

70. Emma Rothberg, "Pauli Murray," National Women's History Museum, https://www.womenshistory.org/education-resources/biographies/pauli-murray; Pauli Murray, "Extending Protection Against Sex-Based Discrimination," June 19, 1970, Speaking While Female Speech Bank, https://speakingwhilefemale.co /testimony-murray.

71. Jo Thomas, "75,000 March in Capital in Drive to Support Homosexual Rights; 'Sharing' and 'Flaunting,'" *New York Times*, Oct. 15, 1979.

72. Matthew Siegfried, "Audre Lorde Speaks! March for Lesbian and Gay Rights Washington D.C. 1979," YouTube, posted May 25, 2015, https://www .youtube.com/watch?v=bQK8yawGQXE.

73. Castle Rock v. Gonzales, 545 U.S. 748 (2005).

74. Congressman Jerry Nadler, "Floor Statement on the Jessica Gonzalez [sic] Victim Assistance Program," July 25, 2007, https://nadler.house.gov/news /documentsingle.aspx?DocumentID=390661.

75. "Violence Against Women Act," National Network to End Domestic Vi-olence, https://nnedv.org/content/violence-against-women-act, accessed on Nov. 20, 2023.

76. "History," BridesMarch.com, https://www.bridesmarch.com/history .html, accessed Nov. 25, 2023.

77. Richard Lezin Jones, "Man Gets Life Term in Wedding Day Killing," *New York Times*, Feb. 2, 2002, https://www.nytimes.com/2002/02/02/nyregion /man-gets-life-term-in-wedding-day-killing.html.

78. "History," BridesMarch.com.

79. Dobbs v. Jackson Women's Health Organization, 597 U.S. 215 (2022), overturning Roe v. Wade, 410 U.S. 113 (1973); Planned Parenthood v. Casey, 505 U.S. 833 (1992).

80. Nicholas O. Alozie, "Political Tolerance Hypotheses and White Opposi-tion to a Martin Luther King Holiday in Arizona," *Social Science Journal* 32, no. 1 (1995).

81. "Martin Luther King Holiday in Arizona," Pima County Public Library, https://www.library.pima.gov/content/martin-luther-king-holiday-in-arizona, accessed Oct. 29, 2023.

CHAPTER SEVEN: PROTESTING VIOLENT POLICING

1. "Fatal Force," *Washington Post*, https://www.washingtonpost.com /graphics/investigations/police-shootings-database, accessed Oct. 20, 2023.

2. Roger Mitchell Jr. and Jay D. Aronson, *Death in Custody: How America Ignores the Truth and What We Can Do About It* (Baltimore: Johns Hopkins Univ. Press, 2023).

3. Alex S. Vitale, *The End of Policing* (Brooklyn, NY: Verso, 2021).

4. William Waller Hening, *Statutes at Large; Being a Collection of All of the Laws of Virginia*, vol. 2 (Richmond, VA: Samuel Pleasants, 1809–23), 270.

5. Act XII, Laws of Virginia, December 1662 (Hening, *Statutes at Large*, 2: 170); In the Matter of Color, p. 39; Herbert Aptheker, *A Documentary History of the Negro People in the United States: From Colonial Times Through the Civil War* (New York: Citadel, 1951); Hening, *Statutes at Large*, 2:270.

6. A. Leon Higginbotham, *In the Matter of Color: Race and the American Legal Process* (New York: Oxford Univ. Press, 1978), 39; Aptheker, *A Documentary History of the Negro People in the United States*.

7. Hening, *Statutes at Large*, 2:270.

8. John Pervis, *A Complete Collection of All the Laws of Virginia Now in Force, 1662–82*, available at http://hdl.loc.gov/loc.mss/mtj.mtjbib026595, 1.

9. US Constitution, Art. IV, Sec. 2 (1789).

10. Aptheker, *A Documentary History of the Negro People in the United States*, 39.

11. Catherine Lewis and Richard J. Lewis, eds., *Women and Slavery in America: A Documentary History* (Fayetteville: Univ. of Arkansas Press, 2011), 101.

12. Gloria J. Browne-Marshall, *She Took Justice: The Black Woman, Law, and Power* (New York: Taylor & Francis, 2013).

13. *Laws of the State of Mississippi* (Jackson: J. J. Shannon & Sons, 1866), 82–86, 91, 165.

14. W. Lewis Burke, "*Pink Franklin v. South Carolina*: The NAACP's First Case," *American Journal of Legal History* 5 (2014): 265.

15. Burke, "*Pink Franklin v. South Carolina*," 269.

16. Burke, "*Pink Franklin v. South Carolina*," 269.

17. State v. Franklin, 80 S.C. 332 (S.C. 1908).

18. "Our History," NAACP, https://naacp.org/about/our-history.

19. Gloria J. Browne-Marshall, *The Voting Rights War: The NAACP and the Ongoing Struggle for Justice* (Lanham, MD: Rowman & Littlefield, 2016), 41.

20. William C. Hine, "*Pink Franklin*: NAACP's First Legal Case," *Times and Democrat* (Orangeburg, SC), May 18, 2014.

21. SC Law Enforcement Officers Hall of Fame, South Carolina Department of Public Safety, https://scdps.sc.gov/hof, accessed Oct. 21, 2023.

22. Margaret A. Burnham, *By Hands Now Known: Jim Crow's Legal Executioners* (New York: W. W. Norton, 2022), 216–17.

23. Burnham, *By Hands Now Known*, 216.

24. Ida B. Wells-Barnett, *Southern Horrors and Other Writings: The Anti-Lynching Campaign of Ida B. Wells, 1892–1900* (Boston: Bedford Books, 1997).

25. Alexis Newman, "New York City NAACP Silent Protest Parade (1917)," BlackPast, Mar. 26, 2017, https://www.blackpast.org/african-american-history/naacp-silent-protest-parade-new-york-city-1917/.

26. U.S. v. Shipp, 214 U.S. 386, 406 (1906).

27. *U.S. v. Shipp*, 413–14.

28. Equal Justice Initiative, *Lynching in America: Confronting the Legacy of Racial Terror*, 3rd ed., 2017, https://lynchinginamerica.eji.org/report.

29. *New York Tribune*, Apr. 24, 1899.

30. Powell v. Alabama, 287 U.S. 45 (1932).

31. Ken Armstrong, "Dollree Mapp, 1923–2014: 'The Rosa Parks of the Fourth Amendment,'" Marshall Project, Dec. 12, 2014, https://www.themarshall project.org/2014/12/08/dollree-mapp-1923-2014-the-rosa-parks-of-the-fourth-amendment.

32. Carolyn N. Long, Mapp v. Ohio: *Guarding Against Unreasonable Searches and Seizures* (Lawrence: Univ. Press of Kansas, 2006).

33. Mapp v. Ohio, 367 U.S. 1081 (1961).

34. *Mapp v. Ohio.*

35. US Constitution, Amendment IV.

36. Radley Balko, *Rise of the Warrior Cop: The Militarization of America's Police Forces* (New York: PublicAffairs, 2014), 54.

37. *Mapp v. Ohio.*

38. Terry v. Ohio, 392 U.S. 1 (1968).

39. *Mapp v. Ohio.*

40. *Terry v. Ohio.*

41. President's Commission on Law Enforcement and Administration of Justice, *Task Force Report: The Police* (Washington, DC: Government Printing Office, 1967), 183.

42. Burnham, *By Hands Now Known.*

43. Johanna Fernandez, *The Young Lords: A Radical History* (Chapel Hill: Univ. of North Carolina Press, 2022).

44. "Who Was Peter Yew?" AAPI History Museum, https://aapihistorymuseum.org/who-was-peter-yew, accessed Apr. 3, 2024.

45. "May 19, 1975: Peter Yew/Police Brutality Protests," Zinn Education Project, https://www.zinnedproject.org/news/tdih/chinatown-police-brutality-protests.

46. Joshua Bloom and Waldo E. Martin Jr., *Black Against Empire: The History and Politics of the Black Panther Party* (Oakland: Univ. of California Press, 2016).

47. Bloom and Martin, *Black Against Empire.*

48. Vitale, *The End of Policing*, 49.

49. Balko, *Rise of the Warrior Cop.*

50. Michael Bronski, *A Queer History of the United States* (Boston: Beacon Press, 2011).

51. Pasadena Police Department, arrest report, Jan. 21, 1953, https://ww2.cityofpasadena.net/2023%20Agendas/Jun_05_23/AR%2012A%20SUPP%20CORR.pdf

52. The organization quickly moved to the forefront of the Civil Rights Movement alongside several other major civil rights groups collectively known as the "Big Five": the National Association for the Advancement of Colored People (NAACP), the National Urban League (NUL), the Student Nonviolent Coordinating Committee (SNCC), and the Congress on Racial Equality (CORE).

53. Tennessee v. Garner, 471 U.S. 1 (1985).

54. Koon v. United States, 518 U.S. 81 (1996).

55. *Koon v. United States.*

56. *Koon v. United States.*

57. Jeff Wallenfeldt, "Los Angeles Riots of 1992," *Britannica*, last updated Aug. 21, 2024, https://www.britannica.com/event/Los-Angeles-Riots-of-1992; *Koon v. United States.*

58. *Koon v. United States*, 89–90.

59. In Re: The Grand Jury Investigation of the Death of Amadou Diallo, Grand Jury #40894/99, Supreme Court, Bronx County, New York, decided: Mar. 3, 1999.

60. Kadiatou Diallo, *My Heart Will Cross This Ocean: My Story, My Son, Amadou* (New York: Ballantine, 2003).

61. Murray Weiss, "NYPD Clears Diallo Cops—with Retraining," *New York Post*, Apr. 26, 2001.

62. "An Act to Amend Title 5, United States Code, to Designate Juneteenth National Independence Day as a Legal Public Holiday," Public Law No. 117-17, 117th Congress (June 17, 2021).

63. Steven Rich, Andrew Ba Tran, and Jennifer Jenkins, "Fatal Police Shootings Go Unreported," *Washington Post*, Feb. 23, 2023, https://www.washington post.com/investigations/2023/02/21/fatal-police-shootings-increase-2022.

64. "Fatal Force," *Washington Post*, https://www.washingtonpost.com /graphics/investigations/police-shootings-database, accessed Oct. 20, 2023.

65. Rich, Ba Tran, and Jenkins, "Fatal Police Shootings Go Unreported."

66. *Washington Post*, "As Fatal Police Shootings Increase, More Go Unreported," https://www.washingtonpost.com/investigations/interactive/2022/fatal -police-shootings-unreported/, accessed June 29, 2024.

67. Benjamin Weiser, "Mixed Motives Seen in Prosecutor's Decision to Release Ferguson Grand Jury Materials," *New York Times*, Nov. 25, 2014.

68. *Washington Post*, "As Fatal Police Shootings Increase, More Go Unreported."

69. Author interview with Lawrence Hamm, Oct. 23, 2023; Lawrence Hamm with Annette Alston, *Lawrence Hamm: A Life in the Struggle* (Newark, NJ: African World Press, 2024).

70. Robert Curvin, *Inside Newark: Decline, Rebellion, and the Search for Transformation* (New Brunswick, NJ: Rutgers Univ. Press, 2014), 164–70.

71. Read more at Mark Wineka, "July 12, 1967: When a Reluctant Salisburian Collided with History," *Salisbury Post*, July 13, 2017, https://www.salisburypost .com/2017/07/13/july-12-1967-reluctant-salisburian-collided-history/.

72. Curvin, *Inside Newark*, 100, 106, 109–10.

73. Curvin, *Inside Newark*, 107; John B. Wefing, *The Life and Times of Richard J. Hughes* (New Brunswick, NJ: Rutgers Univ. Press, 2009), 171.

74. Wes Moore, *Five Days: The Fiery Reckoning of an American City* (London: One World Press, 2020).

75. US Department of Justice, "Federal Officials Decline Prosecution in the Death of Freddie Gray," press release, Sept. 12, 2017, https://www.justice.gov/opa/pr/federal-officials-decline-prosecution-death-freddie-gray.

76. Justine Barron, *They Killed Freddie Gray: The Anatomy of a Police Brutality Cover-Up* (New York: Arcade, 2023).

77. Colin Kaepernick, ed., *Abolition for the People: The Movement for a Future Without Policing & Prisons* (n.p.: Kaepernick Publishing, 2021).

78. Patrisse Khan-Cullors and asha bandele, *When They Call You a Terrorist: A Black Lives Matter Memoir* (New York: St. Martin's Griffin, 2020).

79. Kaepernick, ed., *Abolition for the People*.

80. Cedric Johnson, *After Black Lives Matter: Policing and Anti-Capitalist Struggle* (New York: Verso, 2023); Jesse Hagopian and Denisha Jones, *Black Lives Matter at School: An Uprising for Educational Justice* (New York: Haymarket Books, 2020).

81. Stewart Tolnay and E. M. Beck, *A Festival of Violence: An Analysis of Southern Lynchings, 1882–1930* (Chicago: Univ. of Illinois Press, 1995), 69–71.

82. Abay v. City of Denver, 445 F. Supp. 3d 1286 (D. Colo. 2020); Colleen Slevin, "$14 Million Jury Award for Denver Protesters Could Resonate Around U.S.: There Are at Least 29 Pending Lawsuits Nationwide Challenging Police Use of Force During 2020 Protests," *Denver Post*, April 1, 2022.

83. Robert Samuels and Toluse Olorunnipa, *His Name Is George Floyd: One Man's Life and the Struggle for Racial Justice* (New York: Viking), 2022.

CHAPTER EIGHT: CONTESTING CLIMATE DENIAL AND ENVIRONMENTAL RACISM

1. William B. Huie, *Three Lives for Mississippi* (Jackson: Univ. Press of Mississippi, 2000).

2. Carolyn Goodman, *My Mantelpiece: A Memoir of Survival and Social Justice* (Pacific Grove, CA: WhyNotBooks, 2014).

3. "Andy's Story," Andrew Goodman Foundation, https://andrewgoodman.org/who-we-are/about-andy, accessed Oct. 26, 2023.

4. Jerry Mitchell, *Race Against Time: A Reporter Reopens the Unsolved Murder Cases of the Civil Rights Era* (New York: Simon and Schuster, 2021).

5. Bradley Angel, *The Toxic Threat to Indian Lands: A Greenpeace Report*, 1991, https://www.ejnet.org/ej/toxicthreattoindianlands.pdf.

6. Angel, *The Toxic Threat to Indian Lands*.

7. Colin Crawford, "Uproar at Dancing Rabbit Creek: Battling over Race, Class & the Environment," *Eco-Notes: Environmental Law & Policy* 2, no. 1 (1996): 1–3.

8. Winona LaDuke, *The Winona LaDuke Chronicles* (Ponsford, MN: Spotted Horse Press, 2016), 263.

9. Jean-Baptiste Joseph Fourier, "On the Temperatures of the Terrestrial Sphere and Interplanetary Space," trans., R. T. Pierrehumbert, originally published as "Memoire sur les Temperatures du Globe Terrestre et des Espaces Planetaires," *Memoires d l'Academie Royale des Sciences de l'Institute de France* VII (1827): 570–604, https://geosci.uchicago.edu/~rtp1/papers/Fourier1827Trans.pdf.

10. Joseph D. Ortiz and Roland Jackson, "Understanding Eunice Foote's 1856 Experiments: Heat Absorption by Atmospheric Gases," *Notes and Records, Royal Society,* Aug. 26, 2020, https://doi.org/10.1098/rsnr.2020.0031.

11. John F. R. S. Tyndall, "On Radiation Through the Earth's Atmosphere," *London, Edinburgh, and Dublin Philosophical Magazine and Journal of Science* 25 (1863): 167, 200–206, doi: 10.1080/14786446308643443.

12. Svante Arrhenius, "On the Influence of Carbonic Acid in the Air upon the Temperature of the Ground," *London, Edinburgh, and Dublin Philosophical Magazine and Journal of Science* 41, no. 251 (1896): 237–76, doi: 10.1080/14786449608620846.

13. G. S. Callendar, "The Artificial Production of Carbon Dioxide and Its Influence on Temperature," *Quarterly Journal* 64, no. 275 (April 1938): 223–40, https://doi.org/10.1002/qj.49706427503.

14. G. S. Callendar, "The Artificial Production of Carbon Dioxide and Its Influence on Temperature" (1938), ttps://www.met.reading.ac.uk/~ed/callendar _1938.pdf; https://rmets.onlinelibrary.wiley.com/doi/epdf/10.1002/qj.49706427503; T. Simon et al., "The Marine Heatwave West of Ireland in June 2023," *Weather* 64 (May 3, 2022): 275.

15. John Muir, *Yosemite* (New York: Dover, 2018); Donald Worster, *A Passion for Nature: The Life of John Muir* (New York: Oxford Univ. Press, 2008).

16. Henry Pringle, *Theodore Roosevelt: A Biography* (New York: Mariner Books, 2003); "Theodore Roosevelt and Conservation," National Park Service, last updated Nov. 16, 2017, https://www.nps.gov/thro/learn/historyculture /theodore-roosevelt-and-conservation.htm.

17. Rachel Carson, *Silent Spring* (New York: Mariner Classics, 2022).

18. Carson, *Silent Spring.*

19. Linda Lear, introduction, Carson, *Silent Spring*, xiv.

20. "About Us," Earth Day.org, https://www.earthday.org/about-us, accessed Oct. 26, 2023.

21. Daniel P. Moynihan to John Ehrlichman, Sept. 17, 1969, https://www .nixonlibrary.gov/sites/default/files/virtuallibrary/documents/jul10/56.pdf.

22. Moynihan to Ehrlichman.

23. Lila Thulin, "How an Oil Spill Inspired the First Earth Day," *Smithsonian,* Apr. 22, 2019, https://www.smithsonianmag.com/history/how-oil-spill -50-years-ago-inspired-first-earth-day-180972007.

24. Quirin Schiermeier, Jeff Tollefson, and *Nature,* "How Scientists Reacted to the U.S. Leaving the Paris Climate Agreement," *Scientific American,* June 2, 2017, https://www.scientificamerican.com/article/how-scientists-reacted-to-the -u-s-leaving-the-paris-climate-agreement/.

25. Paris Climate Agreement, The White House, Jan. 20, 2021, https://www .whitehouse.gov/briefing-room/statements-releases/2021/01/20/paris-climate -agreement.

26. Annie Correal, "What Drove a Man to Set Himself on Fire?" *New York Times,* May 28, 2018, https://www.nytimes.com/2018/05/28/nyregion/david -buckel-fire-prospect-park-fossil-fuels.html.

27. Correal, "What Drove a Man to Set Himself on Fire?"

28. C. B. Nielson et al., "Burns: Pathophysiology of Systemic Complications and Current Management," *Journal of Burn Care and Research* 38, no. 1 (Jan.–Feb. 2017): e469–e481, doi: 10.1097/BCR.0000000000000355.

29. Correal, "What Drove a Man to Set Himself on Fire?"

30. Michael Kodas, "Last Earth Day, Wynn Bruce Set Himself on Fire Outside the Supreme Court. I Tried to Understand Why," *Inside Climate News*, Apr. 22, 2023.

31. West Virginia v. Environmental Protection Agency, 597 U.S. 697 (2022).

32. Sackett v. Environmental Protection Agency, 598 U. S. 651 (2023).

33. Jonny Walfisz, "Culture Re-View: When Greta Thunberg Led the Biggest Climate Protest in History," *euronews*, Sept. 20, 2019.

34. Oliver Milman, "US to Stage Its Largest Ever Climate Strike," *The Guardian*, Sept. 20, 2019.

35. Author interview with Michael Waxman, Oct. 25, 2023.

36. Angel, *The Toxic Threat to Indian Lands.*

37. Angel, *The Toxic Threat to Indian Lands.*

INDEX

abolitionists, 58–61, 65, 73, 75, 77–78, 82–83, 150, 214–17
abortion, 226–27, 231–32
Abzug, Bella, 227
"Act for Preventing Negroes Insurrection, An," 148–49
Adams, John, 247
Adams, John Quincy, 65
Adderley v. Florida, 191
adoption, 38–39
affirmative action, 234
Afonso V, 15, 60
African American Civil War Museum, 204
African Communities League, 180
Africans and African Americans, 5; affirmative action, 234; Black Codes, 243–44; Black Lives Matter, 272–73; Black studies, 181, 224; Bloody Sunday attack, 198–99, 222, 234; Civil Rights Act of 1964, 168, 189, 221; defense industry, 155–57, 184; end of Reconstruction, 103, 244; Exodusters, 9, 51–53, 92, 174, 207–9; feminism, 233, 235; highway construction and urban renewal, 289–90; Jim Crow, 82, 152, 180, 183–84, 248; labor and union membership, 107–8, 115, 117–18, 125–27; lynching, 108, 175, 177–78, 183–84, 192, 207–8, 210, 218, 244–46, 274; March on Washington, 185, 189; Martin Luther King Jr. Day, 232–33; military desegregation, 156, 175, 184; military service, 145–46, 148–52, 154; music, 183, 198; Philadelphia (Mississippi) murders, 278; *Plessy v. Ferguson*, 37, 88–91, 107, 151,

174, 178, 183–84; public transportation, 195–97; reconstruction of consciousness, 269–70; Red Summer, 153, 273; Rodney King beating, 192–93; school access, 81–82; school desegregation, 175, 187–88, 197–98; Scottsboro Boys, 251; segregation, 87–89, 106–7, 115, 117, 152, 155, 178, 187–88; self-defense, 58, 69, 145, 148, 250; self-segregation, 180–82; sharecroppers, 199, 206; Tulsa Race Massacre, 124, 200; urban uprisings, 192–93, 253–56, 267–70; Vietnam War protest, 164–66; voting rights and power, 84–85, 102, 117, 199–200, 206–7, 209, 217, 221–22, 243, 247, 253, 278. *See also* slavery and the enslaved; law enforcement abuses; *names of specific people, events, and organizations*
AFSCME (American Federation of State, County and Municipal Employees), 132
AI (artificial intelligence), 142
Ailey, Alvin, 198
AIM (American Indian Movement), 39–41, 258
"Ain't I a Woman?" (Truth), 217
air traffic controllers' strike, 134–35
Airline Deregulation Act of 1978, 134
Alcatraz, occupation of, 39–40
Alcoholics Anonymous, 43
Alexander VI, 15
Algonquian people (Eastern Woodland Indians), 17
Ali, Muhammad (Cassius Marcellus Clay Jr.), 165–66
All Our Relations (LaDuke), 10